THE PRICE OF REDEMPTION

The Price of Redemption

THE SPIRITUAL ECONOMY OF
PURITAN NEW ENGLAND

Mark A. Peterson

STANFORD UNIVERSITY PRESS

Stanford, California

1997

Stanford University Press
Stanford, California

© 1997 by the Board of Trustees of the
Leland Stanford Junior University

Printed in the United States of America

CIP data are at the end of the book

Last number below indicates year of this printing:
06 05 04 03 02 01 00 99 98 97

For Mary Woolsey

Acknowledgments

Within the dense network of interdependency that characterized the economy of early New England, it was not uncommon to be both a creditor and a debtor many times over, and sometimes people found it difficult to tell whether their credits outweighed their debts. The economy of modern scholarship may be similarly intricate and interdependent, but I have no doubts at the moment about the balance on my own ledger. My debts are many and profound, and I am pleased to have the opportunity to acknowledge them here, in the hope that the work that follows will begin to repay them.

This book began as a doctoral dissertation at Harvard University under the direction of Bernard Bailyn, whose infectious enthusiasm for history as a "process of intellection" first drew me to the early American field. Over the years, I have come to appreciate his reluctance to offer his own solutions to questions that I needed to answer for myself. His remarkable scholarship has set a standard to emulate, not a doctrine to imitate. For that, and for his encouragement throughout this project, I am very grateful.

Other teachers provided ideas and early inspiration. Donald Fleming's lectures and seminars on European and American intellectual history offered an expansive context and a wide array of tools for understanding the life of the mind. Andrew Delbanco's subtle readings of Puritan literature taught me how to listen to the voices of my subjects. Lectures by Wallace MacCaffrey and John Brewer introduced me to the economic and religious conflicts that shaped early modern Britain and were transplanted to New England. During the time when most of the research and the initial writing of the book were accomplished, I had the good fortune to be a member of the Harvard Divinity School colloquium on American religious history, led by William Hutchison and David Hall, which was a congenial forum for trying out ideas. David Hall's comments on versions of several chapters and his suggestions for sources to be explored were especially valuable, and I owe a great deal to his innovative scholarship on the Puritans.

A dissertation fellowship from the Congregational History Project at the Institute for the Advanced Study of Religion, University of Chicago, offered financial assistance for the completion of my research. I am grateful to the project's advisory board for its support and for a thought-provoking conference in Chicago in May, 1990. Additional funding was generously provided by the Charles Warren Center, Harvard University. Other resources necessary for this project were made available by New England's research institutions and their librarians, including the Massachusetts Historical Society, the Congregational Library, the American Antiquarian Society, the Essex Institute, the Newport Historical Society, the Westfield Athenaeum, the Beinecke Library at Yale University, and Widener Library, Houghton Library, and the University Archives, Harvard University.

A number of people assisted me in transforming the dissertation into a book. Virginia Anderson and John O'Keefe each read the entire original manuscript and made important suggestions for revisions. Francis Bremer, Richard Bushman, Jon Butler, Richard Fox, Jane Kamensky, and Kevin Sweeney made insightful comments on individual chapters and provided references to valuable sources. Bruce Schulman offered moral support at a critical stage and recommended Stanford University Press as a potential publisher. It has been a pleasure to work with Norris Pope, director of the press, and Peter Kahn, the editor for this project. Richard Godbeer read the manuscript for the press with care and generosity; his criticisms have made this a much better book.

Puritan converts received instruction and encouragement in many informal ways, in small group meetings and through daily contact with friends and neighbors, long before they ever dared to make their public professions. From colleagues and friends, I have received more than my share of this kind of support. Special thanks go to Steve Biel, Tom Brown, Fred Dalzell, Marc Forster, Karla Goldman, Dean Grodzins, Eric Hinderaker, Susan Hunt, Richard John, Susan Lively, Fran MacDonnell, John Martin-Joy, Lou Masur, Jeff Moran, Ben Mutschler, Michael Prokopow, Gerry Prokopowicz, Tom Siegel, Vince Tompkins, Bruce Venarde, and Ted Widmer. The subjects of this book knew family and home to be the deepest source of nurture, the place where the greatest debts are incurred, and I have come to appreciate this lesson while writing it. I want to thank my parents, Elaine Beckstrom and Ernest Peterson, and my sisters, Janet Peterson and Laurie Johnson, for many years of patient encouragement. To John and Ledlie Woolsey I am deeply indebted for their remarkable interest and unflagging faith in my work, and for providing me with an ideal place to write and revise in Petersham, Massachusetts, roughly halfway between Boston and Westfield, where the divergent strands of this book were pulled together. The arrival of Abigail and Thomas slowed the task of revision but made life as a whole much richer. Finally, this book could not have been completed without the constant support of Mary Woolsey. Her incomparable skills as an editor, her keen eye for the logic of an argument, and her sensitivity to historical nuance have improved every page. She has also taught me more about grace and its value than I ever knew before, and I am forever in her debt.

M.A.P.

Contents

Introduction   *1*

1. A "Right Middle Way"   *23*

2. A Temple in the Wilderness   *51*

3. A Garden in the Metropolis   *67*

4. "The Want of All Means Ordained to Help Me"   *96*

5. Keepers of the Vineyard, Gentlemen of Means   *120*

6. "Christ's Curious Garden Fenced In . . ."   *144*

7. Defending the Garden, Cultivating the Wilderness   *163*

8. ". . . With Solid Walls of Discipline"   *191*

Conclusion: From the Covenant to the Revival and Beyond   *219*

Notes   *243*

Works Cited   *297*

Index   *319*

THE PRICE OF REDEMPTION

Introduction

When a man layes out his money unto Spirituall ends, to obtaine the
free passage of the Ordinances of Christ, . . . he thereby sowes to the
Spirit, and shall of the Spirit reap life everlasting.
——John Cotton, *Christ the Fountaine of Life* (1651)

In 1651, the year John Cotton's *Christ the Fountaine of Life* was published
in London, the twenty thousand English colonists who, like Cotton, had
crossed the Atlantic during the Great Migration were settled in some thirty
towns, each with a newly formed Puritan church. Most of these primitive
"plantations" were huddled near the New England coastline, with a few solitary villages reaching up the Connecticut River into the region's interior.
After two decades of settlement, the town of Boston, where John Cotton
was now the minister, still had no press of its own. New England's Puritans
had to rely on English imports for devotional books and for the many other
necessities of their strenuous religion.[1]

A century later, New England's colonial population had grown to three
hundred fifty thousand, and the meetinghouses of five hundred orthodox
churches had sprung up across the landscape. Most of these churches had recently experienced a "Great Awakening," a revival of religion in which the
"spirit of the old writers" like John Cotton was powerfully present in the
preaching of New England–trained ministers, in the hearts of their congregations, and in a steady stream of new publications produced by the dozens
of printers and publishers in Boston.[2] This book is an effort to tell the story
of this remarkable century of growth and adaptation in Puritan religious culture through the experience of two New England churches, one in Boston,
the region's emerging metropolis, and the other in Westfield, Massachusetts,
which in 1651 was an outpost of the fur trade on the colony's remote western
frontier.

A Puritan minister always chose a biblical text as the starting point for a sermon, and then would proceed to explicate its meaning and list the "uses" to which its lessons might be put. In like fashion, John Cotton's words from *Christ the Fountaine* can be taken as a point of departure for this book. In this brief passage, Cotton addresses two distinct but related aspects of what might be called the "spiritual economy" of Puritan New England. Economy, in the sense in which the word is usually used today, means the management of a society's affairs with respect to the allocation of scarce resources—paying attention to what things cost. But economy can also mean more generally the way in which the various elements of a society are organized or integrated, a definition now archaic but in common use in the seventeenth century, especially in a theological context, in which economy could mean "a 'dispensation,' a method or system of divine government suited to the needs of a particular nation or period of time."[3] These two senses of economy inform the two main strands of my story of the evolution of New England Puritanism, for which Cotton's *Christ the Fountaine* is a useful opening text.

For Puritans, religion was expensive. John Cotton's words, originally preached to Puritans in the "other" Boston, in Lincolnshire, England, spelled out the circumstances that some of these future colonists of New England would face: "in case . . . by Gods providence you [are] cast to live in such Congregations, where you cannot have the Ordinances of God but at a great charge."[4] The Puritans who founded Boston in Massachusetts would literally have to "lay out their money" if they were to transplant the religious culture they had known in England to the wilds of North America. The decision to establish Puritan churches in the New World was a costly one, even after the enormous expenses of migration and initial settlement were paid. To maintain a vital Puritan church, the members of a New England community had to invest far more of their resources in religion than did the residents of a comparable Anglican parish. A Puritan church needed at least one and preferably two ministers, and each minister was expected to possess a degree of learning that only an expensive college education could provide. To keep such high-priced clerical talent in remote New England outposts, towns had to spend a large portion of their annual budgets on ministers' salaries. But for a Puritan congregation to thrive, a literate laity also had to be immersed in the Bible and devotional literature. After clerical salaries, public education was often the second largest item in New England town budgets. Bibles and godly books were costly too, but each family had to have them. In addition, enormous amounts of time and effort were spent by clergy and laity alike in preparing for and attending sermons. Public catechism, private devotional groups, daily family worship sessions, the building of meetinghouses and the furnishing of communion tables—all were vital to the maintenance of Puritan piety, and all demanded the expenditure of time, money, and effort by ordinary citizens.

Without the economic resources provided by a vigorous economy, the Puritan movement in America would have died out rapidly. The growth of Puritanism, the continuous nurturing of its inner vitality, and the spread of orthodox churches across the New England landscape *required* the material and cultural resources produced by an expanding commercial economy. The economic growth of early New England, based in large part on mercantile ventures centered in Boston, was the life-blood of its churches as well. Some communities were blessed with greater wealth than others, and therefore had more resources to acquire the means of grace through which salvation usually occurred. But the whole of New England society could maintain its godly character only if it produced the wealth needed "to obtaine the free passage of the Ordinances of Christ." This is one main strand of the narrative, the first aspect of New England's spiritual economy to be explored.

But as John Cotton reminded his listeners, the mere accumulation of wealth would never earn salvation: "if [a man] thinke his money is worthy of Christ, he gets him not."[5] For money to be useful, it had to be laid out unto "spiritual ends"; a man must "sow to the Spirit" to "reap life everlasting." Cotton's metaphor speaks to my other major argument, that a desire to cast the seeds of grace as broadly as possible, an evangelical commitment to convert what they saw as a wilderness into a garden of the Lord, was essential for the growth of individual churches and for New England Puritanism's dramatic ecclesiastical expansion in the century after its initial settlement. In English Puritanism, the evangelical impulse was weak—as a dissenting, minority movement, it had been far more concerned with separating the godly "wheat" from the profane "chaff" of humanity than with broadcasting the seeds of grace. Transplanted to America, Puritans gradually discovered the value of cultivating their religion as widely as possible. This transformation was slow and uneven—some individuals and churches strongly embraced the evangelical impulse, others resisted. But in general, the spread of orthodoxy across the New England landscape was fostered by the steady devotion of precious material and cultural resources to the maintenance of an intense and demanding religion, a devotion made possible by the belief that money sown to the spirit would reap divine rewards. This developing sense of evangelical mission came to characterize the New England spiritual economy in the second sense of the word; it was a new "dispensation" suited to the conditions that Puritans met in the new world.

Taken together, these two arguments suggest that continuity and growth were the accomplishments of devout Puritans who had a deliberate vision of how to channel their material resources into the cultivation of their religion. On the face of it, such a claim would not seem unusual, let alone new or surprising, were it not for the fact that it runs counter to the vast majority of historical writing on this subject.[6] Beginning with the first colonists themselves, and continuing through to the present, the dominant narrative of the history of New England Puritanism has maintained that piety and prosperity were enemies, that the rise of commerce delivered a mortal blow to the fervor of the founders, and that later generations of Puritans fell away from their religious heritage as they moved out across the New England landscape. For nearly four centuries, this story line, the myth of declension, has been repeated so frequently and told with such force and literary grace that it has become deeply ingrained in the American historical imagination. To offer a viable alternative to a narrative that has endured for so long and assumed such a mythic status, it may be useful to account for the declension narrative's power and tenacity, and perhaps to locate within its foundations a new way of seeing the Puritan past.

≈❃≈

The myth-making impulse that produced the declension narrative began with the founding generation, for whom this particular story line served a vital purpose.[7] William Bradford, governor of the Plymouth colony and author of New England's first Puritan history, consciously borrowed Old Testament metaphors to lend a sense of cosmic significance to the Pilgrims' experience of persecution. The opening chapters of his history of Plymouth Plantation provide a clear and powerful narrative of his community's origins in England, exile in the Netherlands, and escape to the freedom of the New World. Yet once his people had arrived in their promised land, his story lost its direction and Bradford was reduced to a mere keeper of annals, bewildered by a flood of events that lacked the meaning, clarity, and promise he had once seen for the future of his colony. Gradually, Bradford began to associate the material gains his fellow colonists made with his growing sense that the spiritual fervor he had once enjoyed as part of a latter-day apostolic community had seriously declined. In the end, he lamented the dispersal of the population through the countryside in search of richer pasture lands, a movement which left the "poor church" of Plymouth "like an ancient mother grown old and forsaken of her children."[8]

Bradford's disappointment with the progress of a colony begun with such great hopes was a natural perspective for the founding generation to assume. Bradford and his fellow colonists frequently likened themselves to

God's chosen people, the ancient Israelites. Worldliness and decay, the worship of false idols, the dispersal of the population, captivity, exile, and destruction—such was the fate of the children of Israel after they had reached their promised land, and such were the available metaphorical constructs that shaped New England Puritans' historical vision of themselves. Given Bradford's intense identification with Moses and the Exodus mythos in his description of the Pilgrims' escape from European bondage, it would have been remarkable if his account of the latter days of their New English Canaan had not taken on an elegiac tone. The part of the prophet lamenting the decline of his people was, in effect, scripted for Bradford already.[9] But this rhetorical strategy served an important function for Bradford, reminding later generations of their religious heritage and encouraging continued commitment to the founders' faith.

The image of a New England soul lost in the colony's material progress created a compelling framework for understanding the region's early history. Bradford's successors among the Puritan clergy did their work thoroughly; their jeremiads made a lasting impression on the way their congregations understood themselves and their own experience. This peculiar form of historical thinking entered the consciousness of ordinary people and framed how they thought about themselves. In this sense, declension can be said to be neither right nor wrong as a way to understand New England's history. It is simply there, an artifact of the conceptual lives of early New Englanders, no more nor less important than the form of their town governments or the average size of their families. Yet more than most artifacts of the past, this Puritan tendency to see history as declension has led subsequent scholars to look for similar patterns in constructing a story, to follow Bradford's Puritan script. Even historians unsympathetic to the souls of the Puritans, who decry Puritan "theocracy" as an oppressive evil happily overcome by the free spirit of commerce, tend to make the same assumptions and tell the same story, if only to celebrate what Bradford lamented.[10]

Like any powerful narrative, the declension model creates meaning by privileging some aspects of past experience while concealing others. William Bradford's viewpoint has encouraged later historians to ask whether the number of communicants in a particular Puritan church decreased over time, but has steered historians away from considering the remarkable numerical proliferation of churches across the countryside, the enduring popular devotion to the unusual form of church polity that Bradford helped to create.[11] Most other European colonists of North America had great difficulty in maintaining any level of commitment to churches as institutions, and failed to create them in numbers sufficient to replicate European patterns. In this light, it becomes difficult to see how New Englanders could manage this singular achievement if the dispersal of New England's population really led, as Bradford insisted, to "the ruin . . . of the churches of God there."[12]

Faults like this one in the declension model have been pointed out before. Many of its constituent parts, especially as formulated by Perry Miller's three-volume history of the "New England Mind," have been carefully scrutinized and revised.[13] From a scholarly point of view, the argument has been poked full of holes, yet for all that, the old ship won't sink. A brief survey of recent college textbooks, perhaps the best indicators of the general framework currently being offered to the minds of Americans, reveals the overwhelming prevalence of declension as the reigning explanation of the fate of New England Puritanism. One textbook, for example, argues for the Halfway Covenant of 1662 as a sign of lost religious fervor, pits mercantile interests against religious belief, and declares that by the 1670s, "the ministers spoke for the past" against a clearly commercial and secular future.[14] Even historians who challenge the traditional interpretation still struggle with its lingering power to invade the very language that they use. One author states that "the rise of maritime New England was a source of pride *even for the clergy*," as though the reader of early New England history would automatically assume that Puritan ministers were so unworldly that they opposed their colony's prosperity.[15] Why, then, does the perspective of William Bradford still hold sway over the historical imagination of twentieth-century scholars no longer steeped in the metaphors of the Old Testament?

The absence of a compelling alternative narrative has been a major reason for declension's refusal to decline. In *1066 and All That*, a "memorable" history of England composed in the 1920s after "years of research in golf-clubs, gun-rooms, green-rooms, etc.," W. C. Sellar and R. J. Yeatman suggested (profoundly) that "history is not what you thought. *It is what you can remember*. All other history defeats itself." The revisionist scholarship on Puritanism, the critique of Perry Miller and the declension model, has been self-defeating in just this sense. Relatively little energy has been devoted to creating a coherent new interpretation with the explanatory scope and the "memorable" quality that give Miller's subtly argued but simple narrative structure its enduring power.[16] To put the Sellar and Yeatman notion into a respectable scholarly framework, we can refer to the work of Thomas Kuhn and other historians of science, who suggest that reigning explanatory paradigms are never supplanted by the critiques and emendations that Kuhn called "normal science." The process of correcting the errors and distortions that any overarching theory is bound to contain actually tends to strengthen the original paradigm, in part because these corrections still view the world within the terms of the prevailing model.[17] Not until an alternative model is imagined, an interpretation in some ways incommensurable with the prevailing view, can the reigning version yield to a new way of seeing. Only then can the accumulated critiques of the old paradigm take shape as part of the groundwork of a new model, or, to translate this analysis into the appropriate conventions of historical knowledge, a new narrative.[18]

The declension narrative derives much of its sustaining power from certain assumptions that are implicit in the way the story is told, assumptions that lie so close to the "facts" it seeks to describe that they rarely are challenged or even seen as assumptions. The particular narrative strategies and unchallenged assumptions that have perpetuated the declension model include: (1) a myth of origins, by which the first generation of New England's settlers are granted a privileged historical position; (2) the problem of the "exemplary life," a biographical genre that distorts the way historians think about social evolution; and (3) a myth of community that frames the assumptions historians have made about the relationships between religion, material resources, and the social order. A close examination of these mythic foundations can, however, provide us with new strategies for reordering facts that have long seemed to make sense only within one very familiar story, and can point us toward new evidence equally worthy of an explanatory framework.

☙

For historians of colonial New England, the question of where to begin the story has typically posed few problems. The tendency has always been to begin at the "beginning," with Plymouth Colony in 1620, with Massachusetts Bay in 1630, and with sufficient backward glances at English history to set a context for New World developments.[19] Yet by commencing this story with the triumphs of the founding generation, set against the background of the Puritan revolution in England, a powerful mythology of New England's origins shapes the way in which all subsequent events are understood.[20] The migration to the New World and the early establishment of New England's religious and social institutions have become definitive standards for the meaning of American Puritanism, against which all changes in New England's religious culture after the Cambridge Platform of 1648 are measured, judged, and usually condemned as decline.[21] Given the Puritans' obsession with "primitive" models of ecclesiastical purity, the tendency of succeeding generations to revere their ancestors' original accomplishments should come as no surprise.[22] But there are excellent reasons to challenge the assumption that the first generation's churches were a normative standard for evaluating the subsequent history of orthodoxy in New England.

First, the evolution of the Puritan movement over many decades in England and America defies the possibility of defining a single normative moment. English Puritanism before the Great Migration went through many phases, shaped by its internal logic of development and by the influence of external conditions. In the early seventeenth century, the more militant political aspects of Puritan reform temporarily subsided; the movement went "underground" and became more of a cultural "persuasion" than a drive for ecclesiastical reform. Yet by the 1630s, the policies of Charles I and Archbishop Laud had forced conforming Puritans into political opposition again. The timing of the migration to New England with these mounting political pressures served to "radicalize" many members of the founding generation and profoundly altered their understanding of religious belief and its institutional underpinnings.[23]

No individual better exemplifies this process than John Davenport, the founder of New Haven. Until the late 1620s, the staunchly Puritan Davenport had opposed the idea of separation from the Church of England. But when Archbishop Laud began to insist that all gatherings of godly people within or apart from the established church constituted separatism, Davenport, like many of his heretofore conforming colleagues, was driven to a radical position.[24] He migrated first to the Netherlands, then to America, where he became the most fervent advocate of strict Congregationalism, separatist for all practical purposes, among the founders of New England. The colony he founded in New Haven has been described as the most Puritan of all New England colonies, "the essence of Puritanism, distilled and undefiled."[25]

The notion that John Davenport was "more Puritan" in 1637 than he was in 1627, or that his earlier positions were "undistilled" or "defiled" forms of Puritanism, is clearly mistaken; it ignores the evolutionary nature of the Puritan movement and unduly privileges its first New England manifestation. It seems more accurate to say that external pressures changed the expression of John Davenport's Puritan beliefs over the course of a turbulent decade. The Puritanism of the founders was not a stable, reified, and distilled set of ideas ready to be implemented in the pure laboratory of the American wilderness, but a complex and sometimes contradictory set of impulses, which in the 1630s had recently moved in a new direction quite unlike that of preceding decades in England.

The self-selecting nature of the migrating group created an unusual population in New England's first generation, providing yet another reason not to think of this period as normative. The great mass of ungodly people, with whom English Puritans had been engaged in ongoing cultural warfare in England, were left behind.[26] The godly in New England were further distinguished by the fervor they shared in their common enterprise, for the migration experience aroused utopian hopes along with daunting anxieties over the tasks of building a new society, lest they "be made a story and a by-word through the world, . . . and shame the faces of many of gods worthy servants, and cause their prayers to be turned into Cursses upon us till wee be consumed out of the good land whether we are goeing."[27] The heightened hopes and fears of this period shaped the emotional lives of the first generation in distinctive ways, but these were not definitive characteristics of the Puritan movement as a whole, nor were they experiences that subsequent generations could possibly have shared.

The political turmoil that engaged Britain from the 1630s through the 1650s also created conditions unique to New England's first generation. The consuming nature of events in England left the crown, Parliament, and the protectorate little opportunity to exercise control over New England.[28] The primary British "audience" for the founders' actions were fellow Puritans who had remained behind in England, and who used New England's successes and failures as arguments in the debate between Presbyterians and Independents over control of the English church.[29] Within these limits, first-generation colonists enjoyed the freedom to develop their Bible Commonwealths without fear of opposition and formed a strong sense of themselves as a distinct and independent people, a development that would have been impossible under closer imperial supervision.

The direct consequence of these unusual circumstances was a radicalization of the Puritan movement in its transplanted form. This change can be seen in the early efforts in Massachusetts to bring the visible church of professing Christians in line with the invisible church of God's elect, a movement that carried the churches toward virtual separatism and went well beyond the original expectations of founders like John Winthrop and John Wilson.[30] Outside the boundaries of Massachusetts orthodoxy, the radical shift went still further. The proliferation of heretical sects in the first generation of New England settlement reflects the ways in which Puritan-inspired beliefs exceeded the limits of what orthodoxy would tolerate, and even pushed the orthodox to take more extreme positions in order to co-opt the radicals' threats to their hegemony.[31]

If the notion of early New England as a "laboratory" for the development of a Puritan society has any value, it is in this sense that the conditions offered to New England's settlers were ideally suited to the flourishing of the Puritan movement's most utopian impulses, a rarefied atmosphere where

many of the harsh conditions of the "real world" of English society were fil-
tered out. But we might better describe first-generation New England as a
"hothouse" designed to cultivate the more delicate flowers of Puritan reform, especially those ideas and beliefs (such as the use of Mosaic Law as a
basis for judicial authority) that would never have survived the pressures of
English society and politics. Andrew Delbanco has argued that the first generation saw migration not as an "errand *into* the wilderness," but as an "errand
out of the wilderness" and into an enclave of purity. Distressed English Puritans hoped to escape from the wasteland they feared their nation had already
become. In moving to a new world, they expected to find new feelings of
closeness to God and to enjoy his ordinances in a pure form unattainable in
the corrupted Church of England. As Thomas Shepard said to his Cambridge,
Massachusetts, congregation in the 1630s, "there is no place in all the world
where there is such expectation to find the Lord as here."[32]

However, the Puritan movement encompassed much more than a desire
to enjoy God's ordinances in pristine purity. The staunch insistence of the
Massachusetts founders that they were not separatists and had no intention of
abandoning the Church of England points to the abiding sense of responsibility to the world that was part of the Puritan reforming impulse. In a later
sermon, Thomas Shepard warned his Cambridge congregation not to "fall
a-dreaming" here in New England, and to oppose the utopian "delusion of
men's brains" and "swarm of strange opinions" that were the product of a society where "we have ordinances to the full, sermons too long, and lectures
too many, and private meetings too frequent." Shepard was not opposed to
New England's pure ordinances and overabundant "means," but he realized
that "golden dreams of grace" were as dangerous to the course of salvation as
"drunken dreams of the world." In Shepard's eyes, the unique circumstances
of the first decade of settlement made utopian delusions a greater temptation
than worldly corruptions.[33]

A full generation of experience was necessary before the most fervent
Puritan colonists would awaken from their golden dreams to realize that the
New World was as much a spiritual wilderness as the England they had left
behind.[34] What caused this awakening were developments that made New
England into a mature society and brought an end to the "hothouse" environment that nurtured the first generation's radical florescence. First and foremost, the Restoration of the Stuart monarchy in 1660 threatened the basic
terms of the colonies' existence, as earlier neglect of colonial matters gave way
to increasing crown supervision of the nascent empire.[35] New Englanders
were aware of the implications of this development from the very start. The
founders, lacking significant opposition from the English government, were

free to mold their colonies according to their religious and cultural objectives. The real test of New England's ability to sustain these objectives came only when the orthodox colonies had to survive against the compromising power of the Restoration monarchy, with its opposition to Puritan religion and its hostility to decentralized self-rule anywhere within the crown's domain. The Anglican merchants and officials who began to appear in Boston reminded Puritans of their differences from mainstream English society and forced New Englanders to make accommodations to the world's demands—demands that had been easy to forget in the rarefied atmosphere of the first thirty years of settlement.

In addition, after a generation of experimentation, New England society had developed institutions and practices that would persist for the next century. In the migration period, colonists had relied upon assistance from the native American population and had looked to the fur trade for income to pay for their import needs, but these transitory patterns had given way to agricultural production and the fishing and trading enterprises that became the enduring staples of New England economic life.[36] By the 1660s, the orthodox New England colonies had formed stable governments, had joined together in an alliance for mutual defense, and had created judicial systems connecting local affairs to colonial power centers.[37] The pattern of settlement for new towns in the interior of New England had been established, and a population growing rapidly through natural increase began to fill up newly acquired lands.[38] A system of schools was taking hold throughout the towns of Massachusetts, and Harvard College, while still a fledgling enterprise, was beginning to train homegrown ministers to replace the immigrant clergy of the first generation.[39]

Finally, the Cambridge Platform of 1648, a written standard of ecclesiastical structure and discipline for the churches of Massachusetts, signalled the institutional maturation of orthodox religious culture.[40] Although the platform stopped short of resolving the problems of baptism and membership of future generations, it pointed toward the Synod of 1662's "Halfway Covenant" as the next logical step in the development of the Puritan church as an institution that could persist through time. In effect, the Halfway Covenant acknowledged that New England's population could not forever be a self-selected body of saints already prepared to be incorporated in churches, as the majority of the migrants had been. Future American generations also had to be prepared for conversion, had to be kept within the "garden" of the church and protected from the dangers of the "wilderness" without diminishing the purity of the church itself. By broadening the eligibility standards for baptism while reserving communion and full membership for those who had experienced saving grace, this is exactly what the Halfway Covenant did.[41]

The challenges faced by the second and subsequent generations in New England were the challenges of a mature society, not an immigrant company. These challenges, while different from those of the first generation, were met with responses no less "Puritan" than the actions of the founders. But in looking for simple continuity or repetition of first-generation events in later years, historians writing within the declension framework have overlooked growth and change that were part of the Puritan tradition. In the 1630s, Thomas Shepard had warned his congregation not to be deluded by "golden dreams of grace." Shepard's sermon can be read as a valuable corrective for modern scholars as well. Just as the purity and plenitude of worship in early New England churches pushed the first generation toward radical delusions of God's kingdom appearing on earth, so historians have been captivated by the remarkable success of New England as a utopian experiment and have taken the events and circumstances of the first generation as a normative standard for American Puritanism. Modern historians did not invent this tendency; the original myth-makers were those like John Davenport who became rigidly committed to the first forms of church polity. To these founders and their immediate descendants, any change from the radical forms of the early New England Way constituted declension from the true church, and they encouraged an almost slavish ancestor worship among subsequent generations. It is their rhetorical emphasis on loss and lamentation that subsequent historians have singled out as the dominant pattern of New England's religious development after the first generation. Yet their myth of origins obscures an equally important counter-narrative. If the Halfway Covenant signalled an end to the "golden dreams of grace," it also marked the emergence of this religious culture's sense of responsibility to the world, a development which paralleled the growing stability of New England society as a whole. By beginning a new narrative of New England Puritanism in 1660, when the "real world" returned to New England with a vengeance, we can remind ourselves that the Puritan movement was not a form of ascetic monasticism, a withdrawal from the world, but rather an attempt to change it, and we can begin to see the efforts of later Puritans in a new light, as an ongoing reformation.

The Puritan notion of the exemplary life, a way of understanding the self and historical development that complements the mythology of origins, has also contributed to the power and tenacity of the declension model.[42] Puritans constantly modelled themselves and interpreted their personal experiences through comparisons to the lives of others. The imitation of Christ, of course, was central to Christian piety, but all Biblical figures, saintly or wicked, were available models against which Puritans could measure their own behavior and beliefs. Although Puritans rejected Roman Catholic idolatry of saints, exemplary lives were still central to their conception of post-apostolic history. John Foxe's *Acts and Monuments* (1563), a chronicle of the endless sufferings of individual Protestants in defense of the true faith, was a central text in the process of Puritan self-fashioning. Its inspirational lessons and images were committed to memory by generations of the godly in both Old and New England.[43]

The practice of writing biographies of the departed became a predominant aspect of the way New England Puritans composed their more general histories. An early instance of this subspecies of historical writing appears in William Bradford's *Of Plymouth Plantation*, which contains a brief account of the life of William Brewster, the Plymouth Church elder, who died in 1643. The subtext of Bradford's veneration of this patriarch was a critique of the rising generation's materialism: "none did more offend and displease [Brewster] than such as would haughtily and proudly carry and lift up themselves, being risen from nothing and having little else in them to commend them but a few fine clothes or a little riches . . . ."[44] John Norton, the successor of John Cotton in the pulpit of Boston's First Church, penned a comparable account of Cotton's life which reminded readers that the death of pious leaders warns of impending destruction: "Sure we are that Josiah was gathered unto his fathers, that he might not see the evil that was to come upon Jerusalem."[45] This genre persisted throughout the seventeenth century, but no one pursued it with greater vigor than Cotton Mather, whose *Magnalia Christi Americana* (1702) contains an immense compendium of biographical sketches of Puritan magistrates and ministers. Mather's biographies make explicit connections between exemplary New Englanders and the Protestant martyrs or Biblical figures whose virtues they embodied—William Bradford as "Galeacius Secundus," or John Winthrop as "Nehemias Americanus."[46] But the implicit message of Mather's entire collection is that the virtues displayed by New England's early leaders were characteristic of a time when "that neglect of the veneration of the Deity, which now marks the age, [had not yet] begun to appear."[47]

To model one's life on these exemplary figures, as Mather hoped his readers would do and as he clearly tried to do himself, was to embrace declension as an organizing framework for one's own personal experience. It meant accepting a vision of contemporary history in which the pious individual was always engaged in a valiant but ultimately losing battle against a vain and wicked world.[48] To internalize this biographical genre therefore made it easy to conflate the life of the individual with the imagined evolution of society as a whole. Cotton Mather, as David Levin has argued, had a remarkable tendency "to identify his own life with the history and prospects of Congregational New England."[49] The title of yet another of these memoir–jeremiads, Joshua Scottow's *Old Men's Tears for their Own Declensions* (1691), neatly summarizes the general tenor of this genre. The psychic representation of the self that the practice of Puritan piety constructed for the individual spilled over into interpretations of historical change, especially when written by men looking back on the events of their own lives.

This image of the exemplary life shaped the way that Puritans interpreted their own history, but it has also profoundly influenced later reconstructions of that history as well. The prolific and engaging writings of colonial New England's leading individuals have made them compelling subjects for biographers. In roughly the past century, there have been at least four large-scale biographical studies of Cotton Mather, along with hundreds of other books and articles on aspects of his life and works.[50] Three biographies of the "ever-memorable" Increase Mather have appeared, along with an essay that labels him a "representative Massachusetts Puritan."[51] There have been four biographies of John Winthrop, with another currently in progress, as well as one of the younger John Winthrop, governor of Connecticut.[52] In addition to ongoing efforts to publish the Mather and Winthrop papers, excellent complementary studies of both these families over the course of three generations have been produced as well.[53] Though few modern biographers make this claim directly, their tendency is to let the individual (or family) exemplify the experience of society as a whole, or to offer the perspective of their subject as a valid interpretation of social development. Even outside the genre of pure biography, general works on Puritan New England often imply that in the lives of individuals, the fate of society can be read. Darrett Rutman's choice of the title *Winthrop's Boston* for a social history of New England's metropolis implies that Boston's history and Winthrop's life bear such an intimate connection that the death of Winthrop marks a definitive break in the town's history. Not incidentally, Rutman's study strongly reinforces the declension narrative that seventeenth-century biographies of Winthrop had already projected.[54] Similarly, Perry Miller's *The New England Mind: From Colony to Province* can be read as a history of the Mather family writ large; the text begins with Richard Mather's "Farewell," ends with Increase Mather's death, and Mather family references fill more than two full pages of its fourteen page index, far outweighing the attention paid to any other person, family, or subject.

Individual lives can be useful tools for historical analysis, but perhaps more importantly, they are also "memorable," as Cotton Mather realized. Everyone bears a personal autobiographical narrative in mind and can easily identify with the vividly told lives of others. Yet once a biographer enters the mentality of the subject, as the demands of the genre require, it becomes difficult to extricate historical interpretations from the viewpoint of the subject; indeed, the finest biographies tend to emerge from intense experiences of identification between author and subject. But there are risks in conflating the fate of individuals with the development of societies or accepting a single family's perspective as the most valid view of an era. To return again to William Bradford, his personal interpretation of the dispersal of the Plymouth population was quite idiosyncratic. To him it meant the dissipation of the particular community of exiles that had been at the center of his own experience, but dispersal did not, in fact, lead to the "ruin of the churches of God" in New England, as Bradford had imagined it would. The economic resources that the settlers sought were eventually responsible for strengthening and expanding the Puritan churches of Plymouth Colony.[55] Yet virtually every history of Plymouth ever written has taken Bradford's emotional reaction as a definitive statement of the character of Plymouth's development.[56] The problem, in brief, is that Puritan biographies projected history as declension, Puritan histories tended to be biographical, and modern scholars have (perhaps unconsciously) relied on these sources for their plot structures when writing both biographies and general histories.[57]

To be able to see the evolution of New England Puritanism differently means escaping the trap of biographically structured narratives. Yet biography's advantage is its concrete immediacy; individual lives allow us the illusion of direct access to past experience that more abstract subjects cannot provide. A solution to this dilemma can be found, however, by centering an alternative narrative on a different kind of "life," an organism of sorts, but one with a potential for perpetual life in this world to which human beings cannot aspire—in other words, the life of the church. It seems an obvious truism to say that the best way to understand the development of New England's religious culture is to look at the experience of its churches. However, relatively few authors in this century have turned their attention to the history of belief, behavior, and practice in specific churches over a long time span. The individual church in New England has rarely been studied as an organism with a life of its own, a life that included a distinctive religious "personality" and a history created and sustained by its ministers, members, and congregation across the generations. We have been treated to numerous biographies of individual ministers and lay people.[58] There have also been thoughtful discussions of more abstract aspects of religious experience, but these are mainly based on a wide sampling of sources from New England's many churches.[59] A focus on churches offers a middle way between these extremes. But just as no individual life can rightly be seen as exemplary, neither can any single church be taken to stand for New England's religious culture as a whole. My tale of two churches is meant to suggest that neither church was exemplary, but that both were integral elements in the spiritual economy of New England. Their common religious aspirations were worked out differently within the range of social conditions that New England's varied local communities offered.

⁂

A focus on the lives of churches avoids the problem of the exemplary individual, but brings to light a third set of assumptions that reinforce the declension paradigm; namely, a constellation of ideas about community, capitalism, and religion that has shaped the writing of New England local history. In the last three decades, prodigious scholarship on New England communities has uncovered a new world of experience and has redefined the field of social history. While religion frequently plays a significant part in these works, most local historians have used the church as a window on social experience rather than focusing directly on the nature of religious life itself. Events in the life of the church have been used as indicators of changes in social structures, economic conditions, or community values within a town. But these analyses have frequently relied on certain assumptions about the relationship between religious life and the social environment, assumptions so basic as to remain untested.

The assumption that commercial capitalism is antithetical to Puritan piety and destructive of its communal ideals pervades the town studies of the "new social history" and reinforces the declension narrative. The common tendency of New England town studies has been to assume that Puritan churches were best suited to the social conditions found in villages cut off from the world of the market, where subsistence agriculture was practiced and communal values associated with pre-modern economic forms predominated. Perhaps the most influential study to advance this position argues that New England's early Puritan towns were intended to be "closed corporate utopian peasant communities," covenanted to the task of mutual cooperation, resistant to change, and anti-commercial. In this formulation, the "peasant" mentality fosters both Puritan piety and economic backwardness, as though these were the religious and economic sides of the same cultural coin. Competition, conflict, and migration away from the original town center for economic gain are taken to be destructive of community and therefore indicators of Puritan declension, a historical analysis that repeats the pattern originally described by William Bradford.[60] The power of this untested assumption can be seen in a study of Springfield, Massachusetts, where the absence of church records allows for little conclusive discussion of the nature of the community's religious life. Here, the presence of contentious commercial behavior among some of the townspeople is taken as proof that Springfield's communal ties were weak, its church ineffectual, and its citizens "generally non-Puritan" in their behavior. Lacking direct evidence, the paradigm provides an answer, a pattern of historical reasoning that ought to arouse suspicion.[61]

Like the other major elements of the declension paradigm, the origins of these ideas about community can be found in the Puritans' own rhetoric and in the inner workings of the Puritan mind. John Winthrop's "Modell of Christian Charity" declared the importance of communal solidarity and denounced the evils of a selfishly acquisitive spirit.[62] The clergy frequently warned their congregations against the dangers of worldliness, and Puritans took to heart the parable of the rich fool, who "layeth up treasure for himself, and is not rich toward God" (Luke 12:21). But to assume, as many historians have done, that Puritanism therefore required pre-modern anti-capitalist village communalism in order to thrive is to miss a subtle but vital distinction. Worldliness was not merely the "laying up" of treasure, but the failure to spend it to sow the seeds of grace. Ideals of communal charity and freedom from worldliness were not prerequisite conditions for the existence of Puritanism, but challenges that the godly gladly took on, challenges that were in many ways made easier by the "treasure" that a thriving market economy produced.

The persistence in later American historiography of the myth of community and its false dichotomy between Puritanism and commerce can be explained in part by the antimaterialism of intellectuals who have written about this problem. The desire for the existence of a pre-capitalist moment in the American past, or for a yardstick against which to measure America's soulless materialism, has been a powerful force behind the tendency to see New England's Puritans as anti-commercial ascetics. American social historians have associated fervent religious belief with pre-modern "gemeinschaft" and have therefore described economic development as destructive of community and religion.[63] But further reinforcement for the belief in a dichotomy between Puritan religion and commercial development emerges from the narrative constructs described above: the privileging of the first generation as a definitive Puritan ideal and the use of exemplary biography as a projection of social history.

Later generations of New England's historians celebrated their ancestors' communal cohesion and unworldly asceticism, but these qualities were not choices made by the founders, and they were not dictated by an opposition to money or markets. Communal cohesion, where it did exist in the first generation, was often a by-product of the experience of migration; in many cases, self-selecting communities organized by charismatic leaders were bound together by their common backgrounds and experiences.[64] The homogeneity of these immigrant companies offers the illusion of aboriginal communal harmony in New England, hiding the fact that many of these Puritans were contentious troublemakers whose beliefs had created turmoil in the Old England of their birth.[65] Similarly first-generation asceticism was not a choice dictated by Puritan religious belief. English Puritans did, of course, abhor the decorative artwork and elaborate priestly vestments that the Church of England still retained. But what they hated was the idolatry, not the wealth and finery, that these Roman Catholic vestiges stood for. John Cotton did not forsake St. Botolph's, the largest non-cathedral church in England, for a log meetinghouse in Boston because he opposed grand buildings and preferred to shiver in the cold, but because he could no longer safely practice his brand of Puritan ministry without molestation from ecclesiastical authorities.[66] John Davenport did not instruct his congregation of pious merchants in London's commercial district to renounce their riches; nor did he leave them for New Haven because he preferred rustic simplicity. The asceticism of early Massachusetts Puritans was not a conscious program of the colonists, but an artifact of the experience of all English colonizing enterprises, the unavoidable "stripping down" of European culture caused by transplantation.[67] The first colonists were ascetics because they had no choice in the matter, and they were communitarians by default, but the mythology of origins and the privileging of the first generation has transformed early necessities into retrospective virtues.

The biographical genre of the exemplary Puritan life also reinforces the tendency to see the passage of time as a triumph of worldliness over piety. Demographic studies of church records have shown that conversion typically occurred at the time in life when people were leaving the protections of adolescence and assuming the responsibilities of adulthood. For women, conversion often coincided roughly with the age of marriage or first childbearing; for men, formal economic responsibilities and the assumption of public office were as important as changes in family status.[68] In either case, the most fervent spiritual experiences of a lifetime were associated with the moment when youth was left behind and engagement with the demands of the world commenced. It is no wonder, then, that at the end of a successful life in which property was accumulated, families were provided for, and civic duties were performed, the publicly active men who most commonly wrote autobiographies should look back and see their spiritual evolution as an early moment of grace followed by a life-long losing battle against worldliness. For highly educated men, the college experience contributed to this tendency as well, for in retrospect, college was a time to cultivate the mind and soul in communal cooperation, while later life's spiritual pilgrimage was more isolated and subject to greater worldly constraints, even for the many graduates who went on to become ministers.[69] The conventions of Puritan autobiography make the belief that prosperity and piety were enemies all the more difficult to shake.

The power of this belief cannot be overcome directly through yet another challenge to the declension model, another study testing whether commercial development erodes communal cohesion and Puritan piety.[70] Again, the problem with asking the older paradigm's questions is that regardless of the answer, the existing explanatory stuctures and narratives remain dominant. To avoid this trap requires not only that old assumptions be challenged, but that they be set aside while new explanatory assumptions are made. For several decades, critics of the declension model have been subtly suggesting the possibility that commercial development may have been beneficial to Puritan religion, and that later generations may well have retained the theological rigor and spiritual fervor of the founders. The time has come to begin by assuming the truth of these notions and asking not *whether* this was the case, but *how* this process worked. When John Cotton preached that "Christ cannot be had for money, yet sometimes without expense of money he cannot be had," he may have been attempting to explicate the contrary demands for striving and passivity implicit in the conversion process, but he was also describing an obvious truth about the social reality of Puritan religious culture.[71] Narratives of declension have always taken Cotton's statement to be a paradox, and have therefore explored the seemingly "insupportable pressures" of trying to be "both a pious Puritan and a successful merchant."[72] This book begins with the premise that in early New England successful merchants with an evangelical commitment to traditional religion were necessary to support the growth and expansion of Puritan churches, and seeks to describe how and how well they managed this task.

✿

The story begins in the 1660s, when second-generation Puritans were forced to grapple with long-term problems of continuity that their parents had avoided. By subtly revising the boundaries defining church membership, and by developing a more evangelical approach to the church's relationship to the larger world, innovative Puritans found ways to apply the wealth of their now-thriving economy to enhance the strength and scope of their religion. But change is always controversial, and there were those who resisted or were left behind by these developments. By tracing the history of two churches, one in Boston, the other in Westfield, I describe the conflicts over these changes while at the same time demonstrating that both churches, though quite different from each other, were part of the same evolving religious culture, two components within a single system.

The two opening chapters describe the controversies surrounding the founding of the two churches, controversies in which their respective positions within the Puritan movement were defined. The founders of Boston's Third Church were proponents of the "Halfway Covenant" and its underlying agenda, an evangelical approach to the church's relationship to the world at large. The Westfield church, led by the Puritan poet-minister Edward Taylor, took an opposing tack and chose to remain a closed conventicle of the elect, rigidly excluding those who failed to meet Taylor's high standards of piety, a position that would create lingering divisions among Westfield's townspeople.

Chapters 3 and 4 demonstrate the Puritan laity's power to shape the religious experience of their communities. The critical elements, I argue, were the laity's access to material and cultural resources necessary for the cultivation of piety, and the manner in which such resources were allocated within the community. Amid the abundance of Boston, the Third Church's lay leadership carefully planned to distribute their religious resources in ways that would expand the size of the "garden" of the church and invite more souls to partake of the means of grace. In Westfield, these resources were relatively scarce and were reserved mainly for the few church members, which contracted the size of the religious community and maintained high walls between those within the garden and those left out in the wilderness.

The focus then shifts to the clergy. Chapters 5 and 6 explore how the availability of material resources shaped the ministers' pastoral work, as well as the strategies used by the clergy for allocating their community's resources. A minister who understood how to make the most of the available resources for a wide range of potential members could help to foster a thriving church, while a minister out of touch with lay expectations and demands for the means of grace could damage a church's vitality, as the examples of Boston and Westfield demonstrate.

Chapters 7 and 8 combine these various elements—the founding visions and the lay and clerical contributions—into complementary narratives of the evolution of each church and its relationship to the larger community from the late seventeenth to the mid-eighteenth century. The Boston church grew and prospered, learned to mitigate conflict, developed successful strategies for internal spiritual renewal, and began to export its resources to other churches within Boston and throughout New England. By contrast, the Westfield church suffered; it dwindled in numbers, became increasingly isolated from other churches, and fell victim to bitter internal conflicts between the laity and their minister.

The concluding chapter reinterprets the Great Awakening of the mid-eighteenth century within the context of the respective patterns of development of these two churches. These widespread religious revivals were not a rejection of an arid system of belief, as the traditional interpretation insists. Rather, the Awakening was the product of the tremendous vitality of the religious culture generated by churches like Boston's Third, the coming to fruition of decades of effort devoted to the cultivation of piety. At the same time, conflicts that accompanied the revivals in some churches were not caused by revivalism itself. Church schisms, like the one in Westfield, were the result of long-standing tensions within many relatively impoverished churches over the proper allocation of scarce religious resources, chronic conflicts brought to the surface by the revival fervor. Such conflicts were not indictments of the religious culture as a whole, but struggles over access to and control of the elements necessary to sustain it—signs of its strength, not its weakness.

From the combined vantage points of Boston and Westfield, we can see the evolution of Puritan religious culture as a whole. These two churches were not only at opposite ends of Massachusetts settlement, but they also occupied extreme points on the spectrum of wealth and evangelical commitment among the colony's churches—Boston, rich and outward looking, Westfield, impoverished and turned in upon itself. Most New England churches fell somewhere between these extremes in one way or the other. Some, like the church in Plymouth, were as poor as Westfield, but through the efforts of clergymen and lay people, still developed a strong evangelical impulse.[73]

Others, like Boston's First Church, enjoyed resources comparable to those of Boston's Third, but lacked the same evangelical purpose. An examination of the two extremes of what remained a single spectrum reveals how New England's spiritual economy was sustained by commercial growth, by the dispersal of the population across the countryside, and by the lasting commitment of its members to replicate their culture in new places among future generations.

CHAPTER I

A "Right Middle Way"

Fundamental Truths which have been the same in all generations . . .
shall be transmitted more clear from age to age . . . until that which is
imperfect be done away. . . . Such addition is no innovation, but an illustration, not new light, but new sight.
     —John Norton, *The Orthodox Evangelist* (1654)

The Third Church in Boston was founded by lay people who wanted to
reform the Puritan church in response to new challenges faced by New England's maturing society. Gathered, covenanted churches consisting solely of
regenerate believers or "visible saints" had admirably suited the population of
the founding generation. Most of the original migrants to New England had
already believed themselves to be among the elect. Their withdrawal from
English society had prepared them to band together as like-minded saints.
But after three decades of settlement, it was becoming clear that the institutional structure of these "primitive" churches was not well adapted to solving
two emerging problems. One was the church's relationship to the growing
population that lay outside the reach of its influence; the other was the status
of the children of church members who had not yet joined in full communion. Both problems essentially concerned the boundary that a Puritan church
created between itself and the world—where should the wall be built and
how high should it be?

In the early 1660s, these problems caused conflict within Boston's First
Church, from which the founders of the Third Church eventually seceded.
Long-standing divisions among the First Church members came to a head
over the issue of the "Halfway Covenant" Synod of 1662. In the ensuing
controversy, the arguments were shaped by the opponents' different interpretations of the nature of the church and its responsibilities to the world. A dissenting minority within the First Church, the faction that favored the Half-

way Covenant, sought to accommodate changing social and political circumstances in New England by modifying the church's relationship to those outside its walls. Their opponents in the First Church majority insisted that any change from the church polity of the first generation was unforgivable apostasy.

The controversy raged for more than a decade, and it appears on the surface to be a dense thicket of abstract argumentation, tangled up with political issues and petty personal grievances in an impenetrable snarl. But a careful retelling of the story, pulling apart the main strands of conflict, reveals the purposes of the Third Church founders, a pattern underlying the decisions they made at each step along the way. Throughout their extended struggle with the First Church majority, the dissenters steadily promoted a program of Puritan reform in New England. They came to see the founding of their new church as an opportunity to institute a "middle way" of church polity that would preserve the purity achieved by the first generation but would also reach out in an evangelical fashion to a world that threatened to leave the Puritan churches behind. The Third Church founders faced the challenge of encouraging adaptation without abandoning tradition—how to change but stay the same. They resolved this dilemma by arguing that reform itself was a way to maintain continuity with the past, and by deliberately linking their innovations to symbols of traditional New England orthodoxy.

❧

Like it or not, change was thrust upon the second generation as it began to come of age in the 1660s. Forces beyond New Englanders' control made them rethink the nature and purpose of their institutions, and these outside pressures inevitably generated conflict. The Restoration of the Stuart monarchy threatened to end the remarkable political independence enjoyed by New England governments in the first three decades of settlement. With order restored at home, the crown turned its attention to regulating the trade and overseeing the laws and liberties of its overseas colonies, including Massachusetts. Charles II reinstituted the Church of England, and the Act of Uniformity of 1662 forced most of England's Puritan ministers into a position of dissent. With their most important English allies now ostracized, the Puritan churches of New England had reason to fear for their own security.[1] The Restoration also brought on social and economic changes. The passage of the early Navigation Acts pointed to the beginnings of an integrated Atlantic economy linking the home country and her American colonies to the maritime markets of Europe and Africa. As this Atlantic economy developed, it became increasingly important to the growth of New England and brought a new set of people to prominence. Anglican Royalist merchants began to compete with the Puritan founders for status and authority.[2]

Along with these external sources of change, the passing of New England's first generation raised further concerns over what the future would hold. The distinctive political and social institutions of the New England colonies were not ancient traditions but recent creations of the early settlers. The new forms of church polity created in the fledgling Puritan colonies had withstood many trials in the first generation, but not the test of time. The men and women who had flocked to the churches in the intense excitement of the early years of settlement were passing on. It was unclear whether their children would live up to the parents' commitment to the church, and whether the parents' vision of the church would be suitable for future generations.[3]

The town of Boston served as a focal point for these changes. As the center of government, the most populous town, and the home of the colony's leading magistrates and ministers, Boston figured prominently in many of the internal changes taking place in the colony. As the leading port and market center for New England, Boston was most directly influenced by the burgeoning Atlantic economy and was always the first place to feel the impact of English developments. Boston's First Church, the only church in town for its first two decades, was located across the way from the Town House, the center of both government and commerce in Massachusetts, at the intersection of Cornhill and King Street, where the major thoroughfare from the countryside met the street leading down to Boston's principal wharf. Strategically placed at the crossroads where people, ideas, and commercial goods moved in and out of New England, Boston's First Church held a powerful and highly visible position as New England's most important cultural institution.[4]

The First Church had been profoundly shaped by continuing contact with English Puritanism in its first three decades. Perhaps more than any other church in orthodox New England, Boston's First Church felt the effects of the radicalization of English Puritanism in the years after 1630. Although the founders of the Boston church in 1630 had not intended to reject the Church of England, the increasingly repressive measures instituted by Archbishop Laud after the departure of the first Massachusetts Bay settlers forced many English Puritans into a more extreme position. The ships arriving in the mid-1630s brought radicalized Puritans to New England, and these new settlers pushed the churches toward virtual separatism. The result was a newly restrictive definition of church membership which limited full communion to those who could satisfactorily describe their experience of conversion, and a movement toward renouncing the Church of England and denying the existence of any authority over the church beyond the gathered congregation.[5]

This movement gained strong support within Boston's First Church, especially after John Cotton arrived to become John Wilson's colleague as minister. Cotton led many of the recent immigrants, including Anne Hutchinson and Henry Vane, in a spiritual revival that culminated in the Antinomian crisis of 1637.[6] The Antinomians were put down through the combined efforts of the colony's magistrates and clergy, but in the aftermath the Boston church retained its tendencies toward radical separatism. In 1646, when the Massachusetts General Court called a synod of churches to write a platform of church discipline for the colony, the Boston church members opposed it as an infringement on the independence of the gathered congregation. Governor Winthrop wrote, ". . . the principal men who raised these objections were some of Boston, who came lately from England, where such a vast liberty was allowed, and sought for by all that went under the name of Independents."[7] Even after the Antinomian crisis, the Boston church maintained a more radical stance than most churches in the colony.

When John Cotton died in 1652, the Boston church's radical tendencies were tempered by his successor in the pulpit, John Norton. Together with John Wilson, Norton pursued a more moderate course of cooperation with the colony's government and other churches. In 1656, the Boston church moved toward a less restrictive definition of church membership by instituting baptismal practices that anticipated the Halfway Covenant. As minister, John Norton proved to be a strong supporter of church councils, ministerial synods, and the enhancement of clerical authority over congregations.[8] In 1662, he served along with Simon Bradstreet as agent for Massachusetts to the court of Charles II, and in his election sermon of 1661, Norton urged his audience to cooperate with the new English government: "God make us more wise and religious than so to carry it, that they should no sooner see a Congregationalman, than have cause to say, *They see an enemy to the Crown.*"[9]

Within the First Church, many members were troubled by these accommodations. Some of the church's leading laymen continued to believe that true churches must exclude all but visibly regenerate saints. In addition, they linked their religious stance to politics by arguing that any compromise with the crown on the political control of the colony constituted a threat to the purity and independence of the churches as well. John Endecott, the colony's governor and a magistrate since 1629; Richard Bellingham, the deputy governor; John Leverett, son of one of Boston's founders and Major-General of the Massachusetts Militia; Anthony Stoddard, another founder of Boston and a leading figure in town politics; all these and many of their "brothers" in the First Church were bitterly opposed to any compromise of the independence that they believed the Massachusetts Bay charter guaranteed.[10]

After the unexpected death of John Norton in 1663, and with the arrival in 1664 of a royal commission to investigate the Massachusetts government, these laymen voiced their protests on both the political and religious fronts. In October 1664, ninety-seven Bostonians including many First Church members petitioned the General Court to express their firm commitment to charter government as a bulwark of their religious liberties.[11] In the minds of these staunch opponents of compromise, defense of Massachusetts' charter privileges was directly linked to the first generation's forms of church polity. They believed that if Massachusetts' churches would only reject the innovations of the Halfway Covenant synod, then God would protect the Massachusetts government "by frustrating the present designe" of the King and his commissioners.[12] But to their dismay, the remaining minister of the First Church, John Wilson, stood in their way, and so they began to seek alternative leadership.

As early as 1662, the radical faction in the church had proposed that James Allen, a young minister from London recently ousted by the Act of Uniformity, be chosen as an assistant to Norton and the aging Wilson. However, at that time, the two senior ministers were thought to be a more than adequate clerical "supply," even for the "great" church of Boston, and the matter never came to open debate.[13] When Norton died suddenly in 1663 and John Wilson followed him to the grave in 1667, the most important pulpit in New England was now left vacant, and the search for their successors became urgent. The more radical group constituted a majority within the church, and in addition to promoting James Allen as a candidate for one of the vacant places, they chose to call John Davenport, the venerable minister of New Haven, for the other post.

By selecting John Davenport, the First Church's majority clearly defined its political and religious sympathies. At age 70, Davenport was an unlikely candidate to begin a new position. He was already bound to the New Haven church, which he had founded and served as minister for thirty years. There were also many younger men, both local graduates of Harvard College and refugees from Restoration England, who could ably fill the post. But Davenport was widely known as New England's most vocal supporter of charter government and of strictly gathered churches.[14] By the 1660s, his position had become virtually reactionary; he opposed unequivocally any variation from his own vision of the proper church and state. Davenport detested the proposed merger of his New Haven Colony with Connecticut in 1663, for it meant enfranchising the unregenerate under Connecticut's broadly defined polity. He abhorred the Halfway Covenant for its inclusive church membership standards and for its implication that a government-sponsored synod held any authority over the practices of individual gathered churches. Anything but the complete independence of New England governments from crown control was for Davenport an absolute threat to the purity of New England's churches.[15] Davenport insisted that his position had been the original purpose of New England's founders, "the first waies of reformation here begun," and that deviation from this standard was apostasy. By devising this rhetorical strategy, Davenport implied that the radicalized New England churches of the mid-1630s were immutable and sacred models for proper church organization, as inviolable as the Bible as guides to pure worship. The Boston church majority, in calling Davenport, expressed their approval of Davenport's version of New England's past and offered him a prominent pulpit from which to propound his vision.[16]

Davenport's quest for strictly gathered churches withdrawn from the world, for absolute purity among the saints in communion, put him at one extreme of orthodox New England Puritan thought on church polity. At the other end of the spectrum lay the desire among godly people to spread their message to the world and to reform both the inner spirit and the outer condition of society. For these purposes, separation from the Church of England or from unregenerate people was an abdication by the elect of their responsibilities to God and to their fellow men and women.[17] This position was just as "original," just as much a part of the "first ways" of the New England churches, as Davenport's. In the first generation, Thomas Hooker, Thomas Shepard, and John Winthrop had been among its champions. In the Boston church of the 1660s, a significant minority of the membership retained their commitment to this position on the spectrum of Puritan belief. They also followed the recent leadership of John Norton, who emphasized a broader, more evangelical impulse with respect to questions of church polity. These lay men and women were devout, pious, regenerate believers, but because they disagreed with those of Davenport's persuasion, they tended to downplay his notion that early Massachusetts offered an "ancient" model that defined a single way, a true form of church polity. Instead, they looked to avoid the more extreme errors of their own times, to find a "middle way" between the desire for purity and the responsibilities of living in the world. They were less likely to equate change with apostasy and more willing to respond to worldly developments. In 1654, John Norton wrote, "even Fundamental Truths which have been the same in all generations, have been, and shall be transmitted more clear from age to age in the times of Reformation, until that which is imperfect be done away. . . . Such addition, is no innovation, but an illustration, not new light, but new sight.[18] In this spirit of ongoing reformation, a dissenting minority within Boston's First Church supported the Halfway Covenant as an adaptation in the church that would promote this "middle way."

Jonathan Mitchell, one of the authors of the Halfway Covenant, stated its purpose in terms that reflected the habit of mind of its proponents: "We make account, that if we keep baptism within the non-excommunicable and the Lord's Supper within the compass of those that have (unto charity) somewhat of the power of godliness, or grace in exercise, we shall be near about the right middle-way of church reformation."[19] Technically, Mitchell's description accurately characterized what the Halfway Covenant accomplished; it allowed the church to look inward to the needs of the godly, for whom the Lord's Supper would provide spiritual nourishment, as well as outward toward the "non-excommunicable," for whom baptism would serve as admission to the benefits of church discipline and worship. But the hesitations and qualifications in Mitchell's statement, his "somewhat" and "near about," reveal the compromising, less than certain attitude about discovering religious truth that characterized this group.[20] Under the guidance of John Norton, the First Church had already moved in the direction of a more inclusive church, and in 1656 had voted for an expanded policy on baptism and discipline of church members' children.[21] To the dissenting minority of the 1660s, the possibility of turning back from "this great Generation truth . . . confirmed by the Synod" meant abandoning their "awful engagement" to maintain their "duty unto the children of the Church."[22] "Confirmed" is the critical word here. In the dissenters' eyes, the Halfway Covenant merely confirmed a principle that their church had already accepted, and now it seemed strange to them that the First Church majority would oppose it. The adaptations made under Norton and by the 1662 synod had been the necessary consequences of a commitment to worldly reformation, in which the best one could hope for was to be "near about the right middle-way." To forsake this commitment in pursuit of an unstable and short-sighted ideal of purity was to depart radically from the middle way. For the First Church minority, accommodation to changing conditions was therefore not an indication of apostasy but a measure of commitment to duty, and the Halfway Covenant was not a half-hearted compromise of a definitive Puritan ideal, but a positive step toward a more perfectly reformed church in New England.[23]

With respect to the political issues of the 1660s, this minority faction in Boston's First Church also tended to favor, for the time being, an accommodating relationship with the Restoration government. John Hull, Joshua

Scottow, Hezekiah Usher, and William Davis were among the First Church dissenters who signed petitions to the General Court expressing their loyalty to the crown and the necessity for compromise with royal officials. They demonstrated their support for this position by contributing money to send Norton and Bradstreet as agents to the crown in 1662.[24] They had no intention of capitulating to imperial demands and were willing to stand up for what they felt to be New England's rights, but they were unwilling to deny that the king had rights as well.[25] They believed that the real danger to self-government and to the preservation of the churches lay not in cooperation with a reasonable monarch, but in needless and provocative defiance of the crown's limited authority. In contrast to the majority's claim to independence based on a strict construction of "ancient" charter liberties, these "moderates" within the Boston church again proposed a middle way, a political stance that exactly paralleled their religious position.

The argument, then, was over whether New England's churches and governments should adapt to changing conditions or hold fast to a narrowly defined version of the ways of the founders. For most of the 1660s, the two factions in the First Church managed to coexist peacefully. While the venerable Norton and Wilson remained in the pulpit, their presence helped to preserve harmony, but with their deaths, conditions changed rapidly. John Wilson's funeral was in August 1667, and by the following month the majority faction had expressed its desire to call John Davenport. To the minority, Davenport was a singularly inappropriate choice and on September 30, 1667, "30 Brethren" stated their objections. They cited Davenport's obligations to the New Haven church, and his age was another concern, for "our church's double experience of her widdow hood, and the difficulty of meat supply, causeth us in prudence to conceive, a person of soe great an age not soe suitable to that end." But the dissenters' objections ultimately rested on their sense of "duty unto the children," which they could not in good conscience abandon by endorsing a vocal opponent of the Halfway Covenant. The majority ignored the dissenters' arguments and went ahead with the calling of John Davenport, who was eager to move to New England's capital.[26] With this, the tensions that had been building in Boston's First Church for at least a decade broke out in a public controversy.

The controversy became bitterly hostile and devolved into a long series of petty squabbles, exacerbated by the personalities and egos of the participants.[27] The struggle degenerated into what Perry Miller called the "most sordid story . . . in the annals of New England."[28] Underlying the surface contention were differences on significant issues in Puritan religious culture that shaped the course of the conflict at each stage. The struggle can be understood as an ongoing argument over three issues: (1) the relationship of the individual believer to the body of the church, and particularly the extent of the authority held by the church over the member's actions and beliefs; (2) the nature of the sacraments as boundaries of participation within the life of the church; and (3) the role of advisory councils, synods, or other deliberative bodies in mediating the affairs of individual churches. By organizing the narrative of the controversy around these three issues, rather than adhering to a strict chronological reconstruction of events, the dissenting minority's persistent pursuit of a new position in the Puritan movement emerges from the sordid squabbling.

❧

The opening stage of the controversy revolved around a single question: what obligation did members owe to a church to which they had bound themselves in sacred covenant but which they could no longer countenance in good faith? The First Church majority saw the church as an institution that demanded uniformity among its members. Religious truth was singular, and any deviation from the revealed way, as determined by the individual church, was punishable as sin or even heresy. In contrast, the dissenting minority envisioned the possibility of unity without uniformity. Honest disagreement could be tolerated within a gathered church about contested matters in worship and church polity, as long as basic agreement existed on the nature and function of the church. The Halfway Covenant and the calling of John Davenport brought these opposing positions into direct conflict.

From the beginning, the First Church dissenters hoped to resolve their differences with the majority through the ordinary means available within the Congregational system of church polity. Their dissent was not an expression of outright opposition. They were not backing a pro-synod candidate for the ministry against the majority's choice of John Davenport. Instead, they recommended laying aside the contentious issue of Davenport's candidacy and waiting to see if they could recruit a famous divine from Britain, "him who is soe much desired," Dr. John Owen. Owen was a minister of the highest stature among English Congregationalists; his calling would have received unanimous consent even in such a fractured church as Boston's First. As an English minister, Owen had no established position on the Halfway Covenant, since he had not had to face the issues that emerged in New England only after a generation of Puritan establishment. To the First Church dissenters, Owen was therefore the perfect compromise candidate—universally respected for godliness and orthodoxy but untainted by connections to local factions.[29] When it soon became clear that Owen was unavailable, the dissenting minority asked to discuss other potential candidates, but James Penn, the ruling elder of the church, "totally refused" to raise the issue in church meetings.[30]

Penn's refusal and the majority's mounting opposition to the dissenters' wishes were based on the premise that a church should be unanimous in its beliefs, a position that left no room for honest disagreement. Anthony Stoddard, a prominent voice among the majority, claimed that the dissenters' objection to Davenport and desire for alternative candidates were "irregular, irrationall and he was ready to say ungodly." Others began to criticize the minority faction, "as if they were called to deale severely with their Brethren dissenting." Citing scripture as evidence, the majority claimed that dissent was an "accursed thing [that] must be removed else God will not be with them." As it became increasingly clear to the minority that their position was not being treated as honest disagreement, the possibility for compromise within the church steadily diminished.[31]

In the meantime, the church majority wrote to New Haven summoning John Davenport to the First Church pulpit; the letter minimized the extent of the conflict among the Boston membership. In response, the New Haven church expressed its reluctance to relinquish its minister, but Davenport himself suggested the possibility of a trial run in which he would preach to the Boston church "for to finde out the minde of God" in the matter. Davenport also took the opportunity to admonish the First Church's dissenters to "walk in the first waies where in you walked according to his Rule under . . . Mr. John Cotton," and not to "fall into divissions amongst yourselves by different principles."[32] This admonition was something of an insult to the dissenters and to the late John Wilson, for Wilson, not Cotton, had been the first minister of the Boston church, and it was Wilson's position that Davenport was now trying to assume. Despite the New Haven church's objections to his departure, Davenport set out for Boston for his trial ministry in the spring of 1668, arriving on May 2 in the midst of a heavy thunderstorm. For Puritans accustomed to reading the heavens for signs and portents, the atmospheric conditions were ominous.[33]

Two weeks after his arrival Davenport preached the Boston Thursday lecture. The Thursday lecture was by this time an established institution in many orthodox New England churches; it offered ministers the chance to discuss current events in a religious context in ways that would have been inappropriate for regular sabbath day preaching, when the focus remained firmly upon "personal salvation through faith in Christ."[34] Although Boston now had a Second Church in the North End, the weekly lecture remained a fixture at the First Church meetinghouse, and the regular presence on Thursdays of the colony's magistrates, merchants, and traders drawn to the Town

House across the way enhanced the significance of the event. The novelty of Davenport's presence, along with his longstanding renown and current notoriety, guaranteed that his audience would consist of "a great part of the Countrey." To the surprise of the First Church dissenters, Davenport launched an attack on them in his prayer before the sermon. He claimed that the dissenters' conditions for choosing a minister were such that "neither Christ himself, nor his Apostles gave any warrant for," and he was convinced that "Satan hath a great hand in it." By demonizing disagreement as willful sin, Davenport eliminated the possibility for compromise. With Davenport acting as a public spokesman for the church's majority faction (though he was still not even a member of the church), the dissenters became convinced that their hopes for an alternative candidate were futile. Consequently, they "began to think if the Lord opened a doore of departure from their relation to the Church, they were called to imbrace it."[35]

The process of departure proved to be far more difficult than the dissenters imagined. Although disagreement over the Halfway Covenant's baptismal policy was the immediate cause of this controversy, the First Church majority insisted that the principle at stake was the location of ultimate authority over the members of the church. They argued that dissent within a gathered church was unacceptable, and on this basis, they attempted to prevent the dissenters from escaping their covenanted obligations.[36] On August 10, 1668, twenty-nine of the dissenting brethren submitted a request to be dismissed from membership in the church. The majority asked the dissenters to leave the meeting in order to consider their motion. The dissenting brethren, along with their wives, cooperated only reluctantly, saying that "if the Church had business to transact that concerned all the Church [that is, anything other than their motion for dismissal] they durst not absent themselves." Despite assurances to the contrary, after the dissenters left the meeting the majority set aside their request for dismissal and instead proceeded with the calling of John Davenport for the ministry. Not surprisingly, the vote in favor of Davenport was now unanimous.

In the weeks after this meeting, the majority frequently met in private to conduct negotiations with the New Haven church in order to secure Davenport's release. During this period, they refused to act upon the dissenters' petition for dismissal and insisted on the church's right to maintain control of its members.[37] Deception now began to creep into the proceedings. Correspondence between the Boston and New Haven churches was concealed from the dissenters and discussed only among the majority in private meetings. The majority sent messengers to New Haven to request a definitive release of Davenport to the Boston church. The written reply the messengers brought back conveyed the New Haven church's continuing reluctance, but this letter was withheld from the body of the Boston church. Later, Davenport and a small group of his allies discussed its implications in private. They decided it was best to keep the letter a secret, and they wrote again to New Haven pressing for a more favorable answer. In the interim, the majority continued to refuse the dissenters' petition for dismissal, saying "that this was not the season" for they were "unlikely to proceed unto [Davenport's] ordination."[38]

In late October 1668, another letter arrived from New Haven, and on the basis of its contents, Elder Penn propounded John Davenport for admission. A week later, when Davenport was formally admitted to the Boston church, Penn read the assembled members the letter from New Haven which seemed to dismiss Davenport. But what he read was actually a carefully edited redaction of the original, complete with a forged signature of New Haven's elder Nicholas Street, which created the impression that the New Haven church was finally ready to let its minister go.[39] In effect, Davenport and his allies were falsely declaring Davenport to be free of his obligations to the New Haven church. In so doing, they were denying the New Haven church's rightful authority over church dismissals, the same authority that they demanded to hold over Boston's dissenting brethren. In secret, Davenport violated the principle of the gathered church's authority for the sake of defending the very same principle in public from a pulpit where his voice would have a greater impact than it would in the wilds of New Haven.[40]

But ironies abounded on both sides of the conflict. For their part, the dissenting minority had argued for the possibility of disagreement and compromise within the body of the church. Failing that, they pressed to be released to form their own church, but their purpose was not a sectarian departure from orthodoxy. This was the irony of the dissenters' position—the program they were promoting, the changes they hoped to make in New England Puritanism, ran counter to the separation they were being forced to make. They favored cooperation among open and inclusive churches, not closed conventicles of the godly. Yet the First Church majority refused to cooperate and left them no option other than secession and withdrawal, the traditional response of separatists and sectarians, as a way to express their commitment to compromise and unity. In forming their own church, these dissenters would therefore need to formulate a plan to overcome the stigma of their separatist beginnings.

❧

Once the dissenting faction expressed its desire to leave the First Church, a second major issue moved to the foreground of the controversy, namely, the meaning and usage of the sacraments. The Halfway Covenant's reform of

membership standards required a reconsideration of the nature of the sacraments because participation in the sacraments marked the boundaries of
church membership. The First Church majority's opposition to the Halfway
Covenant demonstrated its commitment to a clear and wide division between members and non-members. Full membership required the ability to
give an account of one's conversion experience, as well as the courage to
come to the Lord's Supper faced with the biblical injunction that to do so
unworthily was to eat and drink one's own damnation.[41] The privilege of
baptism for one's children went with full-membership, but the children's
membership was only provisional—if they never attested to a conversion experience, then at some unspecified point their connection to the church was
nullified. In this formulation, the gulf between the saved and the unsaved
was wide and the risks involved in taking communion were high.

In contrast, the Halfway Covenant minimized the risks of coming to
communion and allowed for a church that was more inclusive. Under the
synod's recommendation, baptismal privileges were extended to all lineal descendants of full members, not just the children but future generations as
well, regardless of the status of the children themselves. A category of "halfway" membership was created, consisting of baptized children who had
"owned the covenant" and were striving for but had not yet attained the status of full members. In this way, the baptized "children of the church," no
matter how old, would never be expelled so long as the possibility for conversion still existed. With full communion no longer the only form of church
membership, the Lord's Supper's role as a barrier between the church and the
world was reduced. The sacrament of communion remained a standard of
purity within the church and was reserved for those attesting to a conversion
experience, but its displacement as the sole standard for church membership
made it easier for ministers and laymen alike to exercise the "judgment of
charity" in examining potential communicants. The judgment of charity
meant that although saving faith was required for full membership, the least
hint of true saving faith discernible within candidates was enough to allow
their admission. Once within the church, weak Christians would grow in
grace and become more assured in the expression of their faith, due in part to
the beneficial effects of the experience of communion. In sum, although the
supporters of the Halfway Covenant maintained the central importance of
communion as a locus of purity within the church, they also developed a
more charitable approach to the exercise of judgment in such matters, and
consequently, a more inclusive vision of the church.[42]

John Davenport's ordination as minister of the First Church in December 1668 made these differing definitions of the sacrament a source for fur-

ther controversy. The dissenting brethren were now in an even more difficult position. With ordained ministers in the pulpit (James Allen was ordained as Davenport's assistant on the same day) the church could enjoy communion again and the sacrament could be used as a "snare." If the dissenters refused to take communion with the church majority, they would be neglecting God's ordinances and therefore subject to censure. But if they received communion from the new ministers, they would be expressing their tacit approval of their ordination and obviating the need for their dismissal. Either way, the dissenters were stuck. John Davenport openly explained their dilemma in a sermon on January 17, 1669, and then called for the celebration of the sacrament the following Sunday, in effect issuing a challenge to the dissenting minority. On that day, the dissenters expressed in writing their desire to forbear from taking the Lord's Supper, but Davenport and Penn refused to read the letter. When the time came for communion, "all the dissenters after a pause to see if the Elder or Church would offer any ease unto them . . . withdrew themselves except the deacons." The three deacons, Jacob Eliot, Edward Rainsford, and Richard Truesdale, counted themselves among the dissenters, but since it was their responsibility to assist in administering the Lord's Supper, they stayed and performed their duty, "but they durst not partake least they should be ensnared."[43]

Davenport now insisted that in abstaining from communion, the deacons had expressed contempt for the sacrament, for the church, and for his own ordination. In a series of carefully orchestrated meetings in February 1669, Davenport tried to discipline the deacons. Technically, the case was purely an internal church matter to be determined by full church members, but the disciplinary meetings were staged in public with "neer five hundred persons present and diverse not of the Church." Davenport was arguing for the absolute internal autonomy of the church, but he was not averse to letting outsiders be witness to church business if he could score political points. The tone of the meetings was inquisitorial. Davenport "much undervalued" the deacons' arguments and declared them "jejune and poore." The church brethren assailed the deacons with questions, attempted to trap them into saying something censurable, and tried to force them to retract their petition for dismissal. When the deacons refused to desert their fellow dissenters, "the Church concluded them unmeet to be continued in their office, and did therefore vote them out." They were replaced immediately by three new deacons sympathetic to the majority.[44] The majority's use of communion as a "snare" was consistent with a vision of the church as an exclusive refuge for like-minded saints, with absolute authority over its members and complete autonomy as a corporate body. The sacrament became a device for division and exclusion, rather than a means for fostering piety and church fellowship.

After further efforts by the majority to admonish and humiliate their leaders, the dissenting brethren decided to take part in the Lord's Supper the next time it was called to demonstrate their respect for the institution of the church and its ordinances. Immediately thereafter, they renewed their request for dismissal, which the First Church majority again denied. The longer the dissenting brethren pressed their case, the more the majority insisted "that there was no reliefe for a grieved Brother or Brethren in a church unless the Church will relieve them untill the day of judgement." Unprepared to wait that long, the dissenters took matters into their own hands.

✵

In making plans to form their own church, the dissenters also began to formulate a strategy to repair their public image. The concern was that the appearance of separatism in their secession from the church and their seeming insult to the sacrament of communion might damage their larger cause. To counter this tendency, the dissenters turned to one of the traditional institutions of Massachusetts orthodoxy. After their rude treatment at the hands of Davenport, the dissenters petitioned the colony's governor and magistrates to "provoke the churches" of Massachusetts to come to their aid in the form of a church council.[45] A council usually consisted of ministers and laymen representing several neighboring churches, gathered together on a temporary basis to settle disputes within a particular church. This was not the first time in this controversy that a council had been asked to sort out the strife within the First Church. When the dissenters had first objected to the calling of John Davenport, they had requested a church council to mediate the differences between the factions, " . . . it being God's way when any church wants light or peace." But as the controversy proceeded, the question of the power and purpose of church councils became the next contentious issue.

The First Church majority not only insisted on absolute authority over its own membership, but also claimed complete autonomy as an independent church. Technically speaking, all Congregational churches were independent, unbound by any outside authority or hierarchy, but the First Church majority took this position to an extreme, insisting that they were not even obliged to listen to the advice of a council. In contrast, the dissenting minority within the church promoted councils in principle as a way to increase harmony among the churches of New England and to insure that the churches would be united in religious orthodoxy. They also saw the institution of the council as the only practical way to deal with internal church disputes. To them, disputes were inevitable given mankind's sinful nature and the provisional quality of human understanding, but mere disagreement did not imply willful heresy or sinful intent by one of the parties. As the controversy progressed, councils were called at the dissenters' request in the hope of resolving differences, but in each case the majority's opposition to the validity of church councils limited their effectiveness.

When John Davenport first arrived in Boston in the spring of 1668 and the majority wanted to move promptly to ordain him, the dissenters "intreated them not to proceed further without Councill." The majority agreed to a council, but they attempted to control its proceedings by framing the questions for deliberation, insisting that the council would only be consulted "to take advice in order to Censur[e]" the dissenters.[46] This position was consistent with the majority's belief that councils had no binding authority over individual churches, and that the blame for the controversy had already been decided. Yet their desire to regulate the council demonstrated their fear that other churches might interpret a council's authority differently. If the council's opinion favored the dissenters it would strengthen their position.

The first council met in August 1668, and after deliberating on the matter, concluded that Boston's growing population made an additional church necessary. Since the dissenters seemed unable to consent in the calling of John Davenport, they should be dismissed "in order to the propagation of another Church, to be sett up in the Towne of Boston." In the meantime, the dissenters were to be allowed to "have Communion with this church, or some other in the ordinances of God." The council saw "no rule in Scripture" for the First Church "as to proceeding to Church censure" of the dissenters.[47] The impact of this recommendation on the controversy was negligible. Through the winter of 1668–69, the First Church majority ignored the council's advice, ordained John Davenport, and trapped the dissenters with the "snare" of communion.

After the first council, the dissenters had hoped to start a new church with the tolerance, if not the blessing, of the First Church majority. But a winter of increasingly embittered conflict made them see that if they were to form a new church, it would have to be in the face of the First Church's censure. Given their commitment to the ideal of inter-church fellowship and harmony, they felt that in order to proceed with such a radical action, tantamount to schism, they would need outside support. In breaking away from the First Church, they had to demonstrate their allegiance to the rest of New England orthodoxy, and therefore they called for another church council in the spring of 1669.

The dissenters composed a letter to the churches of Lynn, Salem, and Ipswich, three of the oldest churches in Massachusetts Bay, asking for assistance and declaring their loyalty to Massachusetts civil and ecclesiastical polity, despite "such reports against us" that these churches might have heard. Soon other churches nearer to Boston were invited to join, and on April 13, this "2nd Councill" convened.[48] On that day, a flurry of letters went back and forth between the council and the First Church elders. The council asked "againe and againe" for the First Church's cooperation, but Davenport, who did not think they constituted an "orderly Councill," saw no reason to "act with you in matters that concerne this Church." The next day a meeting of the entire First Church was held "to proceed against the dissenters." The council sent a delegation, headed by Richard Mather, minister of Dorchester, with a letter to the First Church. Upon their arrival at the Town House where the First Church members had assembled, they found the doors locked. Davenport refused to let them into the meeting, and would not accept their letter. With no other recourse, the "aged Gentlemen" (Richard Mather was 73 years old) waited outside the door while the meeting went on. Peter Oliver, one of the dissenting brethren, "went to fetch chairs" for the council's messengers to sit on while they waited.[49]

Eventually, Davenport allowed the dissenters' letter (though not the council's representatives) to be taken inside, but then forced through a vote against reading the letter aloud. Some of the First Church members, notably John Leverett, began to feel uneasy about the rude treatment of "these Reverend Elders" waiting outside, and moved to send several members to consult privately with the council's delegation. They met across the street at the house of Hezekiah Usher, a merchant and leading dissenter, and afterwards brought the council's letter back to the church meeting, where the members finally agreed to hear it. The letter itself, signed by eighteen ministers and fourteen laymen, was extremely apologetic in tone. It asked only that the council be allowed to help settle the dispute, and made no specific recommendations. Yet the First Church members "voted to take no notice of it," and Davenport returned to the task of prosecuting the dissenters. He asked, knowing full well the answer, whether anyone "who had any paper of charges against the dissenters would produce them?" Elder Penn, who had prepared for the moment in advance, obliged by bringing forth a "narrative of charges." These ranged from a condemnation of the whole group to specific allegations against prominent dissenters like William Davis, John Hull, and Thomas Savage. But the proceedings went awry as the dissenters strenuously defended themselves, and John Davenport's reasons for leaving New Haven came into question, "which occasioned Mr. Davenport to labour to cleare himself." The meeting broke up with nothing resolved.[50]

Two days later the council dissolved as well, but not before composing a lengthy recommendation, arguing that the First Church's rejection of the council's guidelines left the dissenters free to form a new church. Beneath the specific issues lay a defense of the role of church councils in New England's church polity. John Allin, the Dedham minister, appended an intricate scriptural defense of the councils and the dissenters, and his careful arguments were enclosed with the council's statement in a letter from the dissenting brethren to the First Church.[51] This letter was the dissenters' final plea that their intentions be rightly understood. They claimed that their only desire was "the interprising an Altar of witness and not of Apostasy." They declared their full commitment to the Massachusetts government and to the church platforms of 1648 and 1662, and expressed their resolve "to maintaine due Brotherly love with the first Church in Boston." True to form, the majority ignored the letter, offered more charges, and suggested further censures. Finally, on May 3, 1669, confessing their "shame and confusion" at the extent of the controversy, and admitting "much sinfull infirmity . . . in our late transactions," the dissenters declared their innocence of the majority's charges and announced their intention to form a new church.[52] The majority, unmoved, declared the dissenters "under great guilt," suggested that God would punish them in another world "where the council could not helpe them," voted to excommunicate them and labelled them "scismaticks." The dissenters "heard them patiently and then humbly took leave of the Church. . . ."[53] After two years of conflict, the church had been split.

❧

The definitive break with the First Church left the dissenters with a new set of challenges. To form their own church, they had to request the General Court's approval, call neighboring churches to assist in the church gathering, write a formal church covenant, ordain a minister, and build a new meetinghouse. In addition, the status of the wives of the dissenting brethren, who remained members of the First Church after their husbands' departure, promised to be a vexing problem. But now that the dissenters were free and independent, each of these hurdles could be used as an opportunity to promote their vision of the future direction Puritan churches should take and to repair the damage that the internal controversy had done to their image and their ideals. The dramatic events at the Town House during the second council brought widespread public attention to the strife within the First Church, and the religious controversy now spread into the political domain, where the issues became larger and more complex.[54] Yet the magnitude of the controversy was an advantage to the dissenters, focusing attention upon their actions. The public gestures they made in the process of overcoming the obstacles to building Boston's Third Church helped to define their "middle way" as a means to honor New England's religious tradition while responding to the world's demands for change.

Massachusetts law required government sanction for the gathering of a new church, and the dissenting brethren turned to the magistrates (that is, the upper house of the General Court) for approval. Three of the colony's magistrates had been members of the church councils that supported the dissenters, and the new church found four additional magistrates who were willing to back them.[55] These seven, together with Francis Willoughby, the new deputy governor who was known to sympathize with the dissenters, constituted a majority of the upper house of the General Court. On the basis of their approval, the dissenters sent to five neighboring churches to arrange for the formal gathering of their church. However, the remaining six magistrates, including First Church members Richard Bellingham (now the governor), John Leverett, and Edward Tyng, opposed the new church and attempted to use their power to prevent its formal gathering. The proceedings were scheduled to take place in Charlestown, across the river from Boston, on May 12, 1669—the location was chosen in part to make it difficult for the First Church to interfere.[56] The First Church tried to interrupt anyway by sending a delegation over in the morning bearing letters from the church and from the opposing magistrates who desired "to impede the coalition." The assembly listened to their arguments, but the visiting delegation had little enthusiasm for further conflict, and after a midday adjournment they went home. The dissenters, supported by ministers and laymen from the five neighboring churches, proceeded to the formal gathering.[57]

The founders of the Third Church adapted the rituals of church founding to their own purposes of promoting reform while maintaining continuity. Tradition called for a written church covenant, and most of the specific terms of the Third Church covenant were typical of all seventeenth-century New England churches. But in two points, the founding members spoke to the concerns that had prompted their break with the First Church. First, the founders placed special emphasis on the idea that they were acting not only for themselves but for future generations. The text states that: ". . . for the furtherance of this blessed fellowship we do likewise promise to indeavour to establish among ourselves and *conveigh down to our posterity*, all the holy trueths and ordinances of the gospell." The second distinctive characteristic of the Third Church covenant was its assertion of the importance of solidarity among the gathered churches of New England. The covenant expressed the founders' desire "to hold promote and maintain sisterly fellowship and communion with all the churches of Saints in all those holy ways of order appointed between them by our Lord Jesus to the utmost—especially with those among whome the Lord hath set us, that the Lord may be one and his name one, in all these Churches throughout all generations."[58] This claim departed from earlier New England church covenants, including those of the first two Boston churches, in stressing the importance of inter-church fellowship. Fellowship in this case meant support for synods and councils that would promote harmony among the churches, so that religion would remain unified in all the churches of New England. The Third Church covenant directly opposed the atomistic position taken by the First Church and John Davenport, and described a new viewpoint commensurate with the Halfway Covenant, a vision of cooperation and ordered harmony among the many independent churches of the region.[59]

Following the gathering of the new church, the dispute between the two churches flared up again in political controversy, touched off when John Davenport preached an inflammatory election sermon on May 19, 1669.[60] But in the summer of 1669, not long after this sermon, the Third Church effort to establish its legitimacy was aided by the exposure of Davenport's deception in his dealings with both the First Church and his former church in New Haven. Nicholas Street, Davenport's former colleague in the New Haven ministry, arrived in Boston and brought to public attention the concealment and secret editing of the New Haven letters, which caused the sympathy of Davenport's staunch supporters among the magistrates and clergy to waver.[61] The exposure of this scandal helped to enhance the new church's reputation and to ease the founders' concerns about the righteousness of their enterprise, but it did not end the controversy. The new church members still had to act carefully in their efforts to claim a rightful place within Massachusetts orthodoxy. If their desire to promote a broader vision of the New England Way were to succeed, they had to avoid appearing as "innovators" or apostates, and instead emphasize their continuity with New England's religious traditions. In the remaining foundation work of building a meetinghouse, ordaining a minister, and bringing their wives into the new church, the founders acted consistently to place their church within the mainstream of Puritan religious tradition, stressing the possibility for continuity with the past while carrying out reforms.

The problem of building a new meetinghouse, which was often troublesome even in churches free of controversy, was particularly difficult for the Third Church. The meetinghouse of the First Church symbolically occupied the center of Boston's geography, across from the seat of government in the Town House and at the leading mercantile crossroads. But the Third Church members hoped to claim the centrality of their position for New England's religious future, and to suggest that the First Church had marginalized itself through its quasi-separatist position. However, the typical procedure for allocating land to new churches threatened instead to marginalize the Third Church within Boston. Ordinarily, the General Court stipulated that new churches in Massachusetts towns be given public land on which to build. After considerable political infighting, the Boston town meeting offered the Third Church a plot of open land, but the site proved to be unsatisfactory. The land was located "nigh the windmill" in the extreme south end of town, which "was no way judged convenient" by the Third Church brethren.[62] The new church refused this offer and chose instead to build on private property donated to them by a member. To refuse free land was quite unusual, especially in Boston, where land was a scarce and valuable commodity. Yet the historical and symbolic importance of the privately owned land the church was given explains this decision.

The donor was Mrs. Mary Norton, widow of John Norton, the spiritual mentor of the new church's founders. The Nortons had occupied this site, located on the main street leading out to the town "neck" toward Roxbury (now Washington Street), during John Norton's tenure at the First Church. Before that, the land had been known as the "Green," part of the estate of Governor John Winthrop. John Norton had purchased the site from Winthrop's heirs in the 1650s, and it passed into Mary Norton's hands upon his death in 1663.[63] In the late 1630s, when the First Church was thinking of building a larger meetinghouse, Winthrop had offered this land to the members, but his offer had been rejected. The First Church preferred to keep their meetinghouse at the head of King Street, fearing that a new location would draw trade away from the old center, to the detriment of the merchants who had invested heavily in the marketplace.[64] In 1669, when the newly formed Third Church was seeking a location, Winthrop's site on "the Green" was still available, and Mary Norton generously offered the land as a gift.[65] Both John Winthrop and John Norton had been firm advocates of a church that reached out to the world and upheld its responsibilities to society and to future generations. By accepting this site which the First Church had rejected, the Third Church staked a claim to the tradition of Norton and Winthrop, and defended "the travelling truth relating to duty unto the children of the Church," a truth which they felt Davenport and the First Church had also rejected.

In addition, by placing their meetinghouse on "the Green," the Third Church offered a challenge to the First Church. Unlike the Second Church, which was off in the North End and served a distinct geographical community, the Winthrop/Norton lot was scarcely two hundred yards from the marketplace. It was a less crowded, more attractive site, yet close enough to draw away worshipers from the old church. Had the Third Church accepted the land in the far South End offered by the town, it might have seemed more like the North Church, filling the need for a new parish in the growing town. But the rejection of the town offering in favor of the site on "the

Green" meant that the Third Church's challenge to the First Church was more than just a difference over baptismal standards—it represented a competition for the religious future of the Puritan way in Boston and a major restructuring of sacred space within the town.

This context makes the struggle that ensued over the construction of the meetinghouse more comprehensible. Recently arrived English observers were astounded that men were thrown in prison over a seemingly trivial matter. In late June 1669, the Third Church members began the work of raising the building, but were interrupted when Governor Bellingham signed out a warrant to prevent any further construction. When the members in charge of construction refused to obey, the constable arrested them and locked them in the town jail. The Governor claimed that this private construction of a meetinghouse would be "sundry wayes detrimental to the publique peace, and welfare of the place," and insisted that the project be delayed until the General Court could review it. The Suffolk County Court then tried the two men in charge and fined them £5 in fees and court costs for violating the Governor's warrant. However, the colony's magistrates overruled the court's decision against the builders and gave their written approval to allow the completion of the meetinghouse.[66]

The meetinghouse itself became a major statement of the goals of the Third Church founders. They commissioned "many Brethren in Neighbouring Townes" to bring in some eighty-three "Cartes laden with . . . timber," mostly cedar, from which the building was framed and constructed. By November 1669, the work was completed. Although traditional in design, no expense was spared in the construction of "a large, spacious, and faire meeting house, with three large porches, every way compleately fitted, and covered with sheete lead."[67] The building featured "square pews" on the ground floor, a second-story gallery, and a steeple that housed a bell (price—£18). The total cost of construction was somewhere in the vicinity of £2,000. Divided among the thirty founders, this represents an initial investment of over £60 per member, at a time when £60 represented an acceptable *annual* salary for a rural New England clergyman. The Third Church's meetinghouse was clearly not built to shelter a closed group of narrow schismatics—the enormous initial investment in a capacious and attractive building projected the founders' expectations of rapid growth. Its towering presence at the corner of Cornhill and Milk Streets, with its steeple and bell recasting the visual and aural landscape, announced the beginning of a new religious era in Boston in a way that the farmers and tradesmen who daily passed through Cornhill on their way to market could not have missed. Both the controversy over its construction and its presence in the town served to reinforce in visible terms the meaning of the Third Church's challenge to the First Church. The meeting-house claimed the legacy of John Winthrop and John Norton, just as the new church rested its foundation and expressly based its covenant upon the synods Winthrop and Norton had promoted.[68] The Third Church founders accepted the generosity of Mrs. Norton and built on the land which the First Church had rejected, and they built their religious position within New England society on a plan that the First Church had rejected as well.

The next requirement for the new church was the ordination of at least one and preferably two orthodox ministers. Ideally, the Third Church hoped to find clergymen who could help establish their claim to continuity with New England's first generation. The best available candidate was the former pastor of Weymouth, more recently a member of Boston's First Church, Thomas Thacher. Still only a teenager when he arrived in America in 1635, Thacher was educated by Charles Chauncy, then pastor of the church in Scituate, who trained him for a career in the ministry.[69] His early emigration date, the nature of his education, and his twenty years of service in Weymouth marked Thacher as a holdover from the first generation, despite the fact that he was only fifty years old in 1670, twenty years younger than John Davenport.[70] When his wife died in 1664, Thacher resigned his Weymouth ministry and moved to Boston where he supported himself by practicing medicine. There he joined the First Church, although the majority faction was reluctant to admit Thacher as a member and claimed that he lacked a sufficient dismissal from his pastoral obligations in Weymouth. During the search for a new minister for the First Church in the late 1660s, this allegation was held against his potential candidacy. However, Thacher's support for the Halfway Covenant was in itself probably enough to prejudice this faction against him, for they showed remarkably little scrupulosity about proper dismissals when it came to acquiring John Davenport's services.[71]

During the course of the First Church controversy, Thacher quietly requested and received his dismissal from the First Church to the church in Charlestown. This move eliminated the possibility that the First Church could refuse to dismiss him, which would have forced Thacher either to remain at the First Church or to perform the same act of defiance that John Davenport had recently done in leaving New Haven.[72] Instead, when the Third Church unanimously elected Thacher "to be a teaching officer unto them," Thacher was free to accept, as the Charlestown church wrote a prompt and gracious letter releasing him of all obligations. On December 19, 1669, Thacher preached the first sermons in the new meetinghouse, taking his afternoon text from Psalm 47, "He shall choose our inheritance for us, the excellency of Jacob whom he loved." The minister and his text, like the building in which he preached, further reinforced the new church's claim to be the inheritor of mainstream Congregational orthodoxy.[73]

The most difficult task facing Thacher and the new church members was to make their ideal of cooperation among the churches an established fact.[74] In the years after Thacher's ordination, there remained two obstacles. One was the complicated position of the wives and families of the Third Church founders, the other was the problem of reconciliation between the new church and the old. The continuing opposition of the First Church to the more open and ecumenical principles of the Third Church linked these two obstacles together.

The Third Church founders had separated from the First Church in their own names, exclusive of their wives and families. The founders' wives were left in a quandary; they were still members of a church that refused to recognize the existence of the church of their husbands. Ordinarily, the unity of the family as the first locus of piety was considered essential to Puritan views of church and society.[75] Yet the members of the First Church were willing to risk family divisions for the sake of the principle of church autonomy. Even the demise of John Davenport, who was suddenly "smitten with the dead palsy" on March 16, 1669/70, did not change the position of the First Church members. They used Davenport's death to reinforce their opposition to inter-church communion by rejecting the customary practice of allowing ministers of neighboring churches to serve as Davenport's pallbearers and reserving this privilege to "brethren of First Church." Following Davenport's funeral, the wives of the Third Church founders petitioned for their dismissal, but James Penn and James Allen upheld Davenport's rigid position and denied the women's request. They insisted on the absolute authority of the voting members over all church issues, and once again attempted to use the sacrament of the Lord's Supper as a "snare" to trap the women in a censurable position.[76]

Initial attempts to make a general reconciliation with the First Church fared no better. In August 1670, Thomas Thacher sent an "Essay for Accommodation" on behalf of his congregation to the First Church, but the First Church elders would not accept it. John Oxenbridge, Davenport's successor as pastor, stated that the First Church "desire[d] to heare no more of this matter untill the Lord shall let you see your deviation from these rules and acknowledge and repaire them."[77] Over the next few years, the issue was thrashed about in various public debates, which continued to link questions of accommodation to royal government with the controversy over church polity. On one side, Governor Bellingham established a quarterly lectureship intended to defend the principles of Congregational polity practiced by the

First Church. In response, Urian Oakes preached a sharp tirade against the First Church's position in the 1673 Election Sermon.[78]

In the months following Oakes's sermon, some progress was finally made. The churches corresponded again, and although the First Church elders still refused to admit any wrongdoings, they hinted at the possibility of releasing the wives of the Third Church founders, though not with a formal church dismissal. Instead, they declared that "all the aforesaid sisters . . . are upon their owne irregular choice gone out from us and from any further Authority of this Church."[79] Following this limited concession, the "sisters" consulted with the ministers gathered in Boston for the annual elections in May 1674, who gave them a formal statement of approval to join their husbands' church. Again, they displayed the ongoing reliance of Third Church supporters on the procedures of church councils and inter-church cooperation. With this statement in hand, the women were finally admitted to the Third Church on October 16, 1674, after five years of exclusion from the Lord's Supper and from baptizing the children born to them in this time.[80]

The admission of the founders' wives solved a major problem in the family lives of the members, but it did not bring about a full reconciliation between the churches. Before that could occur, the two churches witnessed the death of John Oxenbridge in 1674, the ravages of King Philip's War in 1675–76 (which brought Samuel Willard to the Third Church as assistant minister to Thomas Thacher), and Thacher's death in 1678. The various disasters of the 1670s, together with the long-standing disputes within the colony, led New Englanders to examine their own behavior to find the cause of "God's controversy" with them. In 1679, the Massachusetts clergy requested that the General Court call a synod of the colony's churches, which met in September and published a long list of New England's sins and backslidings.[81] The synod also voted to adopt the credal statement known as the Savoy Confession, propagated by the Congregational churches of England in 1658 as an adaptation of the Westminster Confession of 1648.[82] In declaring their adherence to this statement of faith, the Massachusetts churches reaffirmed their commitment and connection to the transatlantic English Puritan movement. This expression of inter-church solidarity was consistent with the approach to reformed religion that the founders of the Third Church advocated. Although the First Church participated in the Reforming Synod, its members continued to express opposition to the idea of having synods at all. They declared that "wee doe not see light for the Calling of a Synod att this time," and sent their messengers with the proviso that the synod "bee no further binding to us, than the light of Gods word is thereby cleared to our Consciences."[83] This reluctant participation, though characteristic of the quasi-separatist position it had taken all along, nevertheless represented a degree of compromise on the part of the First Church.

The leaders of the synod, including Increase Mather and Samuel Willard, Thacher's successor and now the sole pastor at the Third Church, were concerned with fostering inter-church cooperation, but they also attended to the needs of particular individual churches, especially in their advocacy of a new form of spiritual revival, the ceremony of covenant renewal. Early in 1680, a large number of the Third Church's "children of the church" came forward to "own the covenant," or affirm their responsibilities and allegiance to the terms of their baptism.[84] In this ritual, the Third Church was finally implementing the principles of the Halfway Covenant on which it was founded, for ironically enough, the circumstances of its founding meant that originally the Third Church did not need the Halfway Covenant—all its first members were full members. But now, a decade later, the church had grown sufficiently that there were a substantial number of "halfway members," baptized but not yet converted. These individuals' decision to own the covenant fell short of full membership, but demonstrated that even people still uncertain of the state of their souls remained devoted to the principle of the particular church.

Several months later, Samuel Willard led the entire Third Church, both full and halfway members, in a ritual of covenant renewal. This ritual was a technique for promoting religious revival by reminding New England church members of their commitment to one another and to God.[85] In form, the covenant renewal emphasized that religion was the province of particular churches; it focused attention on the obligations that the individual members had made to one another. Yet the content of the Third Church's covenant renewal ceremony was heavily influenced by the recommendations of the Reforming Synod, to which explicit reference was frequently made.[86] This ceremony was therefore a visible demonstration that orthodox piety could be shaped by recommendations from all the churches acting in council, but that its specific application, the locus of the relationship between God and man, was always within the individual church. In this sense, the ceremony further served to exemplify the Third Church's Puritan "middle way" between the poles of separatist isolation and presbyterian authority.

The practice of covenant renewal spread rapidly throughout the Congregational churches of New England, and helped to bring about a small religious revival. Typically, the First Church of Boston refused to join in this expression of inter-church fellowship. Yet its isolation in this position, together with the growing threat of royal encroachment on the independence of all the churches, led the First Church to seek reconciliation with the Third Church in April 1682. Asking only that the Third Church publicly declare its adherence to the principle of the church's control over dismissals (Chapter 13 of the Cambridge Platform), the First Church offered to forgive and forget the differences between them.[87] The Third Church was happy to meet this condition and on May 7, 1682, the reconciliation was made official by a vote of the First Church.[88]

In making peace with the newer church, the First Church was not accepting its definition of church polity so much as agreeing to cooperate in the face of common enemies. The First Church still held out against the Halfway Covenant, but this seemed a minor internal difference when compared with the external threats to the New England way posed by King Philip's War or by the looming possibility of imperial intervention in Massachusetts institutions. It took the cataclysmic events of the 1670s, together with the increasing intrusion of crown officials into Massachusetts politics, for the followers of John Davenport to see that they had been treating their allies as if they were enemies. These factors, along with the passage of time and the deaths of the more strident opponents in the controversy, made reconciliation possible.

The Third Church had been formally gathered in 1669, but it was not until this act of reconciliation in 1682 that it was finally established *on its own terms*. It was founded on the premise that godly churches should be cooperative parts of an integrated whole, not isolated cells cut off from the world, and reconciliation with the First Church at last made this vision a potential reality in New England. This newfound unity represented a triumph for the Third Church founders, who had shown that within the context of New England Congregational orthodoxy, changes in church polity were possible without detriment to the principles of the founders.[89] By drawing on the symbols of New England's religious tradition and by acting with a clear purpose throughout the long controversy, the Third Church founders had demonstrated at each step in the process of church formation that the Halfway Covenant would not be a stepping stone toward toleration of heresy, nor would it lead to open and unrestricted church membership. Thomas Thacher and his successor, Samuel Willard, continued to insist on a profession of saving faith as a requirement for full membership. The church did vote to allow slight modifications in the procedure for giving these conversion relations, but this did not change the standards for church admission or allow a wave of hypocrites to invade the church.[90] It has been suggested that the Halfway Covenant was a failure because it did not create enough new full communicants to keep pace with New England's rapidly growing population.[91] But in the context of the 1660s and 1670s, this fact need not be seen as a failure. The steady but limited growth that accompanied the introduction of the Halfway Covenant was probably to its advantage, for a huge influx of new members might have implied excessive leniency and, perhaps, apostasy. The Puritan laity *wanted* full membership to be restricted to the visibly godly, and never expected that everyone would be among the elect. The implementation of the Halfway Covenant by churches like Boston's Third proved that a broader scope for baptism, church discipline, and spreading the means of conversion did not require the abandonment of church purity.[92]

The reconciliation of the First and Third Churches left unresolved the division between the two strands of the Puritan movement they represented. The founding and establishment of the Third Church, long and tortuous though it was, was only a beginning. In the contest over whether or not to adapt to new conditions, the Third Church founders had promoted change and had been forced to secede from the First Church to realize their vision. Although it had caused them substantial difficulties, their act of secession gave them one distinct advantage, reminiscent of New England's founding generation. They were now a community of like-minded believers, fully committed to the Halfway Covenant as a program for reform. The debate over the Halfway Covenant would continue to rage in many other New England churches, but within Boston's Third Church it was settled. The challenge its members faced for the future, then, was not *whether* to change, but *how* best to implement the program of reform to which this Puritan church, more than any other, was fully committed.

CHAPTER 2

A Temple in the Wilderness

The stones of which [the church] is built are fetcht out of the Quarry, or Stone pit of Mankind. The building must not be of pebbles or paultry Stones. God will have all things in his Building proportionably Excellent, & who can imagine that any thing inferior to the Choicest of the Children of Men are intended.

—Edward Taylor, "A Particular Church is God's House" (1679)

At the same time that the argument over Puritanism's future split Boston's religious community and led to the creation of the Third Church, other godly people were attempting to create new churches in what they perceived as a wilderness. New England's steadily increasing English population was beginning to fill up the arable land of the region's interior. In each of the new towns they created, their efforts to replicate Puritan churches demonstrated their persistent devotion to godly religious culture. Despite their frontier isolation, New England's pioneers faced the same problems in creating a church and establishing its boundaries with the world that emerged so clearly in the founding of Boston's Third Church. But the conditions of life, the backgrounds of the settlers, and their religious expectations were different in a new rural community like Westfield, Massachusetts, than they were in Boston, which meant that the Puritan movement in this context would take a different form than it had at other places in earlier generations.

The life of the Westfield church would also be profoundly shaped by the personality and beliefs of its singular leader, the Puritan devotional poet and minister Edward Taylor. Although they were all participants in the English Puritan movement, Edward Taylor and the lay people of Westfield had each been influenced by different circumstances and had developed conflicting expectations for what a godly life should be. As a result, the founding of this new church on the western frontier of New England settlement required an extended process of negotiation between two differing outlooks on Puritan religion, during which certain strains and tensions emerged that would shape the Westfield church for decades to come.

⁂

The town of Westfield, Massachusetts, lies directly west of Springfield along one of the many smaller streams that flow into the Connecticut River. It was first occupied by Englishmen in the 1630s as a trading post called Woronocco, where Puritan entrepreneurs traded with Indian trappers for beaver pelts. A generation later, high demand and overhunting had exhausted the Connecticut Valley fur trade, but as the English began to consider the agricultural potential of the region, the fertile lands along the river valleys attracted new settlers.[1] By the 1660s, the settlement patterns that had characterized the early colonization of the Connecticut Valley were beginning to change. Like the founders of Massachusetts Bay, many of the early Connecticut settlers migrated in cohesive groups built around the leadership of charismatic clergymen or prominent gentlemen. In the mid-1630s, the ministers Thomas Hooker and John Warham led their respective Massachusetts congregations westward to found the towns of Hartford and Windsor, and William Pynchon, a prominent fur trader and a founder of the Massachusetts Bay Company, led a group of Roxbury settlers who established the town of Springfield. The people of these new towns were often united by personal or family ties extending back to their origins in England or at least to the first Massachusetts Bay settlements. But over the course of a generation, these ties were weakened as families migrated to seek better lands and as the leaders who lent stability to these communities, like Hooker and Pynchon, died or moved on.[2]

As the English population grew and the demand for farmland increased, a new pattern of town settlement in the Connecticut Valley emerged. John Pynchon, the son of Springfield's founder, used his father's fur trading business as a base from which to gain a dominant position in the economy of the upper Connecticut Valley. The younger Pynchon invested heavily in land and became the primary figure in the settlement of many of the second generation Connecticut Valley towns. Pynchon would buy large tracts of land with the intention of turning it over to new settlers, who would pay him back once they had established themselves as a town and become profitable farmers. This method insured John Pynchon the most reliable return on his investment and involved relatively little effort on his own part. But for the society of the Connecticut Valley, this settlement pattern replaced the tightly knit communities of the first generation with a new form of social organization. New towns were now formed by more random groups of families, united by a common desire for fertile lands but lacking the group solidarity and inspirational leadership of the earlier settlements. In the middle decades of the seventeenth century, the towns of Northampton, Hadley, Deerfield, Northfield, Brookfield, and Enfield were all established with Pynchon's assistance, and in the mid-1660s, the old trading post at Woronocco became the new town of Westfield in much the same way.[3]

In the early spring of 1668, John Pynchon and a committee of his associates from Springfield went to Woronocco to "settle all matters touching that place," and "make choyce of a meet Number of the fittest Persons for Ordering their Prudentiall affaires." At this time there were about two dozen families living in Woronocco, migrants from Springfield, Northampton, Windsor, Hartford, and a handful of other Connecticut Valley towns, from which Pynchon could select the "fittest persons" to be the new community's leaders.[4] This haphazard grouping of families, all members or descendants of the first-generation settlements, formed the core of what would become the new town of Westfield. They shared a common cultural and religious background and had witnessed similar events over the course of a generation in New England, but few of them had experienced the intense feelings of religious community and allegiance that emerged among the English families who had crossed the Atlantic together.

A generation of experience in the Connecticut Valley had likewise shaped the religious expectations of Westfield's founders. The first-generation towns from which they came had implemented a varied range of standards for church membership and organization. Unlike Massachusetts Bay, where the Cambridge Platform of 1648 established common rules of church discipline, the Connecticut Puritans were notable for their lack of a uniform system— the Cambridge Platform "was hardly noticed in Connecticut."[5] In particular, the Valley churches tended to differ from the strict Congregational form of Massachusetts Bay, where church covenants limited full membership to visible saints who gave public relations of their conversion experiences. Instead, several early Connecticut towns experimented with a parish-based or "Presbyterian" style in which the church served as center of worship for the entire community, and only the visibly *ungodly* were excluded. In the 1660s, then, there was no general colony-wide "Halfway Covenant" controversy in Connecticut to parallel that of Massachusetts, because there was no original platform of church polity to be altered, and because many Connecticut churches already maintained more open membership standards. Within the narrow range of beliefs and practices encompassing English Puritanism, the early communities of the Connecticut Valley operated as locally independent churches, each following its own standards for church membership, practice, and government.

During the first generation, the towns that provided many of Westfield's early settlers experienced these variations in religious polity, played out in the form of frequent local conflicts. Windsor, Connecticut, was led in its early years by John Warham, the minister who helped found the town of Dorchester in Massachusetts Bay and who organized the remove to Connecticut in 1636. Warham's views on church membership and practice wavered back and forth; he began his Connecticut career as a "Presbyterian," favoring a church that would be the center of worship for a parish consisting of the entire town, rather than a gathered enclave of visible saints. Eventually, Thomas Hooker of Hartford convinced Warham to promote a church covenant, restrict membership and baptism, and identify the town's visible saints. But in 1657, declining membership led Warham to adopt more open baptismal standards, broadening church participation. By 1664, Warham had shifted again; he reinstituted a strict form of Congregationalism, required public conversion relations for full membership, and baptized only the children of full members.[6] This last shift alienated many of the townspeople, who withdrew and formed a second church, Presbyterian in polity, under the ministry of John Woodbridge. After Warham's death, conflict between Woodbridge and Nathaniel Chauncy, Warham's successor, continued in Windsor for at least another decade.[7]

In early Springfield, another major source of Westfield's founding population, the community's religious life was disrupted by the religious idiosyncrasies of the Pynchon family. William Pynchon was perhaps the most theologically minded of the men to whom the Massachusetts Bay Company charter was issued, and he also turned out to be the founder most at odds with the religious practices developing in Massachusetts Bay. Pynchon's theological beliefs, for which he was attacked by the General Court, were part of the "rationalist strain" in Puritan thought. In his more extreme pronouncements, Pynchon questioned the reality of Christ's atonement for man's sins, and implicitly denied the idea of the Trinity. In terms of church practice, it seems likely that Springfield's church held more open "Presbyterian" standards for membership than were typical of the Bay churches. Although no records survive from Springfield's church in the seventeenth century, Pynchon's defense of the Presbyterian "Remonstrants" of 1646 suggests an affinity on his part for their beliefs, and in 1652, Pynchon's book *The Jewes Synagogue* challenged the restriction of church membership to visible saints.[8] The General Court censured Pynchon and banned his writings, and he soon left the colony. Springfield suffered without a minister for nearly a decade after the Rev. George Moxon departed with the elder Pynchon.[9] Springfield's religious community offered no settled background, no expectations of unity and stability, to the residents who settled Westfield in the 1660s, and its religious standards and practices tended toward the "liberal" end of the Puritan spectrum.[10]

Northampton, Massachusetts, a third major provider of Westfield's early settlers, had its own problems with church polity. Eleazer Mather, its first minister, was an opponent of the Halfway Covenant and a strong defender of the necessity of conversion relations for full membership. Consequently, Northampton's church during its first decade consisted mainly of Mather and a select group of "Dorchester Men" he had recruited to settle the town. This situation created considerable dissension within the community, and as Mather grew ill in the mid-1660s, a faction within the church forced through a vote to accept a variation of the Halfway Covenant, which extended church discipline and baptism to most of the town and implicitly challenged Mather's ministerial authority.[11] Mather died in 1669, and as his successor, the town hired Solomon Stoddard, whose views on an inclusive church were compatible with those of the majority of Northampton townsmen. Stoddard would become the chief proponent in Massachusetts of an expansive vision of the church for the next half century.[12]

Most of Westfield's first settlers had grown up in these turbulent, experimental religious communities of the Connecticut Valley. They were devout Puritans, but their recent experience of godly life had encouraged lay initiative in the direction of church practices and had exposed them to varied and inclusive forms of Puritan churches that allowed for religious participation by the entire community. In the towns from which they came, Westfield's founders had come to look upon participation in the Puritan church as something of a birthright and had fought with or rejected ministers who tried to convince them otherwise. These were the lay expectations that Edward Taylor would meet upon his arrival in Westfield in 1671, expectations that were ill-suited to his own ideas about what a godly minister's role should be.

Unlike the majority of second-generation New England ministers, Edward Taylor was not born and raised in New England, and with this difference came a competing set of assumptions about the meaning of godly life. From his conversion relation we learn of his birth in England in the early 1640s; his parents were Puritans from Sketchley, in Leicestershire.[13] His conviction of his own election came early in life, and he received some formal education, though where or from whom is uncertain. Taylor was educated for the ministry but was never licensed to preach in England. He was employed as a schoolmaster, however, and in 1662 he lost his teaching position for refusing to adhere to Charles II's Act of Uniformity, about which he wrote one of his earliest poems:

> This sad Dilemma, that new Law did Bring,
>   Displease your God, or else displease your King,
> And men of Conscience need not long to muse
>   What in this case to leave, and what to choose.

As an English dissenter in the 1660s, the young Taylor saw the pursuit of godliness as a matter of removal from the world to join with others who were ostracized by society as "Crack-brain'd Lunatick[s]" for their Puritan beliefs.[14]

Taylor probably belonged to a clandestine dissenting congregation during the years between 1662 and his departure for New England in 1668.[15] In the meantime, he continued his own education and ministerial preparation. On his journey to New England, he frequently read the New Testament in Greek and led prayer services with his fellow passengers on board ship. Taylor landed unobtrusively in Boston in July 1668, only two months after John Davenport's disruptive entry into the town, just as the First Church controversy was heating up. But at the time of his arrival, Taylor's experiences as dissenter and aspiring clergyman were more like those of Davenport and other first-generation ministers who escaped Laudian persecution and fled to New England in the 1630s, than of his soon-to-be classmates at Harvard College, born and raised in the safe Puritan haven of New England.

The three years Taylor spent in Cambridge attaining his bachelor's degree must have socialized him to New England ways and expectations, yet he still remained an outsider at the College. At roughly 26 years of age, he was eight to ten years older than all of his classmates, and his educational background prior to entering Harvard allowed him to finish in three years.[16] He was put in a position of responsibility as College Butler, and was made a "scholar of the house" in his final year.[17] Taylor left a record of only three incidents from his experiences at the college; each reflects the distance he felt from his classmates. When Tutor Thomas Graves suspected the undergraduates of misbehavior, he recruited Taylor as a spy, asking him "to go into the buttery privily and watch who did it." Graves' request left Taylor in a moral quandary; he wanted to offend neither his classmates nor his tutor, and felt inclined toward neither side. On yet another occasion, Graves, who was not well-liked by the Harvard students, tried to take advantage of Taylor's difference from his classmates. When the students (including Taylor) objected to reading an outdated textbook on "natural physics," Graves appealed to Taylor to persuade the others, "seeing he could prevail with me to read it, though they [Taylor's classmates] should continue opposite thereto." Later, Taylor became the subject of malicious gossip, both in the college and in the town, because he spent considerable time and effort ministering to the "troubled spirit" of Goodwife Steadman. Taylor protested that his attentions to the college woodman's wife were entirely innocent, "yet some there were that added afflictions to me by their whispering, back-biting tongues, which made me much desirous to go from Cambridge." Taylor summarized his college experience with the bitter remark that "so long as I remained in the college the Lord gave me the affections of all both in the college and in the town whose love was worth having."[18]

Understandably, Taylor found his closest companions among those whose experience most resembled his own. He became friends with his college roommate, Samuel Sewall, the only one of his classmates not born in New England. Like Taylor, Sewall had emigrated to New England in the early years of the Restoration. Although younger than Taylor at his removal, Sewall retained vivid memories of English life and of the turmoil of the Restoration well into his old age.[19] Sewall seems to be the only classmate with whom Taylor maintained a life-long correspondence. Besides Sewall, Taylor was on good terms with Increase Mather (only three years his elder), with whom he lodged for two nights on his arrival, and who recommended him for the position as Westfield's pastor. Mather had also experienced the pressure of post-Restoration demands for conformity, which forced him to leave positions in England and the Channel Islands and return (none-too-happily) to the poor, remote churches of Massachusetts.[20] But Taylor's closest friend at college seems to have been the President, Charles Chauncy. Chauncy was one of the last surviving first-generation ministers who had suffered under Laudian persecution and found refuge in New England.[21] Upon the eve of Taylor's departure for Westfield, the elderly President's "love was so much expressed that I could scarce leave him, and well it might be so, for he told me in plain words that he *Knew not how to part with mee*."[22]

Taylor's close ties to Mather and Chauncy during his college years suggest that his New England education reinforced his belief that the church was a gathered body of visible saints, an exclusive withdrawal from a sinful world. Chauncy was a champion of the gathered church, as opposed to a tribal one or a "Presbyterian" parish-style church.[23] His New England pastoral career began, significantly, in Plymouth Colony, where the settlers were more inclined toward separatist church polity. Later, he became one of the strongest opponents of the Halfway Covenant's extension of baptism to children of the as yet unregenerate, and his early advocacy of the immersion of infants according to his peculiar scriptural interpretation nearly prevented him from becoming Harvard's president.[24] Increase Mather was also a strong defender of the purity of New England's churches, and like his brother Eleazer in Northampton, he was an early opponent of the Halfway Covenant.[25] The pattern of Taylor's friendships may have made the controversy in Boston's First Church rather bewildering. Mather and Chauncy were staunch opponents of the Halfway Covenant, while Samuel Sewall would eventually follow his future father-in-law John Hull into the Third Church. But in general, we can see that Taylor's closest associates at college were not the majority of his classmates, but the teachers and authority figures who in the 1660s represented some of the more "conservative" (that is, separatist and exclusive) attitudes about the nature of the Puritan church in New England.[26]

Despite his personal background, or perhaps because of the peculiarities of it, Edward Taylor imbibed a large dose of the myth of New England's origins, the reification of the first generation as exemplars of an ideal Puritanism.[27] Taylor was not a son of New England, but his experience as an English dissenter, his early connections in America to such conservative thinkers as Mather and Chauncy, and perhaps his personal temperament all led him to embrace this mythic construction. His late arrival in the midst of a raging controversy may have made it easier for him to accept the myth of a unified first generation, for he did not grow up witnessing the tensions and conflicts that plagued the early years of New England's churches, the memory of which must have made it difficult for native New Englanders to believe wholeheartedly the very myths they were creating.[28] Instead, Taylor was accustomed from experience to the idea that a true Puritan church was an enclave of visible saints, withdrawn from the unregenerate masses, a group which naturally coalesced around the leadership of an educated godly minister, to whom they looked for nurture, direction, and discipline. This was the vision of the church that Taylor brought with him to Westfield in 1671.

❧

By the time Edward Taylor was recruited to be Westfield's minister, the town was desperate for clerical leadership. In the first years of settlement, the townspeople had failed to convince two different ministerial candidates to remain in Westfield. The new community's meager resources for sustaining a minister were partly to blame.[29] In November 1671, the town sent a leading layman named Thomas Dewey to Boston to make another try at recruiting a clergyman. Upon the advice of the General Court and Harvard College, Dewey first approached William Adams, who declined the offer.[30] As a second choice, Dewey was advised by Increase Mather to inquire whether Edward

Taylor would accept the position. Taylor agreed after some persuading to accompany Dewey back to Westfield in December, "the Snow being about Mid-leg deepe, the way unbeaten . . . over rocks and mountains, . . . the desperatest journey that ever Connecticut men undertooke."[31] Despite the brutal conditions, Dewey was eager to hustle Taylor back to the frontier so that Westfield's settlers could gather a church and institute formal worship.

But the combination of Taylor's conception of a Puritan church and Westfield's condition as a newly settled community delayed the process of church formation. Despite the strong pressure from the Massachusetts General Court for every incorporated town to have a church, eight years passed between Taylor's arrival and the formal gathering of Westfield's church. The disruptive effects of King Philip's War on Connecticut Valley life were partly to blame for this delay, but the calling of a church in Westfield was still unusually slow, largely because of Edward Taylor's difficulty in adjusting to his new circumstances.

The early arrangements that Taylor made with the town went smoothly enough, and the people of Westfield seemed happy to have him. He lodged at the homes of several prominent Westfield residents, including Aaron Cooke, David Ashley, and Joseph Whiting, and on the day after his arrival he preached his first sermon.[32] The town made financial arrangements suitable to Taylor's circumstances as a bachelor; he was granted a home lot "in the Most Convenient place" and given fifteen acres for the use of a hired hand. After less than a year of probationary preaching, the town decided to "render their earnest desire of Mr. Taylor's Continuance with us in the Ministry," and to grant him "land, house, and Maintanance." They also arranged to "go on with Building a Meeting house with all Convenient Speed." To these plans Taylor responded hopefully but cautiously. The townspeople understood that "though he was not promist yet he hath and May Continue with us if More be added to procure such help as is necessary to Cary on the Worship of Church as stated."[33]

The meaning of Taylor's ambivalent position became clear soon enough, for despite the townspeople's desires, Taylor felt there were too few visible saints in Westfield to serve as acceptable pillars of a new church. Ordinarily, it took seven men, including the prospective minister, to found a church. The town had at least that many residents who had been members of other churches before their migration to Westfield, but Taylor may not have been satisfied with them for a variety of reasons. Typically, the founding members of a church were also locally prominent men: established, prosperous community leaders who would lend stability to a new town and its church. Taylor may have feared for the community's stability, since some of the most likely foundation men among the early settlers seemed uncertain of remaining permanently in Westfield. Capt. Aaron Cooke, for instance, had already moved three times within New England, and had close ties with Northampton that would eventually draw him back there before Westfield's church was gathered.[34] The age of some of the potential founders may also have been troubling, for neither the very old nor the very young made good candidates. George Phelps, the head of a family that would figure prominently in Westfield's history, and Thomas Gunn, another prospective founder, may have been too old for Taylor's liking; Phelps returned to Windsor before the church was founded, and Gunn, "in that he was so much decayed by age," was replaced by a younger man when a church was eventually gathered.[35]

With Taylor's misgivings holding up the proceedings, several leading laymen, George Phelps, Joseph Whiting, and Samuel Loomis, attempted to speed matters along. First they wrote to Taylor and urged him to continue his work among them, hinting that they were anxious to get on with church gathering, and mentioning "the loss of time already passt" with some regret.[36] Next, they wrote to the church at nearby Northampton and requested that "for further encouraging of Mr. Taylor" one of Northampton's most prominent citizens, Lt. David Wilton, be allowed to settle in Westfield. In this letter, the laymen expressed their sense of the importance of gathering a church; "considering that the main End of N.E.'s undertaking was the servise of God in Gospell Worship," their desire to "Build a Temple" was great. Yet they also knew that "Weak buildings are ready to fall under their own weight." Hence, they called on Northampton to help strengthen them, and cited Biblical precedent for their request, as when "Solomon himselfe sent to Hyram in his necessity to help him both with men & materials for the building of the Temple."[37]

Northampton's response, written by Solomon Stoddard and John Strong, rejected Westfield's request. They claimed that Northampton had already furnished Westfield with sufficient "material" to build a church, and encouraged the Westfield founders to go ahead with their proceedings.[38] Westfield's reply identifies Taylor as the main sticking point. Phelps, Whiting, and Loomis claimed that Northampton's refusal to allow Wilton to settle in Westfield "will put such a demur unto our proceeding, that we know not when we shall get on: for Mr. Taylor is utterly averse to any Coalition into a ch[urc]h state without further encouragemnt, and where to have it, if not of you, we know not."[39] Taylor did not record his own thoughts on these proceedings, but his need for "encouragement" reflects his stricter standards for gathering a church than those of Westfield's citizens or of Stoddard and Northampton's church members, who seemed eager for Westfield to get on with the process. For Taylor, it was not enough merely to reconstitute former members of other Puritan churches into a new church in a new location. To build a new church, he had to have material that was satisfactory to him, which he could mold with his preaching into a new community, a temple of worship made of "living stones."[40] At this point, the process of church formation stalled.

In 1674, after three years of living alone in the wilds of Westfield, Taylor courted and married Elizabeth Fitch, daughter of the minister of Norwich, Connecticut. By his marriage, Taylor established himself more firmly in the Connecticut Valley. He later wrote in his church record, "at length my thoughts being more settled, I determined within [myself that] in case things could go comfortably on, to Settle with them: & in [order thereto] Changed my Condition, & entred into a married State."[41] But if his marriage and decision to stay in Westfield encouraged him to gather a church, these gains were ruined in the following year, when the outbreak of King Philip's War threatened all the English settlements in the Connecticut Valley with complete destruction.

Compared with neighboring towns, Westfield was relatively unharmed by the war itself. Few of its inhabitants were killed in the fighting, and the town, though garrisoned, was never raided by Indians.[42] But the conflict dampened Taylor's hopes for a church gathering:

> . . . tho we lay in the very rode of the Enemy were we preserved; onely the war had so impoverisht us that many times we were ready to leave the place, & many did, yea many of those that were in full Communion in other places, for their number in all being but nine, four of them removed. & worse than this, a sore [tem]ptation was thrust in amo[n]gst us by the Adversary that seem'd to threaten the overthrow of all proceedings unto a Church state, by those on whom that intrest was before, most apparently devolved.[43]

Among those who left Westfield during the war was Joseph Whiting, and his departure caused the "sore temptation" to which Taylor alluded.[44] Whiting had been a partner with Thomas, Josiah, and Jedediah Dewey in a gristmill and sawmill on the outskirts of Westfield. Their partnership agreement stated "that if any are desirous to sell his part the rest of the owners are to have the refusall of it." Nevertheless, when Whiting moved away he sold his share to Capt. Aaron Cooke, which led the Dewey brothers to declare "that wee neither do nor shall att any time Consent that the said Capt. Cooke shall bee any copartner or have any share with us in the said mil."[45] Since Whiting, Cooke, and the Deweys were among the leading candidates for potential church founders, Whiting's departure and the subsequent dispute further undermined Taylor's confidence in the prospects for a Westfield church.

King Philip's War ended in 1676, but in its aftermath, the Connecticut Valley colonists began to revise their settlement patterns to improve their capabilities for defense. In 1677, a small group of Indians raided the new village of Hatfield, north of Westfield, and this event revived fears of hostilities on a large scale. In response, the Massachusetts General Court ordered a "new modelling" of the Connecticut Valley towns for the purpose of self-protection. These towns were originally laid out to take advantage of the broad expanses of fertile land along the Connecticut River and its tributaries, but widely separated farming plots were not well suited for military defense. Westfield was no exception. The early home lots for its settlers were laid out in two main tracts, a central group along what came to be known as the "Fort Side" south of the Westfield River, and another group north of the river called the "North Side." In addition, a handful of settlers, like Capt. Cooke and the Dewey clan, lived off by themselves away from any immediate neighbors. For safety's sake, the more distant settlers were ordered by the "New Modelling" to move their homes back within the stockade on the "Fort Side," and this required the original Fort Side proprietors to give up part of their home lots to accommodate the others. The plan caused tension in the town and required the intervention of John Pynchon to make a settlement acceptable to all parties. By November of 1677, the "new modelling" was completed, but disputes over land ownership continued to disrupt the community for the next two years. These conflicts among the likely church founders caused still further delay in the gathering of Westfield's church.[46]

By the time the land disputes were being settled, Westfield was recovering some of its pre-war vitality. Several more potential foundation men moved in, including one, John Mawdsley, who was given a grant of land "on Condition hee come and setull as an inhabitant in the town."[47] In 1679, a dozen or so families returned to their more distant homes across the river, feeling safe again from Indian attacks.[48] Taylor's salary was raised to £60 in 1677, and then again to £70 the following year—to put it in context, this amount was roughly what *each* of Boston's Third Church founders invested in the initial construction of their meetinghouse. The town hired a schoolmaster and guaranteed to pay him £15 for his efforts, and plans for allocating seats in the new meetinghouse went forward. Although the economic picture was not entirely rosy, partly because of difficulties in getting John Pynchon to pay taxes he owed on his lands in Westfield, the town records suggest that stability, if not prosperity, was emerging in Westfield.[49]

In this new climate, after nearly eight years of residence in the town, Taylor finally agreed to the gathering of a church. But even now, things did not proceed smoothly. The date for the foundation was set for late August 1679, a delay of more than a year after the General Court had authorized Westfield to form a church.[50] Moreover, the foundation ceremonies were marred by a series of minor controversies in which Taylor's position on the nature of a church differed from his fellow townspeople and from his Connecticut Valley ministerial colleagues. The towns to which Westfield sent for "messengers" to witness their church foundation included its near neighbors on the Connecticut River, Springfield, Northampton, Hadley, and Windsor. Also invited were representatives from Norwich, Connecticut, which was not an easy journey away but was the home of Taylor's father-in-law, the Rev. James Fitch. No one from Norwich managed to make the difficult overland journey to attend the ceremony, but all the other towns sent representatives, including the ministers Solomon Stoddard of Northampton, John Russell of Hadley, and Pelatiah Glover of Springfield. Other prominent guests attended, including the deacons of the invited churches, Capt. Aaron Cooke, who had returned to Northampton after the controversy with the Dewey family, and of course, "the Worshipfull Major John Pynchon."[51]

Several problems held up the day's proceedings. The visiting elders, who acted as a supervising committee overseeing the new church's gathering, expressed their dismay over Westfield's preparation for the event, because Taylor had not written out a formal profession of faith for the church. Apparently, his efforts to do so had met with resistance or disagreement from the prospective founding members. He had hoped to proceed simply by declaring Westfield's allegiance to the Westminster Confession of faith and the Cambridge Platform of church discipline, but the visiting elders "did stickle more than was meet" at this, so Taylor hastily drew up a summary of a profession of faith, which was grudgingly approved.[52] The visiting elders may have opposed Taylor's original plan because it failed to show evidence of communal cooperation between the prospective minister and church members. A statement by the minister of adherence to the Cambridge Platform was no substitute for an expression of mutually held beliefs and practices created jointly by the minister and laity.[53]

Once the profession of faith was completed, the individual church founders were called upon to make public relations of their conversion experiences. Here, too, Taylor's desires conflicted with the ideas of the visiting elders. Taylor wanted the relations to be read aloud from prepared texts, while "the Elders & Messengers of Northampton and Hadley Churches drove on to the Contrary." They insisted that the conversion narratives be spoken rather than read, "to give some account of the workings of the Spirit upon our hearts." The visiting elders wanted a direct relation of experience from the members rather than recitations from texts which Taylor had helped to write. For Taylor, the reading of the prepared relations "doubtless . . . would have been to more edification"—in other words, a well-defined standard for the

future members of the church to observe and learn from if and when they decided to join the fold.[54] Taylor's preparations coincided with his vision of a
church in which the minister plays the guiding role in defining standards of
spirituality and belief, set against the visiting elders' and the laity's expectations for more direct popular participation in the life of the church.

After the relations, Taylor preached the foundation day sermon.[55] The
biblical text from which Taylor preached and the contents of the sermon itself expressed Taylor's ideas on the importance of a pure gathered church.
The sermon stressed the need for strictly separating "all of mankinde . . . as
they are either under, or without the Profession of the true God, . . . either in
a State of Wrath or a State of Favour." As Taylor put it, only true saints were
entitled to "Infrenchisation into a City State" as "free Denisons of the New
Jerusalem."[56] Taylor argued at length for the necessity of a conversion relation given before the church members and accepted by them as a precondi-
tion to communion and full membership.[57] Taylor's emphasis on these positions stands in marked contrast to the founders of Boston's Third Church,
who placed greater weight on fellowship, mutual edification, and the claims
of posterity in their foundational documents.[58]

Stylistically, Taylor likened the church to a building, and he sustained this
"architectonical" metaphor throughout his foundation sermon, in contrast to
the metaphor of the church as a garden favored by Boston's Third Church
founders.[59] While both metaphors were common Puritan images of the nature of the church, Taylor's "temple" metaphor was less organic, more rigid
than a garden metaphor. It allowed little room for the idea of the church as a
place where weak believers might grow in grace, and instead emphasized the
purity and sanctification of each member, lest a weak stone undermine the
entire structure. As Taylor put it, "the stones of which [the church] is built are
fetcht out of the Quarry, or Stone pit of Mankind, & hewen, & Squared by
the Axe of the Spirit till they are rightly pollisht & fitted for this building."
He explained that because Christ, the foundation of the church, "is a Pearle
of great price, . . . therefore the building must not be of pebbles, or paultry
Stones. . . . God will have all things in his Building proportionably Excellent,
& who can imagine that . . . any thing inferior to the Choicest of the Children of men are intended."[60] While at several points in the sermon, Taylor
attempted to accommodate the concerns of those struggling to enter the
church, the general tone and dominating metaphor of his discourse tended
to suggest a rigid division between the church and the world. Unless potential members were already "hewn, squared, polished and fitted," they were
not suitable as building blocks for a temple of the lord.

Taylor's foundation sermon made it clear that he was taking a strict Congregationalist position. While the more open view of the Puritan church was controversial in Boston in the 1660s, it was much more the norm in the context of the Connecticut Valley, where various experiments in a looser, parish-oriented church form had been tried, and where Solomon Stoddard was soon to take the lead in this cause again. Hence, Taylor's strict construction, reminiscent of John Davenport's position, was unusual in the upper Connecticut Valley, though diametrically opposed to the position the Third Church founders had taken in Boston a decade earlier. However, the stakes were lower in this small village on the western edge of New England settlement than they had been in the metropolis, and after a decade of controversy, most New Englanders were in a more conciliatory mood about the principles of church polity. Fifteen years later, Taylor would revise his foundation day sermon to attack Stoddard's new call for open communion, but at the time of the Westfield church's founding in 1679, his sermon merely announced the potential for conflict between Taylor and his church members who were accustomed to the prevailing practices of Connecticut Valley Puritans.

At the end of this long day, the ceremonies were drawn to a close. First the gathered elders approved of Westfield as a proper church and then confirmed Taylor as an ordained minister. Here, too, a mild disagreement arose over the form used by Solomon Stoddard to give the "Right Hand of Fellowship," a sign of welcome and approval which the other churches gave to Taylor on behalf of the new church. As Taylor recorded it, Stoddard "gave me it in these words—I do in the Name of the Churches give you the Right hand of Fellowship." Taylor then explained that he would have preferred to have this gesture made "in the Name of Christ. But Mr. Stoddard rather Chose those words having some instance for the use thereof."[61] Stoddard viewed the founding of a new church as an addition to a set of interrelated religious institutions, while Taylor saw the process as an imitation or restoration of the ways of the primitive Christian churches of the Apostles.[62] As Taylor expressed it in the Westfield church covenant, the founding of the church was done "in Obedience unto [Christ's] commands, & in imitation of his Saints, in Scripture."[63] Given this primitivist way of thinking, it was only proper to Taylor that a new church be welcomed among the "Denisons of the New Jerusalem" not "in the name of the churches," but in the name of Christ.

The covenant that Taylor wrote for the new church was unremarkable by New England standards, quite unlike that of the Third Church in Boston. Westfield's covenant expressed the desire of the founders to obey God's commands and through God's grace "to walke together according to the Rules of the Gospel." Like many of the earlier New England church covenants, its terms were cast with reference to the present generation, binding each indi-

vidual who joined the church "so long as we shall remain Members unto the
same Society."[64] But the Westfield church covenant made no reference to the
importance of communion with other churches, nor did it mention the duty
of the church to bring future generations under the means of grace. This is
not to say that Taylor or the Westfield church members were opposed to these
premises that were central to the Halfway Covenant and to the founders of
Boston's Third Church, but to reiterate that for Taylor, the inner life of the
gathered community of saints was the central concern of church formation, a
position that was natural for him given his upbringing and experience as an
Anglo-American Puritan.

"And so the work was accomplisht," wrote Taylor to close out his account of these events. The Westfield community had taken almost a dozen
years from the time it hired its first minister to form a proper church, a very
long time for a permanently settled New England community to go without
the sacraments and church discipline. Even the final step of church gathering
was contentious and marked by disagreements, though these minor disputes
paled in comparison to the controversy over the Halfway Covenant that rent
Boston's religious community. But in the absence of major conflict, why was
it such a struggle for Westfield to gather a church? What did this struggle signify about the nature of Westfield's religious community and its future under
Edward Taylor?

Taylor had a conservative, strict Congregationalist view of the nature of
church life, formed in England and strengthened by his years at Harvard College, a view which he identified, rightly or wrongly, with the founding generation of New England's ministers. The community at Westfield did not see
itself in terms that corresponded well with Taylor's vision. They were not irreligious or "un-Puritan." Their desires for an orthodox church and an established minister were frequently and prominently put forward in the decade
leading to the church gathering. But their experience and expectations for
religious life led them to believe, much more strongly than Taylor did, that
their community was essentially a community of the godly, and that a Puritan church was an organic and natural outgrowth of the social and religious
background they shared. To them, the gathering of a church was a more ordinary (if not routine) event than Taylor made it out to be. Westfield's struggle to form a church reflects Taylor's difficulty in reconciling himself to this
concept. The tensions and disagreements of the foundation day show his de-
termination to hold firmly to his own definition of the church and of his role
as minister, despite indications that his congregation did not share or benefit
from all of his convictions. On this insecure foundation, the people of Westfield would build their temple in the wilderness.

CHAPTER 3

A Garden in the Metropolis

The covenant is, that God owns them, and reckons them among his people, and children, within his visible church and kingdom, and that hereupon he will prune, and cut, and dress, and water them, and improve the means of their eternal good upon them.
—Thomas Shepard, *The Church-Membership of Children* (1662)

O that charming Duty, O that sweet Day is coming, . . . Catechizing Day, I mean that sweet Day.
—Elizabeth Butcher, age 9 (1718)

The founders of Boston's Third Church were faced with a challenge. The controversy from which the new church emerged was essentially over the question of whether Puritan churches should adapt to evolving circumstances. The South Church (as the Third Church soon came to be known) had boldy declared for change, but offered a plan for change within a traditional Puritan framework. Through the intricate maneuvers of the founding decade its members had sketched out a new vision of the future. The challenge, then, was how to make this vision a reality, how to convert reforming impulses into practical new mechanisms for cultivating piety and spreading its influence to a greater proportion of the population. The lay men and women of the First Church's "dissenting minority" had been the motivating force behind the founding of the Third Church, and so it is with their efforts that the story continues.

The language in which Puritans conceptualized their relationship to the church reveals a great deal about how they understood their religious goals. Puritans used a variety of metaphors to describe the nature and function of the church. For Edward Taylor, the church was a temple, raised by founding "pillars" and constructed of members who were "living stones." Others compared the church to a human body, with each member playing his or her assigned part in the organically integrated whole.[1] But for the founders of the Third Church in Boston and for proponents of the Halfway Covenant, the most useful way to describe the nature of the church and its relationship to the surrounding world was to imagine the church as a garden.

Both a garden and a church are organic entities, comprised of living members. A garden consists of nothing but the individual plants in it, just as the members of a church *are* the church—Puritans never mistook a church for the building in which it met. Like a church, a garden transcends the life-span of any individual member and can therefore exist in perpetuity across the generations. Additionally, a garden, like a church, is not wholly different from the "wilderness" around it. Puritans were careful to point out that God did not need the church to save individuals. Salvation could be granted to anyone in any circumstances, just as a wildflower could grow or a fig tree bear fruit in a wilderness. But a garden is where one would *ordinarily* expect to find flowers and fruit trees. A garden provides the conditions where delicate or reluctant plants bloom and prosper, just as the nurturing conditions of the church offer those with the slightest and weakest faith the chance to grow in grace.[2]

Furthermore, that which separates a garden from the wilderness, the "hedge" around the garden, is also an integral part of the garden itself, just as the division between the church and the world was marked by nothing more than the strongest members of the church, those "pillars" or "foundation stones" that were constitutive elements of the church. The common image used by preachers in eulogies for leaders in the religious community was that the departed's untimely death had left "a gap in the hedge," a gap which exposed the church to danger from threatening "wilderness" forces. Unless that gap were to be filled by members of the rising generation, the church as a whole would suffer.[3]

Finally, while the church, like a garden, was a living, organic entity, the creation of the divine hand of God, it was also artificial and required human endeavor in its formation. This meant that if a church were to survive across the generations and grow in size, beauty, and strength, it would need both divine assistance and human commitment. And because the church was essentially a part of the world as a whole, it could through neglect return to a "wilderness" state. Yet with care and attention, more and more of the wilderness could be domesticated. The Puritan clergy frequently advanced this metaphor in their sermons as a way to understand the purposes of the church, and consequently, modern historical accounts have focused on them as the "gardeners" of New England religion.[4] But the laity also understood their part in the church in these terms; they were not merely passive recipients of clerical guidance, but active and self-conscious cultivators who could help to encourage the growth of their communities.

The founders of the Third Church took to heart the lessons and even the metaphors of first-generation ministers like Thomas Shepard whose views on baptism foreshadowed the Halfway Covenant. Their purpose in modifying the baptismal policies that the first generation had instituted was not a rejection of the past, but an attempt to nurture the rising generation in the faith and to bring the means of salvation to those members of the community not yet encompassed within the church. Their devotion to the Halfway Covenant as a "middle way" of church reform was expressed in their efforts to cultivate and expand the garden of the church, and in this regard, the material resources they were accumulating as successful merchants could prove to be very useful. Their goal was to create a "plenitude of means" that would envelop the community and bring all potential saints into contact with an active and vital church, where their propensities toward a godly life would be nurtured and allowed to flourish.[5] These Puritans saw the church as a garden, but they did not think it could flourish only in rural villages closed off from the commerce of the world. The merchants and tradesmen who brought prosperity to New England's metropolis used their wealth to become expert cultivators of religious community as well.

⚜

Who were the founders of the Third Church, and what was their status within Boston society in the later decades of the seventeenth century? The records of the Third Church list twenty-eight men who participated in the church gathering on May 12, 1669. This was an extraordinary number for a New England church founding, which usually required only six or seven founders along with a minister, but because all the founders had been members of the First Church and had suffered together during their years of opposition, all were included in the formal gathering. Of these twenty-eight founders, at least eleven are known to have been merchants, among them some of the wealthier men in the colony, such as John Hull, Peter Oliver, Thomas Brattle, Joshua Scottow, and Hezekiah Usher. In addition, there were at least eleven others who worked at some type of trade and probably engaged in mercantile activities as well.[6] As a group, the founders represented some of Boston's more prominent and substantial men. Even those engaged in less lucrative trades, like the shoemaker William Salter, are known to have been prosperous. Salter had been a freeman in Boston since 1636, and was the owner of Spectacle Island in Boston harbor. Theophilus Frary, a cordwainer, served frequently as a Boston town selectman and as a representative to the General Court, and held positions of fiscal responsibility in the town. Richard Truesdale came to New England as a servant in 1634, but by 1650 he had become deacon of the First Church.[7]

As a further indicator of their social status, at least thirteen of the original twenty-eight founders were members of Boston's Ancient and Honourable Artillery Company, and six of these thirteen served as the company's captain on at least one occasion.[8] Many of these men had reputations of long standing within New England: Edward Rainsford was part of the Winthrop fleet of 1630, and had been a deacon in the First Church, and Thomas Savage, who migrated in 1635, was one of the original members of the artillery company and served as an Assistant to the colony's General Court. Others, like Jacob Eliot and Peter Oliver, were among the first children born in Boston to prominent families and followed their fathers into positions of importance in New England society. Still others, like Edward Rawson and William Dawes, were migrants of the early years who settled in outlying regions, made considerable fortunes, and then moved to Boston once they were well-established.[9] At first glance, the founders of Boston's South Church appear to have been active participants in the commercial culture of New England's leading port city and beneficiaries of its rapidly expanding economy.

The survival of detailed membership lists from the Third Church and of the Boston tax list of 1687 allows for an even closer analysis of the wealth and social standing of the members. The 1687 tax list provides information on the quantity, kind, and value of property owned by the 1226 heads of household in Boston, almost twenty years after the founding of the Third Church.[10] By this time, the church had reached a size comparable to the other Boston churches, and the contention between the First and Third Churches had finally been resolved. From the 1687 tax list, all those heads of household who had a primary affiliation with the Third Church can be identified. By primary affiliation, I mean of course all those in full communion with the church, but this category should also include persons who had owned the baptismal covenant of the church, the "halfway members" who were subject to church discipline and were regular participants in congregational life, but who had not yet testified to the conversion experience that would allow them to join in full communion. In addition, this category also encompasses heads of household who can be positively identified as spouses (usually husbands) of full church members; in many cases these spouses also turn out to have been halfway members themselves.

These last two groups—the halfway members and members' spouses— belong among the primary affiliates of the Third Church because for the purposes of the social and financial position of the church within Boston as a whole, "partial" members were as important as full members. Although each person made individual decisions and commitments with respect to the state of his or her soul, participation in the life of a church was usually a family matter. Formal church records might show only a single member of a family in full communion (often the wife and mother of a family with several children under the baptismal covenant). But closer investigation typically reveals that the entire family attended church together and were part of the minister's regular catechizing visits, that they spent time together in the devotional exercises of family piety, and further, that the material resources of the family, usually under the husband's name, were drawn upon for contributions to the church.

For example, a man named John Hayward is rated at three shillings, four pence on the 1687 Boston tax list, a figure slightly above average for the town as a whole. Hayward's name is not included on any member list or baptismal covenant records of the Third Church, though his wife, Experience Hayward, became a member of the church in full communion in 1685. But as early as 1676, Hayward can be located in attendance at a private devotional meeting along with other members of the Third Church "at Capt. Scottows, where Edward Allin and John Hayward spoke to Prov. 3. 11." Hayward's participation at similar meetings is recorded on several other occasions.[11] John Hayward's name may have been omitted inadvertently from the membership lists, or perhaps he never actually took the step of committing himself formally to the church. Nevertheless, his active involvement in the life of the church demonstrates the need to look beyond the most exclusive definitions of church membership to understand the organization and extent of participation in this religious community.[12] Too often the distinction between full and halfway members created by the Synod of 1662 is taken to be a permanent rift in the churches that adopted it, the beginnings of a spiritual caste system, whereas in the actual life of the church, halfway members were often vital and dynamic participants, spiritual seekers on the road to salvation. By expanding the notion of primary affiliation to include not only full members, but also people under the baptismal covenant and heads of household who were married to full members, we come closer to the social reality of church participation in this period by identifying the *families* that together made up the Third Church.

Under this method of selection, 239 heads of household, roughly one fifth of the total on the 1687 Boston tax list, can be identified as Third Church affiliates.[13] The tax list itself is divided into eight "sheets," or precincts, distributed across the geographical neighborhoods of Boston.[14] In each precinct, Third Church affiliates were on the average rated at higher levels than households not affiliated with the Third Church. For the town as a whole, Third Church affiliates were rated at 43.0 pence, while non-affiliates were rated at 33.2 pence (See Table 3.1). This overall difference in mean tax rates varied from precinct to precinct, and tended to be more pronounced in the precincts

TABLE 3.1
Mean Tax Rates for Third Church Affiliates and Non-Affiliates, 1687
(In pence)

	Households affiliated with the Third Church		Households not affiliated with the Third Church		Total	
	No.	Mean tax rate	No.	Mean tax rate	No.	Mean tax rate
North End						
Precinct 1	12	35.7	132	35.1	144	35.1
Precinct 2	21	34.6	178	31.9	199	32.2
Precinct 3	17	44.5	122	32.9	139	34.3
Center and South End						
Precinct 4	35	39.8	127	32.1	162	33.8
Precinct 5	29	43.3	94	41.7	123	42.1
Precinct 6	45	51.0	124	36.8	169	40.6
Precinct 7	41	42.3	130	27.2	171	30.9
Precinct 8	39	43.1	80	28.7	119	33.4
Totals	239	43.0	987	33.2	1226	35.1

SOURCE: Boston Tax List of 1687.
NOTE: All tax rates have been converted to pence for ease of comparison.

where Third Church affiliates were heavily concentrated. A precinct in the North End of Boston, where the smallest proportion of households were Third Church affiliates (8.3%), also had the smallest difference between the rates paid by Third Church members and the rest of the population (2.3%). By contrast, those precincts in the center and southern parts of town with the largest numbers of Third Church members also had the largest differences between the tax rates of Third Church affiliates and those of the rest of the population. In precincts 6–8, where Third Church affiliates constituted one fourth to one third of the population, their tax rates were on the average from 39 to 55 percent higher than those of the non-affiliated population (See Table 3.2). In short, the Third Church's lay membership appears to have been significantly wealthier than their neighbors who were not affiliated with the church.

The wealth of the Third Church affiliates was based substantially on their active involvement in trade and mercantile activities. The 1687 tax list provides information on the assessment values of several categories of property owned by the heads of household, including "Acres of Land," "Housing, Mills, and Wharves," and "Trades and Estates." By calculating the average values of the assessments for these different types of property, it becomes clear that the unusual wealth of the Third Church affiliates did not lie in land ownership as much as in their participation in commerce. Precinct 6, the precinct with the greatest number of Third Church affiliates, was also the only one on the 1687 tax list for which the values of individual land holdings were recorded, and is therefore the only one in which comparisons can be made between land ownership and ownership of more commercially oriented property.

The tax records suggest a greater tendency among the Third Church affiliates toward ownership of and participation in commercial enterprise. Third Church affiliates constituted 27 percent of the population in Precinct 6, and their land holdings, at 30 percent of the precinct's total acreage, were only slightly higher than what their numbers alone would predict. But their ownership of commercial property was much more substantial. Third Church affiliates controlled almost 42 percent of the precinct's housing, wharves, and mills, and more than 34 percent of its trades and estates, the two categories that reflect commercial property. In comparison with non-affiliates, Third Church members' mean holdings in the housing, wharves, and mills category are twice as large. The 45 Third Church households owned 99 houses, mills, and wharves, more than two per family, suggesting that the typical Third Church family owned both a house and a mill or wharf. By contrast, the 124 families not affiliated with the Third Church owned only 137 houses, mills, and wharves, not much more than one per family, which indicates that few of these families owned commercial property outside their own homes. Similar conclusions can be drawn from the Third Church affiliates' trade and estate values, which are 43 percent higher than those of non-affiliates, while their land holdings are only 20 percent higher than the average holdings of non-affiliates.[15] Given their very high overall tax assessment rates, it should be no surprise that the Third Church families in this precinct score higher than

TABLE 3.2

Percent Differences in Mean Tax Rates Between Third Church Affiliates and Non-Affiliates, 1687

	Percentage of households affiliated with the Third Church	Percent differences in tax rates:	
		Third Church affiliates versus non-affiliates	Third Church affiliates versus all Bostonians
North End			
Precinct 1	8.3%	+2.3%	+2.3%
Precinct 2	10.6%	+8.5%	+7.5%
Precinct 3	12.2%	+35.3%	+29.7%
Center and South End			
Precinct 4	21.6%	+24.0%	+17.8%
Precinct 5	23.6%	+3.8%	+2.9%
Precinct 6	26.6%	+38.6%	+25.6%
Precinct 7	24.0%	+55.5%	+36.9%
Precinct 8	32.8%	+50.2%	+29.0%
Totals	19.5%	+29.5%	+22.5%

SOURCE: Boston Tax List of 1687.

non-affiliates in every category of property ownership. But their holdings tend to be weighted in the direction of commercial enterprise rather than real estate, which indicates the degree to which the overall wealth of the Third Church members stemmed from their participation in Boston's expanding commercial economy.

The very richest men in Boston were not affiliates of the Third Church. Samuel Shrimpton, the highest-rated taxpayer on the 1687 list, was a royalist with strong sympathies for the incipient Church of England establishment in Boston. The expansion of commerce and the extension of royal authority over the New England colonies brought more men like Shrimpton into Boston in the later decades of the seventeenth century.[16] Yet just below this very small group of "high-church officialdom" in wealth and social status lay the bulk of Boston's merchants and traders, men whose vigorous efforts were largely responsible for the rapid growth in the commercial economy, and for the "remarkable diffusion of ownership through the population" of shipping and commercial property.[17] Among this group, members and affiliates of the Third Church clearly stand out as leading participants in Boston's vigorous mercantile community.

The Third Church was founded and grew to maturity in the very years that the New England economy itself was maturing, during the time when Boston was becoming increasingly important as the center of New England's commerce, comparable in scale to all the leading British ports with the sole exception of London.[18] The church's members were vital participants in this remarkable economic growth. But how did this commercial activity and growing wealth influence the life of the church? How did the laity use the considerable material resources at their disposal to cultivate the Lord's garden in Boston? Answers to these questions require us to look beyond numerical analysis and consider the religious behavior of individuals and families whose lives were shaped by strong connections to Boston's expanding commercial economy as well as to its Third Church.

∾❦↬

To view the intersection of commercial and religious life in Boston, we need to become better acquainted with the men who formed the lay leadership of the Third Church.[19] One such man was Captain Thomas Savage. A first-generation immigrant and an early member of Boston's First Church, Savage had been one of the many supporters of Anne Hutchinson during the antinomian controversy, and was among those disarmed by the colony during the crisis. Shortly thereafter he was reinstated into the good graces of church and state and resumed his place of prominence within the merchant community of Boston. Though little is known of his inner life, Savage must have undergone a considerable transformation in his views on the nature of the church in the years between 1637 and 1669. His support of the Halfway Covenant during the founding of the Third Church shows that he had long since abandoned the radical separatist tendencies implied in the antinomian position.

The funeral sermon that Samuel Willard preached at Thomas Savage's death in 1682 emphasized his value to the community, for despite his vicissitudes on church polity, Savage demonstrated a lifelong devotion to promoting religion within Boston. Willard praised Savage for his "long service in publick employment," for "his tender care for the welfare of this people," for "his uprightness towards God as a private Christian," and for "his tenderness and love to his brethren as a member of the Church." But Willard reminded his audience of the implications of the loss of Captain Savage: "that which most of all should affect us, is, that by his removal, the gap is wider, and we left the more naked."[20] In the eyes of contemporaries, Savage's career was valuable, but not particularly unusual. This funeral sermon was but one entry in an extensive literary genre, the lay equivalent of biographies of exemplary clergymen, like those written and assembled by Cotton Mather in his *Magnalia Christi Americana*.[21] The clergy of New England praised and commemorated the virtues of lay men and women whose activities were vital to the survival and prosperity of the churches. These people were the "hedge" that defined New England's churches and protected them from the wilderness threats of heresy, unbelief, or indifference. The death of any one such person always threatened to leave a "gap in the hedge" unless there were willing members of the rising generation capable of filling the place.[22]

At the time of Thomas Savage's death, other prominent first-generation figures who had joined in founding the Third Church were reaching the ends of their lives. Mary Norton, widow of the minister who had guided the dissenters' path, the woman who had donated the land for the church's meetinghouse, died in 1677. Edward Rainsford, a member of the Winthrop fleet, deacon of the First Church for many years, and the first ruling elder of the Third Church, died in 1680. John Hull died in October 1683. The decades of the 1670s and 1680s saw Samuel Willard publish a number of these laudatory funeral sermons and preach many more than were published.[23] But at the same time, the rising generation began to meet its obligations by supplying new members to fill the gaps in the hedge left by the deaths of their elders. In the South Church, the best known of these lay figures to reach maturity in the 1670s was the merchant, magistrate, judge, and diarist Samuel Sewall.

Like Edward Taylor and most of the other members of his 1671 Harvard

College class, Samuel Sewall prepared himself for a career in the ministry and expected that this would be his calling. However, the opportunities offered by marriage to Hannah Hull and partnership with her merchant father convinced Sewall that his vocation lay in the world of commerce.[24] This decision was not, for Sewall, a cynical choice of mammon over the life of the spirit. Sewall's religious beliefs and practices remained constantly at the center of his busy engagement in worldly affairs. Most historians acknowledge the intensity and vitality of Sewall's religious commitment, but there is a tendency to see him as the last vestige of a culture about to disappear from the New England scene, to believe that other men who turned to careers in commerce failed to maintain the religious commitment evident in Sewall.[25] Sewall's distinctive qualities, his prominence in public affairs as merchant and magistrate, make it difficult to offer him as a representative member of the South Church in the later seventeenth and early eighteenth centuries. And yet, as the numerical evidence cited above suggests, the heads of household who joined the South Church did tend, like Sewall, to be wealthier than average with investments in the growing commercial economy of Boston. By looking more closely at Sewall and his fellow members of the South Church, it becomes clear that Sewall was not unique in playing a "quasi-ministerial" role in Boston's religious culture.

The expansive diary kept by Sewall provides unparalleled insights into daily life in Boston from the 1670s through the 1720s, and part of its value lies in the extent to which it is not about Sewall himself. Among his friends and colleagues in Boston mercantile life there were many others like Sewall who were engaged in promoting the life of the church. Some were native New Englanders, born and raised in the (by-now) indigenous religious culture, men like Jacob Eliot. Others were surviving members of the founding generation, like Joshua Scottow. Still others were late-comers, migrants of the Restoration era, brought to New England by its expanding commercial opportunities and by its promise as a last refuge for the godly. Among this last group was Edward Bromfield, an immigrant from London who joined the South Church and became Sewall's close friend and colleague in trade, in affairs of state, and in the life of the church.[26]

A glimpse of prominent lay figures in their collective role as the "hedge" around the garden of the church can be seen at those times when the laity were required to make significant decisions about the future of their religious community. When it came time to choose an assistant and potential successor to the minister Samuel Willard, a group of these laymen gathered to determine the procedure that the church as a whole would follow. On February 5, 1696/7, Sewall records that "This evening Mr. Willard, Bromfield, Eyre,

Sergeant, Frary, Hill, Williams, Oliver, Checkly, Davis, Wally, Stoddard met at my house. . . . Then discours'd what was best to be done relating to the desires of some for a ch[urch] meeting; whether twere best to call one, or no."[27] Some disagreement existed between these members and the minister about whether a church meeting should be called and which of several candidates should be proposed for the job, but the significance of the meeting lies in the fact that neither the minister alone nor the church as a whole was responsible for making this decision and charting the course of action. Instead, this self-appointed group of the most influential men in the congregation gathered to act for the entire church. Nor was this an isolated event; when plans were being made to ordain Joseph Sewall in 1713, the prospective minister's father recorded a similar gathering: "A little after 7. Met at Mr. Pemberton's, Winthrop, Sewall, Sergeant, Bromfield, Stoddard, Sim. Hill, Williams, Checkley, Mr. Nathanl Williams, Schoolmaster, Major Fitch, Mr. S. Phillips, Mr. Borland, Mr. Danl Oliver, Capt. Winslow, Mr. Campbell. Conferred about the Ordination in order to have the Churches' Approbation."[28] Over the course of seventeen years, the composition of the "hedge" had changed a little, but its basic purpose was the same. Like the selectmen of a town, these prominent individuals were routinely entrusted with the care and guidance of the most important matters in the life of the church.

While Sewall's diary is one indicator of the church activities of these prominent individuals, their significance as "quasi-clerical" lay figures in promoting the strength of Puritan religious culture emerges in many other contexts as well. Joshua Scottow, a founder of the Third Church whose career as a merchant spanned the first six decades of New England's history, composed one of the few entries in the Puritan jeremiad tradition written by a layman.[29] In the early 1690s, Jacob Eliot joined Scottow and Sewall in gathering documents and writing a narrative account of the founding of the Third Church.[30] Written after the loss of the original Massachusetts charter and the institution of royal government, both these documents were attempts to remind New Englanders of their religious heritage and to describe a course that would preserve their religious culture despite the loss of state support. Like Sewall, Eliot, and Scottow, many other prosperous and influential Bostonians took advantage of the education, leisure, and material resources afforded them by Boston's commercial expansion to devote themselves to the enhancement of the religious culture they inherited from the first generation. As individuals came forward to fill the "gaps in the hedge" left by the passing of the founding members, they made important contributions to the religion of their community by developing new forms to enrich the means of grace available in the town of Boston, spending their considerable resources in finding ways to insure that the children of the church and all members of their community would be fully encompassed by the institutions of Puritan knowledge, practice, and devotion. A more complete picture of this intensive activity can be gained through a systematic examination of the nature of lay piety and of the laity's use of their material resources to promote a pious society.

～❀～

In Puritan culture, the means of grace were the ordinary forms of religious instruction through which individuals came to know the word of God and its meaning for their lives, the media through which God's saving message was communicated to the elect. The primary form was, of course, the Bible, but the church and its various functions existed to provide a full range of direction and care for the individual soul on its pilgrimage to grace. The laity of the Third Church attempted to enrich Boston's religious culture by creating a dense overlay of care and instruction that would guarantee everyone access to God's message in an all-encompassing variety of forms, so that no potential saints would wither on the vine for want of sufficient pruning, cutting, watering, and dressing. To provide such spiritual nurture, the laity attended to the means of grace at many different levels, from the passing on of devotional practices from parents to children to the development of techniques for spreading traditional messages of piety and belief to society at large. Although historians have already noted this dense network of pious forms and practices within Puritan culture, the focus has tended to be on the clergy as providers and the laity as recipients.[31] But the laity were active providers as well as partakers of the means of grace, and they used the material resources of their growing commercial economy to create an all-encompassing plenum of religious instruction for the population of Boston.

In the few surviving texts that record the conversion experiences of early New England church members, the narrator commonly expresses gratitude for having been born into a godly family, where the habits of piety were inculcated at an early age.[32] Although the practice of family piety is well known, there is relatively little tangible evidence of the way it persisted across the generations. However, a clear example of the strength of this habit among the laity of the South Church can be found in the papers of the Bromfield family. The family was headed by Edward Bromfield, who was born in Hampshire, England, in 1649, and became a merchant in London. Bromfield emigrated to New England by way of the West Indies and arrived in Boston in 1675.[33] Like Samuel Sewall, his lifelong friend, Bromfield combined a successful career in commerce with traditional forms of Puritan piety and devotion. Proof of the former can be found in the 1687 tax list, where Bromfield was rated at eight shillings, more than twice the average for all Bostonians.[34] Evidence for the latter appears in a collection of Bromfield's sermon notebooks.

Edward Bromfield kept detailed notes on the sermons he attended every Sunday at Boston's Third Church, as well as every Thursday at the weekly lecture preached at the First Church meetinghouse. Bromfield also kept notes on occasional sermons, such as those preached at private devotional meetings, funeral services, or on special occasions like Fasts or Election Days. Six of these notebooks have survived, dating from the years 1682, 1683, 1685–86, 1689, 1692, and 1698. Each notebook contains roughly thirty to forty sermons, covering a period of several months. For every sermon, Bromfield would follow the minister's arguments with a thorough outline, keeping track of scriptural citations and adding emphasis to the most significant portions. For example, when Samuel Willard preached a sermon series during the 1692 witchcraft crisis on 1 Peter 5:8, "the devill walketh up and down seking whom he may devower," Bromfield, pious merchant that he was, made special note that the devil is to be expected everywhere: "he is in the house of god, he is In yr shopes &c."[35] Bromfield's notes reinforce our knowledge of the New England clergy's intense devotion to the preaching of conversion in their ordinary Sabbath sermons, their insistence on the need to go beyond reliance on good works or the inheritance of baptism to close with Christ in full church communion.[36]

What is most remarkable and useful to our understanding of the participation of the laity in the church, however, is the fact that these six notebooks, and presumably the many other intervening ones that have failed to survive, were all made by Bromfield *before* he was in full communion with the church. Although Bromfield arrived in Boston in 1675 and began these notes at least as early as 1682, he had no official relation to the church until he became a full member on November 11, 1698, at the age of 49.[37] The last of the surviving notebooks ends in October 1698, just a month before Bromfield joined the church. While it is possible that Bromfield continued to keep sermon notes after he joined in full communion but the later notebooks were simply not preserved, it seems more plausible to imagine that Bromfield's notebooks provided reinforcement and guidance on the spiritual pilgrimage that led him into the church. To have copies of the minister's words for review in private moments of reflection or in the practice of family worship may have assisted Bromfield and others like him in the struggle to know the state of his own soul. These notebooks belie the notion that in the later seventeenth century, fervent piety and spiritual seeking had become the preserve of the diminishing fraction of the population in full membership, while halfway members and non-members languished in secular indifference. Edward Bromfield was clearly a vital participant in the spiritual life of the church, a part of the hedge around the garden, long before he came forward to relate his conversion experience, take the sacrament, and be counted among the saints.

The other sermon notebooks among the Bromfield manuscripts demonstrate that this form of personal devotion was a family practice cultivated across the generations. The first notebook in the collection was kept in the summer of 1687 by Mary Rock, daughter of John Wilson, the original minister of Boston's First Church. Mary Rock was the mother of Edward Bromfield's second wife, and after the death of her husband, she lived with her daughter in the Bromfield household. She attended the South Church with the rest of the family, although she never transferred her formal membership from the First Church.[38] Four additional notebooks covering the years between 1713 and 1721 were the work of Bromfield's son and successor in his mercantile enterprises, Edward Bromfield, Jr. The younger Bromfield recorded sermons in a style that used more shorthand and abbreviations; nevertheless, he paid attention to the converting preaching of the clergy in the same way that his father and grandmother did. In fact, on one occasion in 1720, the younger Bromfield noted the minister Joseph Sewall using the same image that his grandmother had recorded from the words of Samuel Willard in 1687. Where Willard had stated that "the righteous of the saints are as filthy rags, indeed it's only the righteousness of Christ" that earns salvation, Joseph Sewall preached thirty-three years later that "he [Christ] alone Can give you rest, your righteousness are filthy rags."[39] Most significantly, the younger Bromfield, like his father, took these extensive sermon notes during the time when he was under the baptismal covenant by virtue of his father's membership, but was still not a full member, a step which he finally took in 1729.[40]

Taken together, the notebooks illustrate the vitality of this particular form of personal devotion across the generations within a mercantile family of South Church members. They indicate the extent to which the quest for personal salvation was an ongoing part of life in the religious community even (or especially) for those among the congregation who were not yet full members of the church. They constitute tangible evidence of an often intangible element among the available means to conversion, the habits of piety and devotion inculcated within the family by parents concerned about the salvation of their children. In particular, the notebook of Mary Rock reminds us of the role that women played as nurturers of family piety, a role widely understood but seldom demonstrated as clearly as in the notebooks that she and her descendants used as guides on their spiritual pilgrimages.[41]

Expanding outward from the most intimate circle of personal and family devotion, we find another level of practical piety in the ongoing "meetings" into which the church membership divided itself. These meetings were weekly affairs where lay men and women gathered to share their experience of the religious life, including prayers for the health of friends and family, the singing of psalms, and the reading of sermons, either recent preaching taken down by the members in notes, or published sermons of the New England clergy. On occasion, a lay member or visiting clergyman might preach a new sermon to the group.[42] Private meetings were a great benefit to the well-being of the religious community, for they allowed lay people at different stages of the spiritual pilgrimage and with different levels of education to come together, learn from one another, and share each other's spiritual resources. On September 9, 1708, the group to which Samuel Sewall belonged met for the first time at the home of Josiah Franklin (father of Benjamin Franklin), a man of modest means who had recently joined the church. There Sewall movingly "read the Eleventh Sermon on the Barren Fig-Tree."[43] This sermon, one of Samuel Willard's series on this subject, outlined the nature of the church and discussed the responsibility of members to bear spiritual fruit.[44] Reading this particular sermon gave Sewall the chance to instruct a new member on an important subject, while also connecting Sewall to the words of his former minister, who had died only a year before. And the fact that Sewall owned a copy of Willard's publication was no small matter. In a society where books were still relatively scarce and expensive, merchants who lived in the metropolis of Boston were at an advantage over those in outlying regions and therefore had a greater opportunity to bring this material to the attention of other pious lay people.[45] Similarly, on February 7, 1710/11, Sewall went to his weekly meeting despite a great snowstorm "and there read an excellent Sermon out of Mr. Shepard, on the Ten Virgins; against hypocrisy."[46] In this instance, Sewall's offering to the group was a sermon from a series preached seventy years earlier, but still vital to the spiritual life of the meeting.

Sewall was a link in the ongoing chain of religious instruction, passing on knowledge from his own experience to another generation of members. As a young man, Sewall himself had benefitted from the advice of his elders in the church. In December 1676, Sewall attended his first private devotional meetings, where a variety of church members, including "Mr. Smith, Capt. Henchman, Goodm. Needham, Mr. Sanford and Mr. Noyes, Mr. Williams and Wing, . . . spake well . . . to my satisfaction" on various points of scripture.[47] Just as with the sermon notebooks of the Bromfield family, the nurturing value of these private meetings as forms of devotion can be seen in the fact that Sewall began to attend them before he joined the church, and he continued to consult with his more experienced elders on matters of faith as he struggled to commit himself to full membership.[48]

The transition from more private forms of religious devotion—family piety and small group meetings—to full participation in public worship was marked by the Lord's Supper. When a young convert like Samuel Sewall finally felt prepared to make a public declaration of his experience of God's grace, communion was the ritual that signified the new member's inclusion in the body of Christ. Like any rite of passage, the first experience of the Lord's Supper could create intense anxiety, as it did for Sewall, who worried (paradoxically) that God might strike him dead for the feelings of unbelief he harbored as he approached the communion table. Biblical injunctions against taking communion unworthily heightened these fears in converts and perhaps led some otherwise devout people to avoid the sacrament altogether.[49] Yet despite the powerful anxieties that surrounded it, the Lord's Supper could be a nurturing ritual as well. For those like Sewall who managed to brave the risks and cross the threshold into full membership, subsequent experiences of the sacrament might nurture further growth in grace, bringing the communicant into closer fellowship with other church members in the presence of the divine spirit.[50] For those of the congregation not yet in full membership, the regular spectacle of the visible saints performing the communion ritual could be an edifying experience, a reminder of the supreme sacrifice Christ had made for their souls and a demonstration of the benefits to be gained from closing with Christ.[51]

The laity of the Third Church used their considerable material and cultural resources to enhance the availability and the spiritual value of the sacramental ritual. The church's position during the Halfway Covenant controversy encouraged the frequent administration of the sacrament, and lay members like Sewall made it their business to encourage at least one Boston church to offer the Lord's Supper every Sunday in the year.[52] Frequent celebrations meant that the laity would have to bear the increased expense of furnishing the communion table with wine and bread. The church deacons were responsible for acquiring the necessary communion elements with funds drawn from members' contributions, and it was their job to aide the minister during the service in distributing the bread and wine once it had been consecrated.[53] As symbolic representations of the body and blood of Christ, bread and wine were essential to the Lord's Supper, and few if any New England churches were so poor as to miss the sacrament for want of them. But at the same time, few New England churches were able to furnish their communion tables with vessels for serving communion as richly as Boston's Third Church did.

Much has been made of the artistic value of early New England church silver, but its spiritual value as a means of grace has been largely overlooked. The silver cups, beakers, tankards, and salvers used for the administration of the sacrament were complex symbolic objects. Within a religious culture that was otherwise intensely logocentric, communion silver, together with the bread and wine it conveyed, was one of the few visible and tangible ways in which the deepest meanings of the faith were expressed. The intrinsic qualities of these refined, precious vessels subtly reminded both communicants and observers at the Lord's Supper of the terms of their salvation. The purity and permanence of the silver "bearers" of Christ's body and blood symbolized the physical perfection of Christ, and by implication, the weakness and mortality of sinful human beings. And yet part of the promise of salvation was eternal life and the perfection of the body in the afterlife, a promise kept in mind by the common practice of inscribing the names of departed members on the sides of communion vessels they had donated to the church. In this life, converts were expected to strive to live up to God's laws, although original sin prevented anything like human perfection. As Sewall himself put it, recording the words of a sermon he attended, "Christians of the greatest excellency are compar'd to Vessels of Gold. Are pure, precious, will endure the Fire. Are fill'd with all the Graces of God's spirit. Christians that do not excell are compar'd to Silver; persons of Lesser piety, though true piety. Use. Labour to be Vessels of Gold, or at least of Silver."[54] The vessels that graced the communion table bore silent testimony to this injunction. Even their very costliness conveyed a spiritual lesson, reminding sinners of the extreme price Christ had paid in sacrificing himself for mankind's redemption.[55]

The members of Boston's Third Church were in a uniquely advantageous position to furnish their own communion table, and indeed, communion tables throughout New England, with these symbolic objects. New England's silver industry emerged from the shop of Third Church founder John Hull, who, in partnership with Robert Sanderson, was named the official mint-master for the colony of Massachusetts. Hull's control of the coinage gave him ready access to the silver bullion necessary to produce the domestic and ecclesiastical objects that appeared with increasing frequency in New England homes and meetinghouses in the later seventeenth century. The prosperous merchants of Boston's Third Church readily invested their wealth in silver produced by Hull and by the apprentices he trained, many of whom also became Third Church members. Some pieces were commissioned especially for the church, while others, like the silver tankard that Sewall donated in 1730, were originally domestic objects converted to religious purposes. But in either case, the wealth of the membership guaranteed that partakers of the Lord's Supper in the Third Church would always use refined silver vessels.[56] Without silver, the Lord's Supper would still have been served and communicants would still have encountered divine grace. But silver enriched the experience, deepened it, and made it more accessible by opening new metaphors for grasping the meaning of grace.

Although it was hoped that the performance of the Lord's Supper would encourage non-members to join the church, the sacrament was primarily intended to provide spiritual nourishment to those who were already converted. But the South Church laity were committed to finding additional ways to nurture the faith of the rising generation and to offer the means of grace to the unconverted. One of the most important though often ignored ways in which the laity fulfilled this obligation was in the oversight of the church's physical property. The founders struggled to provide a meetinghouse in a suitable location and with appropriate symbolic connotations for the church's mission, but the effort did not end here. In the 1680s, with Boston's population growing rapidly, space at the Third Church's capacious meetinghouse was already becoming scarce. The membership considered it vital that all available room be used to the best advantage. Although the tradition of pew ownership had been in existence since the church's founding, the members now chose to qualify the terms of ownership. If a pew were not in regular use, the church could assign it to another worthy family and arrange for compensation of the pew's value to the original owner. To this end, four prominent laymen were appointed to be the first overseers of the seats in October 1685.[57] Over time, the composition of the seating committee evolved to include distinguished laymen who were not full members of the church, so that halfway members under the church covenant would be adequately represented in the allocation process.[58] The overall effect of this system was to counteract the tendency for Puritan churches to become "tribal," or the exclusive preserve of those families in full communion and their direct descendants.[59] By ensuring that all pews would be used, despite whatever hereditary property rights individuals might possess, and that the seating would be overseen by the congregation of non-members and halfway members as well as by those in full communion, the laity was attempting to maintain a physical plan for the meetinghouse in which the converting preaching of the ministers would reach the widest possible audience. The meetinghouse design and the seating plan were intended to prevent the minister from preaching exclusively to the converted.[60]

In addition to maintaining the meetinghouse, the laity also contributed to the upkeep of the metaphorical "hedge" that protected the body of the church, namely, the exercise of church discipline. The absence of church discipline was one of the primary causes for dissent from the established church at the beginning of the English Puritan movement.[61] Its importance loomed ever larger in the later seventeenth century in New England, when it could no longer be assumed that virtually everyone was part of the godly community. The need for church discipline was expressed in Samuel Willard's *Barren Fig Tree's Doom* sermon series in terms of the garden metaphor. Proper discipline meant weeding out the unfruitful plants, or pruning those in need of correction, to prevent the garden as a whole from suffering and to allow light and room for healthy plants to flourish.[62] The disciplinary tools of excommunication and admonition were meant to be used toward these ends. The laity played a significant role in disciplinary activity and had the last word on the outcome of any case through a formal church vote.

The early records of the Third Church contain remarkably few disciplinary cases, but those few instances that did require formal action demonstrate the extent to which the laity played a part in disciplining themselves. One example occurred in the later seventeenth century and involved a member by the name of Roger Judd. As early as 1688, Judd's inclinations toward the Church of England had aroused concern and caused Samuel Sewall and another lay member, Captain James Hill, to have a "discourse" with him.[63] By the late 1690s, it was clear that Roger Judd was no longer attending services and "was resolved to desert this Church, on some disgust taken." But the course which the minister Samuel Willard followed reflects the importance of the laity to the process of church discipline. Willard first sent the church deacons, Theophilus Frary and Nathaniel Williams, to inform Judd that the church knew of no scandal against him and saw no reason to renounce communion with him. Judd's response was "that if the Church did not renounce Communion with him, he renounced it with them." Willard's further inquiry into the matter was again conducted through the laity; he sent Samuel Sewall to arrange a meeting with Judd at Sewall's home. Judd refused to meet there, and showed further contempt for the disciplinary process on still another occasion by barring Deacon Frary from entering his home to inquire into the reasons for Judd's removal. Ultimately, Judd refused to listen to any intermediaries between himself and Willard, and insisted that if Willard had any grievance with him, he had to come see him alone.

Willard refused to cater to Judd's terms and again sent Deacon Frary and "Brother J. Wheeler" to deliver the same message, which, not surprisingly, received the same answer as before. At this point, Willard thought the matter should be taken up by the church as a whole, and sent Captain Savage and Captain Checkly to inform Judd that he must appear before the church or else meet privately at Sewall's house with Willard. When Judd ignored these last measures, the church voted to excommunicate him, not because he had wanted to leave the church, but because he showed such contempt for the church disciplinary process to which he had submitted himself when he became a member. Willard's conscious choice of intermediaries at every stage of this process reflects the way in which the lay members were essential to the function of discipline in this church. In this case, Willard called on at least six prominent laymen to intercede with Judd, and Judd's excommunication was based on his refusal to accept the authority of either the laity or the minister, a position which threatened the ordinance of church discipline itself. Discipline was not to be a matter of the minister lording it over the members, but a mutual process of watch and care among the members themselves, overseen by the minister but conducted by the laity.[64]

The pattern of the Third Church's prosecution of this case was, in effect, the antithesis of the way John Davenport had dealt with the dissenters in the crisis that led to the Third Church founding. There, discipline had been used as a tool by the minister to ensnare and humiliate disaffected but loyal church members. Here, discipline was offered by the laity as means of reconciliation to a disaffected member who chose to leave the church anyway. Again, the fact that the Roger Judd case even came to a church vote made it quite exceptional. The relative scarcity of formal disciplinary action on the part of the Third Church reflects the success with which the laity independently managed to resolve cases of disagreement or misbehavior without recourse to formal disciplinary action.[65] On a rare occasion when Ebenezer Pemberton, Willard's successor as minister of the church, circumvented the normally lay-controlled process and brought a member's misbehavior to the immediate attention of the whole church, Samuel Sewall expressed his dismay and received assurance from Pemberton "that he would not go in that way again." The function of discipline was to edify the church and maintain its unity as well as to punish the sinning member, and for Sewall and the other lay members, this edification was as much the business of the laity as it was of the clergy.[66]

In most New England villages in the seventeenth century, the population was small enough that a single church could serve the entire community, and the exercise of church discipline therefore helped to uphold the moral order of the town as a whole. Boston was an exception to this pattern. In the later part of the century, as its population neared eight thousand, its three orthodox churches were not adequate to encompass everyone under the regulation of formal church discipline. Although the number of churches would soon expand accordingly to accommodate Boston's demographic growth, the challenges Boston presented to the ideal of a moral community were addressed in other ways as well. The quality of religious life in the town required the maintenance of public morality, and the laity of the churches took it upon themselves to serve watch over Boston's manners. On one level, community oversight might take the form of individuals like Samuel Sewall or Ezekiel Chiever pestering their friends and neighbors who chose to wear periwigs, a fashion that both men "abominated."[67] At times, the moral watch was more elaborate and intrusive. Sewall's diary for February 9, 1707/8, records the following example:

> Mr. D. Oliver, Capt. Keeling, Constable Loring, and my self walk'd in the 7th Comp. to inspect Disorders. Found this to our comfort, that the Widow Harman's daughter Ames is gon to her husband at Marshfield, which was a gravamen for many years, I used constantly to visit them and expostulat with them. I carried ½ Duz. Catechises in my Pocket, and gave them to such as could read, Orphans several of them.[68]

The Widow Harman and her daughter were not affiliated with the South Church, but they were part of the geographical area in Boston that the church ordinarily served, so Sewall and his companions considered it their responsibility to attend to immorality there.[69] Although not formally created as such the way they often were in smaller New England towns, Boston's churches were beginning to act as if they were parishes.

In some cases, the concerns of the laity about public morality conflicted with the views of the clergy. In 1710, during a temporary wheat shortage, a small riot broke out in Boston when a group of dockworkers attempted to scuttle a ship on which Captain Andrew Belcher was exporting grain. Sewall argued that the rioters should be dealt with leniently, and cited Biblical evidence to suggest that Capt. Belcher, his fellow merchant and Third Church member, was the greater offender: "He that withholds Corn, the people will curse him, though I did not affirm that Scripture Justified the Rioters." For this position Sewall was severely criticized by his minister, Ebenezer Pemberton, who insisted that the rioters "were not God's people but the Devil's people," and that "There was Corn to be had; if they had not impoverish'd themselves by Rum." Despite the opposition of his minister, Sewall stood firm in his beliefs as judge in the matter and upheld his view of proper morality.[70]

Later the same year, in a libel case brought before his court, Sewall decided in favor of the plaintiffs (Increase and Cotton Mather), fined each of the defendants twenty shillings, and bound them to their good behavior. Again, Ebenezer Pemberton was upset by the decision and exacted his revenge on the judge by choosing the 58th Psalm to be sung on the following Sabbath, in full awareness that Sewall's position as the church's "precentor" required him to line out the words to each verse in advance of the entire congregation:

> Speak, O ye Judges of the Earth, if just your Sentence be:
> Or must not Innocence appeal to Heav'n from your Decree?
> Your Wicked Hearts and Judgments are alike by Malice sway'd;
> Your griping Hands, by weighty Bribes, to Violence betrayed.
> To Virtue, strangers from the Womb their Infant Steps went wrong:
> They prattled Slander, and in Lyes employ'd their lisping Tongue.

Sewall was humiliated by the experience, but he took consolation from another Psalm, "that God would vouchsafe to be my Shepherd" when his own pastor seemed to leave him behind "in my Straglings."[71]

An ongoing rivalry seems to have developed between Pemberton and Sewall, perhaps because the young minister was wary and resentful of the power that this active and prominent layman had over the church, especially after Sewall's son Joseph became Pemberton's colleague in the pulpit in 1713. But despite the rivalry and the bitterness of their occasional conflicts, Sewall and Pemberton were always able to patch up their differences; the disputes between them caused no major disruption in the church. In a small rural village, such a clash between two sources of religious and moral authority might have been difficult to contain, but the rich array of religious institutions and leaders in Boston helped ease the situation.[72] Through his extensive activities as a "quasi-clerical" figure, Sewall had considerable confidence in his own authority, experience, and judgment. He also had allies among the other Boston ministers, including the Mathers. Nor was Sewall the only prominent layman who attempted to provide moral authority over the town, so in censuring Sewall, Pemberton was not censuring the laity as a whole or attempting to assert a position of superiority over the entire congregation. Neither did Pemberton attempt to make their rivalry an official church matter or use disciplinary measures against Sewall. Though a difference of opinion might temporarily cause conflict between the minister and a church member, there was a general agreement on the necessity of cooperation in the attempt to promote moral order in the town for the sake of the church's prosperity.

In addition to their activities as moral regulators of the community, the laity of the Third Church also provided religious instruction to the townspeople of Boston, as the career of Nathaniel Williams demonstrates. Williams was a medical practicioner, schoolmaster, and prominent member of the Third Church—he was present among the lay leaders at the informal meeting in 1713 that conferred on the ordination of Joseph Sewall—but his importance to the religious life of the community ran much deeper than that. Williams was born in Boston in 1675, the son of Mary Oliver and Nathaniel

Williams Sr., both full members of the Third Church (his father was a dea-con). In 1693, upon his graduation from Harvard, he joined the church in full communion and began to prepare for the ministry. In 1698, he was ordained to be a missionary to a church in Barbados, but the intense heat of the West Indies was too much for Williams' constitution and he returned to Boston in 1700. Instead of seeking a New England pulpit, Williams took up life as a lay-man and devoted himself to teaching and medical work. After several years spent providing private instruction to the sons of "Gentlemen," Williams was hired by the town as the assistant and eventual successor to Ezekiel Chiever, the director of the Latin School in Boston, known then as the South Gram-mar School, situated around the corner and up School Street from the Third Church, in the shadow of the Anglican King's Chapel. There Williams re-ceived a salary comparable to that of many New England clergymen, which together with his medical practice and other investments allowed Williams to amass a considerable fortune. His estate was valued at over £4000 at his death in 1737.[73]

The combination of his wealth, his form of employment, and his clerical training gave Williams the time and inclination to provide religious instruc-tion to the Boston community. On occasion, Williams would fill in at one of the pulpits in Boston to replace an ailing or traveling minister, or even preach the Boston Thursday Lecture. At other times, he would offer public prayers between the two regular services on the Sabbath, or pray at a funeral. He might be called upon to preach a sermon at a private devotional meeting, as he did on December 19, 1707, at the home of Edward Bromfield, or to open militia training days on Boston Common with a prayer.[74] In addition, his work at the Latin School involved religious instruction of the boys enrolled there. The Boston town meeting voted in March 1709/10 to provide assis-tance to Williams from some of the educated gentlemen and ministers of the town, in order "to pray with the Schollars, and Entertain 'em with Some In-structions of Piety Specially Adapted to their age and Education."[75] Eventu-ally, his talents and reputation earned him the honor of being chosen Rector of Yale College in 1723, though he declined the offer.[76] His selection dem-onstrates the respect he gained as a religious educator and highlights the sig-nificance of the "quasi-clerical" role he played in Boston for nearly forty years as a lay member of the Third Church.[77]

Nathaniel Williams was perhaps unusual in the extent to which his career as a layman offered him the opportunity to perform what were ordinarily the functions of the clergy, but he was not alone in this role. Any church member who regularly attended weekly devotional meetings was likely, at some point during the year, to be asked to share some thoughts on a scriptural passage or to advise a younger person struggling with the state of his or her soul. Laymen in positions of secular authority often might open an official meeting or exercise with public prayer, if no minister was at hand. Samuel Sewall became so accustomed to this role that he would occasionally embarrass himself by falling into it automatically. At a large dinner party on December 15, 1708, Sewall began the meal with his customary practice: "I crav'd a Blessing, and return'd Thanks, not thinking of Mr. Corwin till had begun to return Thanks, then I *saw* him, and it almost confounded me—I crav'd his pardon, and paid his Club, saying I had defrauded the Company." "Mr. Corwin" was George Curwin, a clergyman, and Sewall felt he had usurped the minister's proper role in such a gathering.[78] But the ease with which Williams, Sewall, and other members of the church took these tasks upon themselves indicates the extent to which this religious community expected the laity to be instructors and spiritual guides.

The concentration of such a large number of highly trained and spiritually committed laymen with the time to devote themselves to the instruction of others made the South Church an especially rich religious community. Still another aspect of the benefits for traditional Puritan piety that Boston's material wealth provided can be seen in the uses to which books and other printed forms were put by the laity. During his attempts to exercise moral authority over the community, Samuel Sewall might in passing distribute half a dozen catechisms to local families. Again and again in his diary, we see him giving away copies of books, sermons, and pamphlets of religious devotion to colleagues, friends, relatives, servants, and slaves. In March of 1725, Sewall went with Edward Bromfield and Anthony Stoddard to hear the Roxbury minister preach, and while there, he gave the minister a copy of the recently published sermons of Benjamin Colman. On the first of January, 1703/4, Sewall gave away five dozen copies of a sermon preached by Samuel Willard, published several years earlier. Two dozen were given to "Mr. Phillips," and a dozen each to "Buttolp," "Eliott," and "Boon," presumably so that each of these booksellers could in turn distribute them further.[79] During Sewall's ultimately unsuccessful courtship of the widow Katherine Brattle Winthrop, he gave her a copy of Samuel Willard's *The Fountain Opened*, as well as the missionary Thomas Mayhew's "Account of the state of the Indians on Martha's Vineyard." When these failed to win her over, he gave her "Dr. Preston, The Church's Marriage and the Church's Carriage," a 461–page volume published in London in 1638, for which he paid six shillings at auction.[80] In May 1726, the elderly Sewall rode all the way to Ipswich to visit the minister John Rogers, and left him a copy of "Mr. Willard's Body of Divinity," the largest and most expensive book ever produced in North America at the time. And to Rogers' son, who also intended to be a clergyman, Sewall left a copy of "Dr. Owen's Volume printed by Subscription."[81]

Sewall's gift to the younger John Rogers was a volume of sermons preached by a leading English divine of the seventeenth century (whom the Third Church founders had once hoped to recruit to be their minister), a volume that was "printed by Subscription." This subtle reference indicates another way in which the material resources of the South Church laity were used to enrich their spiritual community. The laity were not only consumers and distributors within the developing print culture of New England, they also took part as producers of some of the devotional literature that was vital to the nurture of Puritan piety. A work like the sermons of John Owen or a pamphlet by Samuel Willard would only be published if interested laymen could finance the costs of production, or could guarantee enough advance sales "by subscription" that a printer would take on these costs.

The wealth of the laity in Boston played a crucial role in expanding the availability of religious literature throughout Boston and New England as a whole. The development of more extensive printing allowed creative laymen like Joshua Scottow to add their contributions to the culture's offerings, as Scottow did with his 1691 jeremiad, *Old Mens Tears for their own Declensions*, and his 1694 account of the settlement of Massachusetts. As early as 1675, Waitstill Winthrop published at his own expense a broadside of rather dismal verse, commemorating the efforts of New England soldiers in King Philip's War and reminding readers of the need to repent and turn to Christ for relief from the just punishments of God. Samuel Sewall published a volume of doomsday speculations, *Phaenomena Quaedam Apocalyptica*, in 1697, and a second edition in 1727.

Just as significantly, the ongoing interests of the laity in works of piety and devotion helped to keep traditional forms and beliefs vital across the generations. In 1717, the Boston printer Bartholomew Green, a member of the Third Church, printed on behalf of the publisher Samuel Gerrish, another church member and Sewall's son-in-law, an edition of Hugh Peters' *A Dying Father's Last Legacy*. Peters had been the minister of Salem in the first decade of New England's settlement, and had later taken an active part in the Parliamentary cause during the English Civil War, for which he was executed after the Restoration. Just before his death, Peters had written a devotional manual for his daughter, which was kept in circulation by English dissenters as a general guide to piety. When it was reprinted in Boston in the eighteenth century, the fact that Massachusetts was now a royal colony led the editors to apologize for Peters' politics, but they nevertheless affirmed the value of his text as a model for reformed devotional practice.[82]

In this way, many of the works of Puritan authors from both Old and
New England were kept in the public eye by Boston printers. In 1681, Samuel
Sewall, who was then in charge of the Boston printing press, arranged for the
publication of an early American edition of Bunyan's *Pilgrim's Progress*.[83]
Nathaniel Ward's *Simple Cobbler of Aggawam*, written in 1647, was published in
its first Boston edition in 1713 and went through a number of further print-
ings. Perhaps the most ambitious project of this type was the production of
Samuel Willard's *Compleat Body of Divinity* in 1725. Together with Willard's
successors in the ministry, a number of South Church laymen including
Willard's son edited the 225 sermons Willard had preached in a series of lectures on the Westminster Shorter Catechism, and then completed the additional 25 sermons for which Willard had made notes before he died. Along
with assembling the paper and ink necessary for this massive volume's production, the laymen had to drum up interest and obtain subscriptions for the
book so that the work could proceed. Daniel Henchman, a bookseller in
Cornhill and member of the South Church, provided the financial backing
that made publication possible.[84] Although the audience for this monumental
project was a fairly narrow range of highly educated people, the book was
nevertheless part of the spectrum of religious publications which the mature
Boston economy of the later seventeenth and eighteenth centuries made
available to a widening range of the population.

In 1718, a group of people from the South Church collaborated in the
publication of a small pamphlet entitled *Early Piety; Exemplified in Elizabeth
Butcher of Boston*. This pamphlet illustrates not just the developing use of print
for the enrichment of the religious culture, but also the entire spectrum of
forms and practices that the laity helped to make available in their creation of
a "plenitude of means" for the conversion of the rising generation. Only
twenty pages long, the pamphlet narrates the life and death of Elizabeth, the
daughter of Allwin Butcher, a Third Church member whose parents had also
been members themselves. Elizabeth was born in 1709, four years after her
father joined the church, and it became apparent early in her life that she was
one of the childhood prodigies of religious experience that would occasionally appear in New England.

To begin with, Elizabeth enjoyed the benefit of godly parents who taught
her how to scrutinize herself for signs of sin and redemptive grace: "When
she was about two Years and an Half old, as she lay in the Cradle, she would
ask herself that Question, 'What is my Corrupt nature?' and would make Answer again to herself, 'It is empty of Grace, bent unto Sin, and only to Sin, and
that continually.' She took great Delight in learning her Catechism, and
would not willingly go to Bed without saying some Part of it" (1–2). This

parental instruction was reinforced by print culture. When she learned to read, she began to take her printed catechism to bed with her, and increasingly her parents would answer her persistent questions about spiritual matters by referring her to scripture. Although Bible-reading had a profound emotional effect on her, reading alone was insufficient—Elizabeth required further guidance in order to understand what she read, for "she was not contented with the bare Reading of God's Word, but would frequently ask the Meaning of it" (6, 2–3). When her parents were unable to provide satisfactory answers, they turned to other pious friends and relatives, such as Elizabeth's "Aunt Stone, . . . a Person she had peculiar respect for" (14–15). Again, although men play the most easily identifiable roles in fostering the public presence of the church in the larger community, women are invariably present whenever we get glimpses of the more private aspects of Puritan devotion.

As soon as she was able, Elizabeth did take part in public aspects of worship. "She rejoiced greatly when the Lord's Day came" and began attending Sabbath services at age three, where "she would set with her Eyes fix'd on the Minister, to the Admiration of all that set about her, who said that grown up People might learn and take Example of her" (7, 2). When spiritually troubled, she asked her mother to send for the young minister, Joseph Sewall, who became a steady counselor to her. In the spring of 1718, when her parents told her that soon she could take part in the "Publick Catechizing, she Rejoiced greatly, and would often be speaking of it, drawing near. 'O that charming Duty, O that sweet Day is coming . . . , Catechizing Day, I mean that sweet Day' " (8).

Like many other children in early New England, Elizabeth Butcher fell victim to disease. She first became ill late in 1716, at the age of seven, but her faith gave her patience and understanding through her suffering. Joseph Sewall attended to the state of her soul, and after some fitful wavering, she came to feel that it was "better to be in Heaven with God and Christ, than to be here" (5). After a frightening turn, Elizabeth gradually recovered, but a year later, she was afflicted by another illness. This time she went through more trying physical and spiritual struggles. "When she was first taken, she was in some doubt of her spiritual state, and said, She was afraid she did not belong to God, nor love him as she should." She felt that she had been unable to "keep his Commandments . . . as I ought," and feared that she had disobeyed her parents. At her worst moments, Elizabeth expressed her dismay that "Satan tempts me to Despair of Mercy, because my Sins are so great and Many," and her distress was greatly upsetting to her mother (9–10).[85] But the pains of her illness were no more than what she thought she deserved for her own sinfulness, and she prayed with the South Church's other minister,

Thomas Prince, for a pardon for her sins and "an Interest in Christ." Eventually, through the course of counseling, she began to trust that she felt "a sight of Christ" in herself. From then on, she ceased to fear death and was even able to console and comfort her mother (11–13). As she neared the end, she became more contented, as the ministers helped "prepare me for Death and my great and last Change." On June 15, 1718, her pains abated and she died peacefully, attended by her family, friends, and ministers (16–17).

Elizabeth Butcher's brief and traumatic life demonstrated the basic elements of Puritan spirituality. It also reflected with unusual intensity the impact made by the various forms that this culture used to perpetuate itself in future generations. Her life gave witness to the value of godly parents and family piety, to reading the Bible and godly books, to the need for friends and neighbors to aid in religious instruction, to the importance of attending public worship and clerical counselling, and to the influence that a sense of sin and a striving for obedience could have on the state of the soul. The value of such an exemplary life was not lost on those in positions of authority within this religious culture. The life of Elizabeth Butcher as recipient and benefactor of this plenitude of means was instantly transformed into yet another device to reinforce this system of religious belief and behavior.

No records remain to identify the author who turned the events of Elizabeth's life into a narrative of *Early Piety; Exemplified*. It is possible from the level of personal detail in the pamphlet that her own parents had a hand in the work, and there is evidence that Samuel Sewall took an interest in the project, as did Samuel Gerrish, the Third Church member who first published the text. Once the text was written, its authors called upon the minister Joseph Sewall to write a preface. The younger Sewall knew exactly how to make the most of this material. He spoke directly of the scriptural promise which underlay the Halfway Covenant: "I will pour my Spirit upon thy Seed, and my Blessing upon thy Offspring." Elizabeth Butcher was an obvious example of the truth of this promise, which allowed Sewall to encourage all parents who would read the narrative of her life: "Let godly Parents be excited and encouraged to come to the Throne of Grace, to ask Grace for their Children. . . . What an Obligation is here laid upon us, to give up our Children unto God in Baptism, and then to bring them up in the Nurture and Admonition of the Lord!" (ii). Sewall also saw the uses of this narrative for children of godly parents, members under the church covenant, who had not yet found saving faith. He reminded them to "Be earnest with God therefore to give you that invisible Grace which is represented by water in Baptism," and to know that "if your Lives are among the Unclean, you shall be cast into outer Darkness, tho you are Children of the (visible) Kingdom." The way to avoid this fate was Elizabeth Butcher's way: "to know the holy Scriptures from your Childhood, to learn your Catechism, pray to God, keep the Sabbath holy, be dutiful to your parents, fly the Sins of Pride, Idleness, Uncleanness, Lying, Calling wicked Names, and all other Youthful Lusts; and follow the Things that are pure and holy and of good Report" (iii–iv). In effect, Joseph Sewall was reinforcing the lesson that any godly family in Boston would have drawn from reading this text. What happened to Elizabeth Butcher could happen to any child, and the only defense against such calamity was to prepare oneself and one's family through the means of grace offered by God through the church.

The writing, printing, and publication of this pamphlet thus became yet one more element in the steadily growing and thickening plenitude of means available in eighteenth-century Boston. The pamphlet appeared in Samuel Gerrish's bookshop in Cornhill, just up the street from the Old South Meetinghouse, sometime in the latter half of 1718. By September 1719, Samuel Sewall recorded in his diary that "Mr. Gerrish thinks he must Print Elisabeth Butcher over again next week, though he printed a Thousand of them."[86] The demand for *Early Piety* exceeded a thousand copies in a town that had perhaps twelve thousand inhabitants at the time. Over the course of the next twenty-five years, the pamphlet went through three more editions, the last appearing in 1741, when Boston was in the throes of a great religious revival, and the doubts and fears that plagued Elizabeth Butcher were on the minds of many people, both young and old.[87] The demand for this devotional work, its ongoing utility within the religious culture of Boston, and the readiness of Boston's merchants and booksellers to provide such materials all attest to the achievements of the Third Church laity in cultivating the garden of the church by enriching the means of grace available to all Bostonians.

CHAPTER 4

"The Want of All Means Ordained to Help Me"

Hearing that New England Sinners should have their place in hell, I was startled greatly.
—John Mawdsley, Westfield Church Founder (1679)

Life in Westfield, Massachusetts, in the late seventeenth century was far different from life in Boston. As a Boston merchant, Samuel Sewall lived in the midst of a growing and vibrant town with expanding economic resources and rapidly developing networks of communication. He had friends who shared his intellectual interests and he enjoyed ready access to books and to the colony's center of learning in Cambridge. In contrast, Sewall's old college classmate in Westfield, Edward Taylor, complained of his wilderness life "in these remotest swamps from the Heliconian quarters" and its detrimental effect on his intellect.[1] Books were hard to come by on the frontier, and there were no other educated men in Westfield with whom Taylor could have conversed at a sophisticated level.[2] The fortunate lay people of Boston's Third Church, including Samuel Sewall, took advantage of their involvement in the town's commercial growth and turned their resources to the nurture of traditional Puritan piety. But the residents of Westfield had to make do with much more limited material and cultural resources, and this condition had a profound impact on their religious lives.

The material resources that Westfield had to offer for religious purposes were naturally shaped by the economic development of the town and by the evolving relationships among its citizens. Like other towns on New England's frontier, Westfield struggled to establish itself as an independent and prosperous community. In 1685, almost twenty years after the initial settlement, the Westfield town proprietors finally reimbursed John Pynchon for his contribution as the original purchaser of the town's lands. Pynchon resigned "al my Genll Right Title & Interest in Said Lands" save for the personal grants he had reserved in the original distribution.[3] Having weathered the initial difficulties faced by any new settlement, and having avoided the worst depredations of King Philip's War, Westfield entered upon a long period of growth, in which the town moved gradually from subsistence to stability. Of course, growth that appears steady in historical retrospect did not always seem so to contemporaries. Times of prosperity like the early 1680s were followed by years of cold winters, summer droughts, and poor crops in the 1690s.[4] Renewed Indian warfare and the garrisoning of troops in Westfield brought on a smallpox epidemic in 1690 which killed ten people in a month.[5] Setbacks like these were a recurrent part of frontier life.

Still, Westfield was fortunate to escape the worst dangers of the time. Compared with Deerfield, the neighboring town to the north that was twice destroyed by Indian attacks in its first three decades of settlement, Westfield's setbacks were minor and its population growth was consequently steadier.[6] From a base of 50 families and 200 people in 1679, Westfield almost doubled in size by the turn of the century, and reached 130 families and 455 people by the time of Taylor's death in 1729.[7] Most of this growth came from natural increase. The children of the founders reached maturity, married, had families of their own, and were granted land from the town's initially large reserves. Growth from immigration was less significant. For example, in the land division of 1687, twenty years after the original grants were made, thirty-three men received new lands. Of these, sixteen were established residents, eleven were sons of town founders, and only six were men new to the town. Similarly, a list of families resident in Westfield in 1729 shows that of the 130 households in Westfield, only twenty-five were headed by people whose surnames were not found in Westfield in 1679. Many of these "newcomers" had long since been linked by marriage to original families, like Samuel Bush, who in the 1690s married Abigail Lee, the daughter of one of the town's earliest settlers.[8] Through the course of its first half century, Westfield gradually became more of a "closed, corporate community" than it had been at its founding, as the town developed a stability that its migratory founders had lacked.[9]

Population growth gradually encouraged the geographical dispersal of residents within the town. After the first twenty years, the typical Westfield land grant began to stipulate that the newly allotted land be found at least "two mile[s] from [the center of] towne not hindring other grants."[10] This expansion meant that Westfield evolved into a series of interconnected but distinct settlements, sub-villages within the larger town. The town's original center, known as the "Fort Side" of the Westfield River, had little room to grow. Thirty-four families lived on the Fort Side in 1679; only thirty were there in 1729. In contrast, the north side of the river, where fifteen families lived in 1679, gradually accommodated eleven more families over the next half century to rival the old center in size. But the most rapid growth occurred in "Pochassic" to the west of the original settlement along the "Great River" (i.e., the Westfield River), and in the area south of the "Little River" called (in typical New England terminology) "the farms." Pochassic was unsettled in 1679, but by 1700, fourteen families had residences there. "The farms," likewise undeveloped in the early years, gained a few settlers through the seventeenth century, then expanded rapidly to at least eighteen families by 1729.[11] In addition to the settlement of these fairly well-defined villages, a handful of families moved off individually to more remote areas, often for the purpose of exploiting particular economic resources, as the Deweys did with their milling operations at Two Mile Brook, east of the old town center. Although the population of Westfield increased, its people replicated earlier settlement patterns on new lands rather than clustering near the original center. Half a century after its founding, Westfield still remained an interconnected set of agricultural villages.[12]

The fur trade that brought the first English outpost to Westfield had long since disappeared by 1729. In its place, the residents of Westfield took up a variety of activities in the search for prosperity, or at the very least, for a "competency."[13] The town remained first and foremost an agricultural community. The original land grants of 1668/9 were divided into meadowlands and plowlands, a division which expressed the townspeople's equal devotion to raising grains and pasturing livestock.[14] The annual town meeting to set grain prices for determining the value of "country pay" routinely included prices for "good wintr wheat, . . . indian corn, . . . peas, . . . and sumor wheat," and these cash crops were supplemented by many other kinds of produce, from apple orchards to beehive honey.[15] The town meetings paid extensive attention to the matter of maintaining fences and keeping track of the horses, cattle, and especially swine owned by the townspeople.[16]

In addition to these basic commodities, the people of Westfield experimented with a variety of new ventures in their ongoing efforts to attain reasonable levels of comfort and security. Tobacco caught on as a minor export crop; it could be grown successfully in some of the rich bottom lands of the Connecticut Valley.[17] Very early on, Westfield's residents realized that the many small streams, brooks, and rivers flowing through their township provided opportunities for milling enterprises. In 1669, Joseph Whiting and David Ashley received the first town grant to set up a gristmill, which allowed them 1/14th of all the wheat they ground and 1/12th of all "Indjan" corn in return for their services to the community.[18] Thereafter, grants for the construction of new mills were made with some frequency, and competing claims to the milling rights on local streams became a source of conflict in the town.[19] In addition to gristmills, extensive forest reserves in the region made sawmills a potential source of income, and the two kinds of mills were often built together. Lumber from the sawmills could be used locally for building or shipped to the West Indies where demand for it was high.[20] The local forests also provided resources for industrial enterprises. In the 1690s, the town made several grants of "halve a mille Square of pines" for the purpose of making rosin, used in producing varnish and soap.[21] Some townspeople took advantage of the pine reserves for making turpentine, to the point where the town was forced to institute fines to protect the trees on its common lands from exploitation by turpentine "poachers."[22] On the north side of the river, a brick-making kiln was constructed, and in 1693, the town gave Fearnot King "liberty to make use of what ore is on our Comons" if he could encourage his "kinsman" to come and set up a "bloomery" for making iron ingots.[23]

With these efforts the people of Westfield diversified their economy and connected themselves to local New England and larger Atlantic markets. No Westfield residents were merchants in the sense that the leading members of Boston's Third Church were—they did not own or invest in ships or take part in the organization of long-distance trade. But their attempts to vary the kinds of goods they produced were made with these distant markets in mind. Self-sufficiency was never a realistic goal in the agricultural communities of early New England, and without some reliable forms of trade, the average rural family would have been committing itself to economic ruin.[24] Trade in exportable commodities brought money and goods into Westfield and enhanced the wealth, comfort, and security of the entrepreneurial citizens, though on a scale far more modest than in Boston. Thomas Dewey, the man who recruited Edward Taylor to be the town's minister, was the wealthiest Westfield resident for whom a probate inventory was recorded in the seventeenth-century Hampshire County records. His estate was valued at £793, of which more than two-thirds was invested in land and livestock—a substantial sum, but far smaller than the fortunes being amassed by Boston's leading merchants.[25]

Prosperous farmers in Westfield could make a comfortable living, but there was never "enough" wealth for everyone. The universal quest for competency engendered a certain amount of contention in the town, as individuals struggled to hold on to what was theirs and provide resources for their

growing families.[26] Often the most enterprising men were also the most contentious. Fearnot King (a Commonwealthman by name if ever there was one)
not only sponsored the iron "bloomery" but also operated a gristmill, and he
appeared regularly before John Pynchon's court at Springfield to resolve unpaid debts and personal disputes into which he was drawn by his business affairs. Similarly, the Dewey brothers, who owned and operated various mills in
addition to their farmlands, were among the Westfield men most likely to appear at Pynchon's court.[27] Yet the contention that sprang from the struggle
for competency does not indicate an absence of Puritan religious values or of
a deep commitment to a godly way of life. For as we shall see, the mill-owning
Dewey family, while among the most prosperous and litigious in town, was
also among the most devout families in Westfield's Puritan church.[28]

In the realm of local government and politics, the town's population
growth and geographic dispersal created a larger burden of public responsibilities. With more people, more homes and farms, and a more diverse economy,
the town needed more local officials and regulations. In 1673, Westfield required only a few selectmen "to order the prudentiall affairs of the town,"
along with a constable, a highway surveyor, a town measurer, and a few
"howards" and "sealers."[29] By 1725, the need had arisen for a town clerk, a
treasurer, a moderator for the town meetings, several "Gagers, searchers and
Packers" of export goods, four hog-reives, three tithing men, eight fence
viewers, and committees to oversee tar-making, the laying out of highways,
and the repair of the meetinghouse, in addition to all the original offices.[30]
The increasing burden of these new responsibilities made it more common
for men to shirk their duties and avoid town office, and the town instituted a
fine to prohibit this behavior. In the same vein, some men began to avoid the
town meetings altogether, a pattern which reflects not apathy so much as a
desire to avoid extra work.[31]

Settlement patterns determined the nature of politics in Westfield, which
increasingly focused on the problem of resource allocation within the expanding community. Usually the business of the town proceeded smoothly,
with consensus easily reached on most mundane issues. But at times, Westfield's geographical expansion made it difficult to locate a common purpose
on which the town's cluster of connected villages could agree, especially
when both economic and cultural resources were at stake. In the 1690s, the
town began (rather belatedly) to organize a school for teaching children the
basics of reading and writing. The town meeting arranged to hire a schoolmaster, planned the building of a schoolhouse, and set the fees to be paid by
students: "3 penc a week for each scolar such as are readers and 4 penc for
wrighters . . . , that al boys from six yeers to twelv years of age [are] to pay . . .

whether they bee sent to scool or not."[32] This decision caused the first instance of open dissent in the town meeting. Fourteen men expressed their
disapproval, and although their specific objections were not recorded, a bit of
arithmetic makes it easy to see what troubled them. Among them they had 58
children, a third of all the children in town, and eleven of the fourteen were
"outlivers," residing some distance from the Fort Side where the schoolhouse
was located.[33] As a result, they were required to bear a disproportionate burden of the town's education costs, while the location of their homes made it
difficult for their children to attend school at all. These men continued to
voice their discontent until a compromise was reached in 1705 that allowed
the schoolmaster "to keep his Schoole att the farmes or village," which made
it accessible to more of the town's children.[34] Education was a vital concern
for Westfield's religious culture, since a thriving Puritan church required a
literate laity, but similar issues of resource allocation with respect to more secular matters pervade the town records as well. Decisions to set aside land
grants for new highways, the distribution of rights to land near streams for
mills to serve new areas, and the reapportionment of responsibility for maintaining fences all reflected the town's adjustment to the movement of people
away from the original center. In time, the composition of the board of selectmen came to represent, informally, the scattered villages within the town.[35]

Most of these adjustments to growth were made peaceably. Since the
town meeting was designed to achieve group consensus and was not intended to be a place for resolving disputes, the town records reveal little evidence of internal conflict.[36] During Edward Taylor's tenure, Westfield did
not develop political factions or interest groups of permanent duration.
There was simply an increase in the number of individuals and a greater variety of competing interests to protect. For this, the courts at Northampton
and Springfield, not the town meeting, were the best recourse. Disputes between individuals or even between the town and a resident could be resolved
in court without creating contentious politics within the community. For instance, the town voted to sue Capt. Joseph Mawdsley in the county court
over an alleged misuse of town lands, at the same time that the town meeting
granted him rights to build a sawmill and appointed him to a committee for
resolving the town's border with Springfield.[37] The lawsuit in the county
court did not impede Mawdsley's ability to work on behalf of the town.

However, the degree of the courts' accessibility to all citizens changed
over the course of Westfield's first half-century. Legal proceedings grew more
complex because of changes in the court system. When the Massachusetts
charter was revoked in 1685 and replaced in 1692, the colony's legal system
was revised. The new charter created new courts, jurisdictions, and proce-

dures. As the legal system matured, the use of lawyers replaced simple personal pleading of cases and the expense of taking court action increased.[38] Men like Ebenezer Pomery, who was Sheriff of Hampshire County as well as "His Majesties Counsel" for the District in the early eighteenth century, became important for their ability to perform legal services. People who understood and were familiar with the law had an advantage over their less sophisticated neighbors.[39] Recourse to the law was nothing new to the people of Westfield, but the courts, like the economy, became more complicated as the seventeenth century gave way to the eighteenth. As a result, more pressure was sometimes placed on local institutions like the church or the town meeting for resolving disputes when the courts became less inviting and accessible to the poor and unsophisticated farmers of agricultural villages.[40]

Money, or more typically the lack thereof, was another perennial concern in Westfield, and as the economy of the town developed, new approaches to the problem appeared. As a rule, hard currency tends to drain away from colonial economies, and the Connecticut Valley was no exception. In its early years, Westfield handled this problem by establishing fixed prices for local commodities every year in a town meeting, usually after the harvest was in, and by providing that local taxes could be paid in crops according to these rates. People engaged in trade through the exchange of goods or "country pay," but this was not, strictly speaking, a barter system, for all debts were recorded in monetary figures according to the fixed prices of grain.[41] This system worked fairly well through the seventeenth century, especially while John Pynchon dominated the economy of the upper Connecticut Valley. Most towns were in his debt, for which he accepted "country pay" as payment, thereby facilitating his control over the export of staple crops from western Massachusetts. However, compared with the more sophisticated forms of exchange that were familiar to participants in Boston's commercial economy, this rural system of "country pay" was primitive and limiting.[42]

As time went on, it became more common for people to request the payment of specific debts "in money" or to differentiate between forms of payment. When Westfield hired a gravedigger in 1710, it was stipulated that "he is to have three shillings in Town pay or two shillings in money for each grave." And instead of setting a single fixed price on a commodity for a full year, the town began to adjust commodity prices for specific payments. When the town raised taxes in 1716 to pay Isaac Phelps £20 for keeping school, they agreed to accept wheat and peas at 4s-6d a bushel, but allowed any man a 25% abatement on his rate if he paid in money.[43] The increased use of money payments, which coincided with various colony-wide experiments in the use of paper money, decreased the need for intricate relations of personal interdependence to sustain the market economy. The change became dramatically clear in Westfield in 1721, when the town voted to take part in the new scheme for a Massachusetts land bank. Three trustees were chosen to "Transact on the Towns behalf," and plans were made for "all the bank money . . . to be let out upon interest . . . at five persent." A year later, the town voted to lend out the money accruing to the town in interest at the same rate the principal was lent at the year before. After this time, references in the records to the value of "country pay" are made in an off-hand way: "the stated price of Grain if it so hapen that the abovesaid hundred pounds shall be paid in Grain or any part of it."[44] Now it became routine for payments to be specified "in money" or for that to be assumed if left unsaid. This gradual change in the nature and availability of the money supply made it possible for the people of Westfield to be less directly dependent on one another. The intricate network of mutual debt, personal obligations, and interdependency that characterized the rural economy was loosened by the availability of a "medium of trade."[45] By loosening the personal ties that mitigated against aggressive individualistic economic behavior, the potential for more contention increased.

Social historians have for several decades asked questions about the effects of contentious commercial behavior on Puritan religious belief, and have in most cases assumed that the former undermined the latter.[46] But these investigations have overlooked a more basic question. A certain amount of conflict was an inescapable fact of life in New England villages, where families competed with one another for the relatively scarce resources from which a competency could be gained. Contention or economic individualism does not itself indicate an absence of Puritan religious beliefs or communitarian social values. A devout and precise minister like Edward Taylor was not removed from speculative individual pursuits; his strong interest in metallurgy encouraged him to invest in various commercial mining ventures in western New England, including a copper mine at Simsbury, Connecticut.[47] A more "primitive" system of economic interdependence is not necessarily less contentious than a commercialized economy, and no matter what the level of economic complexity, a strong effort to maintain community cohesion was necessary to counteract the tensions that the universal quest for "competency" created.[48] More to the point is the question of what the relative abundance or scarcity of resources meant for the strength of a community's religious culture and for the success of its communitarian efforts to mitigate the divisive effects of economic competition. Contention itself was no indication of the level of commitment to Puritan religious culture within a community. But increased competition for scarce resources did create a problem for churches by increasing the difficulty of making fair decisions about the allocation of religious and cultural resources as well.

In the seven decades after its founding, the town of Westfield grew larger in population and geographical expanse, its economy became more diversified, and its economic relationships reached farther out into a more impersonal commercial world. The available means for resolving economic conflict became more complicated and tended to be focused outside the town itself in the county courts, while at the same time the courts became less accessible to the poorer members of the community. Despite these changes, Westfield remained essentially an extended agricultural village on the margins of New England settlement, tenuously connected to the markets of Massachusetts Bay and the larger Atlantic economy. Compared with Boston or even with the smaller maritime towns of eastern Massachusetts, Westfield was culturally impoverished. Its leading citizens did not send their sons to college in Cambridge or New Haven, nor did they directly engage in cosmopolitan long-distance trading. If the commercial practices of New Haven seemed quaint and primitive to a Bostonian at the turn of the eighteenth century, then Westfield's economic and social culture was surely even more so. The struggle for economic survival and the material limitations of life in Westfield had a substantial impact on the ability of its residents to maintain a vital church and a healthy communal religious culture. The problem faced by the townspeople was whether, with their limited resources, they could sustain the kind of religious community that would satisfy them.

We can begin to get an idea of the kind of religious community the people of Westfield wanted by examining the records of their participation in the life of the church. Edward Taylor kept very complete records of admissions and baptisms from the church's founding in 1679 through the early 1720s, which reveal in a general way some of the religious aspirations of the town's lay people. In the first years of the church's existence, admission rates were high. In 1679 alone, twenty-seven people were admitted to full membership, including the seven founders, and by 1682, there were forty-three full members out of an adult population of roughly one hundred. Taylor noted that before King Philip's War in 1675, the town had only nine men who had been full church members elsewhere before coming to Westfield. The admission of so many more full members in the church's first years shows a broad base of interest among the original settlers, who had gone without a church for a dozen years and now joined eagerly.[49]

After this initial expansion, membership leveled off. In the late 1690s, there was a sudden growth period as the children of the founding members reached maturity and began to join the church. Another demographically predictable surge occurred in the second decade of the eighteenth century, but in general new admissions leveled off to a rate of about one per year.[50] As death and emigration took their steady toll, the typical year's addition of one or two new members barely kept pace with the losses, and the numbers even dwindled slightly in the eighteenth century. There were forty-eight members in 1699, but only forty-one in 1729, the year of Taylor's death. This pattern of church membership, coupled with the growing population of the town, might suggest on the surface a diminishing desire for connection to the church as time went on. The forty-one members in 1729 represented only one of every seven adults in Westfield. In addition, with the passing of time the composition of church membership began to favor women. In the founding years, the church had more men than women by a small margin, but within only a decade, this had changed dramatically. In 1689, women outnumbered men two to one, a ratio that stayed fairly constant over the next forty years. On first glance these numbers suggest that the church was becoming largely a women's domain. However, the fact that the initial founding of the church required seven men to be the pillars may have skewed the sex ratio at the beginning. In other words, when allowances are made for the requirement that the founders had to be men, it seems that full church membership may have always been more prevalent among women.[51]

These statistics on full membership do not, however, tell the whole story of the church's relationship to the population of the town. For although only 15% of Westfield's adults were full church members in 1729, virtually every family in town contained a church member, was closely related to one, or was descended from one, which made an extremely high percentage of the town eligible for baptism under the Halfway Covenant. The baptismal records bear this out. Unlike the admissions records, they show a steady stream, year after year, of newly baptized members of Westfield's religious community. For instance, in 1718, a year when only one new full member was admitted, twenty-two children were baptized. As of 1729, *every* Westfield family in which there were children, whether the family contained full members or not, had had their children baptized, a fact which indicates a complete overlap between church and town on this basic matter. At the very least, there were no residents of Westfield who remained outside the influence of the church as a provider of the means of grace.[52]

What did the townspeople's continuing devotion to the baptism of their children, coupled with a decrease in full church membership, signify about the religious experiences and desires of Westfield's citizens? Baptism placed a person under the "watch" of the church, subject to its discipline and to preaching and catechism from the minister, but without the privileges and responsibilities of full membership. The main privilege accompanying full membership was the ability to participate in the Lord's Supper, but this was seldom seen by late seventeenth-century New England Puritans as an unqualified benefit. The potential danger to one's soul of coming unworthily to the Lord's Table, along with the social and psychological hazards of exposing one's sins and repentance before the gathered saints, kept many devout, professing Christians from attempting to qualify for full membership. Baptism, by contrast, had few threatening aspects, and served to maintain continuity in the covenanted community from one generation to the next.[53]

The general dilemma facing all New Englanders in considering the sacrament was made more acute by the standards for full membership and sacramental piety maintained by Edward Taylor, who differed on this subject from many of his neighboring Connecticut Valley ministers. Taylor's strict requirements for conversion relations and personal piety in potential converts made it more difficult for Westfield residents to become full members than it was for people in neighboring towns like Northampton and Hatfield.[54] The importance of this fact is highlighted by the skewed gender ratio of the church, for women had an easier time joining the church than men. Men were required to give a personal declaration of their conversion experience before the assembled congregation, while women were allowed the option of private consultation with the minister over the state of their souls. Taylor would then propound their cases to the gathered church, sparing women aspirants the hazards of publicly airing their experiences for evaluation.[55] This difference, together with the increased dangers women faced during childbearing years and the concomitant desire to have their newborn children baptized, made women more likely to brave the risks of entering into full communion, and can account for their prevalence in Westfield's church, as in many other similar congregations all over New England.[56]

The ongoing commitment to and enthusiasm for baptism demonstrated by all of Westfield's families, together with the continuing applications for full membership among women, suggest that the decrease in full membership was not a function of a declining desire for participation in Puritan religious life. Rather, the disparity between baptismal and full membership points to a conflict within the community over one particular (and highly significant) aspect of this religious culture, admission to the Lord's Supper. The membership figures of the Westfield church reveal an underlying desire among the people of Westfield for a more open access to the church than Edward Taylor was ready to admit. The struggle over the founding of Westfield's church in the 1670s had already indicated the potential for this problem. Personal evidence of the religious experiences of the laity allows us further insight into their expectations for participation in the life of the church.

~✻~

Although few records remain from the lives of most of the lay people of early Westfield, especially compared with the wealth of material available on their contemporaries in Boston, we can learn something about the inner lives of those who joined the church in full communion. Most notable among these are the church founders, whose narratives of their conversion experiences were recorded by Edward Taylor. In addition, several members of the Dewey family confided their experiences to Taylor and wrote about their own beliefs. The evidence they left is limited and at times refracted through Taylor's accounts of their experiences. But a careful reading of this material can identify the expectations of these prominent lay people for their participation in the church. It can also allow us to make inferences from their experiences about the expectations and beliefs of others, members and nonmembers alike, and thus provide an idea of what the laity brought to the life of the Westfield church.

There were six men, besides Taylor, who founded the Westfield church, including three militia officers, Lieutenant John Mawdsley, Ensign Samuel Loomis, and Sergeant Josiah Dewey, along with John Root, Isaac Phelps, and John Ingerson.[57] The "relations" of their spiritual conversion that they gave on the foundation day display a varied range of experience and expression, from Isaac Phelps's brief, flat, and formulaic account to Josiah Dewey's emotional rendition of his rapturous encounters with divine grace.[58] Despite individual idiosyncracies, all the relations share some common traits. All six of the lay founders refer to "the Instruction of Religious Parents" as a vital element that introduced them to the need for God's grace.[59] One man, John Ingerson, made brief reference to a sermon he had heard "at Darby in old England" at the age of eighteen, but all six had their conversion experiences in New England, where the action of these relations takes place. Each man describes in some detail how he came under the influence of a godly minister and recounts the Bible verses the minister used to convince him "that certainly I was in a bad state & had need labour to get out of this state."[60] This conviction, frequently reinforced by illness or some other experience which brings home the terrors of death and damnation, is then followed by an experience of grace. The founders often describe a subsequent period of further doubt and temptations from Satan, until finally "it pleased God more & more to draw out my desires, more & more to injoy god in all his Ordinances," leaving the man, in this case John Mawdsley, more assured but not complacent within God's saving grace.[61] Another integral feature of all the relations is the part which family, friends, and neighbors played in encouraging the spiritual progress of these aspiring saints.[62] Major events such as marriage and the birth of children or life-threatening accidents and epidemic diseases played significant roles in the conversion processes of the six lay founders.

In contrast, Edward Taylor's account of his own conversion places little emphasis on the social and cultural context. Instead, Taylor emphasizes the experience of reading the Bible as the key factor in his spiritual development. Taylor's conversion began and appears to have been completed (as much as conversion was ever complete) while he was still in England. Unlike the lay founders' conversion relations, Taylor's says almost nothing about the influence of godly preaching upon him. The persons mentioned as spiritual influences upon Taylor's conversion were, with only one exception, immediate family members. Save for a brief reference to an unnamed "godly able Minister in England," the only other source of spiritual guidance Taylor refers to is the Bible. Taylor's conversion relation demonstrates little evidence of close engagement with a religious community beyond his immediate family, and as a whole stands as an extremely formulaic statement of Puritan spirituality. This is not to say that Taylor did not benefit from communal religious experiences, but rather that he chose not to emphasize them here. His conversion relation was doubtlessly meant to be "edifying" to the congregation, but if so, it served only to remind his audience of the order of salvation which was already familiar to them, without providing a model of the church as a community that would encourage conversion and growth in grace. For such encouragement, the other founders' relations were much more edifying than Taylor's.[63] Their relations demonstrate the extent to which full participation in the means of grace offered by New England's overwhelmingly Puritan religious culture shaped the experience of conversion and guided these laymen on their spiritual progress. Compared with Taylor's, theirs was a characteristically "New England" form of conversion.[64]

Further insight into the religious mentality of the Westfield laity emerges from the details of the individual relations, for interspersed with their recounting of the Puritan order of salvation are incidental revelations about the ways in which formal beliefs were woven into the fabric of ordinary life. The importance of godly parents has already been stressed, but the narratives demonstrate the extent to which religion was a family experience and conversion was part of a maturation process in which one learned to negotiate the hazards of life.[65] John Mawdsley relates that as a boy, "I thought it strange that I, being so young, should pray to God," until an epidemic proved fatal to several neighboring children. At this point, "my parents told me, that my turn might be next & t[hat] I should be miserable for ever & I being exceedingly afraid of death & God's wrath, did set upon the duty of secret prayer again."[66] Yet even with this terrifying experience, it still took Mawdsley years to reach the point of joining a church. Conversion for these men was not an instantaneous transformation from sinner to saint, like Saul on the road to Damascus, but the gradual development of a religious temperament and sensibility, a way of thinking about the self and the community in which the family and the common experiences of early modern life played their part alongside the church and its doctrines. Conversion was not a single event, but a long process, a pilgrimage that took many unexpected twists and turns through the course of an individual life. The encouragement offered by family and friends was part of the process of preparation through which this religious sensibility was cultivated in believers.[67]

We can see how this sensibility developed in John Mawdsley. As he continues his narrative, he states that when a "reall chang" was finally "wrought upon my heart, Now Sabboths [were] not such weary days to me as before, Secret prayer Such a burd[en as] before."[68] Here the Lieutenant confirms what most modern readers have suspected, that even to godly-minded New Englanders, the day-long preaching and prayer that marked every Sabbath and the intense demands for personal piety in Puritan religious culture must have been intolerable burdens at times. What nurtured and sustained the desire for godliness from one generation to the next was the growth in people like Mawdsley of the need to hear and take to heart the message of the minister, and to incorporate this ritualized turning from sin into daily existence. Mawdsley concludes his public relation by claiming that the ordinances of the church have become a necessity for him. He justifies his desire "to ingage in this worke [of church gathering] in this place" by reason of his clear understanding of the "want of all means ordained to help me" against his wicked nature. Without the means of grace offered by church fellowship, Mawdsley fears that he will slip back into sin.

Lieutenant Mawdsley also expresses his belief that by founding a church in Westfield, the interests of future generations will be well served: he hopes "in respect of Posterity, that the Ordinances of God may be carried down unto them."[69] His own spiritual pilgrimage would be sidetracked without the guidance of the church and its means of grace, but he also recognizes that the entire community will lose its way in the future without a properly instituted church. Mawdsley's relation is therefore not just a petition for membership, but also a defense of the church as an institution. Without church discipline to demand adherence to the burdensome duties of Puritan piety, the average individual would never submit to the process of preparation and endure the self-examination necessary for conversion. Though Mawdsley himself does not use this metaphor, his relation expresses a vision similar to that of the authors of the Halfway Covenant who saw the church as a garden for nurturing the faith of potential believers. From John Mawdsley's conversion relation, we get a better sense of why the Westfield townspeople were so eager to form a church and how frustrating Taylor's delays must have been.[70]

Sergeant Josiah Dewey's relation conveys a similar development of sensibility about the self and its place in the religious community, but through very different spiritual experiences. After a period of inner turmoil, the young Dewey experienced a vivid encounter with God's grace. While he sat musing in the fields one day, Dewey "felt a strong perswasion arise in me, of the Love of God in Christ through the riches of Grace, as made me cry out my Lord, & my God, my Saviour & my Redeemer, passing on as it were in an heavenly Rapture." Yet rapture alone was not enough to bring him into the church, for he continued to be plagued with doubts. It was not the ecstatic experience of grace, but rather the growing feeling that he "began to long after Communion with God in his Ordinances" that eventually brought Dewey forward to join the church. Even then he delayed; "yet having some fear I forebore about halfe a yeare."[71] The fear that kept Dewey away from the communion table was the same fear that prevented many devout Christians from ever approaching it. God's assurance was never complete, and Satan's temptations never quite ceased. Josiah Dewey came to believe that his intense experiences were genuine and finally joined the church, but many who lacked this visionary confidence never did, though they continued to attend the means of grace and hope for the best.[72]

Part of what kept potential saints out of full membership in the church was the existence in New England of a certain characteristic form of complacency. John Mawdsley provides a clue to this tendency in his relation. He describes a sermon he heard as a young man, in which, after a discussion of "Sodom & Gomorrah in the day of Judgment ... , hearing that New England Sinners should have their place in hell, I was startled greatly."[73] The minister's sermon jolted Mawdsley out of his assumption that New England was an especially godly place and that its people might therefore escape damnation on judgment day. It is difficult to imagine an English Puritan being startled by a similar announcement, but this complacent sense of self-assurance was available to lay people in New England because of the overwhelming prevalence of the culture of godliness. Year after year, election sermons reiterated the proposition that the "nation" of New England was in covenant with God.

Town and church covenants anchored individuals in their community's corporate connection to the divine. Many New Englanders, especially those in rural villages like Westfield, rarely experienced an alternative to Puritan religious culture, and those alternatives that did exist, from folk magic practices to dissenting sects, lacked the organizational and cultural power of the Puritan churches. Westfield's citizens certainly never felt the external conflict between Puritanism and the Church of England which shaped Edward Taylor's experience of the nature of godly life as a youth in England. For most of the people in Westfield, born into this "tribal" Puritan culture, it may have been enough to be baptized, to attend the word, follow God's law, and make the assumption, so prevalent and tempting even in the conversion narratives of these church "pillars," that there was still time, that one was still young enough or healthy enough or essentially righteous enough to delay closing with God.[74]

This tendency toward complacency was not antithetical to a society comprised mainly of "the godly," but a characteristic part of it. It represented a basic set of religious assumptions on the part of every member, a foundation that served as the point of departure from which the New England pilgrim's journey began. To borrow from Bunyan, it was easy for many New Englanders to imagine that they had already entered through the Strait Gate and were well on the road to the Celestial City, simply by virtue of their birthright in New England's religious culture. But this was not an assumption that encouraged people to think of the church as an evangelical institution. If everyone within the village community saw themselves as equal heirs of a godly legacy, then there was no need for the church to reach out to anyone new. This contrasts sharply with the founding principles put forward by the laity of Boston's Third Church, whose frequent encounters with organized and threatening religious alternatives made the need for evangelical outreach obvious on a daily basis.

From these conversion relations, we begin to get a better sense of the ordinary assumptions and expectations of Westfield's lay people about the place of the church in their lives. In effect, access to the Puritan church and to its means of grace was something they felt entitled to; it was part of their inheritance as New Englanders. The farmers and artisans of the Connecticut Valley considered some degree of membership in the Puritan church to be a birthright which gave them a special relationship with God. This relationship was the beginning of a life-long pilgrimage, a journey along which the pilgrim expected the aid and counsel of family, friends, and ministers, and the discipline and nurture provided by the church. Assurance of salvation was not assumed for everyone, let alone the majority. But the tension between Taylor and the townspeople over the gathering of the church, and the anxious sensibility that commonly delayed the full membership of men like John Mawdsley and Josiah Dewey, indicate that the laity desired greater participation in the church, and perhaps even easier access to communion as another potential means of grace, if not as a mark of their assurance, than the strictest interpretations of Congregational polity might admit.

Like the founders of Boston's Third Church, the Westfield founders expressed their concern that the church conform to the reality of family life and to the desire for future generations to be included within the nurturing garden of the church. But unlike the Third Church founders, Westfield's lay people did not yet see an evangelical program of outreach as a necessary part of their mission as a church. With virtually everyone in their community encompassed under the watch and care of the church, and with little or no organized opposition to orthodox religion, the people of Westfield saw no need for the church to take care of any souls but their own. Their gaze was directed inward in the hope of satisfying their own community's problems rather than outward to the needs of the world at large.

◈

The relative scarcity of material resources in Westfield translated into a rather sparsely furnished religious culture. The rich array of institutional and privately supported means of grace that Bostonians enjoyed was largely absent out on the New England frontier. For instance, neither in the extensive church records kept by Taylor, nor in the descriptions of the experiences of members he recorded in his commonplace book, is there any indication of regular weekday meetings among church members like those that were so prevalent and so useful to the laity in Boston. Of course, the lack of direct evidence does not allow us to rule out their existence in Westfield. But Westfield's dispersed settlement pattern, together with the relatively low numbers of full church members, would have made any regular lay meetings difficult at best, especially in this rural society where heavy demands were placed on the time and labor of each individual. The difficulty the town faced in maintaining a common school for its children is a relevant indicator of the nature of this problem. Furthermore, the limited availability of books and the absence of educated "quasi-clerical" leaders may well have diminished the value of private religious meetings. If they did exist, such meetings might have offered little more in the way of spiritual nurture than the family already provided.

Among the other rich resources that a town like Boston provided for its religious culture were weekday lectures, which became a regular social fixture and provided yet a further way for ministers to educate their congregations in the forms of a godly life. Many rural towns throughout New England managed to sustain weekday lectures as well, but in Westfield, Edward Taylor's efforts along these lines had to be abandoned. In a 1710 letter to Solomon Stoddard, Taylor noted that a number of years earlier, he had kept "a monthly Lecture, [but] the which Lectures proving an Occasion of greate disorder & Sin in the town, & no preventing the Same appearing I let the Lectures Fall." The nature of the sins and disorders that Taylor feared is unknown, but the lectures were probably the only regularly scheduled social event (besides Sabbath-day worship) of any kind in Westfield, and they may have attracted a crowd which included, in Taylor's eyes, less desirable types along with the pious. Lecture days in country towns were usually market days as well, and sin and disorder always appeared as companions of commerce. Taylor replaced the lectures with monthly fast days, a ritual that served a spiritual purpose but turned the Westfield church away from the benefits of commerce and lacked the communal spirit of public edification that lectures provided in other towns.[75]

The limitations of Westfield's resources also caused a significant breakdown in the church's ability to meet the laity's need for an adequate meetinghouse. In Boston, the Third Church members made it their particular concern to ensure that seating in the meetinghouse was available to all potential congregants, and worked to prevent the meetinghouse from becoming the private preserve of families in full membership. In Westfield, this solicitude for the needs of all potential members, whether or not it was a goal of the congregation, proved to be impossible. In fact, evidence from town and church records suggests that many of Westfield's congregants had to stand through the long Sabbath day, and only those who paid for pews received the privilege of sitting through the services.[76] The fact that ownership of the pews was passed down within families made the Westfield church even more closed off to the outside world; it became tribal even with respect to the physical circumstances of weekly worship in the meetinghouse. When after forty years the laity finally decided to rectify this problem by building a new and larger meetinghouse, the town erupted in controversy, based on the contentious politics that were a function of the town's geography, over where to locate the new building.[77] The combination of Westfield's limited economic resources and its dispersed pattern of settlement made it impossible to create a physical space for worship that would have satisfied the needs of the lay community.

Within the Westfield meetinghouse itself, the communion table at which the relatively few church members received the sacrament was humbly furnished. Churches like Boston's Old South had extensive collections of silver

communion plate, and even some of Westfield's neighboring churches like
those in Hatfield, Massachusetts, and Suffield, Connecticut, owned several
silver vessels. But no Westfield church silver from the colonial period survives,
and evidence from contemporary probate records suggests that the church
may not have owned any.[78] Throughout early New England, church silver
was often acquired as a bequest from lay members, who left pieces of domestic silver from their family collections to be used for religious purposes. However, among the Westfield residents in the seventeenth century for whom probate records exist, pewter plates and cups appear on a few estate inventories,
but not even the wealthiest families had any silver.[79] If Westfield's lay people
did not own silver, then the church probably went without it as well, and the
congregation missed a subtle but powerful means of grace, a visible and tangible way in which Puritan spirituality was made manifest in religious ritual.[80]

The weakness of the institutional and material support for religious life
in Westfield, the cultural poverty of the community, is reflected in the lack of
surviving evidence from the spiritual lives of its lay people. We know little
enough about the inner lives of Westfield's church founders, but it becomes
even more difficult to uncover the religious experiences of Westfield's laity in
the years after the church was formally gathered. Taylor described no further
conversion relations in the church records and few townspeople wrote about
the state of their souls. But at least one source of insight remains. Josiah
Dewey, the founder whose conversion narrative was so vivid and compelling,
developed a close relationship with Edward Taylor, who was naturally drawn
toward those in his flock whose sensibilities were most like his own. Throughout Taylor's long tenure in Westfield, there was no one even remotely his
equal in terms of formal intellectual training. Hence his best companionship
came from sympathetic souls devoted to leading a godly life, those who came
nearest to sharing his refined form of Puritan piety. These circumstances
brought Taylor close to Josiah Dewey and his family, and through this window of insight into the experiences of the Dewey clan, we can gain a glimpse
of how Westfield's religious resources were not only kept within the town itself, but were restricted to the benefit of the pious few.

Sometime toward the end of the 1680s, Josiah Dewey, by then a deacon
of the church, went through a difficult spiritual trial during the severe illness
of his daughter Hepzibah. As the town's only learned man, Taylor was frequently called on for medical as well as spiritual advice, and in this case he
tended to the Deacon's soul while easing the sufferings of the daughter. During this crisis, Deacon Dewey once again had ecstatic experiences so vivid
that Taylor recorded them in his Commonplace Book. While Dewey was

praying earnestly for his child's soul, Satan tempted him with the thought that "if she did belong to eternal life she should be saved: but if not all that I could do could not help her." This idea was true in a strictly predestinarian sense, but it denied the efficacy of the Deacon's prayers, and thus threatened to rob him of his sole activity and consolation in this trying time, leaving him on the verge of despair.

Hepzibah's illness was drawn out; she would improve only to suffer further relapses, and when she finally succumbed to the "putrid fever," Dewey took it very hard. He began to "meditate & pray over Gods Dispensation tords us" and was overcome by the wish to see his daughter singing among the heavenly hosts. This wish brought on a vision of her "in the middst of that heavenly company in that happy world," a vision that overpowered Dewey:

> But now my heart was filled with joy unspeakable, & all runing over in such a way as I know not how to express it: something like a Pot over a fierce fire that will soon run all [over] . . . & being sensible the my poor fraile body could not hold this long, my lips moved therefore thus LORD ITS ENOUGH: I KNOW NOT HOW TO BEARE ANY MORE.

But this ecstatic experience, this moment of rapture, was not a permanent and unambiguous source of relief. Soon "Satan laboured to fill me with fears the I had [offended?] God desiring to pry into his Secrets in heaven." Dewey felt strengthened by God to resist this temptation, but he still could not rest easy, and felt a sense of his unworthiness of God's grace, mercy, and blessings, just as he had expressed in his conversion relation a decade earlier at the time of the church founding.[81]

Josiah Dewey's religious sensibility, revealed in these two experiences, was very similar to the combination of ecstacy and self-doubt that Taylor cultivated within himself and that formed his view of the proper condition for a full church member. For example, in a meditative poem composed in September 1698, Taylor's first stanza glories in a vision of divine riches, but then turns back to examine the self:

> My mentall Eye, spying thy sparkling Fold
>   Bedeckt, my Lord, with Glories shine alone,
> That doth out do all Broideries of Gold:
>   And Pavements of Rich Pearles, and Precious Stone
>   Did double back its Beams to light my Sphere
>   Making an inward Search, for what springs there.

What the second stanza then reveals is the self's unworthiness to receive such precious gifts:

And in my Search I finde myselfe defild:
Issues and Leprosies all ore mee streame.
Such have not Enterance. I am beguild:
My Seate, Bed, Saddle, Spittle too's uncleane.
My Issue Running Leprosy doth spread:
My upper Lip is Covered: not my Head.[82]

Like Taylor in his poem, Dewey has learned to take his ecstatic visions of the divine and "double back" their beams by making an "inward search" of himself and exposing his own failings, thereby bringing him closer to an understanding of his need for Christ's salvation, lest he not have "Enterance" into the kingdom of God. The ecstatic vision of the riches offered by God, followed by an inward conviction of utter unworthiness, has the paradoxical effect of convincing the aspiring Christian that through the sacrifice made by Christ, that "pearl of great price," the faithful believer is made worthy of these riches after all.

Josiah Dewey's position as a founder and deacon of the church, along with his ability as a lay person to live up to the standards of piety Taylor expected of church members, would make him the most likely candidate if we were to search early Westfield for "quasi-clerical" figures like those who were so prominent in the life of Boston's Third Church. Yet Deacon Dewey's power to shape the religious life of his community in the way that men like Samuel Sewall, Edward Bromfield, Nathaniel Williams, et al. were attempting in Boston was limited by the conditions of life in Westfield. If he received more than his fair share of godly riches, he was in no position to distribute them further among the members of his community; in fact, he could barely survive there. In the mid-1690s, economic hardship struck the Dewey family. Another unexpected death, coupled with the need to settle his children on adequate lands, forced Deacon Dewey to move to a new settlement in Lebanon, Connecticut. Although Dewey fully intended to "promote God's ordinances" in the new community, the loss of the Deacon was a hardship for Taylor and the Westfield Church as well. From the earliest years of the settlement, Taylor had feared that the town would have too few "pillars" to give the church a strong foundation, and now in the case of Josiah Dewey, these fears proved to be well founded.[83]

Dewey's removal was the only such event recorded by Taylor in his Commonplace Book, though many other church members also moved away during Taylor's tenure, which emphasizes the significance of Dewey's departure to Taylor's hopes for the church. The importance of the presence of men like Dewey in the town is connected to the potential for support that prospective church members might find in their struggles to enter in full communion. In Boston, when Samuel Sewall sought to join the church, he received inspiration, consolation, and examples of spirituality not only from his minister and family members, but from the extensive array of friends and elders with whom he was familiar in his daily life. It was through the "importunity of friends" that Sewall finally found the courage to join the church, despite his own "unfitness and want of Grace."[84] Without an extensive network of encouragement and support provided by friends for spiritual growth, the churches in rural villages like Westfield were that much more likely to become "tribal" entities, where membership was for all practical purposes confined to families already within the fold.[85] The departure of a single pillar of lay piety like Deacon Dewey would seriously damage the ability of the community to nurture the next generation in the faith—the temple's foundation was weakened, a gap opened in the hedge that might not be replaced.

In this case, however, disaster was averted in Westfield, if only temporarily. Josiah Dewey's nephew, David Dewey, moved into the town shortly after his uncle's departure and took his place as a pillar of the church. He became a full member in 1700 and eventually a deacon as well. Josiah's departure was thus compensated for by the arrival of his nephew, but only for a dozen years. David Dewey died young. He was thirty-six when he fell victim to an epidemic in 1712, but the circumstances of his death preserved evidence of his own religious sensibility and the strength of his relationship with Taylor. Taylor wrote a rather touching elegy upon his friend's death and appended it to a collection of Dewey's spiritual meditations which was published as a small pamphlet, probably in 1713.

The pamphlet shows the continuity of the religious sensibility displayed by Westfield's founders into the eighteenth century, at least for one of the more prominent church members. In particular, it stresses the importance of the family and the nurturing role of godly parents in passing on this sensibility and helping it to grow and withstand life's hazards. The sixteen "Meditations" in the pamphlet are organized to "reflect the passage of human life and its basic concerns."[86] In addition, Dewey wrote a series of "Exhortations, Pen'd and Left . . . as a Legacy to His Children," which were included in the pamphlet posthumously. Reminiscent of the founders' conversion relations, Dewey's exhortations emphasize the need to "Remember your Creator in the Days of your Youth." Even in his dying hours, as Taylor attended his bedside, Dewey's concerns were for his family's spiritual welfare. As Taylor described it in his elegy, at "our last Fast for Zion's cause attended," a quiet moment fell:

> . . . sweetest Breathings in thy closet still'd
> And Family, like Incense, Christ's Ears fill'd.
> Thy Lips dropt Dewy Rhymes, which then did fall
> In Admonitions, on thy offspring all:
> To bring them up to Christ, as Dews in th' Morn
> Do hang bright dangling Pearls on ears of Corn.[87]

The nearly contemporaneous date of publication and the obvious similarity of intentions between this pamphlet and *Early Piety; Exemplified in Elizabeth Butcher of Boston* suggest a comparison of the social and cultural circumstances in which they were produced.

While the Elizabeth Butcher pamphlet displays the complete range of the means of grace through which Bostonians attempted to propagate their religious culture, the Dewey pamphlet's focus is entirely on family as the source for religious inspiration and nurture. Unlike Joseph Sewall's preface to *Early Piety*, Edward Taylor's contribution to the production of Dewey's pamphlet does not turn the experiences of Dewey outward as an exhortation for all New England or even all of Westfield, but instead gives personal comments on Taylor's connection to Dewey and praises the strength of the Dewey family's devotional practices. Taylor's elegy on the Deacon is "more directly focused on the actual events and significance of the deceased's life than is true of other elegies of this period," which tend to treat the deceased's life as exemplary for the community and his or her death as a reason to chastise society at large.[88] In other words, Taylor was less accustomed than Sewall to "improving" the death of a pious individual for the spiritual edification of the community.

The reason for Taylor's and the other townspeople's failure to capitalize on the exemplary nature of Dewey's life and turn it into yet another means of grace for the community of Westfield is grounded in the difference between the material and cultural conditions in Boston and Westfield. It was obviously much easier to get a pamphlet published and widely distributed in Boston than it was from New England's remote rural frontier. We know virtually nothing about the publication of the Dewey pamphlet; the only extant copy was recently discovered, missing its first three pages, including date and place of publication. The only reason this obscure text was ever properly identified and attributed is the intense interest among literary scholars in Taylor the poet.[89] But the fact of its obscurity highlights the difference between this pamphlet and *Early Piety*, which went through numerous editions and thousands of copies. The meager circumstances of its production, the limited ambitions of its author and of Taylor for turning this material to evangelical ends, its exclusive focus on the family as the source for religious inspiration, nurture, and continuity, all help to demonstrate the relative paucity of means available in Westfield.

The conditions of life on the New England frontier forced severe limitations upon the town and reduced the ability of its citizens to provide the resources that would make its church a nurturing garden for spiritual growth. Many if not all of Westfield's families sought the chance to participate in the religious community, but only a few favored souls managed to attain the heights of Puritan spirituality that Edward Taylor expected of the converted, and even they lacked the economic stability to turn their attention to enriching the larger community. With a minimal supply of educated, prosperous, godly leaders, the "hedge" around Westfield's garden was weak, and the extent to which the laity demonstrated the capacity to tend to their fellows' souls was small. The burden of this responsibility would therefore fall heavily on their minister, Edward Taylor.

CHAPTER 5

Keepers of the Vineyard, Gentlemen of Means

The church voted to give £200 out of their treasury to the children
of Samuel Willard.
— Records of the Third Church of Boston, December 7, 1693

He knew how to be a Son of Thunder to the Secure and Hardned;
and a Son of Consolation to the Contrite and Broken in Spirit.
— Ebenezer Pemberton, Funeral Sermon for Samuel Willard (1707)

The founding of Boston's Third Church was accomplished by lay people
with remarkably little clerical involvement in the process. During the controversy within the First Church that led to schism and separation, the dissenting
members charted their course with advice from sympathetic ministers of other
churches, but without a clerical leader of their own. However, once it was
formally organized, the Third Church expected guidance from its ministers.
If the church was a garden, then the minister was its "tender," according to
Samuel Willard's use of the metaphor, or the "vineyard keeper" or the "faithful shepherd," as other pastoral metaphors would have it. The Third Church's
clergy were committed to the "middle way" program of church reform that
stood as the principle behind the Halfway Covenant synod; this was the direction they would lead their flock, the plan on which they would cultivate their
garden.
    Like the laity, the Third Church clergy were affected by the material cir-
cumstances of life in Boston, but their aims and responsibilities within the
church were different from and more extensive than the laity's. It was their task
to nurture the faith of those already in full communion, to convert the rising
generation of "children of the church," and to bring the means of conversion
to those outside the church's walls. To see how the ministers met these obligations requires a focus on three significant aspects of their clerical work: first,
the pastoral duties of the ministers in nurturing the spiritual growth of the

flock; secondly, the content of the messages they preached to the congregation; and finally, the new forms the clergy developed to deliver their messages
to a growing and diversifying population in Boston, forms that depended on
the ready availability of material resources provided by the church laity. These
resources made it possible for the clergy to perform their tasks with unusual
devotion, and in so doing, they followed in the tradition of the minister as
"orthodox evangelist" outlined by John Norton: "orthodox" because they remained committed to traditional Puritan definitions of the nature and order
of salvation and the purity of the church; "evangelists" because they saw it as
their duty to spread this message beyond the church's current boundaries and
extend the scope and impact of the means of grace.[1]

⚜

In the years following its establishment, Boston's Third Church was
blessed with a series of talented and capable ministers, clergymen who were
strongly committed to building on the traditions defined by John Norton,
Thomas Shepard, Jonathan Mitchell, and other leading first-generation proponents of the Halfway Covenant. In the persons of Thomas Thacher, Samuel
Willard, Ebenezer Pemberton, Joseph Sewall, and Thomas Prince, the Third
Church was guided through its first century by preachers loyal to its founding
impulse, ministers who maintained the theological continuity and expanded
the social mission of the South Church. The church members discovered
among the sons of New England, and indeed among the members of their
own congregation, a more than adequate "supply" for their religious needs. It
was rare for a New England church to hire ministers from among its own
membership. The Old South's success in this line suggests that as a religious
community, it served to nurture its clergymen as much as the ministers nurtured the church by creating an ideal atmosphere for men with clerical aspirations. A closer look at the material support and working conditions provided
for the clergy by the Third Church members confirms this picture.

The structure for a Congregational church described in the Cambridge
Platform of 1648 and defined by the leading clergy of the first generation
required a church to have three "elders." Two of the elders, the pastor and
teacher, performed the functions ordinarily associated with ministers: preaching, leading public prayer, administering the sacraments, catechizing, visiting
the sick, and offering spiritual counsel. The duties of the third elder did not
require the special training in ancient languages and biblical exegesis necessary for ministers, and thus fell to members whom we would ordinarily think
of as laymen. This was the office of the "ruling elder," whose primary respon-

sibility involved the maintenance of church discipline. Despite the differences in function and skills, all three were solemn offices and required official elections by the voting members of the church and ceremonies of ordination.[2]

In practice, the churches of New England rarely lived up to this ideal. On one level, material constraints limited most congregations' ability to afford two ministers. Many clergymen had to haggle with impoverished townspeople to collect a salary sufficient to live on. Most churches in rural villages thought of adding a second minister only when their pastor was too old or enfeebled to fulfill his duties. Nor did many of these churches ever ordain a ruling elder, as few laymen could be found who would take on this responsibility. It was often difficult to find a church member who, without any special training or qualifications, would accept the burden of a permanent, unpaid calling which required him to sit in judgment over his friends, neighbors, and relatives. The risks were great, the rewards were slim, and the office of ruling elder consequently fell into disuse throughout most of New England. In addition, many of New England's churches became occasional battlegrounds between clergy and laity over issues of religious and social authority, and few clergymen were keen on relinquishing control of the effective tool of church discipline to a layman who might be overly sympathetic to his fellow members.[3]

Boston's Old South Church proved to be an exception to this pattern by actually trying to achieve this ideal for much of its first century. The new church was founded by laymen who were unafraid to take an active role in church affairs, men who could stand up to powerful clergymen like John Davenport. Thus it is no surprise that they were able to find a ruling elder in the person of Edward Rainsford, who was ordained along with Thomas Thacher in February 1669/70. Rainsford was a venerable figure in Boston, a member of the Great Migration fleet of 1630, and consequently a natural choice for such a weighty position.[4] However, after Rainsford's death in 1680, the office of ruling elder remained vacant, and despite periodic efforts to revive it, fell into disuse just as it did throughout New England at the end of the seventeenth century. But unlike most New England churches, the absence of a single ruling elder in the South Church may have reflected the presence of too many rather than too few qualified candidates for the role. Instead of a single ruling elder, the functions of this office were performed in the South Church by an unofficial quasi-clerical committee.[5]

More significant and successful were the Third Church's concerted efforts to maintain two clergymen. Although the new church had only about thirty members at its founding in 1669, these few members must have anticipated considerable potential for growth when they expressed their immediate desire to find a colleague for Thomas Thacher. Small in number, the church was not lacking in resources to support two full-time clergymen, for among the membership were some of Boston's wealthiest merchants. Yet despite their financial resources, their initial efforts to hire an English dissenter met with mixed success. John Owen, their first choice, could not be convinced to leave England for the American wilderness. Two years later, they succeeded in luring Dr. Leonard Hoar across the Atlantic, only to lose him to Harvard College, where he served as President for a short and unhappy tenure.[6] It was not until after King Philip's War of 1675–76 that the Third Church finally hired a colleague for Thomas Thacher.

Samuel Willard, son of a leading Massachusetts merchant, fur-trader, land-magnate, and magistrate, had been the minister in the frontier village of Groton, Massachusetts, until it was destroyed in the war.[7] With his congregation decimated and scattered across many New England towns, Willard moved to Boston. His considerable talents quickly earned the respect of the Third Church membership and he was ordained as Thacher's colleague on March 31, 1678. With Willard's ordination, the Old South joined its parent church as one of the few New England religious bodies to maintain two prominent clergymen. Sadly, Thomas Thacher died unexpectedly only six months later. No permanent replacement was found for over a decade, but Willard was assisted throughout this period by temporary preachers, as Boston was a magnet for visiting ministers and young candidates seeking experience in the pulpit.[8] When Ebenezer Pemberton was finally ordained as Willard's colleague in 1700, the Third Church once again had two permanent ministers, a practice which became a fixture through the eighteenth century, as Joseph Sewall was installed after Willard's death, and Thomas Prince succeeded Pemberton in 1718.

Despite the increased cost of supporting two ministers, the Old South Church maintained its clergymen rather handsomely. Unlike the rest of Massachusetts, where all townsmen were taxed to pay the local minister's salary, the churches of Boston were financed by voluntary contributions. In New England's rural parishes, the minister's salary was voted on by the town government, including church members and non-members alike, and was collected by the town's constable or treasurer, either in money or in "country pay." Ministers as a class were not impoverished, but this system of maintenance kept clerical salaries at fixed levels, and the clergy often found their salaries difficult to collect and subject to the vagaries of crop prices and economic fluctuations. As the century wore on, salary issues became a source of steady, low-level conflict between pastors and their flocks throughout the New England Congregational establishment.[9] However, through the first few decades of settlement, the people of Boston were wealthy and generous

enough not to require taxation to support their ministers and churches, making Boston the exception to the Massachusetts taxation system. Once Boston
churches began to proliferate with the town's expanding population in the
later seventeenth century, voluntarism became the only practical method for
supporting Boston's churches, so this system was retained in contrast to the
mandatory taxation practiced elsewhere in Massachusetts.

The Third Church members' voluntary contributions maintained the
ministers as richly as anywhere in New England. In addition to the basic contributions for salary and firewood that were typical throughout the region,
the Old South ministers were given additional expense accounts for entertaining visiting dignitaries who passed through Boston. The church's account
book shows that "The Ch. allowed Mr. Willard £10 p annum for Entertaining the Elders, besides abt £6 for Every Election," and Willard's successors received comparable consideration.[10] Despite the fact that the regular salaries
of the Old South's ministers were reasonably high by New England standards, the members found additional ways to enhance their ministers' material well-being. In 1693, "the church voted to give £200 out of their treasury
to the children of Samuel Willard," and raised an additional £136 "in money
or plate to be forthwith presented to Mrs. Eunice Willard . . . in testimony of
Our respects to her, to be her own forever." These gifts, which amounted to
several times the typical annual salary of most New England ministers, were
given in gratitude for "the Faithfull and Painfull Labours of the Reverend
Mr. Samuel Willard in the work of the Ministry among Us . . . being sensible
of the Obligation we lye under both to God and him, for so great a blessing."[11] The money was to serve as a trust for Willard's wife and for his children's education, an unusual act of generosity in New England, where many
highly educated ministers could not afford to send their sons to college.[12]

The effect of this generous financial support on the Old South Church's
ministers was not to make them overly worldly, but to free them from the
constant worry over money matters that plagued many New England ministers and kept them from their clerical duties. Because Thacher, Willard, and
their successors did not have to become part-time farmers or traders to support themselves and their families, they were left with more time and energy
to devote to their careers as ministers. In their own church, the Old South
ministers took advantage of their working conditions to provide a strong tradition of pastoral support for their congregation. They offered spiritual nurture and counsel to the families of the church's congregants and endeavored
to draw new families into the congregation from the surrounding neighbor-
hood. In addition, the ministers benefitted from their circumstances in ways
that reached beyond the church itself. The resources of the Third Church al-

lowed them to serve as scholars, theologians, historians, and leading public figures in the religious and cultural life of New England. From Thomas Thacher through Thomas Prince, the Third Church's ministers compiled a remarkable record of service not just to their own church but to the religious culture of Boston as a whole.

Beginning with Thomas Thacher, the clergy of Boston's Third Church maintained a steady devotion to their responsibilities for tending to the souls of their congregation. Thacher was noted for qualities suited to the nurturing role of the pastor—his prayerfulness, humanity, watchfulness, patience, piety, and charity. His own spiritual life was characterized not by a dramatic moment of conversion, but by a slow and gradual growth in grace begun in childhood under the influence of godly parents, and it was this model of spirituality that Thacher attempted to foster as a pastor.[13] Within his own family, he was particularly devoted to religious education and tended closely to his family's spiritual concerns, raising two sons who became ministers.[14] Within his congregation, this concern made itself evident in what Cotton Mather referred to as the "one excellency that shined above the other glories of his ministry, . . . that excellent spirit of prayer which continually breathed in him."[15] Much has been made of the significance of the Puritan minister as scholar, as theologian, and as preacher by twentieth-century historians. Each of these roles was important, and in pursuing them Puritan ministers left behind some of the most fascinating and accessible evidence available to modern scholars. However, this emphasis underestimates the importance of pastoral prayer and counseling to the religion of early New England.[16] This aspect of spiritual life was often spontaneous, was usually performed in private, intimate settings, and left behind little evidence. But Cotton Mather's description of Thacher's prayerfulness begins to reveal the significance of pastoral work, and suggests to the modern reader that even ministers like Thacher who were not prolific authors or publishers of many sermons still had a major impact on the lives of their congregations.

Samuel Sewall's diary confirms Mather's assessment of Thacher's distinctive abilities. As a young man uncertain about the state of his soul, Sewall turned to the older minister for guidance: "Mr. Thacher . . . took us up into his Chamber; went to prayer, then told me I had liberty to tell what God had done for my soul. After I had spoken, prayed again. Before I came away told him my Temptations to him alone, and bad him acquaint me if he knew any thing by me that might hinder justly my coming into Church. He said he thought I ought to be encouraged, and that my stirring up to it was of God."[17] Shortly after these encouraging discussions, Sewall felt confident enough to come forward and join the Third Church. Thacher died within a year of

Sewall's admission, but the memory of his ministrations continued to influence Sewall's life. On one occasion, a surprise visit from a distant relative put Sewall "in mind of the Rev'd Mr. Thomas Thacher's expression—The Lord who comforteth all that are cast down, comforted us by the coming of Titus."[18] It is not unusual that Sewall should recall his minister's characteristic expression of comfort and solace at this moment. What is remarkable is that Sewall's recollection occurred in 1729, a full fifty years after Thacher's death. Sewall's memory attests to the powerful and enduring impact that Thacher's "excellent spirit of prayer" made upon his congregation.

Samuel Willard, Thacher's colleague and successor in the Third Church pulpit, was equally devoted to the pastoral mission of the church. Unlike Thacher, Willard was a prolific author, overshadowed only by Increase Mather among his contemporaries in the volume of his published works. Willard (like Mather) enjoyed the economic support of a prosperous urban community, which afforded him the freedom to build close relationships with his parishioners yet still have time for extensive scholarly pursuits. Again, Samuel Sewall's diary attests to the remarkable frequency and significance of Willard's pastoral visitations. On any given day, Willard might be called upon to visit, comfort, and pray for a dying child, attend a private worship meeting among church members and preach an impromptu sermon there, or speak to the spiritual concerns of a young adult preparing for membership. Willard and Sewall formed a special bond and were fond of each other's company. Sewall would single out the minister for invitations to family picnics or "treats" for local dignitaries. Their close friendship might explain the extensive time and effort that Willard spent tending to the souls of Sewall's family, such as the time he "discoursed" with Sewall's daughter Betty when "she was afraid she should goe to Hell, her Sins were not pardon'd," or when he comforted Sewall's equally distraught son Sam who "was weeping and much discomposed" over his difficulty in finding a suitable calling. Yet Willard served the same function for all of the church's families. On a Friday in October 1688, Willard was presiding at a private fast day at "Mr. Airs's" when he was "call'd out to Isaac Walter who lay dying." In 1692, Willard went with Sewall to "visit loansom Mr. Torrey," whose wife had recently died. And although Puritans considered marriage to be a civil matter and not a sacrament, by the later seventeenth century clergymen were accustomed to performing in Boston area weddings, and Willard presided at many of these. In 1699, "Mr. Willard married Atherton Haugh and Mercy Winthrop," and his comments at this wedding were typical. He reinforced the importance of attending to personal spiritual matters by giving "very good Advice and Exhortation; especially most solemnly charged them never to neglect family Prayer." These few examples offer only a glimpse of the regular daily activities of Samuel Willard as shepherd over the Third Church flock.[19]

Even Willard's scholarly work, the theological writings that have received extensive attention from modern historians, had a specifically pastoral character as well.[20] His greatest work was the posthumously published *A Compleat Body of Divinity*, a series of two hundred fifty sermons preached over the course of twenty years and compiled into one volume by Willard's successors in the Third Church pulpit. Yet this work, treated by modern scholars as a textbook of theology, "the closest thing to . . . a *Summa Theologiae* that Puritan New England ever produced,"[21] was preached as a series of public lectures. These lectures were neither the regular Sabbath-day sermons preached to the church, nor were they Willard's contribution to the weekly Thursday lectures at the First Church that were a Boston institution. Instead, Willard began this series as a special exercise, to be given one Tuesday afternoon a month at the Old South meetinghouse, explaining the tenets of the catechism and providing useful applications of doctrine for the lives of Boston's lay people. As the preface to the published edition states, Willard would close his lectures by demonstrating "the farther beauty use and excellence of the Truths explain'd, by reducing them to a suitable Practice and applying them to the Hearts and Lives of his Hearers." Just as on earlier occasions when Willard had explicated the catechism for the benefit of the church's children, he began this lecture series as a way to apply these eternal truths to "Riper and stronger Minds, of more enlarg'd Capacities and more advanced Knowledge."[22]

Willard's congregation received these lectures in this catechizing spirit, as Sewall's diary attests. In 1699, a twice-postponed dinner party was finally arranged on a Tuesday, which conflicted with "Catechising day" and caused Sewall to miss "the company of Mr. and Mrs. Willard." In 1705, Sewall declined to participate in the "drinking of healths" at the Council Chamber in order to attend "Mr. Willard's Catechising Lecture."[23] In addition to these monthly exercises, many other Willard publications were originally sermons or educational talks given as part of Willard's pastoral duties, including his *Brief Directions to a Young Scholar Designing the Ministry* and his *Sacramental Meditations*. Willard's enormous scholarly output should be viewed not just as the chief focus of an intellectual's career, but also as an extension of the minister's primary role as pastor to his church and to the people of Boston at large.

Willard's colleague and successor, Ebenezer Pemberton, carried on these traditions after Willard's death in 1707. Sewall's diary records how Pemberton, a year after his ordination, went to visit and pray with Sewall's daughter Betty, whose spiritual troubles had been tended to by Willard in earlier years.[24] In similar fashion, Pemberton took up many of Willard's pastoral duties, and gave the senior minister needed assistance once Willard became acting president of Harvard College in 1701. The energy and commitment which pastoral labors required can be seen in a typical afternoon in 1713, when a group of five Boston area ministers gathered on a Monday to pray with the ailing Peter Sergeant. According to Sewall, they "Began between 1 and 2 p. m. Candles were lighted before Mr. Pemberton had ended."[25] Although this was winter and night came as early as four or five o'clock, the episode is still suggestive of the extent to which pastoral work dominated the lives of Boston ministers.

Ebenezer Pemberton died in 1717, and a year later the Old South Church ordained Thomas Prince, who joined Samuel Sewall's son Joseph in the pulpit. Joseph Sewall, schooled by his father in the importance of family worship, brought a strong commitment to pastoral care to his office, and together with Thomas Prince, built on the Old South Church's traditions. Numerous examples could again be provided to demonstrate the importance of these duties to their ministerial lives, but the purpose of this discussion is not to prove that the Old South's ministers were more committed to their pastoral responsibilities than were other New England ministers. The emphasis the Third Church clergy placed on this role was common throughout New England, perhaps more common than many historians have realized.[26] But in Boston's Third Church the material and social resources offered by the religious community allowed the ministers to fulfill their duties under nearly ideal conditions.

In 1719, Thomas Prince recorded his daily schedule. He would rise at 5:00 A.M., pray and read the Bible for an hour, lead family prayers, have breakfast, and then spend five hours working in his study. Every afternoon, he would "at 2 Dress and go abroad till candle-Light," thus leaving himself anywhere from three to six hours a day for visiting, praying, counselling his parishioners, and attending the frequent sermons and lectures preached each week in Boston and vicinity. At times he might "Do something about the House," but nowhere in his daily schedule did Prince have to allot time for plowing or harvesting.[27] An interleaved almanac from 1737 in which Prince recorded his daily activities confirms that his schedule of 1719 accurately described his regular habits. The 1737 diary shows the steady preoccupations of his life to be preaching, both his own and that of the many other ministers whose sermons he attended weekly, along with visiting parishioners on his regular round of travels.[28]

Prince and his colleagues in the South Church were faced with few of the financial concerns, routine chores, or heavy labors that many contemporary ministers in less wealthy towns or rural parishes had to contend with on a daily basis.[29] Both Samuel Willard and Joseph Sewall received support for their families from generous church subscriptions. Ebenezer Pemberton was wealthy enough to own a slave named "Cophee" who provided Pemberton with an extra £40 a year in money by purchasing his time from the minister.[30] In fact, Pemberton had the wherewithal to assemble one of New England's finest libraries, consisting of over a thousand volumes, at a time when rural New England ministers were still copying borrowed books by hand.[31]

Along with the greater freedom that accompanied larger personal wealth, even the purely "ministerial" chores that every clergyman faced could be divided between two ministers at the Third Church. When William Clark, an Old South member, had his son baptized in 1718, Thomas Prince performed the ceremony, as "He begins his Month to baptise this day."[32] In other words, the two clergyman took turns performing baptisms in alternate months, thereby sharing the burden of this duty. The greater resources offered by a church like Boston's Third did not make its ministers more pious or more devoted to their pastoral duties, but it did allow them the luxury to give more of their time and energy to the practice of their calling. As a result, the clergy of the Old South Church, together with their colleagues in the other orthodox churches in and around Boston, created a network of pastoral care and watch over the lives of Boston's families, a network which grew as the Old South Church and Boston's other religious societies expanded and proliferated in the late seventeenth and early eighteenth centuries.[33]

While the performance of pastoral work was vital to the success of the Third Church ministers' mission, equally important were the content of the messages they taught and preached and the audience which they envisioned as the target of their messages. Left to their own devices, the laity tended to stray from the difficult doctrines of orthodoxy, and it was the clergy's job to keep them in line. In addition, the Third Church ministers faced the challenge of imagining and identifying their proper audience among the growing population of Boston, and then shaping the content of their preached messages in order to reach that audience, without diluting the purity or vitality of their religion in the process. In the dissenting conventicles of English Puritanism, and in the rarefied atmosphere of spiritual revival which characterized the early churches of New England, the ministers had enjoyed the luxury of preaching to the converted. English Puritans could easily identify their audience as the saving remnant of "godly people" engaged in cultural warfare against the worldly and unregenerate masses of the nation. In England, Puritan ministers found their audiences coming to them, in the form of zealous lay people who went "gadding after sermons."[34] Similarly, the process and experience of migration engendered an overwhelming interest in preaching among New England's first Puritan settlers, and the ministers tailored the form and content of their messages to the needs of this self-selecting group.[35]

In the later seventeenth century, as the first group of immigrants grew old and died, the clergy discovered a new problem. Orthodox New England's overwhelming commitment to Congregational Calvinism had largely prevented the development of an "ungodly" population hostile to the religion of the Puritans. Most of the outright opposition to the New England Way in the first half-century of settlement came from individuals who were at least as devoted to a form of godliness as were the orthodox, usually a more radical program than the authorities would allow.[36] The problem that developed in the later seventeenth century, then, was not opposition to the New England Way so much as indifference to its traditional messages. A sense of complacency developed in the wake of the remarkable success of the churches, resulting in a loss of the fervor of the early days, or so it seemed to those who could remember the vitality of English dissent and early New England's spiritual turbulence.[37]

For a minister like John Davenport, whose own beliefs had been forged in the religious and culture strife of the 1630s, the only way to restore the church's former vitality was to preserve the forms of worship, preaching, and church polity that were products of those earlier struggles. Yet as the controversy over the Halfway Covenant and the Third Church founding demonstrated, Davenport's position failed to comprehend the nature of the problem and made enemies out of those who were essentially friendly to his cause. The Halfway Covenant was not a complete solution to indifference or complacency, but it did correctly identify the nature of the problem. The ministers of Boston's Third Church began from a position which supported and defended the Halfway Covenant, but they did not see this reform in the definition of church membership as the end of their work. Instead, they built upon the Halfway Covenant by developing a style of preaching and an approach to the sacraments designed to encourage a renewed commitment to godliness, and they aimed their message at as wide an audience as possible within New England society.

Samuel Willard's attempts to bring this evangelical approach to the Third Church stirred up controversy in Boston. In 1682, Edward Randolph, the royal emissary and unremitting opponent of New England's Puritans, wrote a letter to the Bishop of London in which he described the religious situation in Massachusetts and assessed the prospects for success of an Anglican mission.

Randolph claimed that "We have in Boston one Mr. Willard, a minister, brother to Major Dudley, he is a moderate man and baptiseth those who are refused by the other churches, for which he is hated."[38] Randolph was a biased observer of New England life, and the "hatred" of Willard by the other ministers he described may have been the lingering residue of the Third Church founding controversy, since the reconciliation between the First and Third Churches occurred only weeks before Randolph dated his letter. While it is impossible to find any corroborating evidence that Willard was hated by anyone in the Massachusetts religious establishment, Randolph's statement about Willard's baptismal practices was nonetheless accurate. In the early 1680s, Willard took on the task of defending broadly based infant baptism against recent attacks by a fledgling group of Particular Baptists in Boston. In 1681, he published a pamphlet in response to the "New England Anabaptists' late Fallacious Narrative" against Congregational orthodoxy. Willard followed this up the next year by publishing his sermons on covenant renewal, in which he argued that scriptural authority endorsed taking infants into the covenant through the sacrament of baptism.[39]

Later in the 1680s, Willard described more fully the implications of his views on baptism in a sermon series entitled *The Barren Fig Trees Doom*. The purpose of widespread infant baptism, even for the offspring of parents who were not full church members but who professed belief in orthodox doctrine, was to extend the size of the garden of the church and make its nurturing environment available to as many visible professors as possible. As Willard put it in the first "Use" of the second sermon in the series, "How injurious they are who deny them a room in the Vineyard. . . . Are we wiser than [Christ], . . . shall he say, I have planted these in my Vineyard, and shall we say they are in the Wilderness?"[40] Willard saw widespread baptism as a way to expose many potential believers to the beneficial effects of the means of grace.

Similarly, Willard encouraged greater participation in the ordinances of the church by adjusting the requirements for full membership and communion. He did not propose to do away with the relation of an experience of conversion, or a testimony to a work of saving faith wrought in the professor's heart by God. He did, however, lessen the anxiety which many lay men and women felt in giving such a profession before an entire congregation. Willard's method allowed persons to give their conversion relations to the minister in private, who then would judge the potential member's worthiness and report his decision to the church.[41] This change was not designed to alter the meaning of full membership or suggest that the Lord's Supper was a "converting ordinance," as Solomon Stoddard would later argue. Rather, it was meant to soften the intimidating effect of what many perceived to be a barrier to church membership, and perhaps to allow some neglected believers in the "wilderness" a chance to enjoy the benefits of the "vineyard."[42]

Willard's policy on relaxing access to the sacraments implied a view of the church as a mixture of saints and sinners, the elect along with the unregenerate. Convinced of the limits of human ability to identify the truly regenerate, Willard reminded his listeners in the Third Church that "there are those that are planted in the visible Church, that bear no fruit," including hypocrites, legalists, and unregenerates. Consequently, the focus of much of Willard's ordinary preaching throughout his career was to remind both full church members and those within the broader church covenant not to rest complacently in their positions. The covenant was no assurance of ultimate salvation, and it provided threats as well as promises to those within it. "There is an hell which God hath prepared for the exalting of the glory of his revenging Justice in, . . . thus, the tree that brings not forth good fruit is hewn down and cast into the fire."[43]

At its heart, this position argued for a particular approach to the allocation of the church's religious resources. Willard favored spreading the church's "means" as widely as possible, offering everyone the opportunity to benefit from them, but this distribution of means was not intended to be indiscriminate. The recipients were enjoined to make the most of the "goods" they received. As Willard described it, church members who enjoyed the sacraments not only had the most to lose from their failure to repent, but they actually harmed the church by wasting the efforts of those employed in providing the means of grace, when other more responsive recipients might be going without. For this reason, members were expected to improve upon the promise of baptism and the means of conversion offered to them under the church's auspices. In the metaphor of the vineyard, each plant in the garden was obliged to "bear fruit." This fruitfulness would manifest itself in the sanctification of the individual and would be evident in the godly life and in the good works and community service that sanctified individuals would perform. But Willard was careful never to imply that salvation was *accomplished* through these outward manifestations of godliness. Willard reminded his listeners that "All the endeavors which are used by men for the rendring of Sinners fruitful, are uncertain as to the issue," for "men cannot convert whom they please." Instead, this uncertainty was to be used as a reminder for all to avoid "carnal confidence," to refrain from judging men's inner faith by their outward successes, and to place one's expectations for salvation not on human actions but on God's grace. Doing good works was man's duty and could even bring others the means of grace, but it was not a way to salvation.[44]

The minister's role in this process was to encourage people to enter the

church and enjoy its benefits, to serve as their mentor and nurture their growing faith, but also to keep them from "the desperate madness of secure sinners," lest they "continue unfruitful . . . [and] perish without remedy, without
pity."[45] Willard's combination of the "judgment of charity" in church admission together with a strong emphasis on preaching the necessity of conversion
has been described as "sacramental evangelism."[46] As the body of Willard's sermons demonstrate, the changes he proposed and helped to carry through in
matters of church polity did not sever the vital link to earlier generations with
respect to the message of his preaching. His efforts to encourage growth in
church membership and growth in grace within the church were not made at
the expense of reformed Calvinist doctrine. In sermons like *Morality Not to be
Relied on For Life*, he continued to remind his audience "how far a natural man
may go in the improvement of his Moral Powers, and yet miss of eternal life
at last," for "the legal Moralist is not only a stranger to, but an enemy of this
faith."[47]

Willard's message to halfway members not to be satisfied with their position was delivered in peculiarly vivid form in *Impenitent Sinners Warned of their
Misery and Summoned to Judgment*. This set of two sermons had been preached
upon the sentencing and execution of a young Bostonian convicted of infan-
ticide, a woman who had been baptized by Willard and raised by a godly family in the Third Church. Willard reminded this woman, and by implication,
all those under the covenant who had not yet closed with God, "what an
egregious fool you have been. . . . You have sat under the clear Dispensations
of the Word of God, in which you have been many a time over, told of your
sinful courses, and the certain destruction that they would lead you to . . . , yet
how have you *despised instruction* and scorned reproofs . . . and you must now
dye, as one that would not be instructed . . . Cry out then bitterly of this your
own foolishness."[48] And yet, while Willard thundered about man's account-
ability for his own sins, he repeated the message that salvation came only
through grace, which God could grant even to the most heinous sinner. In a
lengthy sermon series on the parable of the prodigal son, Willard described
"those secret wayes wherein God carries his Decree of Election," and warned
his listeners to "beware that we rely not upon our selves and our duties, but to
renounce all, and fly to the Grace of God in Christ." As Harry Stout has suggested, Willard's regular Sabbath preaching, together with his sermons on
special occasions and his lecture series on the Westminster Catechism, "reveal
an enduring concern with the doctrine of conversion and unconditional election that conforms closely to the pietistic preaching of the founders."[49]

This mixture of spiritual nurture and zealous conversionist preaching
was the message Willard brought to his congregation both in his preaching

and in his pastoral role. According to his successor Ebenezer Pemberton, Willard "applied himself to *Wounded Consciences* with great Skill . . . , as became a Wise, Tender, and Faithful Physician, And he knew how to be a Son of Thunder to the Secure and Hardned; and a Son of Consolation to the Contrite and Broken in Spirit."[50] The tone Willard set in his thirty years as the South Church's minister was maintained by his successors in the pulpit for the half-century after his death. First Pemberton, and then Joseph Sewall and Thomas Prince remained remarkably devoted to the message preached and taught by Willard. While the personal characteristics of each of these ministers shaped his style and approach to his work, their collective commitment to sacramental evangelism lent continuity to the religious life of Boston's Third Church well into the eighteenth century.

Ebenezer Pemberton was one of the first to call for the publication of Willard's Catechism Lectures as "one of the *BEST* Bodies of Divinity that has been known."[51] A student and friend of William Brattle, Benjamin Colman, and John Leverett, Pemberton has been described by modern scholars as "liberal," but his liberalism, like Willard's, was confined to matters of church polity. To his dying day, Pemberton rested all hope for human salvation, including his own, "only upon the merits of Christ."[52] His published sermons, of which there are few, hint at a greater tendency toward "legalist moralism" than Willard would allow, but as Harry Stout has suggested, published sermons from this generation were often those delivered on public occasions which "emphasize themes of moral reform and waning piety," while obscuring the message of "salvation of the soul and the life of sanctified obedience" preached in regular Sunday sermons.[53] Thus, while a sermon like *A Christian Fixed in His Post*, preached at a public lecture in 1704, might emphasize the need for reformation of manners and the performance of duties, Pemberton's *Advice to a Son*, delivered at the gathering of a family whose son was about to leave on an overseas voyage, argued the premise that only "the gracious presence of the Lord Jehovah" offered any hope for prosperity, and encouraged the departing son to seek diligently after grace.[54] In the eyes of his contemporaries, Pemberton's "natural temper was all *flame*, and *zeal*, and *earnestness*," and his "brave soul was ill-lodged in a distemper'd body," which may have made him a more abrasive pastor than Willard. But beneath the differences in temperament, the message he offered remained the same.[55]

Joseph Sewall, son of the famous merchant, judge, and diarist, was ordained as Pemberton's colleague in the Third Church pulpit in 1713. Pemberton was not altogether happy with this choice of a junior colleague, and was less than impressed with the young Sewall's potential for scholarship. However, the judge's wishes carried great weight in the Third Church (which may have been what bothered Pemberton to begin with), and Joseph Sewall quickly established a strong reputation, if not for advanced scholarship, then for his intense piety and emotional style of preaching.[56] The younger Sewall earned the nickname of "the weeping prophet" from his tendency to break into tears over the goodness of God in granting grace to undeserving sinners.[57] Sewall's emotional style was coupled with a great reverence for traditional New England theology. As an early biographer put it, "He dwelt upon the great articles of the christian faith in preaching and conversation; and dreaded the propagation of any opinions in this country, which were contrary to the principles of our fathers."[58] Other Boston clergymen looked to Sewall's conservative position as an anchor against drifting too far from tradition. Cotton Mather suggested that "his objections to our Interpretations, may be of use to us, to prevent our going too Easily into mistakes."[59]

A sermon which Sewall delivered to his church in 1722, on a fast day "to Ask of GOD the Effusion of His SPIRIT on the Rising Generation," demonstrates Sewall's commitment to the tradition of sacramental evangelism developed by Samuel Willard. This sermon, entitled *The Holy Spirit the Gift of God*, was preached on the doctrine that "God our Heavenly Father will most certainly give his Holy Spirit to them that Ask Him." On the face of it, this would seem to suggest a belief in the potential for universal human salvation based on the performance of duties. But Sewall insisted that "the Asking here spoken of is a Duty which none but the Children of God, who have the Spirit of Adoption, can discharge aright; and they are obliged to ask that they may receive the Holy Ghost in more plentiful measures." Only the elect could ask for grace properly, yet Sewall made it clear that the duty of asking was required of all, saint and sinner alike: "Unregenerate Persons are also indispensibly obliged to attend this moral Duty of Prayer, and to ask of God the Spirit of Grace and Supplication, that they may do it in a right manner. . . . Who knows, but that you may be the happy Subjects of this great Benefit."[60] Sewall's preaching, like Willard's, was orthodox in its emphasis on the necessity of conversion and God's sovereignty in the granting of grace, yet it was aimed at a mixed audience of the converted and the unregenerate and it was meant to encourage the uncertain members of the "Rising Generation" to take advantage of the benefits offered by the church.[61]

In October 1718, Thomas Prince was ordained as Sewall's colleague in the South Church. Prince and Sewall had been friends in college, where their religious interests and beliefs had been cultivated under the guidance of Samuel Willard.[62] Prince was more cosmopolitan than Sewall, having spent almost a decade after graduation travelling and preaching in the West Indies and England. He was also more scholarly than Sewall, and took a strong interest in collecting documents and writing history, particularly the early history of New England. Yet despite these differences, Prince shared Sewall's fundamental outlook on the nature of religious experience, the necessity of conversion, and the role of the church in the process of salvation. Prince's "anglicization" served to make him somewhat more tolerant of religious diversity than other New England ministers, yet it also reinforced his belief that the New England Way was superior to all other religious systems. On his arrival in London, Prince was captivated by its grandeur and by the variety of entertainments and diversions unknown in New England. However, after a few short months of taking in Anglican services, seeing plays at the theatres, and visiting "the stupendious Church of St. Pauls," Prince established ties with English dissenters in the East Anglian countryside, where he remained for most of his time in Britain.[63] Despite this opportunity to preach in Suffolk, Essex, and Cambridgeshire, areas traditionally known for Puritan belief, Prince longed to return to New England, and his descriptions of life in the New World convinced some thirty members of his congregation in Suffolk to migrate with him to New England.[64]

In these experiences, Prince's early career was reminiscent of the formative years of Increase Mather, or even of the founding generation of New England ministers who led their own groups of converts to the New World.[65] Like Mather, Prince's cosmopolitan experiments left him firmly convinced of the truth of the New England Way and one of the most ardent defenders of its traditions. In effect, it reaffirmed his identity as a New Englander and clarified his sense of New England's distinctive character as a religious society. Upon his return to New England in 1718, Prince met with immediate acclaim, received calls to the pulpit from a number of New England churches, and was quickly settled as Sewall's colleague at the Old South Church. Their long co-pastorate, lasting forty years until Prince's death in 1758, was noted for the harmonious relations between Sewall and Prince, who renewed and maintained the friendship they had formed in college.

Prince shared Sewall's devotion to sacramental evangelism, and together they advanced the theological traditions that were shaped by Samuel Willard. Although numerous sermons and publications might be cited to confirm the orthodoxy of Prince's and Sewall's preaching, perhaps the strongest evidence of this devotion is the part they took in the effort to publish Willard's series of catechetical sermons. *A Compleat Body of Divinity*, published in 1726, was the largest and most ambitious publication effort undertaken in America up to that time. Together with Willard's son and other church members who had kept notes from the original sermons, Sewall and Prince worked to decipher Willard's manuscripts from the 225 lectures that he actually preached and to edit the additional 25 manuscripts that Willard had prepared before he died. This monumental effort was worthwhile to Willard's successors because of their belief in the continuing usefulness of Willard's brand of "systematical divinity." Willard's lectures, in their opinion, demonstrated his "superiour Abilities, his consummate Judgment, his uncommon Penetration, in an Age of the greatest Light, at least since the Apostles Days." Hence, their publication was "to communicate the same celestial Light and Heat to others, which so eminently shone and wrought in [Willard] himself."[66]

As theologians and as pastors to the members of the Old South Church, Sewall and Prince maintained the traditions developed by their predecessors in the pulpit. Similarly, their view of the proper audience for their message required that the church attempt to convert the community as a whole. If the Third Church's "middle way" were to succeed, the clergy's devotion to traditional theology, pastoral care, and converting preaching were essential. But in the later seventeenth and early eighteenth centuries, the Third Church clergy developed new techniques and expanded the scope of older methods in order to encourage godliness among the growing and changing population of Boston. The publication of *A Compleat Body of Divinity* represents just one example in a range of sophisticated and ambitious efforts by the ministers of the Old South Church to extend the plenitude of means and foster piety in local Boston society. Their program for reform encouraged an ever broader distribution of the culture's religious resources, and the strength of Boston's commercial economy provided them with new opportunities to achieve this goal.

Some of the new techniques that the clergy encouraged have already been mentioned. Prominent among these is the development of the covenant renewal ceremony, of which Samuel Willard was a chief proponent. In a series of sermons from 1680 to 1682, Willard emphasized the spiritual value gained when a church and its members publicly renewed their covenant with God.[67] While this ceremony was technically not an innovation but a recovery of forms used in the founding generation and among English Puritans, its utility in reinforcing the obligations of membership in the covenant to the minds and hearts of the laity made it a complement to the sacramental evangelism of Willard and his colleagues.[68] The payoff to these "seasons of renewal" came in the laity's increased devotion to the practices of Puritan piety, and occasionally, as in the Third Church's covenant renewal ceremony of 1680, an influx of "children of the church" into full membership brought on by the revival in piety.[69]

Similarly, the clergy at the Reforming Synod of 1679 recommended a renewed commitment on the part of ministers to the pastoral watch, instruction, and nurture of the laity.[70] While these were traditional functions of the clergy, the Synod's call for renewed attention spurred many ministers on to vigorous efforts, as when John Cotton, Jr., minister of Plymouth, organized all the heads of families who were under the church covenant into study groups to answer doctrinal questions.[71] In Boston, Samuel Willard took this recommendation and applied it in a way that was suitable to his large and diverse congregation when he began his series of "catechetical lectures" on Tuesday afternoons. By formalizing religious instruction in this manner, Willard could reach a wider audience than was possible in small groups like those Cotton organized in Plymouth, and this wider range was essential if the ministers were to have an impact on Boston's expanding population.

The eventual publication in 1726 of Willard's catechism lectures points to the most significant form in which the Third clergy worked to spread their message widely within the community, that is, the publication of ordinary sermons. Again, this tactic was not an innovation but a more vigorous and thorough employment of a means of conversion that earlier generations had used. The rapid expansion of the publishing industry in Boston made the press generally more accessible to New England ministers, and yet even with this growth, the press was always more available to Boston ministers than it was to their rural colleagues. A striking example of this fact can be seen in the publishing career of Samuel Willard. Willard published only one small collection of three sermons in the thirteen years he spent as minister of the remote frontier town of Groton. But after he moved to Boston, Willard became one of the colony's most prolific authors, publishing over forty works in the next thirty years.[72] Part of this change might be attributed to his maturing skills as a preacher and writer, but the increased amount of time available to spend on scholarship and the immediate access to the press that a Boston pulpit provided were greater influences on his publication level.

George Selement has demonstrated the preponderance of Bostonians among those ministers who were the most prolific publishers in the first five generations of Puritan New England. Not surprisingly, Third Church clergymen were among the two or three most prolific authors in their respective generations, with the exception of Ebenezer Pemberton, whose death at an early age cut short his career just before he reached "prolific" levels.[73] The majority of the South Church clergy's publications were sermons, and the great bulk of these were simply ordinary Sabbath-day sermons that were sufficiently elegant, timely, or forceful that the minister or his congregation felt they deserved a wider audience. But the publications of the clergy were not limited to works on spiritual development alone. In 1731, Thomas Prince wrote and published *The Vade Mecum for America: or a Companion for Traders and Travelers*. This highly useful pamphlet contained a guide to currency values and exchange rates throughout British America, a table of simple and compound interest, another table showing the "value of any quantity of any commodity, ready cast up, from one yard or one pound to ten thousand," a listing of the major roads from New Hampshire to Virginia, along with a schedule of meeting times for county courts throughout the colonies, a guide to Boston's streets and principal commercial establishments, and a "correct table of the kings and queens of England, from Egbert the 1st King of England to his Present Majesty King George II." Prince's *Vade Mecum* suggests the remarkable familiarity and ease with which the Boston clergy operated in the commercial world surrounding them, and their publishing ventures demonstrate how they used these opportunities for the promotion of Puritan religious culture.

From the pulpit to the press was literally a short journey for the sermons of the Third Church clergy. Among the regular auditors of Willard, Pemberton, Sewall, and Prince were leading Boston printers and publishers, men like Bartholomew Green, Daniel Henchman, and Samuel Gerrish, whose shops were just down the street or across the way from the meetinghouse.[74] The printers Kneeland and Green and the publisher Daniel Henchman were responsible for producing Prince's *Vade Mecum* along with most of his other works. Other wealthy church members were ready to subscribe to publications and distribute copies among the townspeople. With all these advantages of metropolitan religious culture, the Third Church clergy and their colleagues in the other Boston pulpits were responsible for the vast majority of all the sermons published in New England from the mid-seventeenth to the mid-eighteenth centuries.[75] Through their use of the press, these ministers found a way to give their traditional messages a more permanent and widespread impact upon society, and thus to increase the availability and cultural saturation of a significant means of conversion.

Another way in which the Third Church clergy used the medium of the printed word to extend their message deserves special mention, namely, the work of Thomas Prince as a historian of New England. Just as Cotton Mather in an earlier generation had thought of himself as the "Lord's Remembrancer" in writing the *Magnalia Christi Americana*, so Prince understood the value of history as a reminder to a covenanted people of their obligation to God.[76] In 1730, Prince had the honor to preach the Massachusetts Election Sermon on the hundredth anniversary of the settlement of the colony. Prince reminded his audience of New England's corporate identity and made use of the colony's historical experience as a tool to encourage piety and devotion to traditional religious forms.[77] His most ambitious historical work, *A Chronological History of New England in the form of Annals* (1736), was seen as something of a failure because it ignored most of New England's recent past in its voluminous effort to place New England within the frame of providential history, "from the Creation: Including the connected Line of Time, the Succession of Patriarchs and Sovereigns of the most famous Kingdoms and Empires, the gradual Discoveries of America, and the Progress of the Reformation to the Discovery of New-England."[78] By the 1730s, a sense of historical identity had become an integral part of New England's religious culture and a source for pious devotion, as evidenced by the republication of the works of famous first-generation divines like Thomas Shepard and Hugh Peter.[79] Thomas Prince's historical publications, whatever their literary successes or failures, served as a further reminder of the vitality of this heritage, and thus played a part in the evangelical efforts of the Third Church clergy.

A final way in which the clergy extended the reach of their pastoral message can be seen in their attempts to create general resurgences in popular piety. Boston's orthodox ministers would occasionally shift from their usual focus on the individual believer and instead single out a class or category of lay people for special attention and encouragement. In 1721, the South Church ministers joined with other Boston clergymen to preach a series of special sermons designed to address the young people in town who were not yet in church communion. The sermons were well publicized and the "audiences were considerably crowded." During the course of these lectures, a smallpox epidemic struck Boston, the first in over eighteen years. Because of this long hiatus, the younger people in town were especially vulnerable to the disease, having never developed an immunity. The sermons for converting the young were promptly rushed into print, were eagerly bought up by the townspeople, and "many of the younger people especially were then greatly awakened" and came forward to join the church.[80]

Similarly, in 1726, the Boston clergy embarked on another specialized lecture series, designed to encourage the practice of religious devotion within the family. Then on October 29, 1727, New England experienced a severe earthquake. Just as in the smallpox epidemic, the clergy hastened to "improve" this natural disaster by calling fast days, preaching, and printing sermons:

> The Ministers endeavoured to set in with this extraordinary and awakening Work of GOD in Nature, and to preach his Word in the most awakening Manner; to show the People the vast Difference between Conviction and Conversion, between a forced Reformation either in Acts of Piety, Justice, Charity, or Sobriety, by the meer Power of Fear, and genuine Change of the Frame and

Relish of the Heart by the Supernatural Efficacy of the Holy Spirit, to lead them on to true Conversion and unfeined Faith in Christ.[81]

The ministers were not suggesting that the panic experienced by people in response to natural calamities was the same as conversion. Rather, they were arguing that the panic was God's way of showing people their *need* for conversion, awakening them from spiritual torpor to a realization of their own desperate unconverted state. At the Third Church, Thomas Prince's strategy was to take advantage of natural fears, the conviction of human sinfulness inspired by the disaster, and use it as a tool to demonstrate what true salvation was, in the hope that those among the population with saving grace would search their souls and make the effort to close with Christ.[82] The success of this strategy can be seen in the church records: from November 1727 to March 1728, fifty-three new members joined in full communion, and in the remainder of 1728, forty-two more people joined, the largest influx in the church's history since its founding in 1669.[83] In general, these specialized forms of preaching and the efforts to "improve upon" epidemics, natural disasters, and public calamities were further ways in which the clergy of the Third Church strove to expand the community of the church and its means of conversion.

One source for our knowledge of these ministerial efforts to capitalize on epidemics and natural disasters is a historical narrative written by Thomas Prince during the Great Awakening. At the time that he wrote this account, Prince was looking back from the perspective of the remarkable religious revival that swept Boston in the wake of George Whitefield's visit in 1740. Prince was attempting in his magazine, *The Christian History*, to justify the recent awakenings as a true work of God against its spate of detractors.[84] In addition, he hoped that his magazine would encourage the further growth of these astonishing outpourings of grace upon God's people. Given this agenda, it was in Prince's interest to look back on the decades leading up to the great revivals as a "dead time," an era of languishing spirits when what appeared to be true revivals were really false alarms. Prince's attitude is not unlike that of the revolutionary partisan determined to forget the era of reform that preceded the deluge in the interest of heightening the current drama and casting the *ancien régime* in the worst possible light. Yet despite his attempts to characterize the two decades before the Great Awakening as an era of "great tranquility" in Boston's religious life, his decision to single out the series of events that foreshadowed the revival is significant and revealing. The drama of Whitefield and the Great Awakening made it difficult for Prince to appreciate the influence of what had happened earlier. However, if we divest ourselves of the perspective of the extraordinary and enthusiastic outpouring of religious feeling in the early 1740s, we can gain a new understanding of the meaning of the clergy's influence on Boston religious culture in the preceding era.

The long-term effect of the decades of orthodox evangelism on this religious culture, and particularly on the clergy themselves, was to create a climate of feeling in which most of the time their extensive efforts seemed to go unrewarded, as religious sentiment among the population languished in a "dull" or uninspired state. However, this orthodox evangelism also created a set of *expectations* among the clergy that their efforts would occasionally be rewarded in popular upsurges of religious sentiment and devotion, especially in response to public crises and at cyclical intervals when substantial portions of the population were reaching the typical age of church membership. The clergy's long years of devotion to the pastoral nurture of the flock, their unwavering efforts to preach the message of conversion and to offer the sacraments as both an encouragement to piety and a standard of purity, and their attempts to find new forms for spiritual renewal of the population as a whole, all served as an elaborate, extended "preparation" of the entire community for a "conversion experience."[85] Though the temptation to do so is strong, the tendency to focus on the blinding moment of conversion and ignore the necessary preparatory work is an error which the Third Church clergy themselves would have denounced. Just as conversion for individuals was a lifelong process in which preparation and subsequent sanctification were as important as the precise moment of grace, so for entire communities the extensive preparatory work was as much a part of the culture of revivalism as was the season of grace that marked its culmination. For the Third Church as a whole, it is important to see that through the late seventeenth and early eighteenth centuries, the activities of the clergy as orthodox evangelists tended to promote a revivalist mentality in the religious culture that would come to fruition in the 1740s.

Revivals, like individuals conversions, were not just private events. They occurred within the larger context of New England religious culture, and were profoundly shaped by religious politics and social developments. In order to understand fully the Third Church's "preparation" for this event, it is necessary to turn from the internal life of the church, the efforts of laity and clergy to sustain the church over time, and look to the public life of the church. In the decades between its founding and the Great Awakening, the ministers and members would face various conflicts, controversies, and crises in New England's larger religious culture. The Third Church members would be forced to confront opposition from forces hostile to Puritan culture as they attempted to prepare an ever greater proportion of New England society for conversion and the godly life. The difficulties of this task, and the extent to which the internal resources for this type of communal preparation were unavailable in other parts of New England, can be seen by comparing the work of the Third Church's clerical gentlemen of means with the more frustrating labors of Edward Taylor.

CHAPTER 6

"Christ's Curious Garden Fenced In . . ."

Where I have one thought of spiritual concerns, I have twenty laid
out upon the things of the world.
——Edward Taylor, *Treatise Concerning the Lord's Supper* (c. 1693)

For on the Towers of these Walls there stand
Just Watchmen Watching day, and night,
And Porters at each Gate, who have Command
To open only to the right.
——Edward Taylor, *Gods Determinations touching his Elect* (c. 1680)

To Edward Taylor, the town of Westfield seemed more like a wilderness
than a garden upon his arrival in the winter of 1671. His overland trip from
Cambridge had been graced by "fair and warm weather all the way," but
heavy snow lay on the ground and the traveling party had inched its way across
the frozen Connecticut River with the newly formed ice cracking at every
step. Half an hour after Taylor's arrival in Westfield, a storm blew up, and
"there came such gusts of winde . . . as I scarce ever heard. . . . I know not that
ever I heard such gusts and shuffs of winde as blew then." The fearsome
weather was not the only hostile element. Within a month, the home of
Thomas Dewey, the man who recruited Taylor to be Westfield's minister, had
burned to the ground.[1]

Life in Westfield would not always be storms, fire, and ice, but Taylor's
initial encounter set the tone for his relationship to the community he would
serve for the rest of his life. The first sermon Taylor preached in Westfield was
drawn from Matthew 4:16–17, a message to "the people which sat in darkness
. . . and to them which sat in the region and shadow of death. . . . Repent: for
the kingdom of heaven is at hand."[2] The image of the western frontier as a
howling wilderness and of its people sitting in darkness would be reflected in
Edward Taylor's career as pastor. The resources available to Taylor amid the
primitive conditions of life in western Massachusetts would limit the extent
to which he could devote himself to pastoral duties. His devotion to the writing of meditative poetry would further influence the way he performed his

pastoral labors. In these circumstances, Taylor's vision of the nature of the church, of the need to protect its purity, and of the limited potential for converting the local population would determine the kind of religious community that Taylor hoped to cultivate in Westfield. Boston's Third Church was unified behind a program of evangelical reformation and its clergy had the means and will to carry it out. By contrast, the Westfield church was of no single mind about the kind of institution it wanted to be. Edward Taylor lacked the desire to spread the community's religious resources widely, and faced with a shortage, he chose to confine participation to a privileged few.

❧

As the minister of a small rural village, Edward Taylor occupied a highly visible position in community life, but aside from his clerical duties, he made few concerted efforts to be a leader in Westfield's affairs. In the years after the Westfield church was finally gathered in 1679, Taylor played a very minor role in the formal business of the town. He seems not to have participated in town meetings, held no town offices, and was mentioned in the records only rarely, as when the town voted on who was to collect the "rate" for Taylor's salary.[3] This was the one subject on which Taylor had regular dealings with the town meeting, for like most rural New England ministers, Taylor had recurring difficulties in collecting his salary, especially when bad harvests or wars created economic hardships. In 1692, for instance, the town voted to give Taylor his usual £80, but added their "desire that Mr. Taylor would abate 10 pound thereof," and requested Josiah Dewey and Nathaniel Weller "to treat Mr. Taylor about it."[4] A salary of £80 was reasonably generous when Taylor began his ministry in the 1670s, but the amount became something of an automatic fixture. As Taylor lived on into the eighteenth century, its relative value declined, and Taylor's successor in the 1720s began his career receiving £100 per year.[5]

The town's request for a salary abatement in 1692 touched off an intermittent struggle that lasted nearly a decade. Taylor refused to accept the cut in pay, but the townspeople, whose tax burden had been increased by the colony's participation in the war against France, were hard pressed to come up with his full salary. Many families evaded their taxes, claiming inequitable assessments, and in 1697/8, the town voted to pay Taylor in "current pay," the devalued local currency.[6] Eventually, Taylor made intimations that he might quit or leave Westfield if his salary was not better maintained. In January 1698/9, the town reaffirmed its commitment to pay Taylor adequately and expressed its "desier [for] Mr. Taylors continuance and setlment amongst us in the work of the ministry."[7] The difficulties Taylor faced in collecting his salary, although not unusual in rural New England, indicate the limitations that rural life placed on the pastoral work of ordained ministers.

Furthermore, Taylor, unlike his urban colleagues in churches like Boston's Third, was forced to support his large family by farming his own lands and selling the commodities he raised.[8] The town facilitated this effort by giving him extra land grants through which he gained some income from rentals, but he still had to engage in agriculture himself to maintain his own family's competency. In addition to raising a variety of crops, Taylor kept livestock and experimented in beekeeping. Samuel Sewall, his old college friend, served as his representative in marketing his livestock in Boston.[9] As the town's only college-educated gentleman, Taylor was also frequently pressed into service as an amateur doctor and lawyer, for which, if he was paid at all, he was probably paid in kind.[10] This work was not incompatible with Taylor's pastoral duties, for in tending to the townspeople's physical ailments and social conflicts, he could also minister to their souls.[11] Nonetheless, the combined weight of Taylor's responsibilities for caring for the town's needs and maintaining his own family cut into the time and energy he could spend on strictly pastoral duties:

> I find I am called to set mine affection on things above, and not things upon the earth. . . . But alas, I find it otherwise with me. . . . Where I have one thought of spiritual concerns, I have twenty laid out upon the things of the world. . . . While we have these bodies of clay to look after, and are betrusted with the concerns of families, towns, and public duties in our hands, they necessitate our thoughts; so that we lay out a great deal of our contemplative substance all the day long upon them, and are constrained to put off spiritual concerns. . . . I doubt not but it is thus with many a thousand of the choicest of God's children that are singled out by Him to eminent service for Him that the managing of the concerns of their particular callings are so circumstanced with difficulties and attendants, which with the circumstances of their personal refreshment summon, maybe, out from them a thousand thoughts for one bestowed upon spiritual things, save in a transient way.[12]

The heavy demands of family and community that were part of life in a rural New England village kept Taylor away from the purely spiritual endeavors he would have preferred to pursue.

Still, Taylor did not suffer undue economic hardship. His second marriage to Ruth Wyllys brought him a substantial dowry, and toward the end of his life he may even have owned a slave, to whom he referred as "Agnes my Neger Servant."[13] It is unclear whether Agnes was a slave or served under a less permanent form of indenture, but at any rate, her presence in Taylor's household does not mean that he was a rich man. His estate at his death was valued at £236, which put him among the middle rank of contemporary

Westfield men; by coincidence, it was exactly £100 less than the trust fund given to Samuel Willard by Boston's Third Church in 1693.[14] Even compared with his Northampton neighbor, Solomon Stoddard, who received a £100 salary from the beginning of his contemporaneous tenure and whose estate, exclusive of a large library, was valued at £1,126, Taylor's fortune looks rather paltry.[15] Making ends meet must have been a struggle, and he could never afford to send any of his sons to college, leaving them less well educated than he had been. When Taylor was old and enfeebled, the town voted to give £10 to his daughter "to inable her to provide help to tend Mr. Taylor," as the family's accumulated resources were insufficient to care for the minister in his old age.[16] The town treated Taylor decently and he was not poor, but neither was he handsomely maintained. Taylor's modest wealth made him dependent on keeping in the good graces of his congregation, lest he be left shivering in the cold for want of firewood, and he remained well below the economic rank of Westfield's more prominent citizens and other western Massachusetts figures. The honorary "Mr." with which the town records prefixed his name was a tribute to Taylor's learning and dignity, not to his wealth and social prominence.

Even in this honorific distinction, Taylor was isolated in Westfield. Compared with his contemporary colleagues who remained in Boston and its environs, Taylor had few fellow ministers to consult with, few "quasi-clerical" gentlemen in Westfield to aid him in his labors, and less time for devoting himself exclusively to spreading the means of grace among the townspeople in his charge. Taylor shared the challenge of these limiting circumstances with other ministers similarly placed in rural communities all across New England, and indeed, in English parishes as well.[17] As leaders of their local religious communities, Taylor and other rural ministers simply had fewer available religious resources to allocate than the ministers of Boston's major congregations possessed. But the way in which Taylor responded to this challenge and conducted his pastoral labors was shaped by his own introspective temperament, by his refined religious sensibility, and by his understanding of the nature of the Puritan church, which he expressed in the writings that became the organizing principal and focus of his life.

∾❧∽

After straining to catch a glimpse of the religious experiences of Westfield's settlers from the fragmentary evidence that remains, turning to examine the spiritual life of Edward Taylor can be overwhelming, like stepping out from a cave into blinding sunlight. Taylor wrote thousands upon thousands of words in his lifetime, many of them intended to capture his deepest emotions and express his most fervently held beliefs. His poetry, for which he is today most famous, amounts to some forty thousand lines. The surviving prose fills several substantial volumes, including his lengthy church records and at least three sermon series collected into thematic treatises. These surviving sermons represent only a portion of the hundreds he must have written and preached in his lifetime. Besides these major works, there are diaries, commonplace books, notes, an attempt to write a "Harmony of the Gospels," and even hand-written copies of books he borrowed, ranging from travelers' accounts of China to works on metallurgy.[18] From this massive production, it is obvious that Taylor must have spent an immense amount of his time and energy with pen and paper in hand. One would expect all this introspection and self-expression to provide a detailed view of Taylor's life and the world he lived in.

Yet for all that he poured out his soul in his "Preparatory Meditations," Taylor the man seems strangely out of focus, difficult to imagine in a real place and time.[19] Like his classmate, Samuel Sewall, Taylor's writing dwelt on humble, mundane, ordinary things. In calling for God to remake his soul, Taylor turned to homespun metaphors:

> Make me, O Lord, thy Spining Wheele compleate.
> Thy Holy Worde my Distaff make for mee.
> Make mine Affections thy Swift Flyers neate
> And make my Soule thy holy Spoole to bee.
> My Conversation make to be thy Reele
> And reele the yarn thereon spun of thy Wheele.[20]

But Sewall filled his diary with the people and events that shaped his daily life, while Taylor's writing excluded this kind of detail. Though he used mundane imagery, Taylor's concern was not for the commonplace in and of itself, but for the way ordinary objects turned his thoughts to things eternal.[21] In all of the volumes of Taylor's own writing, what remains of his daily life and closest associations in Westfield are a few poems about his first wife and his family, several entries in his commonplace book, a handful of elegies, and his church records, which were not written to express his feelings about his congregation or record his pastoral labors.[22] Although his grandson Ezra Stiles claimed that Taylor "was a vigorous Advocate for Oliver Cromwell, [and] greatly detested King James, Sir Edmund Andross and Randolph," his politics are not directly evident in his writings.[23] His church records contain a brief discussion of King Philip's War, but he does not dwell on this elsewhere, nor does he ever directly describe frontier life.[24] Given Westfield's precarious position on the western edge of New England settlement, the infrequency with which Taylor mentions Indians in his writing is rather remarkable, but it illustrates how little attention he paid with his pen to the buzz of the world around him.[25]

Instead, Taylor intently directed his thoughts toward matters of eternal importance, the struggle for personal salvation and God's plan for human-kind. The bulk of his extant writings can be described in these terms under three rough headings. First, Taylor's concern about his own salvation, his personal relationship with God, emerges from his "Preparatory Meditations." These, Taylor's best poems, were written regularly over a forty-year span, beginning in 1682, as a way for Taylor to prepare himself for his approach to the sacrament of communion. In these meditations we can see the centrality of the sacrament to Taylor's personal religious experience. Secondly, Taylor's attempt to understand God's word and to act as a means for his congregation to receive it can be seen in the treatises he delivered in the form of sermons. His *Christographia*, a meditation on the nature of Christ, his *Treatise Concerning the Lord's Supper*, and his examination of biblical typology in *Upon the Types of the Old Testament* all fall under this heading, as do his attempts to versify portions of scripture and his analysis of the "Harmony of the Gospels." Also in this vein is his long poem, *Gods Determinations touching his Elect*, which recounts the Soul's reconciliation with God, effected by God's Justice and Mercy, ending in "The Joy of Church Fellowship rightly attended." While both the "Harmony of the Gospels" and *Gods Determinations* might have been useful and edifying for his congregation, we have no evidence that Taylor ever shared these works with the people of Westfield.[26] Finally, Taylor was also concerned with Christian history, more particularly, with the idea of the properly instituted church as the culmination of God's plan for man on earth. He wrote his longest poetical work, a *Metrical History of Christianity*, as an attempt to versify two well-known Protestant histories, Matthias Flacius's *Magdeburg Centuries* and John Foxe's *Actes and Monuments*. His extensive writings on typology and the contents of *Gods Determinations* also reveal his conception of Christian history. Although Taylor experimented in a variety of other forms, these general categories describe the primary focus of Taylor's literary endeavors: his own salvation, the nature and meaning of God's plan for mankind, and the manifestation of this plan in God's churches, including, most especially, his own.

In the past half century, enormous scholarly labor has been lavished on Taylor as poet and author. Indeed, the immense project of publishing all of Taylor's works is still not complete, as his manuscripts continue to turn up in unlikely places.[27] The majority of this scholarship has focused on assessing Taylor's literary merits, placing him within various poetic and theological traditions, and evaluating his influence on American letters, rather than on describing Taylor's career as a minister in Westfield. Major studies of Taylor's poetry and prose tend to leave this aspect of his life in the background, resigning themselves to a "meager" or "skeletal" outline of his biography.[28] To reverse this tendency, we can use Taylor's writings to understand his life as a member of a religious and social community, as the pastor of a Puritan church on the New England frontier.

The sheer vastness of his accumulated works suggests that Taylor responded to the wilderness of Westfield by turning inward to a life of contemplation and literary production.[29] Of course, not all of his writings should be judged as inward or private. As we have seen from the publications of Boston's ministers, clerical scholarship often had a pastoral character, and certainly Taylor's sermons fit this pattern. The fact that Taylor, unlike his Boston colleagues, never published his sermons merely indicates the difficulty that all rural ministers faced in bringing their works to the press, not an opposition on his part to publishing in general.[30] Nevertheless, the focus of much of Taylor's literary effort had no specifically pastoral purpose. The great achievement of his lifetime as a poet came in the series of meditative poems he wrote as part of his own preparation for receiving and administering the sacrament of the Lord's Supper. In these intensely personal poems, composed at regular intervals over a span of forty years, Taylor charted the course of his soul in its relationship to the divine.

For Taylor, the sacrament of the Lord's Supper was central to life's pilgrimage, and as he grew older it became the chief focus of his religious experience. The "Preparatory Meditations," his most inventive, engaged poetical works, are the most obvious testimony to this. They were written to prepare him for and celebrate his impending approach to the communion table.[31] Communion was, for Taylor, far more than the ritual reward a saint received for having been converted. Rather, as a direct approach to a symbolic offering of grace, communion was an incredible gift from God, incommensurate with man's merits, and therefore something for which the sincere believer struggled to prepare. In his Preparatory Meditations, Taylor would characteristically bewail his sinfulness or the deadness of his soul in the face of this gift:

> My Flame hath left its Coale, my fire's gone t'bed:
> Like Embers in their ashic Lodgen gray.
> Lord let the Influences of thy head
> Most graciously remove this rug away.
> If with the Bellows of thy grace thou blow
> My ashes off, thy Coale will shine and glow.[32]

Taylor perceived the spiritual deadness of a self bound by sin as a barrier to the experience of communion. If he could not discern the presence of God's grace in his soul, Taylor knew that his own sinful nature could not possibly merit his receiving such a gift.

In a passage that was familiar to all New Englanders, Paul's First Epistle to the Corinthians (1 Cor. 11:27–29) warned against coming to communion unworthily, for to do so was to eat and drink one's own damnation. Taylor took this injunction to heart and used the writing of devotional poetry to scrutinize the state of his soul in preparation for the sacrament. His meditations often reflect the scouring introspection Taylor associated with preparation for communion:

> Unclean, Unclean: My Lord, Undone, all vile
> Yea all Defild: What shall thy Servant doe?
> Unfit for thee: not fit for holy Soile,
>   Not for Communion of Saints below.
>   A bag of botches, Lump of Loathsomeness:
>   Defild by Touch, by Issue: Leproust flesh.
>
> Thou wilt have all that enter to thy fold
> Pure, Cleane, and bright, Whiter than whitest Snow
> Better refin'd than most refined Gold:
>   I am not so: but fowle: What shall I doe?
>   Shall thy Church Doors be shut, and shut out mee?
>   Shall not Church fellowship my portion bee?

As the end of the second stanza suggests, Taylor directly linked the practice of anxious self-examination to the requirements for communion. Consequently, he abhorred Solomon Stoddard's idea of opening communion to all professing believers in the hope that the sacrament itself would encourage further spiritual growth. In another poem, also written in the 1690s, Taylor called Stoddard's idea "Presbyterian apostasy . . . where open Sinners vile unmaskt indeed/ are Welcome Guests (if they can say the Creed)/ Unto Christs Table." To Taylor, this approach to church membership was no better than the English Prelacy he had fled a generation earlier.[33] His scornful use of the term "Presbyterian" in the 1690s, at a time when even traditionalists like Increase Mather were encouraging reconciliation between English Independents and Presbyterians, shows how mired Taylor was in the ecclesiastical politics of a bygone era.

To Taylor, conversion or church membership required a willingness to enter a life of devotion, a pilgrimage on which the sacraments were milestones. His "Preparatory Meditations" represent the most refined record of a life committed to such devotion that we have from early New England. As far as we know, however, these poems were never seen by any of Taylor's contemporaries. Although they often bore a direct connection to the sermons Taylor preached on sacrament days, the poems themselves were too closely tied to his own personal condition to be shared with others for their benefit.

In this light, Taylor's poetic opus bears comparison to Samuel Willard's equally massive work, *A Compleat Body of Divinity*. Like Taylor's poems, Willard's posthumously published work was not part of his regular preaching as the Third Church minister, but an additional task which he took upon himself. Like Taylor's poems, Willard's lectures were begun in the 1680s and produced at regular intervals over many years. The major difference, of course, is that Willard's lectures were conceived and designed for the purpose of public instruction in spiritual growth, while Taylor's "Preparatory Meditations" were highly personal works of art produced for his own spiritual benefit. The source of this difference must be attributed both to the personalities of the respective ministers and to the possibilities offered them by the social and cultural conditions of the communities they served.[34] Still, taken together, these "Preparatory Meditations" serve as Taylor's model of an exemplary inner life, in which the Lord's Supper stands out as the symbolic focus for the individual's growing desire to leave the world behind and come ever closer to God.[35] But as the intensity of Taylor's meditative poetry suggests and as the declining number of admissions to the Westfield church affirms, this model was an extremely difficult example of spiritual life for ordinary citizens to live up to, even in a godly society. Its effect was to make the church an exclusive preserve in which only those with the most rarefied religious sensibilities might fully participate.

Given the importance of the sacrament to Taylor's understanding of godly life, it is not surprising that he supported the Halfway Covenant's continuing protection of the sanctity of communion. His early life in England conditioned him to think of the church as a community withdrawn from the world, and he brought this attitude with him to Westfield. Yet Taylor realized that the Halfway Covenant's purpose was also to draw the hyperscrupulous into the church and to create a systematic approach to encouraging backward saints to come forward and claim their rightful place among the elect. His desire to reserve communion for visible saints did not come from any scorn for the non-elect, but from his immense regard for the sacrament and his desire not to dilute its attractions for potential believers. Taylor likened the sacrament to a wedding where the communicant is the honored guest, receiving "royal entertainment, noble society, and hearty welcome with sweetest familiarity imaginable. Oh! What Sweet, what heart-ravishing and soul-enlivening delight will here be unto thee?"[36] For a sinful person to come to such a feast with anything but a repentant and grateful heart and an earnest desire to know God's grace would be an intolerable desecration.

Yet Taylor knew the difficulty of attaining such a state, and recognized the fears of earnest Christians who felt themselves unworthy of such gifts.

Early in his career, perhaps even before the Westfield church was gathered, Taylor wrote *Gods Determinations touching his Elect*, an extended poem dealing with the problems faced by various kinds of elect souls (or "ranks," as Taylor called them) as they struggled to fend off Satan and come nearer to God.[37] Taylor understood the common difficulties faced by ordinary believers in New England, and in *Gods Determinations* he laid out his vision of the soul's progress into church fellowship in order to overcome the typical reluctance that impeded ordinary Christians from joining the church.

The difficulty faced by many religiously minded non-members was that although they may have experienced inclinations toward God and a desire for communion, they feared that putting themselves forward as visible saints was presumptuous, especially if they still felt they were sinful at heart. Such individuals cannot believe that they are worthy of salvation and fear that approaching the Lord's Table would be hypocritical. Out of their own moral scrupulosity they avoid the matter entirely, hoping someday to receive more light. Taylor's poem, with its discussion of "Mans Perplexity when calld to an account" and its extended description of the various ranks of timid sinners on their slow progression toward salvation, was intended to assuage the fears of these overly scrupulous souls and usher them into full church fellowship. These Christians might in effect be called "false hypocrites." They have the requisite religious sensibility for full membership, but they doubt themselves and are overwhelmed by the awesome meaning of the decision to join the church. Once again, we cannot know if Taylor's congregation ever saw or heard this poem, which like virtually all of his work was unpublished in his lifetime, but we might safely assume that his preaching and pastoral counseling at the time reflected these ideas, thereby registering Taylor's sympathy with the overly scrupulous portion of his congregation.[38]

Despite Taylor's sincere efforts to understand and reach out to the typical believer, the vision of the church he portrays in *Gods Determinations* and elsewhere in his writings is more exclusive, less inviting and encouraging than that offered by the more evangelically minded ministers of Boston's Third Church. Like his Boston colleagues, Taylor on occasion resorted to the metaphor of the church as a garden planted by God in which the elect might grow in grace. Toward the end of *Gods Determinations*, when the exemplary "Soul" is finally convinced to overcome his backward and fearful nature and seek church fellowship, Taylor describes the church as "Christ's Curious Garden."[39] Yet compared with the typical evangelical use of this metaphor which emphasizes the nurturing qualities of the garden for weak Christians, Taylor's depiction of the garden/church highlights its forbidding deterrents to outsiders:

Hence now Christ's Curious Garden fenced in
    With Solid Walls of Discipline
Well wed, and watered, and made full trim:
    The Allies all Laid out by line:
    Walks for the Spirit all Divine.

Whereby Corruptions are kept out, whereby
    Corrupters also get not in,
Unless the Lyons Carkass secretly
    Lies lapt up in a Lamblike skin
    Which Holy seems yet's full of sin.

For on the Towers of these Walls there stand
    Just Watchmen Watching day, and night,
And Porters at each Gate, who have Command
    To open onely to the right.
    And all within may have a sight.

The forbidding tone outweighs the much less fully articulated image of the garden as a "Paradise set with Choice slips and flowers."[40]

As Taylor goes on to describe how "The Soul . . . Enters into Church Fellowship," he drops the garden metaphor and turns briefly to an image of the church as a "City, bespangled with Graces," and then more extensively to the "Joy of Church Fellowship" as a ride to heaven in Christ's Coach:

In Heaven soaring up, I dropt an Eare
    On Earth: and oh! sweet Melody:
And listening, found it was the Saints who were
    Encoacht for Heaven that sang for Joy.
    For in Christ's Coach they sweetly sing;
    As they to Glory ride therein.[41]

Here, the image of church fellowship is a more inviting one, but the exclusive aspect of the Puritan church is again reinforced in the image of the church as a coach, an aristocratic form of transportation which few people in Westfield might ever have seen, let alone taken a ride in.[42] In the highly stratified world of the seventeenth century, where sumptuary laws were still used to distinguish the prerogatives of various social ranks, the notion of the church as the elect's coach bound for glory was a firm reminder that full communion was reserved for the spiritual elite.

Taylor would return to the metaphor of the garden in later years when he composed his "Preparatory Meditations," but here again his usage of this common trope for depicting the church often turns from a general description of the pleasures of church fellowship to a highly personal plea for an infusion of God's grace. In 1708, Taylor wrote two successive meditative poems based on Canticles 5:1, "I am come into my garden. . . ." In the first four stanzas of Meditation II.83, Taylor describes the "Garden-Church, set with Choice Herbs and Flowers" and tells how Christ's entry into the garden makes "all Plants of Grace gust out like Spice / Their sweet perfumed breath." But in the last two stanzas, Taylor personalizes the metaphor:

> Make mee thy Garden; Lord, thy Grace my plant:
> Make mee thy Vineyard, and my plants thy Vine:
> Then come into thy Garden: View each ranck:
> And make my Grape bleed in thy Cup rich wine.
> When thou comest in, My Garden flowers will smile
> And blossom Aromatick Praise the while.

Then in his next meditation, composed from the same biblical verse, the metaphor is entirely devoted to the state of the poet's soul, beginning with the question, "Hast made mee, Lord, one of thy Garden Beds?"[43] Given the devotional context in which these poems were written, the fact that Taylor would turn this common image of the church inward to question the state of his personal relationship to God is not unusual, but it does convey the sense that Taylor's spiritual temperament was highly personal and idiosyncratic, more interested in the soul's relationship to Christ than in the communitarian aspects of church fellowship.

Although Taylor did recognize the need for encouraging weak Christians in their progress toward faith, the overall thrust of Taylor's poetry was inward, removed from the world, and mystical in ways that reflected his own religious sensibility but may well have repelled some members of his congregation. Despite the encouragement which *Gods Determinations* attempted to provide by arguing potential saints out of their fears, Taylor upheld as a standard for church admission the anxious, self-scouring sensibility which he revealed in his meditative poems. This sensibility has been described by Karl Keller as "humility ritualized, self-searching formalized." In Keller's words, Taylor worked "artfully to implant . . . a morbid, hope-filled self-consciousness, an alert and anxious attention to spiritual nuance, a life-dominating watchfulness, a spiritualized masochism."[44] While a few Westfield lay people like Josiah and David Dewey were able to rise to this challenge, the majority of the population was bound to be excluded from the church as long as full membership was linked to such a demanding inner life.

Taylor's approach to the problem of the unconverted in *Gods Determinations* differed from contemporary jeremiads like Michael Wigglesworth's terrifying *Day of Doom*. Taylor did not intend to jolt complacent sinners into a concern for their souls, but to ease the passage of the already anxious soul into the church. But there were complacent people in Westfield for whom Taylor's poem and his general outlook offered little sympathy, and for whom his staunch defense of the purity of the sacrament must have seemed like a permanent and insurmountable barrier to church fellowship. Here it is helpful to think of the complacent not as ungodly, unchurched people, not atheists or scoffers or worldly minded "Yankees," but instead to remember John Mawdsley and his assumption that New Englanders could trust in their inherited godliness to fare better than Sodom and Gomorrah on judgment day. Many of Westfield's citizens were presumably never jolted out of such an assumption, or were content to base their religious life around following the law, attending lecture, fearing God, and observing the Sabbath. To such people, "Puritan" or "precise" by contemporary English standards but "Hypocrites" or "Lawful Men" should they try to join the Westfield church, Taylor's poem and his vision and defense of the sacrament would have offered little encouragement.[45]

Among Taylor's ministerial colleagues in the Connecticut Valley, complacent Puritans might have encountered a much more nurturing environment. Even in the earliest days of the region's settlement, before the passing of the first generation ever suggested the need for a Halfway Covenant, there were ministers who were not content to cultivate the souls of the converted and guard the church closely against encroaching unbelievers. For first-generation ministers like Thomas Hooker, evangelical preaching that could draw the complacent and unconverted into the church was an essential part of the Christian mission, which required a concern for those people whose sensibilities were not already attuned to the enigmatic and rarified sermons of a John Cotton or a Thomas Shepard.[46] Hooker's colleague and successor at Hartford, Samuel Stone, was still more lenient than Hooker on the matter of qualifications for church membership, and in Windsor, Connecticut, John Warham, the town's minister, frequently wavered on this issue, causing dramatic changes in the structure of the local church and constantly throwing the town into turmoil.[47] As we have seen, many of Westfield's early families had come from these valley towns where alternative experiments in ecclesiastical polity had been tried. In fact, the public relations of several of Westfield's founding pillars single out the preaching of Hooker, Stone, and Warham as the means to their conversion.[48] While we have no direct evidence of how the lay men and women of Westfield were influenced by this more open evangelical tradition, it remained a continuing force in the religious life of the Connecticut Valley.

During Edward Taylor's tenure as Westfield's minister, this tradition came to be embodied in the person of Solomon Stoddard of Northampton.

Over a forty-year span, Stoddard raised a series of proposals for expanding the scope of the church far beyond the boundaries defended by Taylor and other "conservatives." As a result, Stoddard became the figure against whom Taylor explored and refined his standards and beliefs on the sacrament and church membership, and with whom he engaged in an extended intellectual controversy that had profound effects on the religious community in Westfield. Edward Taylor's gradual turn inward and his increasing emphasis on guarding the purity of the sacrament coincided directly with Solomon Stoddard's experiments in freeing the benefits of church life from exclusive standards of admission.

Beginning in the late 1670s, Solomon Stoddard began a series of changes in the church polity of his Northampton congregation and advocated his measures as a way to reform religion in New England as a whole. Over the course of several decades, Stoddard's beliefs on the reason for declining membership and on the problems with New England's ecclesiastical polity evolved through a shifting series of positions. Stoddard considered the exclusivity of communion and the requirement of conversion relations for full church membership to be unscriptural, and sometime in the 1680s he abandoned such requirements in his own church. Instead, he accepted into full membership all persons who showed an understanding of the gospel and lived a godly life, without further requirements or tests. In addition, Stoddard began to raise the idea that the Lord's Supper was a converting ordinance, that it was efficacious in bringing about the conversion of those who received it. The concept of individual church covenants and the gathered church as a completely self-governing body also seemed unscriptural to Stoddard, and in 1700, his *Doctrine of the Instituted Churches* rejected this basic tenet of New England Congregationalism and offered an innovative alternative in the form of a national church with an organized ruling clergy.

Although he eventually backed away from this proposal for lack of support, Stoddard never ceased to seek out ways to bring more people into the church and to reduce the obsessive commitment to strict church admissions that he felt was destroying the vitality of New England's religion. To this end, he strongly emphasized evangelical preaching, which resulted in at least five significant "harvests" of new members in his Northampton church during the course of his ministry.[49] These positions brought Stoddard into a state of frequent conflict with New England's conservative ministers, particularly Increase and Cotton Mather, his relatives by marriage but his enemies on matters of doctrine and emphasis within Puritan religious culture.

The Stoddard-Mather conflict was fought out in the public press and was as well known to contemporaries as it is to modern historians.[50] Edward Taylor's opposition to Stoddard, though consistent with and more sophisticated than the Mathers', was characteristically a much more private matter. The arguments Taylor raised against Stoddard's innovations were at least as cogent and thoughtful as those of the Mathers, but they were not made available to a broad audience. Unlike the Mathers, who published incessantly, and Stoddard, whose Boston background and connections gave him frequent access to the press, Taylor's isolated position in Westfield and his unwillingness to travel annually to Boston as Stoddard did left him little recourse to public debate.[51] As Stoddard proposed one "heresy" after another, Taylor's responses came in the form of sermons to his own congregation, private correspondence with Stoddard, or detailed refutations of Stoddard's arguments written for only himself to see.[52] The most significant of these responses for Westfield's religious community came in the years between 1688 and 1694 when Taylor preached a series of eight sermons which he later revised and which are collectively known as a *Treatise Concerning the Lord's Supper.*

These sermons stand as an extended defense of the sacrament as Taylor understood it. He argued that the founders of New England had come to America for the sake of enjoying pure ordinances, that a restricted sacrament was perfectly scriptural, and that Stoddard's view of the Lord's Supper as a "converting ordinance" was a "Popish error" to be banished from New England.[53] In these sermons, Taylor defends the need to restrict communion to the saints and describes how saints should prepare for their approach to the Lord's Table by cultivating the forms of devotion exemplified in the "Preparatory Meditations."[54] The moderately encouraging position on church admissions that Taylor put forward early in his career in *Gods Determinations* had by the 1690s evolved in response to Stoddard's "apostasy" into this much more restrictive argument for communion limited to the elect few. The *Treatise Concerning the Lord's Supper* emphasizes the purity of the "wedden garment" that the converted saint must prepare for him or herself. Above all, Taylor argues for the doctrine "that no reason can be given of approaching to the wedden supper without the wedden garment." By contrast with Stoddard, the *Treatise* discourages the idea of the Lord's Supper as a source of spiritual nourishment or growth in grace.[55]

Taylor's enunciation of his position on the sacrament must have made it clear to the members of the Westfield congregation, if there were any who did not know it already, that they lived under a stricter form of church discipline than did their neighbors in Northampton and in a growing number of other Connecticut Valley communities.[56] As time went on, Taylor grew increasingly protective of the Lord's Supper and its attending qualifications, and the proportion of Westfield's citizens in full church membership decreased.

Consequently, the difference between the Westfield church and Northampton with its open admissions and periodic revivals must have become increasingly apparent. The early encouragement that the ideas Taylor expressed in *Gods Determinations* may have provided to potential church members in Westfield could not have been enhanced by the knowledge that in neighboring towns the leading ministers were endorsing a more accommodating way. The spiritual experience that Stoddard hoped to foster in the individual believer, the sense of man's utter depravity and helplessness in the face of God's justice and the requirement of salvation through faith alone, was perfectly orthodox and not significantly different from Taylor's understanding of true religious conversion. But in Stoddard's view, admission to the church and all its ordinances was the proper way to encourage people in a godly society to follow this path to God. An exclusive church was an artificial barrier that discouraged the qualified from setting forth on the road to salvation. Thus, the controversy between Taylor and Stoddard, played out in private correspondence between the two ministers and in Taylor's sermons before his Westfield congregation, demonstrated to the people of Westfield that their minister's vision of the church was separating them from the mainstream religious culture developing around them, limiting their access to this culture's main benefits and restricting those benefits to a few privileged saints within the community.[57]

The Stoddard controversy affected Taylor as well, leaving him increasingly isolated in the Connecticut Valley. Although Taylor had powerful conservative allies in the Mathers, there were no vocal defenders of his strict Congregationalism in western Massachusetts. Alone in his position, Taylor's natural tendencies toward solitude were exacerbated. The fact that he wrote so very much and published virtually nothing is indicative of Taylor's introspective cast of mind. Publication was certainly more difficult for frontier ministers than for residents of the Bay, but Stoddard and many others were able to manage it. Taylor, as far as we can know, lacked any interest in the social aspects of public debate or in adapting his beliefs and ideas to the demands of the changing world. Increase and Cotton Mather wrote at least as prolifically as Taylor did, but their efforts were unceasingly directed toward a public audience and were actively engaged in current events. Certainly self-aggrandizement figured into the Mathers' efforts, but so did an active concern for shaping society at large, whereas Taylor seems rarely to have looked beyond his own congregation, and kept some of his finest and most exhaustive efforts even from them. Perhaps Taylor's initial impression of Westfield as a wilderness and his continuing belief that he lived in an intellectual vacuum discouraged him from believing that his entry into public debate could have a discernable impact on his community. Or perhaps his quietist spirituality and the individual orientation of his piety left him content to focus his pastoral energies on those few souls, like the members of the Dewey family, who nurtured the seed of saving grace in a way that he approved. But the controversy with Stoddard left him further convinced that true piety was slipping away in New England and made him all the more determined to defend his own embattled beliefs.

⁓✤⁓

Given the disturbing changes he saw taking place in New England in the late seventeenth century, it is not surprising that Taylor, like Cotton Mather, would turn to history and try to examine (or imagine) a past when the saints led heroic lives and willingly gave themselves up to God's will. But unlike the *Magnalia Christi Americana*, in which Mather attempted to defend present positions by rehearsing New England's past glories, Taylor's *Metrical History of Christianity* was a private exercise, an enormous effort to versify the *Magdeburg Centuries* and Foxe's *Acts and Monuments*, "two of the most reactionary [works] of church history from a Protestant point of view."[58] In its nearly 20,000 lines, Taylor's poem recounts an endless series of stories of Christian martyrs from apostolic times through the beginnings of Protestantism in the sixteenth century, but it stops before the English Puritan movement and the migration to New England.[59] While Taylor had the greatest respect for the founders of New England, by the time he began the *Metrical History* in the 1690s he was unable to see New England's subsequent development as a triumph of the Reformation, given the apostasy he saw all around him. Instead, his history is static, a gruesome record of man's constant struggle with Satan, continuing until the final judgment which human effort can do little to bring about.[60] Ultimately, the *Metrical History* was an immense failure, universally regarded as Taylor's worst poetry, a mass of doggerel written according to a rigid, laborious system and grimly disconnected from the world around him.[61]

Taylor's extended sermon series on biblical typology, preached over the course of fourteen years from 1692 to 1706, similarly displays little evidence that Taylor identified New England with biblical Israel, as his old classmate Samuel Sewall and other Puritan typologists tended to do.[62] Rather, Taylor was a "devotional typologist," who saw Old Testament figures as models for the spiritual strivings of the individual soul, properly reflected through Christ and his gospel.[63] Since Taylor did not imagine that events in New England might be fulfilling biblical prophecy, he had little reason to believe that expanding the scope of the church to bring new souls within its walls would hasten New England's progress toward becoming the New Jerusalem. Such a step would only impede the spiritual pilgrimages of individual saints, in whom Taylor's true interest lay, by cheapening the value of the sacrament. Taylor preferred to remind his congregation how high the price of salvation was, how dear the sacrifice of Christ's body and blood, effectively suggesting that it was beyond their means.

Taylor's attempts to explore the historical dimensions of Christian life, expressed in his *Metrical History* and in his sermons on typology, were ultimately futile efforts to find useful meanings that might be applicable to New England as a social entity. Like Taylor, Thomas Prince of Boston's Third Church struggled to write history that would place New England in a meaningful Christian context, and his massive *Chronological History of New England* also failed to make coherent connections between New England's development and the grand sweep of God's providential plan. But Prince, unlike Taylor, constantly strove to find a spiritual meaning for the fate of his church, for his community, for New England as a whole, and in his historical narratives of the revivals of the 1740s, he eventually succeeded.[64] Taylor, by contrast, never looked for more than the relationship between the individual and the divine. His history was the story of individual martyrs, his typology was meant for personal devotion, and his vision of the church placed the preservation of its sanctity for qualified individuals ahead of enlarging its scope for the sake of the community. The initial impression he received of Westfield as a wilderness remained with him throughout his life. While he hoped that God would make him "one of thy Garden Beds," he never imagined that the whole community of Westfield would become "A Garden, yea a Paradise indeed."[65] As Karl Keller bluntly put it, "The world is crap on which a few flowers of Puritan color will grow. This is the legacy that Edward Taylor saw for early America."[66]

The image of Taylor that emerges from his life and writings is that of an intensely personal, inward-looking man, increasingly isolated in his wilderness outpost from the public events which engaged the participation of his contemporaries. This is not to say that Taylor lacked interest in the world around him, but his interest was often expressed passively, in collecting and copying down tales of wonder, marvels, and prodigies in his commonplace books.[67] He did take an active part in some aspects of local life, most notably as town physician, and he also served on the occasional church council to resolve neighboring church disputes.[68] From the effort he put into his sermons and from the intensity of his own spiritual life, it is clear that he had a deep commitment to his ministerial role and to the nurture of his congregation. Yet the terms in which he understood the godly life, especially the importance of communion, together with his reverence for the church polity created by the Massachusetts Bay founders, made it unthinkable for him to condone the changes he saw taking place in the surrounding towns, or to accept the evangelical approach that the Third Church of Boston championed. His conception of his pastoral role, like his understanding of history, was both retrospective and static. The proper form for a Christian church had been established long ago, and there was no need to make accommodations to a changing world. Despite Taylor's desires, he could not turn back the clock or recreate the Puritan conventicles of his youth in Britain, but by staunchly maintaining his conservative and introspective position, he had a profound impact on the religious community of Westfield. This can be traced most clearly in the church's disciplinary records, where we get an intimate look at the everyday life of the religious community and the gradual decay of the relationship between Edward Taylor, pastor, and his flock.

CHAPTER 7

Defending the Garden, Cultivating the Wilderness

The twenty pounds, the price of my redemption, was raised by some
Boston gentlemen and Mrs. Usher, whose bounty and religious char-
ity I would not forget to make mention of.
—Mary Rowlandson, *The Sovereignty and Goodness of God* (1682)

Voted—That twenty Pounds be given to Mr. Josiah Cotton, to encourage his settlement at Providence; provided, he accept of the call
. . . given him to the work of the Ministry there.
—Records of the Third Church, Boston, March 15, 1728

Boston's Third Church had more resources than it really needed. Its am-
ple supply of ministers and of laymen qualified to be ministers, its rich church
treasury, its spacious meetinghouse, its extensive collection of communion
silver, and above all, its hundreds of devoted families giving voluntary support
to the entire endeavor made the Old South Church known and envied by Puritans on both sides of the Atlantic. Located in the heart of Boston's commercial district, within sight of the Town House and on a busy commercial street
where farmers bringing produce from the countryside passed it every day, the
Old South Meetinghouse held a prominent place in the public eye. Because
of its prominence and its multifarious riches, the Third Church had the potential to be a powerful influence far beyond the corner of Milk Street and
Cornhill. New England's religious culture was an amorphous network of beliefs and practices perpetuated by the continuing adherence of individual
churches, rather than a fixed set of doctrines and institutions controlled by a
higher authority. The actions of particular churches could therefore have a significant impact on the development of religious life in the region as a whole.
The clergy and lay members of the Third Church were conscious of their
powerful public role, and the reforms that had inspired the church's founding
and shaped its internal life also gave direction to its actions in the larger world.
The Third Church members set out to promote and defend their "middle

way" of church reform through the positions they took on major social issues and matters of religious politics in the later seventeenth and early eighteenth centuries.

For its relationship to other Puritan churches and to the "wilderness" beyond the enclosed gardens of the churches, the Third Church's commitment to the Halfway Covenant and the "middle way" of reformation required three things. First, it called for unity, though not uniformity, among the orthodox churches of the region. The Third Church covenant declared that cooperation and compromise were essential to the churches of New England when faced with controversial questions, so that "the Lord may be one and his name one, in all these Churches throughout all generations."[1] The promotion of unity required the toleration of minor differences among orthodox churches for the sake of mitigating disruptive strife within the whole religious community. As religious and political controversies threatened to divide the orthodox community, the Third Church ministers and laity would consistently act to resolve disputes among the Puritan churches of New England without sacrificing the basic tenets of orthodoxy itself. The Third Church members also worked actively to create an atmosphere of fellowship among the independent churches, bringing them out of their separate cells into an ecumenical culture of the godly in Boston.

A second significant aspect of the Third Church's public life was its opposition to encroachments upon New England orthodoxy from alternative religious cultures. The Third Church community tolerated diverse opinions among those who could demonstrate allegiance to the Westminster Confession and the Cambridge Platform, but it rigorously opposed forms of belief and church polity outside these boundaries. Notwithstanding their desire for harmony among Congregational churches, the founders of the Third Church were notorious for their hostility to Quaker and Baptist radicals. This posture toward sectarian challenges continued into the eighteenth century, but a more potent and subtle threat to orthodoxy gradually emerged from proponents of the Church of England. The Anglican Church represented not only alternative doctrines and church polity, but also a cultural challenge to traditional Puritan forms of behavior, a challenge that was more dangerous because it was more enticing than the austere ways of Quakers and Baptists. Yet in following the "middle way" the Third Church steered clear of both radical sectarianism and Anglican formalism. The church developed a combative public stance toward the Church of England and Anglican ways, so much so that a Puritan culture of opposition can be said to have formed for the first time in New England in the later seventeenth century. Godly New Englanders used the rising challenge of "anglicization" to help them redefine what it meant to be a New England Puritan, both through overt responses to the rise of Anglican institutions and through the development of rituals and patterns of behavior that served to demarcate traditional Puritan culture from newer Anglican forms.

The Third Church's reform program also called for an effort to reach out to the larger community and to the region as a whole, to extend the blessings of orthodoxy into the "unchurched" areas of New England. This program of outreach depended on the substantial material and cultural resources of institutions like Boston's Third Church. Gradually, and in an increasingly organized fashion, the church put its surplus of resources to work to insure that poorer churches, churches in frontier regions, in heterodox Rhode Island, and among communities of praying Indians would receive preaching, godly books, and the encouragement of other churches: the "means of grace" that were essential to the growth of religion.

The public life of the Third Church, its relationship with the outside world, was often cast in the same garden metaphor used to describe its internal life. If the Third Church members and ministers saw the Puritan churches as gardens in a wilderness, then the aim of their public life was first to reduce the high wall that separated one Puritan church from another, secondly to reconstruct the wall in defense of all the gardens of the Lord against the wilderness temptations of a maturing society, and finally, to cultivate previously uncharted parts of the wilderness for inclusion within the garden of the church.

∼✻∽

Over the course of three generations, the members of Boston's Third Church strove to live up to the legacy of John Winthrop and John Norton, which emphasized the importance of solidarity among the churches of New England. The contention over its founding in the 1660s guaranteed that the Third Church would face severe challenges, and these were compounded by rapidly changing political circumstances in New England. During his brief pastorate, Thomas Thacher, the church's first minister, began to craft a public position for the Third Church in response to these initial challenges that would establish the ecumenical goals of the founders as a model for a new New England Way.

In the midst of the foundation controversy, Thacher was appalled by John Davenport's manipulative use of the forms of church polity, and by Davenport's willingness to break the very rules and guidelines he had helped to define. The depth of his feeling on these matters is clear from a vehement letter to Davenport which Thacher drafted sometime in 1669 or 1670 but chose not to send. He preferred to blow off steam about this "horrible crime" in private

rather than exacerbate an already contentious issue.[2] The Davenport controversy and its impact on the Third Church's public image were still on Thacher's
mind when he wrote a preface to Thomas Shepard's 1672 Election Sermon.
Shepard's sermon was a sharp attack on the supporters of the now deceased
Davenport. It emphasized the long history of church councils and synods as
valid parts of New England's tradition, and claimed that in the first generation
of settlement, "it was not then accounted an *infringement of the Liberty of the
Churches*" for councils to intervene in church disputes. Shepard insisted that
the absolute autonomy of individual churches created a structure in which
"two or three men shall continue to disturb the peace of a whole Congregation," and asked, "is there no redress for this?" He argued that redress for
troubled churches properly came in the godly practices of "the help, watch, &
assistance either of the Civil Magistrate above them, or of the neighbour
Churches about them." Taking a final dig at the Davenport faction's obsessive
concern for the liberty of individual churches, Shepard wrote, "let the liberty
of Churches be preserved, but care continued for conversion of those that are
out of the Church visible," an evangelical obligation which Davenport's supporters were guilty of neglecting.[3]

Thacher's preface reinforced Shepard's arguments. He argued that the
liberties of the churches in New England had been excessively protected during their forty-year history, and that what was actually in short supply in New
England was not liberty but "the spirit of Union, and the Spirit of Subjection
to Gods order."[4] While such a call for unity over liberty might sound authori-
tarian, this unity was to be constructed through accommodation among basically like-minded believers, and stood in contrast to the absolute dominion
over individual members that the Davenport faction claimed for each gathered church. With his preface to Shepard's sermon, Thacher demonstrated his
commitment to a view of the church as one among many cooperative bodies,
where disputes could be resolved by councils of churches in a spirit of compromise and harmony. This public position was the logical consequence of
the church's actions during the founding struggles, when they turned repeatedly to church councils as the proper way to resolve the frustrating disputes
with the First Church. As its first minister, Thomas Thacher established the
new church's public stance in New England religious culture, in which the
desire "to walk on in brotherly love and communion" with other orthodox
churches outweighed the abstract legal rights of a particular church over its
members.[5]

The public image of the church was created by the laity as well as by the
clergy. In developing a harmonious religious community among the orthodox, the lay people of the Third Church played two important roles. The first

was their willingness to participate in the institutional forms of inter-church cooperation. When the 1679 Reforming Synod of churches was called by the Massachusetts General Court, the South Church sent four of its lay members to attend the proceedings and paid for their expenses out of church funds.[6] By contrast, the First Church very grudgingly sent representatives to the Synod and refused to be bound by its conclusions in any way.[7] Synods were relatively rare in colonial New England, but more common formal expressions of inter-church cooperation came in the calling of councils to settle disputes within individual congregations. In April 1686, Samuel Sewall and Third Church Deacon Jacob Eliot accompanied Samuel Willard to a council in Malden, where the minister, Thomas Chiever, was dismissed for his "very scandalous Evils."[8] In cases like this one, the laity of the Third Church demonstrated their willingness to fulfill the responsibilities of inter-church fellowship, to maintain the watch and care over neighboring religious institutions that was meant to parallel the discipline provided for family, friends, and neighbors within one's own church.

In addition, the laity created a unified religious community through more casual forms of fellowship. In the routine activities of everyday life, the laity of Boston established strong connections among the town's growing number of orthodox churches. In December 1723, Samuel Sewall attended services and took the sacrament at a recently founded church, and afterwards "humbly bless[ed] GOD that I have had the Opportunity to show this Respect to Seven of the Churches of Boston."[9] During Sewall's lifetime, the number of orthodox churches in Boston rose from three to ten, as his own church went from being the "new" church to the South Church to the "Old South." In the fifty years between his own entry into full communion at the Third Church in 1677 and this act of inter-church fellowship, Sewall filled his diary with notes of his endless round of visits to other churches and his discussions with ministers and members of other churches on sermons and points of scripture. Sewall's extensive array of friends and acquaintances among the godly people of Boston shared this way of life. The steady course of fast days and thanksgivings, of funerals and marriages, of lecture days and private meetings brought the members of the various Boston churches into a collective experience of religious life that tended to minimize distinctions among individual congregations.

When Ezekiel Chiever, the Boston schoolmaster, lay on his deathbed in 1708, he was attended by Sewall despite the fact that Chiever belonged to the First Church and Sewall to the Third. After Chiever's death, the leading members of the First Church came to Sewall and "earnestly solicited me to speak to a place of Scripture at their private Quarter-Meeting in the room of Mr.

Chiever." Sewall thought it might be unsuitable "because I was not of that Meeting," but in the end he complied with their wishes.[10] In effect, the willingness of the First Church members to have Sewall participate in Chiever's funeral represents a triumph of the Third Church's vision of ecumenical fellowship. Through cooperative acts like these, the churches had come to reconcile their differences in the generation since the contentious founding of the Third Church.[11] The years of steady interaction among the membership of the orthodox churches allayed earlier fears that the liberty of individual churches would be endangered by a loosening of church boundaries, and helped to create an ecumenical religious community that linked the individual churches.

The Third Church solidified these connections by offering support to other churches and their members in distress. Life in early New England held the prospect for many calamities, and Third Church members were financially better prepared to meet them than most people. During King Philip's War, the regions of New England hit hardest by the conflict were the frontier towns that could least afford to recoup property losses or ransom families taken captive by Indians. When Mary Rowlandson was captured in a 1676 attack upon Lancaster, Massachusetts, her husband appealed to friends in Boston for aid in securing her return. After negotiations were completed for her ransom, Mary Rowlandson was thankful that "the twenty pounds, the price of my redemption, was raised by some Boston gentlemen and Mrs. Usher, whose bounty and religious charity I would not forget to make mention of." Her use of the term "redemption" implied both her physical and her spiritual salvation, for her faith was ultimately sustained as much by the cultural resources of Puritan society as by her knowledge of God's word; had she become a permanent member of her captors' society, she may have lost her religious bearings as well.[12] The identity of the "gentlemen" who purchased her redemption is unknown, but Mrs. Usher was the widow of Hezekiah Usher, a merchant, bookseller, and founder of the Third Church.[13] Later, after Mrs. Rowlandson's children had also been redeemed from captivity, the family's housing needs were supplied by charitable church members: "Our family being now gathered together, (those of us that were living), the South Church in Boston hired an house for us." Here they lived for another nine months, in a house that belonged to a member of the South Church congregation.[14] Mary Rowlandson "thought it strange to set up housekeeping with bare walls, but as Solomon says, 'Money answers all things,' and that we had through the benevolence of Christian friends." The ability of Boston's Third Church to supply money and sustenance for victims of calamity was taken to be a blessing from God, both by those who received and by those who gave.[15]

Similar acts of generosity were made on behalf of churches suffering from dramatic losses. On the night of October 2, 1711, a terrible fire swept through the center of Boston and destroyed both the Town House and the meetinghouse of the First Church.[16] The following week the Third Church held a fast, where "A Collection was made for sufferers by the Fire," and the church raised over £260 in contributions. In addition, the Third Church voted to allow the ministers of the First Church to alternate with their own minister in preaching on the sabbaths. The Brattle Street Church made a similar offer and together these two churches absorbed the displaced congregation of the First Church until their new meetinghouse was built.[17] The value of this inter-church fellowship tended to offset differences among congregations on ecclesiastical principles or specific practices. In this case, the actions of the Third and Brattle Street Churches strengthened their ties with the First Church, helped to erase the contention that had marked each of the newer church's origin, and built a sense of cooperation for a united purpose among the orthodox congregations of Boston.

The constant interaction among Boston's godly lay people, together with these occasional examples of solidarity in times of crisis, give reason to revise the emphasis historians have placed on disputes among the clergy in the later seventeenth and early eighteenth centuries. It is easy to read theological arguments as dramatic conflicts that undermined the unitary New England Way, especially when powerful and articulate ministers exchanged pamphlets that propounded hostile points of view.[18] Yet just as a dispute between Samuel Sewall and his minister Ebenezer Pemberton could be easily diffused within Boston's dense religious culture, so could arguments among the clergy of various churches diminish in importance within the context of a well-established tradition of fellowship.[19]

Several clerical and inter-church disputes of the late seventeenth century have been singled out as milestones on a road leading to the disintegration of New England's unitary Puritan culture. Chief among these are the development of "liberal" ideas in New England theology and ecclesiology and their embodiment in the Brattle Street Church in 1699, along with the clerical movement for standing bodies of ministerial consociations, the "Proposals of 1705." Undoubtedly, these issues were sources of conflict in New England's religious politics, especially among the leading ministers who argued the opposing sides. But to focus only on the conflict is to ignore the strength of forces working to accommodate change within the bounds of orthodoxy. The ministers and laity of the Third Church, as leading proponents of harmony and church fellowship, took a public stand in each of these controversies that minimized divisiveness and reinforced the potential for unity among the New England churches.

In the 1690s, several ministers and intellectuals, particularly those associ-

ated with the younger tutors at Harvard College, developed a new perspective on New England church polity, which caused a public controversy when
several Bostonians with recent connections to Harvard College formed a
new church in Brattle Square in 1699.[20] Its founders held to more "liberal"
ideas of church polity; that is, they dispensed with the church covenant and
the tradition of conversion relations as a qualification for full membership.
The new Boston church hired as its minister the young Benjamin Colman,
another recent Harvard graduate, who had been previously ordained for this
purpose by Presbyterians in England. Colman's ordination departed from
New England's traditional practice and capped a trend that had long been
developing to take the power of ordination out of the hands of laymen in the
gathered church. For Increase Mather, the new church's innovation was too
radical to be tolerated, and he responded to this (and to the similar position
taken by Solomon Stoddard in Northampton) with a series of public decla-
rations of his opposition.[21] Despite his earlier involvement in plans for unit-
ing English Presbyterians and Congregationalists, Mather was unwilling to
condone a church that embodied this development on American soil.[22]

Samuel Willard, on the other hand, took an active part on behalf of the
Third Church in drawing the Brattle Street innovators into the orthodox
Boston community. He organized a fast day at the new church in January
1700 and brought its founders together with its opponents, the Mathers and
James Allen, who was still pastor at Boston's First Church. At the fast, Willard
"pray'd God to pardon all the frailties and follies of Ministers and people; and
that they might give that Respect to the other churches that was due to them
though they were not just of their Constitution." The two Mathers then followed Willard's lead in their preaching and prayers and spoke "to the same
purpose."[23] Through Willard's judicious handling, an event that might have
split New England's religious culture was made far less divisive, and instead a
ritual mode for recognizing cooperation among members of the orthodox
community was created.[24]

The conflict over the establishment of the Brattle Street Church (or the
analogous debate between Solomon Stoddard and the Mathers over church
polity) may seem dramatic and divisive when viewed as intellectual encounters, yet in the daily lives of the members of the churches involved, these conflicts had little bearing on ordinary religious experience, and even clarified
the laity's commitment to essential principles of the faith. During the founding of the Brattle Street Church, Samuel Sewall took time to "Expostulat"
with Benjamin Colman on his objections to the new church's "Manifesto."
Colman convinced Sewall that they were basically of the same mind, but
Sewall still maintained that Colman "did not express such an Approbation of

the N.E. way as I desired: Many in England conform'd to things they profess-edly disliked." Still, the new church remained faithful to the Westminster Confession, and therefore, at the fast day for the new church, laymen from all the Boston churches attended, including "Mr. Russell, Mr. Cooke, Col. Hathorne, Sewall, Addington, Sergeant, Col. Foster, Lynde, Saffin, Em. Hutchinson, Walley, Townsend, Byfield." Just like their clerical leaders, these prominent individuals, who acted as the "hedge" around the garden of their individual churches, now joined together in their public roles to welcome a new society to the fellowship of churches. Sewall's concluding thoughts to Colman on the new church were: "If God should please by them to hold forth any Light that had not been seen or entertain'd before; I should be so far from envying it, that I should rejoice in it."[25] The course of discussion with Colman had brought him back to a founding principle of his own church, ar-ticulated in its controversial gathering thirty years before, that orthodoxy was not a rigid commitment to the forms of the past, and that further light on the nature of the true church was always possible. The "new light" that the Brattle Street Church brought to New England came in Benjamin Colman's emo-tional preaching within the confines of orthodox theology. Colman demon-strated that despite alterations in church polity, the new church could join Boston's established religious fellowship. Its members, many of them drawn from the Third Church and other Boston churches, continued to participate in local religious culture as before, and its ministers, first Colman and then William Cooper, became leading figures among the Boston clergy known es-pecially for their promotion of traditional piety.[26]

As minister of the Third Church, Samuel Willard strongly supported clerical solidarity as a way to enhance fellowship among the churches and promote orthodox piety. During his years as acting president of Harvard Col-lege (1700–1707), Willard trained a large group of future ministers who would eventually fill pulpits all across New England and form a "cortege of country support" for Willard's efforts to create new institutions for clerical coopera-tion.[27] In the last years of his life, Willard devoted himself to creating a formal system of clerical organization in New England, made necessary by the new Massachusetts Bay charter of 1691. Although the new charter technically guaranteed the liberty of Massachusetts's Puritan churches,[28] it was clear that the presence of a royally appointed governor and toleration for the Church of England would prevent the colony's government from upholding orthodoxy as it had done under the old charter.[29] In order to maintain tradition despite diminished government backing, Willard encouraged the clergy to embrace the idea of ministerial associations, to re-create on their own the "establish-ment" that the colony government no longer had the ability to support.

Opinion on the validity of ministerial associations, like most matters of Puritan ecclesiastical polity, had been subject to the constantly shifting pressure of events in both Old and New England. In England in the 1650s, the Independents' opposition to any remaining vestiges of prelacy became less urgent during the chaotic religious splintering of the Commonwealth period. Consequently, in 1655, the first Ministers' Association among English Congregationalists was formed in Cornwall, and Independents throughout England began to think of resolving their differences with Presbyterians in a number of unification attempts.[30] In New England, the question of the validity of clerical associations followed a different logic, but by the later seventeenth century, the trend toward a reconciliation between the Puritan movement's main competing factions showed greater promise of success.[31] The establishment of the Brattle Street Church proved that there was support within Massachusetts for a compromise between the Congregational and Presbyterian poles, and Solomon Stoddard's idiosyncratic version of Presbyterian polity in Northampton also demonstrated the flexibility of thought on this matter. Stoddard, the Brattle Street group, and Samuel Willard at the Third Church shared a common belief that the churches of New England, now lacking the unqualified government support which the old charter had given, required a new basis for the maintenance of orthodoxy. One solution was to be found in forming associations of ministers that would connect the orthodox churches of New England in a more organized fashion.

Early in the eighteenth century, the rudimentary association of Boston area ministers that had been meeting since 1690 created a proposal for the ecclesiastical reorganization of the colony.[32] In 1704, Willard moderated several meetings that sent circular letters to the Massachusetts churches. These letters recommended a renewed commitment by the clergy to pastoral watch, catechism, and discipline, and called for the formation of regional ministerial associations so that churches could have a forum for regular communication on matters of importance. The following September, several newly founded ministerial associations met in Boston, where Willard again moderated the meetings and drew up "The Proposals of 1705." The Proposals called for ministerial associations to review clerical candidates for orthodoxy and to encourage inter-church correspondence "so that the state of Religion may be better known and secured in all the Churches."[33] In addition, they recommended that standing councils or "consociations" of churches be formed to resolve disputes in an authoritative way. Where offending churches refused the consociation's decision, these new bodies would have the power to "excommunicate" the church as a whole from the community of faith.[34] In short, the ministerial associations proposed a strengthened position for church councils within the ecclesiastical polity of New England. Individually, none of these powers was entirely new, but the Proposals of 1705 recommended a permanent formal structure and authoritative powers which the churches themselves had previously lacked and which the Massachusetts government could no longer uphold.

Several clergymen, most notably Increase Mather and John Wise of Ipswich, wrote pamphlets attacking these clerical efforts at consolidation, and the plan was never ratified by the Massachusetts legislature.[35] But the idea behind the proposals was not a failure, for on a voluntary basis, the movement for ministerial associations throughout Massachusetts took off dramatically from this point. The associations began to engage in the activities that Willard's circular letters of 1704 had recommended, including the examination of ministerial candidates, deliberation on points of doctrine, and inquiry into the state of religion on the local level.[36] As a means of safeguarding orthodoxy and encouraging piety in the churches of Massachusetts, the association movement proved to be a successful legacy of the work of the Third Church, yet another piece in the ongoing program to encourage cooperation and unity among the Congregational churches. From its members' daily interaction with their co-religionists in Boston, to the church's negotiation of controversial subjects in Massachusetts religious politics, to these larger plans for restructuring New England's ecclesiastical polity, the Third Church consistently encouraged the growth of an ecumenical religious culture that united New England Puritans in a common cause.

The churches of New England would no longer have been identifiably "Puritan" if they did not exclude someone; a completely ecumenical culture was unthinkable. The toleration and cooperation endorsed by the Third Church had its limits, and these were nowhere more clearly defined than in its response to "wilderness" threats from outside the garden of the orthodox churches. The development of closer ties among the godly of Boston's churches was intimately connected to a growing opposition to anything that undermined New England's Puritan heritage. The connection between these two attitudes can be seen, for instance, in a small incident that took place in 1714 on the day after Christmas.

In that year, December 26 fell on a Sunday, the Puritan Sabbath. Not long before, a new Congregational church had been formed in the North End of Boston. On this Sunday, the new church celebrated communion, and

Samuel Sewall and Edward Bromfield decided to worship at the New North instead of at the Old South. Sewall recorded the day's events and his purposes in visiting the new church:

> I did it to hold Communion with that Church; and . . . to put Respect upon that affronted, despised Lord's Day. For the Church of England had the Lord's Supper yesterday, the last day of the Week: but will not have it to-day, the day that the Lord has made. And Gen'l Nicholson, who kept Satterday, was this Lord's Day Rummaging and Chittering with Wheelbarrows &c., to get aboard at the long Wharf, and Firing Guns at Setting Sail. I thank God, I heard not, saw not any thing of it: but was quiet at the New North. I did it also to Countenance a young small Church, and to shew that I was pleas'd with them for having the Lord's Supper once in four Weeks, and upon one of the Sabbaths that was vacant. Had a very comfortable Day.[37]

Sewall was disturbed that the Anglican Church had celebrated Christmas, a pagan invention in Puritan eyes, by holding communion on Saturday the 25th rather than on Sunday, the Lord's Day. General Nicholson, the Anglican military commander of royal troops in New England, chose to flaunt Boston's Puritan rules for Sabbath-keeping by laboring noisily on Sunday after attending the Christmas mass on the preceding day. Sewall, as a respected magistrate and judge, hoped to set a contrasting example of proper respect for the Sabbath by showing his support for a new church that was struggling to uphold traditional ways. The pleasure Sewall took in finding that the new church held monthly communion on a Sunday when no other Boston church did so highlights one of the benefits of inter-church cooperation. Now at least one Boston church would offer communion every Sunday of the year, and therefore orthodox church members might partake of communion on any Sabbath, a dream of evangelical ecumenicism that the Third Church members had been pursuing ever since John Davenport had arrived in Boston and reduced the frequency of the communion celebration.[38]

Rarely were the two complementary aspects of this evolving position combined so neatly as in this episode, but each aspect appears repeatedly in the behavior and attitudes of the members of Boston's Third Church. The increasing involvement of Boston in the Atlantic commercial economy brought new men and new influences into the closed Puritan world of Boston and New England. With these stronger connections to the outside world, Boston society was becoming "anglicized."[39] That is, it began to take on more characteristics of the society in which the Puritan movement originated as an oppositional culture. In the later seventeenth century, the men and women who hoped to carry the Puritan faith into future generations began to develop, for perhaps the first time in New England, an "oppositional mentality." As threats to their religious culture mounted from external sources, churches like the Third Church of Boston took the lead in encouraging the defense of traditional Puritan ways.

In the late seventeenth century, dangerous challenges to the New England Way were encroaching upon Boston society. Radical elements on the fringes of Puritan belief were not new to the second generation in New England; they had plagued the orthodox leaders of Massachusetts Bay from the colony's beginnings.[40] However, the Restoration of Charles II raised the possibility that radicals might receive official license in the form of enforced toleration. This was a new danger and required a new kind of response. Advocates of the Halfway Covenant like the Third Church members tended to allow for a certain amount of variation within orthodoxy, but they were adamantly opposed to tolerating deviant forms of belief or church organization.[41] In the 1670s, Thomas Thacher, the church's first minister, had been one of the fiercest opponents of Quaker and Baptist radicals among the clergy of New England, and the laity supported Thacher's position.[42] In December 1676, John Hull entertained Samuel Willard and Joseph Rowlandson at his home, where these refugees from the recent Indian war discussed with Hull the need for "Reformation" of society in the wake of God's calamitous judgments. The group decided that "the disorderly Meetings of Quakers and Anabaptists" had to be put down, and that "if all did agree, i.e. Magistrates and Ministers, the former might be easily suprest, and that then, The Magistrates would see reason to Handle the latter. As to what it might injure the country in respect of England, trust God with it."[43] More than twenty years later, Samuel Sewall displayed the same mentality when he voted in Council against a petition for building a Quaker Meeting House in Boston: "I oppos'd it; said I would not have a hand in setting up their Devil Worship."[44]

Quakers and Baptists continued to disturb orthodox Congregationalists in Massachusetts well into the eighteenth century, but the more serious threat to New England's religious traditions, at least from the perspective of Bostonians, was the growing Anglican presence in the colony.[45] Backed by royal governors, customs officers, and soldiers, the Church of England posed a challenge more organized and formidable than isolated groups of Baptists and Quakers could ever mount. Radicals and Anglicans were equally erroneous in the eyes of the orthodox, but in the late seventeenth and early eighteenth centuries, the Anglican challenge appeared to be more threatening.[46] In addition to (or perhaps because of) their royal patronage, the Anglicans posed a greater cultural challenge to orthodox New England. The growing prosperity of Bostonians encouraged them to display their wealth in a manner closer to the cultural style of Anglicans than to the more austere Quaker or Baptist sects. Furthermore, because the Congregational churches were attempting to resolve their own problems of establishment and authority within New England society, the Church of England seemed less distant from traditional New England practices than did the extreme sectarians who rejected establishments out of hand. In short, the challenge from the Church of England promised to be more subtle and persistent and was promoted by more powerful and pervasive forces than were the sectarian alternatives to orthodoxy.

In response, the members of Boston's orthodox churches strove to maintain their commitment to the faith by adopting a posture of opposition to the encroaching Anglican trend. Concerted efforts were made to resist the formal establishment of Common Prayer worship in Boston, but these efforts alone were not enough. The promoters of traditional Puritan ways within the Third Church found it necessary to define themselves as constant opposers of a culture hostile to their own, to remind themselves of their religious identity and affirm its distinctiveness as the New England Way.

At first, the Anglican challenge to New England orthodoxy was not very subtle at all and brought a dramatic response from Boston's Puritan churches. Early in the 1680s, Samuel Willard preached a number of public sermons in which he reminded his listeners of their important place in the worldwide Protestant cause, currently facing setbacks on many fronts including the encroachments of the crown on their own colony. "When you hear how God's cause is the present suffering cause, and seems to go down the wind," said Willard, "so much bloodshed in one place, so much powerful adversary in another, be not now distressed." The remedy for these setbacks was the certainty of God's promise to his covenanted people. Willard encouraged New Englanders to renew their church covenants in a sincere and faithful manner, and called on the colony's magistrates to enforce strict adherence to orthodoxy. Specifically, he urged the prevention of Quaker, Baptist, and Common Prayer worship as well as enforcement of moral laws and scrupulous observation of the Sabbath.[47]

The arrival of Edward Randolph in 1680 as royal customs collector began a long series of events that pointed ominously toward the revocation of the Massachusetts Bay Charter of 1629, the bulwark of the colony's religious independence. In October 1683, news arrived that a writ of *quo warranto* had been issued, but the king announced that if Massachusetts would submit the charter for revision, the colony could avoid legal proceedings and keep its charter in an altered form.[48] The Massachusetts General Court divided over whether to submit to revision or stand fast against any alteration. The ministers of the Boston area met at Samuel Willard's house for a day of fasting and deliberation. Most were in favor of submitting the charter to the king, "so the

Essentialls of the patent might be continued."[49] The ministers believed the liberty of the churches could be retained under a modified form of colonial self-government. Increase Mather, however, disagreed on this political strategy, and preached against it before the Boston town meeting.[50] Willard sided with the majority of the clergy, but to no avail, as the General Court rejected the king's offer of revision. Edward Randolph returned to England with this news, and the threatened legal proceedings were carried out. The Massachusetts Bay Company's charter was revoked on October 23, 1684, making way for its replacement by a new royal government, the Dominion of New England.[51]

Following the charter's downfall, the first efforts to establish an Anglican church in Boston were conducted with a remarkable lack of sensitivity to the strength of New England's religious culture. In May 1686, Edward Randolph returned to Boston with an Anglican minister named Robert Ratcliffe and immediately instituted Common Prayer worship. Ratcliffe asked the Massachusetts Council for the use of one of Boston's Puritan meetinghouses, but the Council denied this request and offered the east room of the Town House as a substitute. When Edmund Andros, the permanent royal governor, arrived later in 1686, the struggle intensified. Samuel Willard and Increase Mather informed the new governor that his request to use one of Boston's churches was out of the question. But after holding Anglican worship at the Town House for several months, Andros decided in March 1687 that these arrangements were unsatisfactory. As Easter approached, Andros took over the meetinghouse of the Third Church by force. The decision to invade Willard's church was partly based on the building's convenient location and recent construction, but the vigor of Willard's and the Third Church laity's opposition further encouraged Andros to humble this particular church. Consequently, the Third Church's large congregation had to share their meetinghouse with a paltry number of Anglicans, who frequently kept the members standing in the streets waiting for Common Prayer service to end.[52]

Willard could not prevent Andros from seizing the meetinghouse, but he led the Third Church's opposition to Anglican inroads on Puritan culture. He disregarded Andros's orders prohibiting fast days and continued to call them for his own church, and he denounced the Anglican practice of swearing on the Bible which the new royal government had introduced into the courts.[53] On May 20, 1688, Willard preached from the text, "Ye have not resisted unto blood, striving against sin," which Sewall noted in the context of other comments on the Anglican takeover of their meetinghouse.[54] In addition, Willard initiated his innovative series of catechetical lectures early in 1688, shortly after the beginning of Anglican worship in Boston. Although the course of these sermons followed the logic of the Westminster Shorter Catechism, Willard found ways to apply doctrine to current events. On April 23, 1689 (five days after the overthrow of Andros), Willard reminded his listeners of "how very unsuitable it is to represent the Divine Nature by any corporeal similitude; I mean in Pictures or Images," and of "the unlawfulness of imposing upon men stinted forms of prayer and publick service to God because indeed it is not to God, but against him." The obvious criticisms of Anglican worship suggest the public and political nature of these ostensibly abstract theological expositions.[55]

The Third Church laity responded to the Anglican takeover of the meetinghouse in their customary fashion, by forming a committee to address the governor. The committee included the church deacons, Jacob Eliot and Theophilus Frary, along with Nathaniel Oliver, Ephraim Savage, Benjamin Davis, and Samuel Sewall. The laymen brought Andros the original deed of the church property to demonstrate that the meetinghouse was privately owned and could not be seized by the government without consent. Andros ignored their claims to ownership and forced the Third Church sexton to open the meetinghouse for Anglican worship on Good Friday, 1687. In case anyone doubted the sincerity of his intentions, the governor threatened the members with thinly veiled references to the massacre of French Protestants who had refused to yield to royal demands.[56]

In response to the hostile occupation of their meetinghouse, the Third Church members declared their open animosity to the Church of England and its institutions. When Anglicans attempted to buy land in Boston on which to build their own meetinghouse, Sewall refused even to hear the idea, especially when they offered to purchase the site on which John Cotton's home had once stood. In the context of this conflict, real estate became sacred space to be defended against profane violators. The women of the church were also emboldened to express their opposition to Andros's takeover. Mrs. Anna Joyliffe and Mrs. Dorcas Grecian sought out Andros to "expostulat with Him about his Design," but to no avail. Andros even had the gall to solicit contributions from Third Church members toward the building of an Anglican chapel, figuring that wealthy and generous merchants would gladly give money if it would free their church from the imposition of Common Prayer services. Surprised by the Puritans' refusal to contribute to this effort, Andros inartfully complained of "folks backwardness to give, and the unreasonableness; because if any stinking filthy thing were in the House [they] would give something to have it carried out, but would not give to build them an house." Besides being an unflattering description of his own form of worship, Andros's statement reveals how badly he underestimated the tenacity of the Puritan

oppositional mentality. The Third Church laity preferred to suffer the indignity of an illegal invasion of their own church's property rather than pay for
the legal establishment of a form of worship they abhorred.[57]

The laity also opposed the introduction of high church ritual into public
life, sometimes at great personal cost. Upon the death of Edward Lilley, a
prominent local merchant, in the winter of 1688/89, the Anglican minister
attempted to read the Common Prayer funeral service at the burial, despite
the wishes of the family, who "Unanimously informed him that it would be
very Offensive to them to be so Imposed upon therein." When Ratcliffe persisted, Theophilus Frary, deacon of the Third Church, came forward and attempted to stop him, and "with fitt words desired him to for-bare." Frary was
arrested and threatened with stiff fines for his actions. Had the rebellion of
April 1689 not occurred, Frary would have been financially ruined as pun-
ishment for his act of defiance. One concerned Bostonian asked, "What does
the proclamation for liberty of Conscience doe, if such impositions are allowed! This is a very tremendous thing to us."[58]

When rebellion against Andros eventually broke out in April 1689,
Samuel Willard and many members of the Third Church joined with prominent laymen from other Boston churches in united opposition to Andros's au-
thoritarian rule. With Increase Mather away in England attempting to negotiate a new charter, Samuel Willard was the most prominent minister in Boston
during the uprising, which followed upon the news of William of Orange's
successful invasion of England and the overthrow of James II.[59] Among the
Third Church membership, Simon Bradstreet, Peter Sergeant, John Joyliffe,
Wait Winthrop, Nathaniel Oliver, John Eyre, and Andrew Belcher played important roles on the Committee of Public Safety that overthrew Andros and
acted as an interim government until a new charter was acquired. Samuel
Sewall was away in London at the time; otherwise, he undoubtedly would have
joined his fellow members of the "hedge" around the garden of the church in
this moment of crisis.

The rebellion had causes beyond the underlying religious issues, but its
outcome served to galvanize and clarify Bostonians' allegiance to New England's religious culture. During the period of provisional government before
the new charter arrived in 1691, Willard continued to preach against "formal
worship" and delivered a sermon expressly intended to discourage Anglican
religious culture from persisting after the overthrow of its political backing.[60]
The Third Church laity gave strong support to Willard's leadership during
the crisis. Some church members like Theophilus Frary were active opposers
of the Andros regime. Others found that the political crisis helped them confirm their religious and cultural allegiances. Two members of the Committee

of Public Safety, Waitstill Winthrop and Peter Sergeant, had long-standing but still somewhat ambiguous connections to the Third Church before the rebellion. Neither was a full member of the church, but Winthrop had joined under the baptismal covenant ten years earlier, and Sergeant appears to have attended the Third Church since his arrival as an immigrant from London in 1677. Both men were among the wealthier Bostonians of the time, and their fortunes, their business contacts, and their personal tastes aligned them closely with the royalist merchants who were beginning to enter Boston society.[61] Yet the dramatic events of 1689 convinced them of their devotion to the traditional culture of Puritan New England. In the summer of 1689, only a few months after the rebellion, both men were moved to give public accounts of their conversion experiences and join the Third Church in full communion. They took this important step in their spiritual lives long before the crown gave its approval to the actions of the insurgent colonists, at a time when it was uncertain what fate the rebels would suffer at the hands of the new monarchy.[62] To join the Third Church in the summer of 1689 was not a matter of expediency. Winthrop and Sergeant expressed their commitment to the Puritan oppositional mentality that appeared in the church's stance against Andros's invasion and that propelled the successful overthrow of the Dominion of New England.[63]

Although the overthrow of Andros was ultimately ratified by the crown, the new charter that Increase Mather negotiated for the colony mandated a royally appointed governor for the colony. The Church of England, which had established a foothold in Boston under the Andros administration, now gained the sanction of official toleration under the new charter. In the years following the rebellion against Andros, dramatic confrontation gradually gave way to intermittent cultural strife between those devoted to traditional Puritan beliefs, morals, and behavior, and the growing number of Bostonians indifferent to, unconnected with, or opposed to the Puritan way of life. This ongoing hostility bore an interesting resemblance to the conflicts between Puritans and the ungodly majority in the early Stuart period in England.[64] During the reign of James I, the English Puritan movement, forced underground by a hostile monarch, turned from the politics of ecclesiastical reform to the cultivation of godly living and behavior among the masses. This program of reform caused friction between Puritans and those who resented the demanding, disciplined and exclusive culture of the godly, and this friction further served to reinforce the Puritans' sense of distinctiveness. Similarly, the conflict in provincial Boston between Puritans and Anglicans helped those of the Puritan persuasion maintain their own distinct identity as a godly people, and reminded them of their connections to their Puritan ancestors who founded Massachusetts. Of course, the terms of this conflict were reversed from the days of the first King James—New England's Puritans remained a dominant majority as they fought off Anglican encroachments. Yet the memory of former conflicts, the sense of connection to a Puritan past, added to the ritualistic process by which these latter-day Puritans developed symbolic ways to maintain distinctions between two cultures that were in danger of blurring together. Puritans demonstrated their discontent with the presence of Anglican rituals or practices in Boston, often by removing themselves from or speaking out against circumstances they considered offensive. They also responded vigorously to assaults on their own way of life from new and hostile forces within the society. Just as in the Third Church's founding when its leaders had manipulated symbols of New England's religious tradition to establish their commitment to orthodoxy, now in the struggle against the Church of England the Third Church members cultivated a symbolic opposition to a "profane" and "ungodly" culture.

The establishment of Anglican worship introduced new public rituals previously unknown in Massachusetts Bay. The weekly Common Prayer service remained enclosed within the walls of the newly constructed King's Chapel, largely unseen by Puritans attending their own churches on the Sabbath. But other Anglican "superstitions" took place in public and could not be ignored by their Puritan detractors. Funeral services, like the one which brought Theophilus Frary into danger early in 1689, frequently became settings for religious antagonism. On August 28, 1708, Sarah Taylor, the late wife of Col. William Taylor, was buried. Taylor was a devoted member of King's Chapel and eventually became Lieutenant Governor of the colony, but both he and his wife had family connections to members of the Puritan churches. The late Mrs. Taylor was the daughter of Nathaniel Byfield, a "dissenter" and author of an account of grievances against Edmund Andros's government.[65] The funeral was attended by notables from both parties, and the burial itself took place in Dorchester at the family tomb of William Stoughton, another stalwart of the "dissenting" Puritan culture. Yet at the grave, the King's Chapel minister read the Common Prayer service. Samuel Sewall saw this as "an Indignity and affront done to Mr. Stoughton and his Friends," and refused to enter the burying place, as did John Leverett, the newly installed president of Harvard College. While this was a minor protest on the part of Sewall and Leverett, it nonetheless marked their desire to keep Anglican ritual separate from places sacred to their own religious culture. Four days later, Sewall had the misfortune to repeat this form of protest. Nathaniel Byfield's other daughter, Mrs. Deborah Lyde, died suddenly, and rather than risk encountering another Common Prayer funeral, Sewall slipped away from the burial party. In

Sewall's eyes, the Anglican funeral rite was "a Lying, very bad office; makes no difference between the precious and the vile."[66] For those of Sewall's persuasion, separating the precious from the vile was becoming an increasingly necessary part of living a godly life in Boston.[67]

Leading members of the Third Church held positions in the royal government, and the rituals of state sometimes competed with their allegiance to Puritan ways and forced them to defend their religious culture. Such was the case when the Governor encouraged the members of the Council to drink toasts to the health of the Queen on her birthday, forcing men like Sewall and Bromfield to stay home or to attend "Mr. Willard's Catechising Lecture" instead.[68] On another occasion, Bromfield, Sewall, and Aeneas Salter entered a Boston tavern to stop the drinking of healths on the Queen's birthday, which happened to fall on the eve of the Sabbath when all such carousing was outlawed. The most vehement member of the offending party was one "John Netmaker, Gent." Netmaker was fined for publicly cursing the constable's assistant, who refused to drink the Queen's health. When arrested, Netmaker expressed contempt for the charges and refused to cooperate with the legal proceedings, so Bromfield and Sewall ordered him thrown in prison. However, John Netmaker happened to be the private secretary to General Francis Nicholson, who demanded Netmaker's release. Ultimately, the Governor coerced the Council to countermand Sewall and Bromfield's order, but the more devout members of the Puritan party "were hardly drawn to it," and Waitstill Winthrop refused to comply altogether.[69] The controversy came to a peaceable ending, but it served as another marker of the differences between these two cultures.

In many cases, these cultural distinctions were maintained by more subtle actions. With the introduction in the 1680s of the Anglican celebration of Christmas, Puritan Bostonians developed their own ritualistic non-observance of this "pagan" holiday. At the height of Andros's tyranny, the royal government went so far as to shut Boston shops on Christmas and to drive the town schoolmaster out of the school for a forced Christmas holiday.[70] But in the years after the overthrow of Andros, Sewall would note with pleasure in his diary that on December 25, "shops open and business carried on as at other times" (1691), or that "Carts of Pork, Hay, Coal, Wood come to Town as on other days" (1694). While business within the town went on as usual, families used the occasion to create an anti-Christmas ritual. During the Sewall family's daily devotions on December 25, 1697, Sewall "took occasion to dehort mine from Christmas-keeping, and charged them to forbear." His son Joseph, the future minister of the Third Church, told Sewall "that most of the Boys went to the Church [i.e., to King's Chapel to see the Christmas mass], yet he went not." As a reward for this pious obedience, Mrs. Sewall suggested that Joseph be allowed to read the Psalm for the day, which his brother graciously conceded.[71] Seventeen years later, Joseph Sewall "expostulated" with his own family about forbearing from the celebration of Christmas. This ritual of avoidance remained intact in New England into the nineteenth century, and further served to set the heirs of Puritan culture apart from the new Anglican element.[72]

The importance of these forms of cultural differentiation can be seen in their continuing impact on New Englanders, even on those who went abroad and experienced English culture first-hand. Thomas Prince's cosmopolitan experiences in England and direct exposure to Anglican culture only confirmed his commitment to the New England Way. Although curiosity and a sense of wonder encouraged him to attend London theatres and visit the "stupendous church of St. Paul's," his New England training eventually placed him among English dissenters and drew him back to his rightful home in Boston.[73] All in all, Boston's more traditional Puritans developed a variety of oppositional responses to the Anglican presence within their society and the "anglicizing" influence of the Atlantic commercial economy, ranging from the non-celebration of Christmas to the effort to prevent ship captains who entered the harbor after sundown on Saturday from blowing their trumpets and disrupting the Sabbath.[74] Even customs that were not essential to Anglican belief but were part of the more relaxed or "indifferent" culture of Anglican society met with opposition from Puritan church members. After a Thursday lecture in November 1716, two laymen, "Mr. Welsteed and Capt. Wadsworth," informed Sewall and Bromfield that the organist of King's Chapel was hosting a dance, and asked them "to prevent the Gov'r being there." Andrew Belcher joined Sewall and Bromfield in their consultations with the newly arrived Governor Shute, who finally agreed not to attend out of respect for Puritan custom. In return, they rewarded the Governor with the gift of a beef.[75]

Puritan hostility to Anglican culture was not always met with the cordiality Governor Shute displayed. At times, Anglican newcomers lashed out against the godly, which reinforced the Puritans' sense of solidarity in their animosity toward this culture. On April 23, 1706, the military guard appointed to attend the royal governor decided to celebrate St. George's Day and rode into Boston with crosses fixed to their hats. Out of contempt for this Anglican custom, someone in the crowd attached a cross to the head of a dog. When the column of soldiers rode by, the Governor's boatswain was so angered by the impious dog that he struck it down, then entered the nearest shop and assaulted the first person he saw, a carpenter who was innocently minding his work. The boatswain was arrested and fined ten shillings by Judge Jeremiah Dummer, a devout member of the First Church.[76]

Other attacks from opposers to Puritan ways were less violent but just as divisive. One morning in 1699, Sewall awoke to find playing cards strewn across the ground in front of his house, retaliation for his having broken up a card game in a tavern the previous Saturday night. In February 1712, the "monstrously profane" John Green performed a mockery of a Puritan sermon on the Anglicans' Shrove Tuesday, then had the mock sermon printed and scattered about the town. Five years later, on the day when the dedication of the meetinghouse of the New South Church was to take place, a sarcastic poem was found nailed to all three doors of the building, which called the members of the church a "Canting Crew" of "sower-headed Presbyterians."[77] Attacks upon traditional culture from new elements made Puritans aware on a daily basis that they no longer had complete authority over New England society. Especially in urban centers like Boston, these challenges would become increasingly prevalent and would require constant resistance. Yet the awareness of this opposition could and did serve to strengthen the commitment and solidarity of those who remained devoted to traditional religious beliefs and customs.

In 1722, when several members of the Yale College faculty announced their conversion to the Church of England, the Boston churches responded by coming together to bewail this event. A fast was held at the Old North Church. Cotton and Increase Mather preached and prayed, as did Benjamin Colman. Though these men stood at opposite ends of the ecclesiastical spectrum *within* orthodox Congregationalism and had been enemies in 1699 when the Brattle Street Church was formed, they came together in cooperation against a much more tangible threat to the New England Way and ignored their differences in favor of collective opposition to the Church of England. In so doing, they demonstrated the intimate connection between the growth of an ecumenical culture of orthodoxy in provincial New England and the posture of opposition toward those religious elements that could not be tolerated or included within traditional definitions of Puritan identity. The result was a religious culture that was simultaneously critical of outsiders and supportive of its own, a mentality that explains the dual purposes of Samuel Sewall and Edward Bromfield's attendance at communion in the New North Church on the day after Christmas, 1714.

ﻌﯽﯖ

If the culture of godliness were to maintain its dominion over New England and prevent the encroachment of Anglicans and radicals, then the Puritan church would have to expand into new areas and convert the wilderness of the world into the Lord's garden. The principle behind the Halfway Covenant's broadened scope for baptism pointed in this direction. If more of the population of any region was baptized and subjected to church discipline, then the souls of more potential saints would receive the necessary cultivation to bear spiritual fruit. In the later years of the seventeenth century and in the early decades of the eighteenth, the Third Church laity gradually realized that their material wealth made it possible to sponsor missionary activities to unchurched peoples and regions of New England. The membership of the church found new and more systematic ways to ensure that all of New England, and not just a declining remnant of the first gathered churches, would become and remain a godly people.

As home to the Massachusetts General Court and to the richest men in New England, Boston had long been seen as the place for distressed settlers in outlying regions to find aid and relief. When Indian wars, natural disasters, or crop failures struck rural communities, the victims turned to the colony's metropolis for financial and spiritual assistance. Even in ordinary circumstances, when a new frontier town needed to hire a minister, the natural tendency for the pioneer inhabitants was to send a messenger to Boston for advice from the leading ministers about an appropriate candidate, as when Thomas Dewey was sent by the town of Westfield to recruit Edward Taylor. But as the seventeenth century wore on, Bostonians realized they possessed the ability to do more than give sporadic aid to people in distress or respond to requests from those in need of assistance. Leaders in the Boston religious community began to examine new ways to broaden the reach of their religious culture. They found methods to extend the "plenitude of means" they had developed within their own local society to people previously untouched by a godly way of life, or to places lacking the resources to sustain godliness on their own. From unorganized and piecemeal beginnings in the later seventeenth century, this impulse gradually took the form of a program of missionary expansion of orthodox religious culture among "unchurched" people throughout New England.

This effort was aimed largely at two distinct groups, the Indian population of New England that was yet to be organized into praying towns, and the remote, frontier, or heterodox regions of English settlement that were unlikely to gather and maintain orthodox churches of their own accord, although the poor and downtrodden of their own community received attention and nurture as well. Members of Boston's Third Church played a major role through their financial and personal contributions to the cause. They provided material resources and energetic leadership to this program of outreach through their support of missionaries, their publication and distribution of Bibles and pious books, and their personal involvement in the over-sight of these programs.

Much of the early work for the conversion of Indians to Christianity was funded and directed by the New England Company, an English corporation chartered in 1649 by the Long Parliament, which raised and invested money to pay missionaries in America. Its directors were English Protestants of a dissenting cast of mind, and its missionary endeavors were overseen in America by the Commissioners of the United Colonies, the military organization that linked Plymouth, Massachusetts, Connecticut, and New Haven. The Commissioners were responsible for distributing the funds sent over by the New England Company. In the early years, funds were raised by requesting contributions from parish churches throughout England, based on the implicit assumption that the newly founded churches of New England were too poor to carry out this work for themselves. Indeed, the most active of the New England missionaries, John Eliot of Roxbury, not only received support for his efforts from the Company, but also sought financial aid independently by writing pleading letters to wealthy friends and associates in England. For the first half century of New England's settlement, then, most of the missionary work toward the Indian population was carried out by a few extraordinarily devoted individuals, associated with and financed by New England Company funds. The Company not only paid the salaries of missionaries, but also provided money for printing Indian translations of the Bible and other pious works produced by Eliot and his colleagues.[78]

In the later years of the seventeenth century, however, the maturation of the New England economy gave local churches a wider range of resources, and in turn, the laity of New England churches began to contribute to the New England Company's efforts and to sponsor their own independent aid to missionaries. Several members of the Third Church took on significant roles in the New England Company in the late seventeenth and early eighteenth centuries. Samuel Sewall kept the business records for the company, recording the disbursement of the Company's money as well as the contributions made by New Englanders to the general fund.[79] Sewall also played a major role in the Company's ongoing publication of the Bible and pious tracts translated into Indian languages, though it made him unusually fearful of the prospect of fire, as his house was filled with "Hundreds of Reams" of the paper necessary for this enormous publishing enterprise. In addition, Peter Sergeant, Anthony Stoddard, and Daniel Oliver took on the duty of overseeing the work of the Company's missionaries, and of appointing suitable individuals, usually young college graduates, to bring the gospel into new areas.[80]

But the contributions to missionary work made possible by the church's

growing resources went much further than this, and can best be seen by examining the career of one of the many missionaries of the early eighteenth
century, men whose work was not famous or groundbreaking like that of John
Eliot, but who were vital links in the ongoing effort to spread the New England Way to the natives of New England. One such missionary was Joseph
Seccombe, who was born in Boston in 1706, the son of Mehitable Seccombe,
an Old South Church member. Joseph showed intellectual promise and was
also a pious youth; he joined the South Church in full communion at the early
age of seventeen. However, his father was poor and Joseph would have received little formal education were it not for his family's affiliation with the
church. Over the years, the church developed the practice of collecting
money on occasional fast and thanksgiving days for charitable purposes. In
March 1726, the church voted to formalize this practice to create a fund "to
be bestowed on pious uses, for the advancement of Christ's Kingdom among
the poor and other proper objects of such a Charity." Edward Bromfield and
Daniel Oliver, together with the church deacons, were appointed the first
trustees of this "Evangelical Treasury."[81] Given his talent and early piety,
Joseph Seccombe seemed like a natural candidate for this charity and was
among its first recipients. In June 1726, the church paid for him to board with
a minister, Samuel Wigglesworth of Ipswich Hamlet, for preparatory study.
Two years later, Seccombe entered Harvard College, where his tuition and
expenses were paid in large part by the South Church, supplemented with a
Hollis Scholarship from the college.[82]

After graduation, Seccombe taught school in Ipswich for a short time
but was quickly recruited for missionary work. In 1731, Benjamin Colman of
the Brattle Street Church was commissioned by the Scottish Society for
Propagating Christian Knowledge to appoint three missionaries on its behalf. Joseph Seccombe was the first to come forward and offer his services,
and that winter he sailed for Fort St. George's in Maine, where he became
chaplain to the military garrison as well as missionary to the local Indians. His
expenses were paid by the Edinburgh Society and supplemented by contributions from the Third Church. He learned to speak the local Indian language and began his mission work in the traditional New England style,
which involved not only preaching but the attempt to "civilize" Indians with
instruction in English, reading, writing, and arithmetic.[83] After nearly two
years at Fort St. George's, Seccombe and the two other appointees of the Edinburgh SPCK were called back to Boston for ordination in a public ceremony at the Old South Church, presided over by Joseph Sewall.[84] The efforts of these missionaries, publicized by this ceremony and by reports in the
New England Weekly Journal, brought popular acclaim which led to further

charitable contributions from New Englanders and from interested English supporters. Seccombe remained in his post as a missionary for four more years, battling with French Jesuit missionaries over the souls of the native population, before finally taking a more tranquil position in Kingston, New Hampshire.[85] Without the South Church's charitable fund, the education and preparation of Joseph Seccombe to conduct this work would have been impossible.[86]

In addition to Indian missionary work, the Third Church supported the spread of the gospel to unchurched regions of English settlement in New England. While conversion of Indians received much attention from interested parties and organizations in England, there was no institutional support for the spread of the gospel among English settlers. Each New England settlement was technically responsible for providing religious instruction to its own people, but the poverty of rural life often made it difficult to maintain even minimal support for a minister in the newer frontier towns. Furthermore, from the point of view of Massachusetts orthodoxy, there were whole regions of New England suffering in darkness for lack of the right kind of religious instruction. Most offensive in this light was the colony of Rhode Island, where a growing number of orthodox people were beginning to settle in search of economic and commercial opportunity.[87] In addition to Rhode Island, the remote frontiers of New England harbored many settlers who had minimal ties to Puritan orthodoxy or who actively favored radical sects or the Church of England. And the poor or transient people right in Boston were also in danger of slipping through the safety net of orthodox religious instruction. In the early decades of the eighteenth century, the Third Church used its material resources to cultivate gardens of piety in these several kinds of wilderness.

Among the poor of Boston, the church took to using the charitable fund established in 1726 as a way to provide religious instruction to those who might otherwise miss out. The church vote which established the "Evangelical Treasury" called for the overseers to help the poor "by putting into their hands Bibles, Catechisms and other Books of piety; or by promoting Religion among them any other way as you shall agree and determine."[88] Although newly established as a formal practice of the church, this vote merely regularized what the public-spirited laity had been doing privately for years. More innovative was the use of this treasury for the support of ministers in outlying frontier towns. The Third Church members had always been quick to provide aid for fellow religionists suffering from unexpected calamities, but now they began to commit their charitable funds to the permanent support of clergymen and churches that could not afford to keep a minister any other way. In the wake of the establishment of this permanent fund, the church regularly disbursed money to newly settled towns like Ashford, Easton, and Dunstable.[89]

Still more ambitious was the effort of the Boston laity to gather and support churches in Rhode Island, where traditional hostility to Massachusetts orthodoxy prevented the establishment of any Congregational church throughout the seventeenth century. The first Congregational missionary to Rhode Island to receive aid from the Boston churches was Nathaniel Clap, a Harvard graduate of the class of 1690. In January 1695/6, with the advice of the ministers of Boston, Clap went to Newport and began preaching to the few Congregationalists who had established residences there.[90] Over the next two decades, Clap received steady encouragement and support from the Boston churches. When Samuel Sewall visited Bristol County, Massachusetts, on his judicial circuit rounds, he made special efforts to stop in nearby Newport, visit Clap, and distribute supplies of pious books.[91] On other occasions, delegations of Boston clergy and laymen would visit to lend their support to the minister and encourage him to gather his congregation into a formal church, which finally occurred in November 1720. When conflict over communion privileges and admissions practices divided the Newport congregation in 1728, the Boston churches sent a council of ministers and laymen to intervene and resolve the dispute.[92]

Once the Newport church was established, other Rhode Island towns followed, and these received further and more direct financial aid from Boston. In March 1728, the South Church voted to provide £20 to Josiah Cotton, another recent Harvard graduate, to "encourage his settlement at Providence," where he had received a call from the local Congregationalists to preach.[93] Cotton accepted and within a few months had prepared for a day of ordination and church gathering, which drew a large crowd of interested clergy and laity from Boston and the surrounding area. Third Church minister Thomas Prince presided over the ordination, which was attended by more than a thousand people, including many Rhode Island dissenters curious to see the establishment of this new church in their midst. Josiah Cotton remained in Providence and continued to receive much of his salary from the Old South Church's Evangelical Treasury.[94] Similarly, when a colleague for Nathaniel Clap was ordained in Newport in 1732, Joseph Sewall and many fellow Third Church members attended and Sewall prayed at the ordination service.[95] In 1738, the South Church, in addition to its usual contributions, provided £60 and some expert legal advice in order to defend the rights of the Rev. Samuel Torrey, the Congregational minister in Kingston, Rhode Island. An Anglican minister had brought a lawsuit claiming that only a person ordained by a bishop could receive the support of lands that had been set aside by Congregationalists for an "orthodox" minister. In Massachusetts, the definition of orthodoxy as "Puritan" would have been unambiguous, but in Rhode Island, the Congregationalists needed vigorous support from Boston churches to defend themselves in a case eventually decided by the crown in Torrey's favor.[96]

The Third Church's efforts to reach out and bring new people and regions of New England under the influence of the means of grace culminated in these various forms of missionary work. Together with the development of an ecumenical religious culture among the godly and the defense of the faith against heterodox challenges, the program of outreach completed the Third Church's work of preparing New England society for conversion and revivals. The internal life of the church, nurtured by the clergy and by the lay leadership, was designed to cultivate a revivalist mentality within the church, and now the public life of the church spread this impulse outward in an ever larger and denser network of evangelical religion.

In the progress toward salvation, an individual's inner life was mirrored by his or her outer life. On the road to the celestial city, Bunyan's Pilgrim learns to cultivate godly associates, to defend himself against enemies, and to realize the Christian's evangelical calling.[97] In its public life, the Third Church of Boston turned the resources and purposes that had sustained its inner development outward to New England society at large. The church members cultivated a community of godliness, battled against opponents of orthodox Puritanism, and extended their hands to convert more of the "wilderness" into a "garden." The ultimate aim of this extensive preparatory work was to unite the individual believer, the gathered church, and society as a whole in a common progress toward salvation. Within the Third Church, in Boston itself, and throughout much of New England at large, the results of long years of preparation, begun with the Halfway Covenant and fueled by the overflow of resources from Boston's commercial economy, would soon emerge in the experience of the Great Awakening.

CHAPTER 8

" . . . With Solid Walls of Discipline"

The church had another leader besides me to rule them.
—Edward Taylor, Westfield Church Records (1713)

Compared with the Third Church of Boston, Westfield's Puritan church can hardly be said to have had a "public life." The reclusiveness of its minister virtually guaranteed that few of its actions would be known beyond the confines of the town, and with its limited resources, the church was in no position to reach out beyond its garden walls to provide charity to anyone but its own. The extent of the church's public role was therefore confined to the town of Westfield and manifested itself principally in the attempt to regulate public behavior through the exercise of church discipline.

Discipline was a fundamental element of any Puritan church. Along with preaching, public prayer, and the administration of the sacraments, discipline was one of the ordinances that defined the church and gave it its special character as a godly institution. When properly applied, discipline was useful in correcting church members who had gone astray and in maintaining the harmonious relations that were appropriate to a body of persons in communion with Christ. Discipline also shaped the church's relationship to the outside world by regulating its members' actions in the community at large and by making church fellowship an attractive model to those outside its walls. To achieve these goals, the lay people and ministers of a church had to share a common vision of the godly life, because the work of church discipline, while formally in the hands of the church elders, required the participation and consent of the members. Without this cooperation, church discipline could degenerate from a fundamental basis for the church's existence into a direct threat to its continuity. At its worst, a poorly applied disciplinary sanction could alienate individual members, divide a community, undermine a minister's authority, and even poison a church's relationship with other churches and with the outside world.[1]

In these terms, the records of a church's disciplinary cases can be read as a measure of the health of the religious community, judging not by the quantity or the nature of particular offenses in disciplinary cases, but by the church members' ability to resolve conflict in a peaceable and mutually satisfactory way. In most early New England churches, the worst-case scenario of church discipline gone wrong was seldom played out. Ministers and lay people usually cooperated to define standards that kept order in the church and disciplined individual members without dividing the community. For much of Edward Taylor's tenure at the Westfield church, this generalization holds true. The majority of the disciplinary cases that Taylor recounted in his "Church Records" were ordinary examples of sinful behavior on the part of one of the church members. In these cases, everyone, including the offender, agreed on what the sin had been, why it was wrong, and how to rectify matters through confession and conciliation.

Nevertheless, the tensions in Westfield's religious community that were present from the founding of the church gradually began to emerge in the details of successive disciplinary cases. As time went by, conflict within the community, often involving scarce material or cultural resources, began to affect the church in ways that the church became increasingly incapable of resolving, in large part because of the growing division between Taylor and the laity over participation in and control of the church. As a result, the religious community of Westfield slowly degenerated into conflict among members, between the membership and Taylor, and between the Westfield church and the other churches of the Connecticut Valley. A close reading of Taylor's records of the disciplinary cases, beginning with a review of the early cases where the community's inner conflicts begin to emerge, followed by a detailed examination of a traumatic case in the early eighteenth century when the community was seriously disrupted, demonstrates how the conflicting expectations for a godly life held by Edward Taylor and the laity, when exacerbated by the limited material and cultural resources of this rural town, undermined the Puritan religious community in Westfield.

～❧～

Edward Taylor began recording disciplinary cases in 1682, three years after the foundation of the church. The people of Westfield had "scarcely slipt into the Temple Doore before the Adversary [Satan] had brought us to the need of this Corrosive," that is, the censures of the church. As Taylor described it, even converted Saints are still "but part flesh; & that Satan by his poysonous darts doth oft make it ranckle & grow proud Flesh." Human pride and sinfulness required "Sensures of the Church to take it down, thereby to recover the Poore Soule from his wound," and "also to keep the Holy Place Clean from being defiled by unclean ones."[2] The language here is typical of Taylor's view of the church and the human condition; it contrasts the diseased state of the individual sinner with the need for purity in the gathered church. Taylor's record of disciplinary cases was thus in his own view a continuing report on the health and purity of Westfield's religious body.[3]

For most of its first two decades, the church was virtually self-regulating in disciplinary matters; the members maintained its good health with little need for Taylor's intervention. The eight cases recorded for the period between 1682 and 1697 tend to deal with economic or social behavior among church members that was dishonest, immoral, or caused offense to others, behavior brought to the church's attention by the aggrieved parties. The first recorded case involved Lt. John Mawdsley, one of the founding pillars of the church. Mawdsley attempted to take advantage of the "New Modelling" of town land in the late 1670s and acquire an undeserved land grant by sending a petition couched in half-truths to the Massachusetts General Court. But when the General Court referred the matter to the Hampshire County Court, suspicions in Westfield were raised, and a copy of the petition was attained and read to the Westfield church members' meeting. The church formed a committee "to gather up the offences therein Contained, & present them to the Church as offences, & to treat Brother Mawdsly about the same."[4] Mawdsley had temporarily moved back to Windsor, Connecticut, but he was still a Westfield church member and was dealt with as such. He responded to the charges by confessing his guilt and his heartfelt repentance, and renounced the false claims by which he had hoped to gain special favor. Taylor was required to step in only to make a clear statement of where Mawdsley's offenses fell within the ten commandments, and to propound Mawdsley's confession to the church members, who acknowledged their acceptance "& the Confirming of their Love to him by a lifting up of their hands."[5]

Most of the other cases in this period involved similar offenses and were handled as simply. Thomas Dewey, Josiah Dewey's brother and the man who had recruited Taylor to come to Westfield, was so angered when a new millworks built upriver from his own mill began to ruin his water supply "that he went one morning, & cut down their Dam & hid their tools." The offended parties settled the civil matter in court, but brought Dewey's aggressive behavior to the church's attention. After Taylor preached a sermon on Romans

12:19 ("Dearly beloved, avenge not yourselves, but rather give place unto wrath: for it is written, Vengeance is mine; I will repay, saith the Lord"), Dewey saw the error of his ways, confessed his fault, and was forgiven.[6] Similar cases included that of a town constable who negligently mishandled town funds, along with further contention over conflicting mill rights, a business in which "Satan had been busy."[7] In all of these early cases, the economic contention that inevitably emerged in a growing rural community was kept from disrupting the church, largely because of the agreement between the church and other institutions of social order—the town meeting and the county courts—on the nature, meaning, and remedy for the offenses committed. The community as a whole was cohesive enough that these institutions overlapped in their duties and did not compete with each other for authority.

Other cases recorded in the first two decades reflected isolated instances of unsavory personal behavior. Joseph Pomery was censured for drunkenness in 1687, and in 1697 Abigail Bush was charged with dishonoring her father, stepmother, and brother with her "undutifull Expressions." In 1686, David Winchell uttered "very unworthy & unchristian Words" against the minister of a neighboring town, where he had moved while still in full membership at Westfield. These cases of personal misconduct, like those of economic contention, were brought before the church by the offended parties, after which the guilty members confessed and were forgiven without much ado. In all these cases, Taylor's role was simple: he clarified the offense, propounded the case for a church vote, and offered a "briefe exhortation" to the offender and to the church as a whole.[8] The ease with which these matters were handled indicates that the members were capable of disciplining themselves. The institutions of the church were sufficiently respected for the church to be able to resolve disputes and maintain harmony within the community. So although Taylor alluded frequently to "the Adversary" or "the old-Madobato" in the church records, at this stage in the church's life, Satan seemed rather easily beaten back and the minister felt called upon to do very little direct prosecution of misbehavior within his church.[9]

In the late 1690s, the beginnings of a shift in the church's handling of disciplinary cases can be discerned. Taylor was now over fifty years old, and had been in residence in Westfield for twenty-five years. His first wife, Elizabeth Fitch, had died in 1689, and in 1692 Taylor married Ruth Wyllys.[10] The 1690s were trying times in Westfield; the town witnessed a smallpox epidemic, suffered through the dangers of another war with the French and Indians, and lived with soldiers garrisoned in the town. The consequent economic hardships made this the most difficult period for Taylor to collect his salary.[11]

Taylor's controversy with Stoddard was also developing at this time; from 1688 to 1694, he preached his "Treatise Concerning the Lord's Supper" and wrote his "Animadversions" in opposition to Stoddard's innovations.[12] In 1693, Taylor began his "Second Series" of Preparatory Meditations, which, compared with the earlier series, showed a decided inward turn and an increased focus on his rarified approach to the sacrament of the Lord's Supper.[13] It was in a 1696 letter to Samuel Sewall that Taylor complained of the intellectual isolation he faced in Westfield, "far off from the Muses' copses, . . . in these remotest swamps from the Heliconian quarters, where little save clonian rusticity is a la mode."[14] In this context, the disciplinary cases recorded by Taylor began to change. Taylor himself began to feel personally threatened by the controversies that arose at this time, and he gradually came to occupy an increasingly adversarial role within the town. In putting down challenges to proper church discipline and to his own authority, he also found himself alienated from his congregation and from neighboring churches.

The first such case stands out in Taylor's records by the unusual title he gave it. Previously, he headed each entry with a descriptive phrase like "Brother Pomeries Case" or "Brother Thomas Dewey's Case," but in 1697, Taylor was faced with a new kind of problem which he called "Suffield Concerns." The trouble arose when several residents of nearby Suffield, a newly organized town (then in Massachusetts but now in Connecticut), wrote to Taylor asking for advice. They had planned to gather a church there under the ministry of Benjamin Ruggles, "an able, hopefull, & promising young gentleman," until Ruggles "declared that his Principalls are presbyterian principalls: & desires to gather a presbyterian Church: & to bee settled a presbyterian Minister."

Although they had no disagreements with Ruggles' theology, the Suffield residents were fearful of taking this new step in matters of church polity, and wanted Taylor's advice on "How far we may Comply with Mr. Ruggles his desires, without Sin, & breach of Rule?" Given the lack of a Presbyterian establishment in New England, the absence of other Presbyterian churches to form an ecclesiastical organization above the level of the individual church, it is difficult to say exactly what Ruggles' "principalls" would have meant for Suffield's church. Without such a hierarchy, the Suffield church would have been a *de facto* Congregational church, in the way that Anglican churches in New England, in the absence of a bishop, were also "congregational" for most practical purposes. However, Ruggles' "principalls" presumably might have included a more open, parish-style form of church membership. He may have favored forgoing a church covenant and placing greater authority in the hands of the minister over church matters, akin to the system of "Instituted Churches" that Solomon Stoddard would advocate, if never quite achieve, in Northampton.[15]

Taylor objected strenuously to the idea of making any concessions to Ruggles' desires. Interestingly, Taylor's defense of Congregational polity, expressed in the letter he wrote to Suffield, was not based on biblical analysis but on the authority of the founders of New England, "those Worthy, & Renowned men of God, . . . who for Natural Abilities of Choicest Endowments, who for Acquired Accomplishments of Depth of Learning; who for Supernaturall Qualifications of Sanctifying Grace, [were] inferiour to few in the learned part of the World." Here more than anywhere else, Taylor displays the influence that the mythology of New England's founding had on his own thinking. His praise of New England's founders demonstrates his personal identification with them; like himself, the founders suffered persecution ". . . sustain'd for the Discipline of Christ in his Churches under Prelacy in their Native Countrey, . . . [and] left Father & Mother, Brethren & Sisters, Friends & Relations, Homes & Lands, to follow Christ in a Wilderness."[16] In fact, Taylor's description here is really more characteristic of his own experience than of the founders, many of whom brought family, friends, and relations with them to New England. But with this heritage of sacrifice for the sake of church discipline behind him, even if his imagination embellished the founders' sufferings, Taylor was not ready to let the introduction of "Prelacy" in a neighboring town go unchallenged, and he urged the Suffield townsmen not to bend to Ruggles' wishes.[17]

The matter would not rest here. Upon Suffield's request, the Hampshire County Court recommended calling a church council of neighboring clergy, which would include Stoddard and Taylor, William Williams of Hatfield, Daniel Brewer of Springfield, and Samuel Mather of Windsor, to meet in April 1698 and advise the town on how to proceed. Ruggles, in an alternative strategy, wrote to each of these ministers individually and asked them to appear in Suffield on the day chosen for this meeting, not to hold a council but to assist in gathering his church and ordaining him as its minister. This ploy to circumvent the workings of the council "caused great displeasure" to Taylor. He "took no notice of it," and planned to go to Suffield only "to make peace," not to gather a church. Illness prevented him from attending at all, but the other ministers who did go to Suffield brought Ruggles around to compromise on a more traditional Congregational standard. With this agreement made, a day for church gathering and ordination was set up for the following month.

When the ordination day came, Taylor was not among those invited to attend, despite the proximity of Westfield to Suffield and the presence of many former Westfield residents in the new town. In addition, Taylor refused to give those Westfield church members now resident in Suffield a full dismissal and recommendation to join the Suffield church. Instead, he left them "onely their liberty" to do what they thought best. John Hanchett and his wife chose to remain members at Westfield, while two others, David Winchell and Thomas Smith, joined the Suffield church. What most irked Taylor was that several Suffield founders who had been members of "Bay Churches" joined the new church without any kind of dismissal; according to Taylor, "This was the first instance in these parts, if not in the whole Countrey, of Members in express Covenant Relation with other Churches that were torn away without Dismission or liberty."[18] Of course, Taylor was incorrect in his claim, for in fact, the Suffield affair bore a minor resemblance to the much larger controversy over the founding of Boston's Third Church in 1669, when the founding members were denied proper dismissals from the First Church. But claims that particular kinds of controversies were unprecedented in New England were part of the standard litany of complaint that supporters of the declension argument often made—the past was a golden age of benevolent cooperation, the present, a degenerate era of betrayal, against which the pious remnant fought to maintain a last refuge of godliness.

These "Suffield Concerns" were at best only marginally a matter of church discipline in Westfield. The few Westfield church members involved had technically done nothing wrong. Nevertheless, Taylor chose to devote more space in his church records to this case than to any other matter to date. His unusual attention to this quarrel suggests the degree to which Taylor, by the late 1690s, was beginning to feel isolated and embattled in his conservative position; his neighboring ministers were willing to participate in practices he considered unscriptural, and members of his church acted against his better advice. While the Suffield case was not a direct challenge to Taylor's authority in Westfield, it differed from the earlier disciplinary cases, which had been simple matters of chastising and forgiving sinners who knew they had done wrong. In the "Suffield Concerns," Taylor was faced with ministerial colleagues and godly lay people acting in ways he found distasteful, if not exactly sinful. From these more complex changes in Westfield and the surrounding communities, other issues soon emerged that Taylor would perceive as direct challenges to his authority.

In 1698 and 1699, Taylor's salary problems became particularly severe, reaching the point where the minister even threatened to leave Westfield unless something was done about it.[19] The townspeople affirmed their desire to keep Taylor and strengthened their commitment to maintaining his salary, so for the moment Taylor was satisfied.[20] But shortly thereafter, another ambiguous disciplinary case arose, involving what Taylor called "Pochassuck Matters." A group of Westfield men petitioned the Northampton Court of Sessions for an order to have "an Highway laid out from Westfield town to the upper end of Pochassuck Meadow," which would connect the distant but rapidly growing settlement to the older town center. The petitioners had already been denied such a highway by the town selectmen, but continued to protest the inconvenience and cost involved in the current way of getting to town: "For now we cannot persue the work of our Calling, nor do these Civill Duties which are required of us, nor attend the publick worship of God without being counted trespassers." This petition "did create no small stir in the Church," and brought quite an outburst from Taylor, who called it "This Scrible nonsensicall, tautologicall & illogicall writ by Pomery the Lawyer full of Falshoods & Untruths from the first to the last of it."[21]

A number of prominent church members had signed this petition, including Isaac Phelps, the last surviving foundation man, yet few of the signers actually lived at Pochassuck, and among the signers were the very selectmen against whom the petition complained. Ebenezer Pomery, "the Lawyer" mentioned here by Taylor, had been engaged to write the petition on behalf of these townsmen who were seeking a more convenient and economical way of conducting their ordinary business. This case differed from John Mawdsley's earlier petition for land grants, in that now a group of men were acting in concert and taking what should have been a matter for the town meeting to an outside authority in order to readjust boundaries and property rights within the town. That Isaac Phelps, the town's most prominent citizen and oldest church member, should head the list must have been disturbing to Taylor, and Taylor took it upon himself to censure this group for their "Errours in point of truth" among the convoluted claims of the petition. But unlike John Mawdsley's case, where all agreed that Mawdsley's actions had clearly been sinful, there was nothing obviously wrong with the petitioners' desire for a new highway; their fault lay in the means they used and the language in which they expressed their wishes. Instead of working out a consensus on the matter within the town meeting, the petitioners went directly to an outside authority, the Northampton Court of Sessions, and employed a professional, "Pomery the Lawyer," who stretched the truth in his description of the petitioners' circumstances.

The fact that the petition's subscribers had sworn to a falsehood for their gain was what made this incident into a case of church discipline. The vehemence of Taylor's response, however, indicates that he took personal offense at the matter, despite the relatively minor nature of the case. Taylor's response may have been prompted by his growing concern that as townspeople moved away from the old center, church participation became more difficult to maintain and communal harmony was threatened by geographically based factions.[22] This underlying problem may have been a greater source of Taylor's ire than the way in which the petition distorted the facts. Additionally, the influence of Ebenezer Pomery may have irritated Taylor by bringing a new source of expertise and authority into his previously unchallenged domain. But in the outcome, it became clear that the church was having greater difficulty resolving an ambiguous case like this one than the earlier cases of economic contention.

In the final reckoning, there was "some debate" among Taylor and the church members before the offenders came to see their errors and confess. The presence of debate, unusual for these disciplinary proceedings, suggests a lack of consensus within the congregation that the "Pochassuck Matters" were properly a case for church discipline at all. The lawyer's "Scrible nonsensicall, tautologicall & illogicall" might in actuality have seemed quite sensible to the petitioners themselves. Their signatures may be read as their agreement to the sense and purpose of the document, rather than to the truth of every word of the lawyer's arguments about precedent and rights of way. At last, the accused petitioners "acknowledged their Errou[rs] in point of truth"; that is, they admitted that their petition was not entirely accurate, but they did not retract their desire for the Northampton court to grant them rights to a new highway. With debate concluded, the church voted to reinstate the offenders in its good graces, ending this case amicably but leaving greater ambiguity over the role of church discipline within the life of the community. The church encompassed a shrinking percentage of the town as participants in full membership, and the town continued to spread away from the original center, making the degree to which town and church formed a unitary authority less clear. Although this was the first case in which Taylor recorded debate within the church over a disciplinary sanction, it would not be the last.[23]

In 1710, after a relatively peaceful decade, a more direct challenge to Taylor's authority came from two of the younger church members.[24] Sgt. Joseph Mawdsley, son of the foundation man, and Ensign Steven Kellogg, a relative newcomer to the town, "did somewhat boggle at our Church fasts which in the wintertime wee had attended once a month ever since we were in a Church State." Eventually, these two men stopped attending the fasts altogether. They claimed that the monthly fasts were "stated" fasts; that is, holidays set by custom and tradition rather than by scriptural mandate or in response to particular events, like the "occasional" fasts proper to a Puritan church and approved by the Massachusetts Bay elders. Mawdsley and Kellogg even brought

Taylor a book (of unknown title) from which they had derived their opinions. Armed as they were with authorities, Taylor could not persuade Mawdsley and Kellogg of their errors, and when he threatened them with a church censure for "Breaking of Covenant," they asked for a church council to resolve the matter. Taylor replied that "I stood in no need of Councill as to my proceeding," but they insisted on an outside opinion. As there were no other qualified sources of authority within Westfield, the two men turned to Solomon Stoddard, asking for the opinion of a man known to disagree with Taylor on other points of church polity. In this case, however, Mawdsley and Kellogg were disappointed. While he differed from Taylor on the issue of admission standards, Stoddard opposed attempts by the laity to gain control over church practices, and believed strongly in the unique qualifications and responsibilities of the clergy to guide such matters.[25] Stoddard backed Taylor's claim that the monthly fasts were "occasional," and the two dissenting brethren, "having now received light in the matter," apologized and promised to attend the fasts in the future.[26]

It is difficult to know what motivated Mawdsley and Kellogg's challenge. Neither one had been among the Pochassuck petitioners censured by Taylor a decade before, and there is no evidence that they held any long-standing grudge against the minister. If they had been "horseshed Christians," the type of persons who simply did not want to bother with church fasts, it is unlikely that they would have become full members to begin with, especially given Taylor's rigorous membership standards. Rather, their behavior seems to have come from genuine religious conviction, though it is odd that they would try to be more orthodox than the ultra-conservative Taylor. Their position might indicate their wish to have religion based on "scripture and nothing but"; that is, a desire for heart-rending preaching and scriptural simplicity rather than preparationist devotion, a trend seen among some groups of the laity in New England in the eighteenth century that would later characterize various "New Light" and "Separate" churches during the revivals of the Great Awakening.[27] Or, as members of a younger generation, they may have been expressing a general dissatisfaction with Taylor as representative of older ways. In typical Puritan fashion, they may have looked to an even earlier model, the polity of the colony's founders, as inspiration for their own "further reformation," unaware of Taylor's own feeling of connection to the first generation. Finally, it is possible that their objections to the fast days were not aimed against this ritual per se, but were an expression of discontent with the fact that the fasts had replaced the lecture days which Taylor had discontinued because of their tendency to create disorder within the town.[28]

This unusual case represents another example in the growing tendency for the laity to assert their authority over church practice, to challenge Taylor's role as minister, and to look beyond the boundaries of the local church for support for their positions. As Taylor's vision of the church became more exclusive, the church's connection to the ordinary life of the community at large was reduced. But Taylor, accustomed to his position of authority over matters of morality and public behavior within church and town, was unwilling to accept the implication that a narrowed church membership meant a narrowed scope within the community for his own control. The troublesome disciplinary cases of the 1690s and 1700s emerged from these gray areas where the authority of the church was uncertain. They demonstrate that the tension between Taylor and the town over the definition of the church and its role in the community, already present at the founding of the church, was becoming increasingly problematic as the town grew, as the town's connections with the outside world became more complex, and as the allocation of the church's resources became more difficult to manage.

By the time of this latest challenge from Mawdsley and Kellogg, Edward Taylor was nearly seventy years old. He had outlived most of his fellow town founders, with the exception of Capt. Isaac Phelps, who was roughly Taylor's age and still served as town selectman, clerk, treasurer, and sometime schoolmaster.[29] The first decade of the eighteenth century had seen renewed warfare in the region, most notably the attack on Deerfield in 1704, but Westfield was spared again. The potential danger did not discourage more families from moving to the outskirts of Westfield, where extensive new land grants were made in 1709 and 1710. At about this time, the Stoddard–Mather debate erupted again in a flurry of pamphlets, to which Taylor responded in his idiosyncratic way by writing "his last major anti-Stoddard manuscript, 'The *Appeale* Tried.'" In this private argument, Taylor turned again to New England's founders in defending restricted communion and denying that the Lord's Supper was a "converting" ordinance.[30] In 1711, an influenza epidemic hit western Massachusetts, and among its victims were both of Westfield's deacons, Nathaniel Weller and Samuel Root.[31] Thomas Noble and David Dewey were quickly elected by the church as their successors and ordained in May 1712, but by November Dewey had also succumbed to disease, robbing Taylor of his close friend and spiritual ally.[32]

It was at this juncture, late in Taylor's life, with the spirit of godliness as he knew it threatened from a variety of sources, that a minor squabble over the inheritance of a local resident's meager estate snowballed into an enormous controversy within the church. This case would create a deep and abiding rift in the religious community of Westfield and effectively mark the end of Taylor's usefulness in the ministry. In the church records, Taylor called the affair "Brother Benjamin Smith's case," but initially, it concerned not Benjamin Smith but another church member, the elderly Walter Lee, and his contentious extended family.

Walter Lee was one of Westfield's first Puritan settlers. He moved there from Northampton in the 1660s, worked as a stone mason, farmed his own small plot of land, married, and raised a family. After more than thirty years' residence in town, he joined the church in 1696. Shortly thereafter, Lee's wife died and he moved in with his eldest son, John. Walter Lee made a "covenant" with John, deeding his estate to him in return for future care and assistance. This arrangement broke down when Walter became dissatisfied with John's care. John and his family used up the "Barrell of Pork" which Walter had brought them, and when this was gone, Walter feared he would "have no meate to live upon."[33] He decided to move to the home of his daughter Abigail and her husband, Samuel Bush, where he stayed for about five months until he remarried in 1697. Walter Lee's second marriage created further problems; Abigail was censured by the church for saying that her father "married not for Love. And that he was as hot as a Skunk, & the woman as hot as a Bitch"(188). After this insult, Walter and his new wife went to live by themselves; John continued to help, but only with the heavy farm work, and his haphazard assistance brought further complaints from Walter.

Walter Lee outlived his second wife, Hepzibah, and after she died Walter once again needed someone to take care of him, but the situation was now more complicated.[34] His son John died in 1711, leaving a widow, Sarah, whose family was now all the more dependent on inheriting Walter Lee's estate. Yet at first, Walter refused to live with Sarah, for Sarah's daughter (i.e., Walter's granddaughter) "had told him to his face that he w[as] not worth the Droppings of his nose"(209). Walter once again tried to live with his daughter Abigail Bush and her husband, but soon Walter was "offended" by Abigail and went back to Sarah. Abigail must have offended Walter deeply, for he refused to make any payment for his upkeep during the time he spent with Abigail and Samuel Bush.

After this last family reshuffling, Abigail and her husband felt taken advantage of. Samuel Bush had supported his father-in-law for several months, and now Walter Lee refused to "make any satisfaction to his Son Bush for what he had done for him" (209). Bush was aware of the "covenant" Walter had made with John Lee years before, and therefore knew that if he did not receive payment while Walter was alive, he would not get any of the estate after Walter's death. For this reason, Samuel Bush decided to take the matter to court and filed suit against his father-in-law in the summer of 1711.

To protect her family interest in the estate, Sarah Lee, John's widow, engaged the services of Ebenezer Pomery of Northampton—"Pomery the Lawyer," as Taylor called him. Pomery came up with the idea that Bush's suit could be dismissed "if Walter Lee was not a Man in Law, but was put under Guardian by the Court at Northampton" (210). In other words, if Walter Lee could be declared a ward of the court, incapable of caring for himself or making his own decisions, he would not be subject to lawsuits and his estate would pass directly into Sarah Lee's control, according to the "covenant" Walter had made with John. To this end, Pomery drew up a petition to the Hampshire court, and enlisted the aid of his friend Benjamin Smith. Smith was particularly useful to Pomery; he was a full member of the Westfield church, and his uncle happened to be Samuel Partridge, the senior judge of the Hampshire County Court of Sessions, from whom he hoped to get a favorable judgment.

At Pomery's urging, Benjamin Smith brought the petition to Edward Taylor in the hope that the Westfield minister would sign it and add the weight of clerical approval to their request. Taylor, however, believed that Lee was capable of managing himself, and that it was "a very unrighteous thing" to make a man "shut out of the law" when he had committed no crime (211).[35] Yet Taylor was still concerned that Walter Lee might foolishly sell off land to pay his debts, land that had been rightly deeded to his late son John. Urged on by Smith, Taylor wrote his own letter to the court, requesting that the court prevent Walter Lee from alienating his land, if this were possible without making Lee a ward of the court. Taylor was rather naive when it came to legal matters. He knew little about them and feared that he was being manipulated, but he lacked the expertise to prevent this from happening. Taylor would later write, "I fear mine ignorance hath been dishonestly interpreted to bring about unrighteous Designs" (212).

At the next Court of Sessions at Northampton, Pomery and Smith presented their petition together with Taylor's letter as if both documents had the same intention—to make Walter Lee a ward of the court. Taylor's letter was ambiguous enough for the judge, Samuel Partridge, to read it as further support of Pomery and Smith's petition. His decision led to the dismissal of Samuel Bush's suit, which left the unfortunate Bush to pay court costs and attorney's fees and with no hope of ever collecting anything from his father-in-law.

When Taylor heard about these proceedings, he was furious with Benjamin Smith for having abused his intentions. He felt that he "ought not to let such abuse alone & not to looke into the Case," and asked Smith to come to his house where they would discuss the matter in the presence of a neutral witness. Taylor described the meeting as follows:

> I treated him about it as abusing me in producing Goodman Lee to be laid un-
> der Guardians by the letter that I wrote & he knew that I would never have
> wrote if I had thought it should have been made to serve such a Design. He de-
> nied that he had done it, & many unhandsom things then being vended, I for-
> bade him the appearing to the Lords Table till he had manifested his repentance
> for such abuse (210).

At this point, concern over the welfare of Walter Lee rapidly disappeared from
this case. Now, what had been a legal matter for the civil courts became a
moral issue, a case of church discipline that would rapidly escalate to involve
the entire congregation of Westfield. Although the legality of Pomery and
Smith's maneuvers remained an issue, and the question of whether Walter
Lee had been made a "man out of law" was left unsettled, none of the principal participants seemed actively concerned about Lee's future or about the
injustice done to Samuel and Abigail Bush. Instead, the focus shifted to Taylor
and his insistence that his personal authority within the church had been in-
jured by Smith's actions. The abruptness with which Taylor suspended Smith
from communion on his own authority, rather than bringing the matter to
the church members for discussion, demonstrated a concern for his personal
honor and clerical authority that denigrated the role of the laity in maintaining church discipline and widened the gulf between Taylor and his congregation as the controversy grew.

Taylor next wrote to Colonel Partridge, the judge in the case, to explain
that his earlier letter had been used falsely and in opposition to his wishes, especially in putting Walter Lee "out of the Law, to the dammageing of such as
had laid out any Credit upon him" (210). Colonel Partridge wrote back to
Taylor, but the minister "could not english the meaning" of Partridge's reply,
for its legal language was unintelligible to him. Still, Taylor reached the conclusion that Partridge was against him, for Partridge, "being kin to Smith,"
had been made Smith's "side man" (213).

At the next regular meeting of the Westfield church members, Taylor
confronted Benjamin Smith about his behavior. Smith immediately requested that the letter Col. Partridge had sent to Taylor be publicly read.
Taylor refused, and Smith responded insolently, charging that Taylor had "de-
famed" him. Taylor asserted that Smith had clearly acted to put Walter Lee
"under guardians," and that this was unrighteous and ought to be censured.
Taylor attempted to put the church to an immediate vote on this charge, but
the church members were not ready to accept this interpretation. In particular, three prominent members of the community, Captain Isaac Phelps, Captain Joseph Mawdsley, and Ensign Steven Kellogg, protested the absence of
proof that Walter Lee had actually been put "out of the Law." Unable to re-

solve this hostile situation, Taylor dismissed the meeting and called on Smith to appear at the next meeting with a copy of the Court Act regarding Walter Lee. According to Taylor, Smith drew a number of members aside as they were leaving, asked them in private whether he had offended them, and offered his apologies if he had done so. "This," said Taylor, "he did Subtilly that he might say that the Church had nothing against him," a small episode that would loom larger as the case developed (215).

At the next church meeting, the copy of the Court Act did little to clear the air. Its meaning, to these untrained readers, "was so dark, that it did not appear whether [Walter Lee] was put under Guardians, or no" (215). Taylor conceded the ambiguity, retracted his accusations against Smith on this matter, but would not drop the case. Instead, in a remarkable shift, Taylor moved his argument against Smith onto new grounds, and censured Smith for his insolent responses in the prior church meeting. Taylor charged Smith with "thrusting yourselfe into the Officers work: & taking his Work away from him in determining of & propounding matters to the Church" (215). In Taylor's eyes, Smith's brief private discussion with the other members at the end of the last meeting had been a subversion of Taylor's ministerial authority, a flagrant attempt to circumvent the minister's right to control disciplinary procedures within the church. This issue would remain at the forefront of the rest of this controversy, and alienate Taylor from more and more of his congregation in his insistence on ministerial control over church matters.

Initially, Benjamin Smith denied these new charges and claimed never to have detained the church and propounded his case to them. Taylor, in recording what happened next, wrote "At length Brother Samuel Bush said you did say so, & gave him [Smith] his words" (215). This is a telling passage. It suggests that the church was already out of sympathy with Taylor, for it was only "at length" that any of them spoke up to admit what all must have known to be true, that Smith had indeed addressed them on this matter. And of all people, the only member to speak out was Samuel Bush, whose interest Taylor had indirectly been defending all along. In the new charges Taylor was pressing against Smith, the minister could not have had a great feeling of support from the church members.

Faced with Bush's testimony, Smith apologized, but Taylor was unsatisfied. Taylor asked Smith "whether he was heartily sorry for it," to which Smith "smartly replied" that Taylor "had nothing to do with his heart" (215–16). Taylor insisted that without a heartfelt apology, Smith could not be forgiven, and propounded the case to the church, asking them to vote either for or against Smith. To Taylor's chagrin, "the Church voted not at all, neither ways," leaving the situation unresolved. Again, the church members' impassive response indicates their lack of sympathy with Taylor's conduct, and suggests that they might have judged the state of Benjamin Smith's heart in a different light than the minister did.

At this point, Taylor had several options. In his own words, he could either "Call a Councell" of outside churches to advise on the matter, or he could "Suspende the Administration of the Lords Supper" (216). Another option was possible: Taylor could have backed away from the whole matter, but this seems never to have occurred to him. His honor and personal authority were too bound up in this issue to let matters stand as they were. Taylor was not about to allow outsiders into this case, and therefore rejected the idea of a council. Instead, he declared to his church: "I should not administer the Lords Supper to them & turning to Smith I Commanded Smith in the Name & by the Authority of Christ to repent of his Sin" (216). This, claimed Taylor, "was not an Ecclesiasticall Admonition; but a ministerial admonition," done on the weight of his own authority as elder of the church. To Smith's protests that Taylor was overstepping his official bounds, Taylor replied, "I would not come to him to teach me my office work" (216). Taylor felt confident in the righteousness of his own authority, and was willing to use the Lord's Supper as a tool for disciplining the entire church, thereby demonstrating his absolute control over admission to the sacrament.[36]

The animosity between Smith and Taylor grew still more intense. Smith now claimed that he had held a grudge against Taylor for some years running, dating back to a time when he had been gravely ill and Taylor had tended to his medical needs. Apparently, Taylor had urged Smith to review what was "amiss" in his past life rather more strenuously than was pleasing to Smith, who took offense at this "& kept this upon his Spirit rankling till now." Given the overall "paucity of means" that characterized Westfield's religious culture, it may well be that Taylor's demand for intensive soul-searching during this time of illness seemed intrusive to Smith, a rare event in a community where individuals were not used to others prying into the state of their souls. At any rate, Smith told Taylor that "he shold never be reconciled to [him] again." This was the last straw for Taylor, and he immediately forbade Smith "ever to approach the Lords table till he had repented of this" (216).

Several more church conferences could not resolve the matter. Smith would not repent and refused to sign any confession that Taylor would accept. Exasperated, Taylor put the matter to the assembled church to vote on whether Smith's "carriage" was offensive to them. But even here, the vote was handled in a way that exacerbated the tension. Taylor called for those *not* offended by Smith to "signify it by the lifting up of their hands." When no one responded, Taylor asked those who "judged him to have offended to signify it

by their silence" (217). In other words, this system required anyone who disagreed with Taylor to come out in open defiance of his authority, and allowed
no easy expression of sympathy for Smith. With this "vote" in hand, Taylor
now placed Smith under a "Church admonition" (more severe than the earlier ministerial admonition) which carried the threat of excommunication
unless Smith would confess in an acceptable manner (217).

Taylor had clearly taken a very hard line by insisting on complete ministerial control over all aspects of the church's disciplinary procedures. This approach began to disturb some prominent church members, including "Old
Captain Phelps," the last surviving founder, who was so "netted" by Taylor's
declaration of the church admonition "that he could hardly tarry till prayer
was done & being done out he went shucking as he went." Additionally, the
church deacon, Thomas Noble, "openly opposed" Taylor (218). Taylor's rigid
position forced Smith and his supporters to take their case beyond the confines of the Westfield church.

For assistance, Benjamin Smith turned to his uncle, Col. Partridge, and to
the ministers in neighboring towns. In Taylor's opinion, this only made a bad
situation worse: "Now the Greate Encouragement to Smith in this his Evil
Case seems to me to be Colonall Partridge, his Kinsman, & Mr. Stoddard, Mr.
Brewer, & Mr. Woodbridge" (225). Smith, backed strongly by Isaac Phelps
and several other townsmen, wrote letters to these outside authorities, attempting to win their influence. Solomon Stoddard reviewed a copy of Smith's
confession, which Taylor had rejected, and at Smith's request wrote to Taylor
and urged him to change his mind (218). Smith also attempted to gain admission to communion at John Woodbridge's church at West Springfield without Taylor's knowledge. Woodbridge wrote to Taylor, asking about Smith's
status in the church, and Taylor in reply told Woodbridge that "the Church
had voted [Smith] an offender, & that he could not regularly administer the
Lords Supper to him" (220). Upon receiving this, Woodbridge wrote another
letter to the Westfield church (not addressed to the pastor as was the custom),
"inquiring after the same matter of the brethren"; in other words, asking for
the opinion of the church members apart from their pastor, which indicates a
growing outside awareness of the split in the Westfield church between minister and laity.[37] Benjamin Smith gathered the other church members together and obtained a vote stating that they were satisfied with Smith's confession and would allow him to take communion with Woodbridge's church.

To Taylor, the unwanted intrusion of these neighboring ministers was an
attempt to subvert his authority and a personal affront as well. In a phrase
Taylor would repeat more frequently over the years, a phrase that echoed
John Davenport's words in the crisis over Boston's First Church, Taylor told

Smith: "they might take Councill that needed it, I knew the rule of my proceedings" (218). Taylor also opposed the intrusion of Colonel Partridge, a civil magistrate, into a church matter. In a letter to Taylor, Partridge tried to minimize Smith's offenses, calling them "triviall" and suggesting that Taylor's misunderstanding of the legal details in Walter Lee's case caused all this trouble. To Partridge, the fact that "the greatest part of your Church hath declared themselves satisfied" with Smith's confession should have been sufficient for Smith's reinstatement. By standing above the laity in the exercise of ministerial authority, Taylor was, in Partridge's words, assuming powers "more than any . . . Presbyterian Ministers have acquired to themselves" (226–27). To Taylor, Partridge's letter was "full of mistakes & of offenses in his spirit that he hath received from his kinsman Benjamin Smith, whose case he espoused, & was a back to him making him bold and impudent" (227). Clearly, Taylor could see nothing but harm coming from persons and authorities outside the Westfield church, but his defensive behavior was making the Westfield church into an isolated cell, the fortress of discipline that his poems depict, rather than an evangelical garden of inter-church fellowship.

Nevertheless, Taylor did want to resolve this matter, so he agreed in principle to a church council. After bickering with Smith over who would be invited to compose a council, Taylor finally acquiesced in an informal meeting with Brewer and Woodbridge at Smith's house. At this meeting, Brewer and Taylor initially lashed out at each other, but after the shouting died down, Brewer drew up a confession for Smith. Taylor rejected it. Brewer revised the confession, and now Taylor accepted, though in his words, the new confession "did not please me," for "I can't see sufficient reason to thinke that it flow'd from Evangelicall Repentance" (219). Smith's confession was accepted by the Westfield church at their next meeting, but not without some grumbling by the laity over Taylor's handling of the case. Smith was reinstated, but Taylor still would not let matters rest. He wanted to call a day of fasting for the entire church to repent for their contentious behavior, yet the laity seemed to feel that the conflict was Taylor's responsibility.

Taylor turned to the church members and addressed them directly, saying "Your Actings have been very grievous, irregular, & greatly wounded mee." He listed their specific offenses and focused on their usurpation of his rightful duties as church officer, which, Taylor claimed, makes a "bad example to others to rise up against their officers judgment, that tends to bring in all disorder & confusion in matters of Church Discipline." He warned them not to repeat this behavior, then offered them the choice of a day of humiliation or a church council "to direct us about these things" (222). Isaac Phelps objected; he claimed that Taylor had promised not to bring up these specific grievances in calling for a fast day. Now an open argument broke out. As Taylor described it, Capt. Phelps "entred upon a discourse very unbeseeming to him" which laid bare the essentials of this conflict. According to Phelps, the church members were not blameworthy at all, for they had only done what Taylor had asked them to do in dealing with Smith's problem. Taylor rejected this interpretation, saying he had given them leave to urge Smith to make a more sincere confession, but not "to meet together in distinct meeting & plot with [Smith], . . . to draw up letters to other Elders & Churches against me." In essence, claimed Taylor, "the Church had another leader besides me to rule them," and he cited Hebrews 13.17 as evidence that they must submit to his judgment. Unfazed by Taylor's use of scripture, Capt. Phelps's reply was sharp: "Not as Lords over God's Heretage," he said, calling on 1 Peter 5:2–3 to suggest Taylor's own failings in attempting to rule by force rather than by example (223).[38]

Phelps also cited New England tradition to show that Taylor was overstepping his bounds. Phelps claimed "the Bay Ministers say that three things Elders [i.e. ministers] may not Doe, viz., they can't Elect Officers, they Can't Admit Members, & they can't Suspend." Taylor countered this with a logical argument about the minister's role, and in fact, the Cambridge Platform and the Reforming Synod of 1679 backed up Taylor's position.[39] Yet Phelps was still not satisfied, and argued that if the clergy could suspend members on their own authority, then "there was no power in the Church." Taylor claimed that the church's power lay in deciding matters that the minister brought before them, "but such things as are not committed to the Church by the Elders . . . , the Church . . . have nothing to do at all in ordinary Cases." Taylor made one last stab; he accused Phelps of competing with him for leadership of the church, and claimed (yet again) that "I knew my office & would not come unto him to learn my duty"(223). Taylor went ahead and appointed the fast day without Phelps's approval, an unusual event within an ecclesiastical system in which most decisions were made by consensus. On that day, Taylor preached a sermon calling for repentance, then appointed the following Sabbath for communion after a lapse of about four months caused by this extended conflict.[40]

Four months later, Taylor preached two disciplinary sermons to the church, in which he discussed systematically the roles of the minister and the laity in matters of discipline and obedience, and went so far as to recapitulate the events of the Smith case in detail, pointing out where specific individuals had gone astray. This was Taylor's attempt, once passions had subsided, to get the last word on the matter, and to lay out his vision of proper church order once and for all. Sadly for Taylor, his sermon fell on deaf ears. For the remaining dozen years of his career as Westfield's minister, the important issues faced by the town and church created divisions along the lines exposed in the Smith case, and the residents and church members of Westfield continued to find ways to circumvent or override Taylor's authority. Controversies over building a new meetinghouse and hiring a minister to succeed Taylor became particularly embittered, and on both of these major issues, Taylor lost out to the opposition of Capt. Phelps, Capt. Mawdsley, and others who supported Benjamin Smith in the controversy of 1713.

What had begun as a family dispute involving the settlement of a small amount of property escalated rapidly to the point where Captain Isaac Phelps, one of the oldest and most respected citizens of Westfield, accused the equally ancient and venerable minister of acting as "Lord over God's Heritage." Taylor in turn took to describing Captain Phelps as "the Master of Miss rule" (235). Why did this minor event take such a strange turn? Why did this challenge to Taylor's authority happen at this time, and why did it create such a lasting and irreconcilable rift in the community?

The context of Westfield's social and religious development over the course of fifty years makes it possible to explain the peculiar nature of the Walter Lee/Benjamin Smith case and the unusual vehemence with which the people of Westfield fought over its initially trivial issues. First of all, the fact that Walter Lee faded so rapidly from the controversy can be understood by considering that while Lee and his family were a contentious lot, their sins were neither unusual nor of the kind that threatened Taylor's position or disrupted the church. The family squabbles and selfishness that marked their behavior were simply a reflection of sinful human nature, and were similar to the cases of discipline that the church had handled peaceably in its early years.

The preceding disciplinary cases help to explain why Taylor focused his anger on Benjamin Smith. Taylor had already expressed his disdain for "the lawyer Pomery" in the "Pochassuck matters," and while Pomery as a resident of Northampton was beyond Taylor's reach, Smith was a ready substitute, a member of Taylor's church acting in concert with the lawyer to bring about an unethical financial transaction. It was not simply a personal grudge that Taylor held against Pomery and Smith. What comes through in the record is Taylor's dismay over his own incompetence before the complexities of the law. When he reviewed the letter which he had initially written at Smith's urging, Taylor could see that the language he used was disturbingly similar to that used by Pomery: "I had forgot the speciall terms used in the letter, it being a twelve month before we had any debate about it, ... & in the treating Smith in the Matter I used such terms as Lawyer Pomery & Smith now use about it. ... Hence in my letters I used the term put under guardians, but I meant further consideration."[41] As Taylor goes on in this vein, it becomes clear that the ambiguity and misuse of his letter in court may have been his own fault, a product of his ignorance of legal language.

The most obvious targets of the resentment that this confusion and incompetence created in Taylor were Benjamin Smith and Ebenezer Pomery. Associated with them in Taylor's mind was Colonel Samuel Partridge, Smith's uncle and "Side man." Together they stood for a legal and judicial establishment that acted in ways and dealt in ambiguities that were beyond the scope of Taylor's expertise and created issues that eluded simple classification under the ten commandments. Capt. Joseph Mawdsley, by contrast, was perfectly comfortable with these ambiguities, for at this very time he was being sued by the town for misuse of lands while working on the town's behalf. It was Mawdsley who confidently stated at one point in the proceedings that "Lawyers oft say in their pleadings, what was not." Not surprisingly, Mawdsley opposed Taylor in the Smith case, as he had a decade before over the calling of fast days.[42]

Benjamin Smith also stood for an understanding of the church and a religious mentality that disturbed Taylor. By his full membership in the Westfield church and by his ongoing desire for communion with John Woodbridge's church, even when he was out of favor with Taylor, Smith demonstrated that he was not an ungodly person or a scoffer at religion, but a man with a real devotion to the church and its ordinances. However, as a member of the Westfield church, Smith had moved beyond the town limits into West Springfield. The movement of the members away from the town center threatened the church's limited vitality, a problem that had plagued Westfield from the beginning, which perhaps accounts for some of Taylor's anger over the "Pochassuck matters." What made things worse in Smith's case was that in moving away, Smith acted to contradict Taylor's belief in the importance of particular church covenants. Smith attempted to receive communion in Springfield's West Church without a proper dismissal from Westfield, calling to mind Taylor's objection to the earlier "Suffield Concerns." This disregard for the sanctity of a particular church covenant was an insult to Taylor's high opinion of the Lord's Supper and the church's supposedly "solid walls of discipline," and a signal to Taylor that the more open view on church polity championed by Solomon Stoddard and other Connecticut Valley ministers was beginning to prevail even in Westfield.

Furthermore, what lay behind Smith's actions, as Taylor understood them, was an inadequate religious sensibility. This element emerged in Taylor's discussion of the grudge Smith had long held against him. Smith had become angry years earlier when Taylor, in the role of physician, had urged him to search his own soul for evidence of sin and to try to repent. For Taylor, this was what any properly religious person would do, but Smith had taken the suggestion as an insult and held it against Taylor for years. When Taylor heard this, his immediate response was to forbid Smith "ever to approach the Lords table till he had repented." And when Smith's apologies were not "heartfelt" enough for Taylor, Smith insisted that Taylor "had nothing to do with his heart."[43] For Taylor, the fact that a full church member held such views meant that a "hypocrite" had slipped in past him, and had to be kept from defiling the Lord's Table until he showed true signs of repentance. But Benjamin Smith was obviously of a different mind, and was determined to take the sacrament elsewhere if Taylor would not comply. Here, Smith demonstrated a relative indifference to the fear of taking communion unworthily that seemed to plague so many scrupulous New Englanders, a scrupulosity encouraged by Taylor's approach to the sacrament. In Smith's case, the view promoted by Stoddard of the Lord's Supper as a nurturing or converting ordinance seems to have prevailed over Taylor's tendency to reserve communion for the few and to use it as a disciplinary tool. The conflict here was not between a secular future and a sacred past, but between two differing religious sensibilities, two competing definitions of the nature and meaning of the sacrament for participation in the church. Smith's actions were prompted by sincere beliefs, closely aligned to the positions of Taylor's opponents in the controversies of the preceding decades.[44]

The fact that the rest of the church members backed Smith so strongly must have been even more disturbing to Taylor. The lay members showed that their disagreements with the minister included issues of church discipline along with control of the sacrament. Smith's attempt to take a church vote on his confession without Taylor's approval, and the resistance of Phelps, Kellogg, and Mawdsley to Taylor's desire for a penitential fast day must have exacerbated for Taylor the earlier challenges to his authority made by the same people. Their actions indicated a willingness to take church matters into their own hands and to circumvent Taylor's authority. By holding private meetings, corresponding with neighboring ministers, and making church decisions without consulting Taylor, the brethren were expressing their disagreement with the way Taylor handled church business. Smith's insistence that outside opinions on his case be gathered, and his consultation with Stoddard, Woodbridge, and Brewer without Taylor's knowledge were further signs that Taylor's control over his own church was slipping away, the culmination of a trend that had been developing for more than a decade. The laity's rebellion against Taylor's absolute authority, expressed in Isaac Phelps's assertion that Taylor was ruling as a "Lord over God's Heritage," demonstrated their dissatisfaction with Taylor as an exemplary figure, a rejection of his particular brand of religiosity as a model to live by.

Finally, the complicity of the neighboring ministers in the "designs" of Smith and the church brethren may have been the most galling thing of all to Taylor. Even if they disagreed with him on the need for conversion relations or church covenants, Taylor must have expected his fellow ministers to support his effort to maintain control of church discipline. And yet Stoddard approved Smith's confession, which Taylor had thought inadequate, before consulting Taylor, John Woodbridge exchanged letters with the Westfield congregation without Taylor's knowledge, and Daniel Brewer vehemently attacked Taylor's attempt to prosecute the case. Arguments and language that Taylor might have excused in "illiterate persons" he was now hearing from a fellow minister, "him that had learned the Arts & rules of reason."[45] The slow development of Taylor's isolation among the Connecticut Valley clergy, beginning in theological controversy over the sacrament and extending to matters of church practice, discipline, and personal authority in the "Suffield Concerns" and the fast day dispute, reached its culmination in the Smith case. Taylor's only remaining recourse was the phrase he uttered repeatedly to the various parties in this controversy, "I knew my office & would not come unto [them] to learn my duty."[46]

The two lengthy disciplinary sermons that Taylor preached five months after the controversy ended were essentially an extended commentary on this self-justifying phrase.[47] But there is little evidence that these sermons were persuasive. Taylor had been accused by Captain Phelps, the oldest surviving church member, of acting as "Lord over God's Heritage," and Taylor had in turn called Phelps the "Master of Misrule." Such a drastic breach in the town's religious community would not be easy to repair. Neither side was eager to make amends, and there were no strong third parties within the community to smooth things over. Compared with Boston's Third Church, where a direct confrontation between Samuel Sewall and his minister Ebenezer Pemberton could be diffused by other important figures in the community, Westfield's religious culture was too shallow and too brittle to withstand such a break.[48]

The remaining disciplinary cases Taylor recorded in the years after 1713 involved Ensign Kellogg in several episodes of drunkenness and a very odd personal dispute between Abigail Dewey and her neighbors, a case where Taylor's attempt to conduct disciplinary proceedings was once more challenged by the parties involved.[49] Nothing so disruptive as the Benjamin Smith case appeared again in the remainder of the church records. The town records, however, reveal another controversy which became at least as involved and contentious as the Smith case, brought on in 1717 by the need to build a new meetinghouse.

In many ways the controversy over the meetinghouse was even more bitter than the Benjamin Smith case, but its impact on Westfield's religious community was not as great, simply because the damage to the church had already been done. The rift between the brethren and the minister was merely widened by these further events, which can be traced in the town records. The growing population required a new church building; repairs and extensions on the old one were no longer adequate or feasible. But the attempt to build a new structure led to a long and bitter struggle over its location; Taylor insisted on building where the old meetinghouse stood, while a majority of the townspeople favored a new site. The leaders of the opposition to Taylor were, as might be expected, Isaac Phelps, Joseph Mawdsley, and Steven Kellogg, and their leadership created a division in the town meeting which ultimately required a committee of outsiders to settle the matter. As it turned out, the final recommendation on the matter was made by Col. Samuel Partridge, Taylor's nemesis in the Smith case. Partridge recommended that the meetinghouse be built on land owned by Joseph Mawdsley, which the town then purchased at a rather inflated price. The new meetinghouse was far different from the rough and simple structure of the early years. A great deal of money was spent to procure a bell for the tower, replacing the drum that was once used to call people to meeting.[50] The town also voted to "seal up the windows below & above & the rest to whitewash," and to "face the pews & the fore seets & the back seets with wainskut work," luxuries unknown in earlier days.[51]

When the building was finally completed, Taylor refused to preach in it. In October 1721, a committee was formed to persuade him "conserning his removeing to the new meeting house to atend the worship of God there,"[52] but Taylor was so affronted by the town's actions that it took many months of argument and coaxing before he agreed, urged on by correspondence from his old friend, Samuel Sewall.[53] Surprisingly enough, Taylor wrote nothing about this lengthy controversy in the church records. He stopped recording disciplinary cases in 1720, when the meetinghouse controversy was well under way, but never mentioned this issue at all, nor did he formally accuse any church members of wrongdoing, despite the similarities to earlier cases. We might speculate that the lack of support from the brethren in the Smith case prevented him from acting more strongly in this matter.

Taylor's strong opposition to this project demonstrated his diminishing concern over whom and what the meetinghouse was for, a disregard for the evangelical purposes that a more spacious and well-appointed church building would serve. The old meetinghouse, familiar as it was to Taylor, was neither well situated nor large enough for Westfield's expanding population. As an enclave for the elect few, the old building may well have been sufficient, but if the church were to grow with the community, the meetinghouse had to be more commodious. The new bell, extravagant as it might have seemed to Taylor, could be heard as a call to worship across the expanding reaches of the Westfield settlements, and the finished pews and benches could seat all of the town's people, never before possible in the old building. The overall effect of the meetinghouse dispute was to confirm the developments of the past two decades. It defined the laity's desire for a more inclusive religious community, which, in the building of the new meetinghouse, they demonstrated that they could finally afford. But the dispute pushed Taylor even further aside from the central role he had once played in Westfield.

Taylor's declining health may have prevented him from pursuing the meetinghouse controversy as a case of church discipline. In 1720, at the age of seventy-eight, he suffered through a severe illness, and shortly thereafter began to write "A Valediction to all the World preparatory for Death." For the next half decade, he continued to revise this poem as his health wavered and death drew near. These late poems reflect the beginning of his final withdrawal from the world. Taylor's valediction focuses on celestial bodies, the air and the sky, and the material world to the relative exclusion of family and friends. His first version devotes more lines to the moon than it does to his wife, children, and congregation, perhaps indicating that his connections to the society around him were growing less important as he approached eternity.[54]

As Taylor's health declined, the town took steps to find a successor. In 1722, smallpox and "the Distemper" threatened the town, and Taylor was not up to dealing with this as a physician. The town was forced "to send down to Roxberey for Docter Tomson or to som other man of skill . . . to help us in our dificulties." For the first time it was the townspeople rather than the minister who took the initiative "to keep a day of humiliation upon the acount of Gods hand that is out against us in the small pox."[55] At the same time, the town began to look for a candidate to be Taylor's assistant and eventual replacement. Typically, Taylor was reluctant to relinquish control. Several times committees were appointed to "discours with Mr. Taylor concerning giveing a minister a call."[56] In 1723, Isaac Stiles, a recent Yale College graduate, was hired to assist Taylor, and efforts were made to secure him as Taylor's successor. But there was some disagreement over his qualifications, and in one extended town meeting, twice adjourned for week-long recesses, the town voted to hire Stiles for half-time, then voted again for Stiles to "undertake the whole work of the ministrey," from which thirteen townsmen dissented, including Captain Isaac Phelps.[57] The fact that Stiles married Taylor's daughter Keziah suggests that the aged minister may have favored Stiles as his successor, and that the old Captain was battling him one last time. At any rate, the dissenting townsmen were a "sufitient Discoragment" for Stiles to give up the chase, and he left to settle in West Haven, Connecticut. Within another year, the town acquired Nehemiah Bull, another recent Yale graduate, and after further negotiations Bull was permanently settled and ordained as the town's minister.[58]

In May 1726, the town chose a committee that included a Captain Dewey, a descendant of the man sent to Cambridge in 1671 to hire Taylor, "to go to Mr. Taylor & discors with him to see whether or no he be wiling to lay Down preaching."[59] Lay down preaching he did, and although his son Eldad claimed that "many persons came to him for the resolving of their doubt, for council and direction in the conserns of their souls after his last confinement to his house," Taylor's powers declined, he no longer wrote poetry, and by 1728, his daughter required money from the town "to tend Mr. Taylor."[60] Confined to his home in a weakened condition, Taylor had no strength to protest when his successor put the following question to a church vote: "Whether such persons as come into full communion may not be left at their liberty as to the giving the chh. an account of the work of saving conversion i.e. whether Relations shall not be looked upon as a matter of indifferency." The motion passed in the affirmative. In addition, the church voted to create a standing committee of five lay members to consult with the minister "about the issuing cases of difficulty" in matters of church discipline, thereby giving the brethren a formal platform for voicing their opinions and shaping church decisions.[61]

Thus, with Taylor in his "last confinement," the church voted to overthrow his strict requirements for approaching the Lord's Table and to end the minister's personal authority over the congregation. These were the two aspects of church life that Taylor had fought longest and hardest to defend, but which had also prevented the church from meeting the community's religious needs and maintaining harmony between itself and the town. What had been a lifelong commitment to Taylor had become a "matter of indifferency" to his successor and his former congregation. Taylor's views on admission to the sacrament and church discipline had been essential to creating a Puritan church in the England of his youth, but were obstacles to maintaining and enhancing the church's growth so many years later in a very different new world. Mercifully, Taylor "fell asleep" for the last time, as his gravestone reads, "June 24, 1729 in the 87 year of his age."

More than a century before, the Anglican bishop Richard Hooker had written a penetrating critique of the English Puritan movement. Hooker understood that those called "Puritans" differed from conformists not in their theology, not even necessarily in their spiritual sensibilities, but in their belief that for a godly person, nothing in life was a "matter of indifferency," least of all the proper forms of worship.[62] By this standard, Taylor's successor and the Westfield church members were no longer Puritans. Edward Taylor would have seen it that way (and historians have tended to agree with Taylor's position), but Taylor's understanding of the issue and his vision of New England's history was a partial one, shaped by his own experience and his personal definition of a godly life. The vote taken by the Westfield church was not an expression on their part of indifference to the culture of godliness which produced the Puritan movement. In the circumstances of their homogeneous rural community on the New England frontier, it made little sense to maintain restrictive standards for church membership. Rather, their vote represented another step in their continuing effort to take control of the resources that sustained piety and to define their religious lives within the world of their own experience, an effort which Taylor had largely opposed.

In the first five years of Nehemiah Bull's tenure, there were thirty-three church admissions, equalling the number in the last seventeen years of Taylor's ministry. Then in 1735 the Connecticut Valley revival began, and forty-three new members were added to the Westfield church in one year alone, a feat repeated in 1741 and 1742 during Whitefield's revivals.[63] These figures are merely indications of the thriving godly religious mentality and the desire for participation in the life of Westfield's church that existed beyond the rigid boundaries defined by Taylor during his ministry.

The depth and content of Westfield's lay religious culture can never be defined with precision or explored in elaborate detail in the way we can examine Edward Taylor's religious beliefs. Instead, we get glimpses of the lay mentality here and there; in the few surviving conversion relations, in David Dewey's meditations, in Mawdsley and Kellogg's peculiar concern for keeping proper fast days, or in Captain Phelps's detailed knowledge of the determinations that the Cambridge Platform's authors made sixty-five years earlier.[64] But in the impoverished religious climate of this rural village on the New England frontier, Westfield's population suffered from the lack of resources that would have helped them to emulate the devotional life exemplified by Taylor. For Taylor, conditioned to see the godly life as a withdrawal from the world into a sanctified community, nothing less than this ideal would suffice. But in holding fast to this belief, he failed to see that a people who thought of themselves as part of a godly nation could not forever maintain the siege mentality necessary to sustain such a withdrawal, and would not tolerate the inequity of restricting the community's religious resources to the elite few. This Richard Hooker saw in the 1590s, and this Solomon Stoddard understood and effectively acted to correct a century later, when he opened the church to participation by all while still trying to cultivate heartfelt repentance in the lives of sinners.

The sparks of revival coming from Stoddard's Northampton were fanned into flames by his successor, Jonathan Edwards, illuminating the eagerness of the people of the Connecticut Valley for a vital, emotional religious life. But when Edwards, like Taylor, would attempt to restrict access to the church, to control the language and definition of true conversion, and to question the sincerity of many of the revival's converts, the people of Northampton would reject Edwards even more firmly than Westfield had rejected Taylor.[65] In Westfield, Taylor's lifelong commitment to a vision of the church that was formed in an earlier and much different historical moment had prevented the cultivation of a more open and vital religious community. This problem, exacerbated by the limiting conditions of life in a frontier village, had led to a divided church that turned inward upon itself. In the conflicts of Taylor's later years, recorded in the cases of church discipline when these divisions finally emerged, one can read beneath the surface of petty argument and controversy a consistent desire among the laity for a more accessible church, attuned to the realities of their social experience and their religious desires. The people of Westfield would never encounter a bishop, would never witness the rituals of high church Anglicanism, would never experience the threat of the enemies that had shaped Edward Taylor's world. If there was an arbitrary religious authority and worshipper of idols in their experience, it was Taylor himself and his reverence for a bygone phase of the Puritan movement that was out of place in Westfield. In their rejection of an earlier vision of the Puritan church, a vision that was largely foreign to them, but which had been the formative experience of their minister's life, the Westfield laity demanded a wider gate to "Christ's curious garden" than Edward Taylor's "solid walls of discipline" would allow.

Conclusion

FROM THE COVENANT TO THE
REVIVAL AND BEYOND

The people of Westfield have till now above all other places, made a
scoff and derision of this concern at Northampton.
—Jonathan Edwards, "A Faithful Narrative of the Surprising
Work of God . . . in Northampton" (1735)

Bless the Name of God for spiritual Blessings already received in the
remarkable Revival of his Work among us, . . . that it may go on and
prosper, 'till the whole Land shall be filled with the blessed Fruits of
the Spirit.
—Joseph Sewall, "Sermon Preached in the South Church" (1742)

In the 1730s and 1740s, churches and congregants all across New England
experienced a Great Awakening. But the vital religious feelings they were
awakened to, their convictions of personal and corporate sinfulness and their
responses to divine grace, were not unfamiliar emotions. In the decades between the Halfway Covenant of 1662 and the extraordinary revivals of the
mid-eighteenth century, the evangelical churches of New England had thoroughly prepared the region's population to anticipate, recognize, and improve
upon a sudden outpouring of God's grace. Yet each person's reaction to the
awakening was shaped by his or her disposition, preparation, and position
in the world. For some, the awakening brought on spiritual crises and moral
reformations, leading them to embrace the promise of grace and dedicate
themselves to traditional forms of piety. For others, it restored the vitality of
conversions first experienced many years before. Still others gave up old ways
of life to follow itinerant evangelists or split off from churches in which they
had complacently worshipped for many years.
    Similarly, each New England church, like each individual, responded to
the Great Awakening in ways shaped by its experience and preparation, by its

history as a religious community. Revivals were by definition a communal experience, based on the idea that God would occasionally pour out his spirit on groups of believers who had gathered together in a covenanted relationship.[1] The two communities of Boston and Westfield each responded differently to the challenges of life in a maturing New England society, challenges that were first addressed in the decade of the Halfway Covenant. In subsequent decades, the conflicts and negotiations between clergy and laity that shaped the practice of religion created lasting patterns within each local community's religious culture. These developing traditions helped make revivals possible, and determined the course of events in each community when they did happen. This distinction is important to keep in mind, for the causes of revival were often separate from the causes of the contention that split churches in the revival's wake. By tracing the distinctive features of the revivals in these churches, we can review the results of these long years of development, and also begin to see what linked individual communities together in the larger system of New England's social and religious evolution. During the awakening, our two churches experienced similar outpourings of piety because at least some (if not all) of the members of each community had been taught to expect them. But the effects of revival in Boston and Westfield were quite different because of the differences in the way they were prepared.

❦

Edward Taylor did not concern himself extensively with preparing the people of Westfield to anticipate a great and sudden outpouring of God's grace upon the community at large. He did cultivate an intense and at times ecstatic form of spirituality, but only within the context of a church that was an exclusive withdrawal from the world, where only a few chosen saints could expect to be so favored. Consequently, the Westfield religious community was divided between those few families who could approximate something like Taylor's form of spiritual introspection and devotion, and a larger body of believers who looked for a more inclusive way to salvation within the church. In the first few years after Taylor's death, the church's membership standards were revised under his successor, Nehemiah Bull, and a substantial influx of new members joined the church, though not in revivalistic proportions.[2] But in 1735, the revival that began under Jonathan Edwards' direction in nearby Northampton seems to have spread to the church in Westfield. We learn this from the admissions records, which list an unprecedented forty-three new members in 1735, but also from oblique and telling references to Westfield in Edwards' famous *Faithful Narrative of the Surprising Work of God . . . in Northampton and the Neighbouring Towns and Villages.*

Edwards' *Narrative*, first published in London in 1737 and republished countless times in America, was originally composed as a private letter to Benjamin Colman in Boston. In an abridged version of this letter which Colman sent to English correspondents, and in published versions of the text, Westfield is listed among the "Neighbouring Towns and Villages" that experienced awakenings. Nehemiah Bull is said to have informed Edwards "of a great alteration there, and that more had been done in one week than in seven years before."[3] But in Edwards' original letter, the terms were more ambiguous: "Mr. Bull of Westfield [said] that there began to be a great alteration there, and that there had been more done in one week before that time that I spoke with him than had been done in seven years before. *The people of Westfield have till now above all other places, made a scoff and derision of this concern at Northampton.*"[4] That Bull merely reported that an alteration (not a revival) had *begun*, and more significantly, that the people of Westfield had been notorious scoffers at the Northampton revival, were purposely omitted from Edwards' published text, probably to highlight the appearance of harmony in an event that actually must have been quite chaotic.

Given the context of Westfield's religious development under Edward Taylor and the divided community that was his legacy, it should not be surprising that some Westfield citizens were caught up in the revival, while others derided the doings in Northampton.[5] The long years of controversy in which Taylor had attacked Solomon Stoddard's inclusive definition of the church and his revivalistic approach to converting the population had failed to prepare the whole community of Westfield for anything like what Northampton was experiencing. But aside from the fact that Nehemiah Bull testified to the veracity of Edwards' *Narrative* in a preface to the Boston edition of 1738, this is virtually all we know of the first stirrings of revival in Westfield.[6] Bull, a contemporary of Edwards at Yale, was friendly to the revival impulse and would presumably have welcomed George Whitefield during the Grand Itinerant's dramatic tour of New England late in 1740. But the ailing Bull died in April of that year, leaving the Westfield pulpit vacant at the time of Whitefield's arrival.[7]

During the westward swing of his first tour through New England, George Whitefield did manage a brief stop in Westfield on October 20, 1740, after a more extended visit to Edwards' Northampton church. In his journals, Whitefield noted that at Westfield he preached "to a pretty large Congregation, and with considerable Power at the latter End."[8] The Westfield church records indicate that in the year or two following Whitefield's visit, the membership rolls displayed high levels of new admissions, equalling those of the revival in 1735.[9] But compared with Whitefield's visits to other Connecticut

Valley towns, the impact of his preaching on Westfield was rather limited. Here, for instance, is Whitefield's description of his preaching in nearby Hadley:"... reached Hadley, a place where a great work was carried on some years ago; but lately the people of God have complained of deadness and losing their first love. As soon as I mentioned what God had done for their souls formerly, it was like putting fire to tinder. The remembrance of it caused many to weep sorely." Similarly, when Whitefield preached in Northampton, he discovered that "when I came to remind them of their former experiences, and how zealous and lively they were at that time, both minister and people wept much."[10] In these cases, Whitefield's enormous success was predicated on the power of earlier revivals led by the local clergymen. This prior work of God's grace prepared the people for further spiritual harvests, and supplied Whitefield with the knowledge of the emotional effects he could achieve simply by reminding the community of its collective past and its need to turn to God for renewal.[11]

Although Whitefield had moderate success in Westfield, the inadequacy of Westfield's preparation for a community-wide awakening, especially when compared with Northampton, where Solomon Stoddard had been gathering spiritual harvests long before his grandson took over the pulpit, helps to explain why the Westfield revival was a more subdued affair. The absence of an ordained minister at the time of Whitefield's visit further dampened the town's response to the Grand Itinerant, for all across New England, the typical revival pattern required local ministers to carry forward the religious fervor in the wake of Whitefield's and other itinerants' whirlwind visits.[12] Until John Ballantine was ordained as Nehemiah Bull's successor in June 1741, there was no one in the Westfield pulpit to improve upon Whitefield's visit and encourage the local revival, and Ballantine's unfamiliarity with his congregation must have further limited his immediate effectiveness as a spiritual guide.[13]

John Ballantine was an orthodox Calvinist and a favorer of the revivals.[14] At the time of his ordination, he was particularly eager to distance himself from the taint of Arminianism that still hung over the First Church of Springfield from the recent controversy surrounding its ordination of Robert Breck, a suspected Arminian, in 1735.[15] But Ballantine's support for the revival and his religious orthodoxy were cast in a moderate mode. He tended to downplay the importance of doctrinal disagreements, and he encouraged tolerance for minor variations in church polity, a position consistent with his youthful membership in Boston's Brattle Street Church, but at odds with the stance Edward Taylor had promoted in Westfield.[16]

The new minister's ecumenical outlook pleased those Westfield congregants who had longed for a more accommodating church, but it could not have appealed to those trained by Edward Taylor to see the church as the exclusive refuge of the saints. It should not be surprising, then, to discover that Westfield was one of the few Upper Connecticut Valley towns in which a separatist schism occurred in the Awakening's aftermath.[17] Furthermore, the self-appointed leader of the secession from Ballantine's church was Jedediah Dewey, a member of the Westfield family that had through several generations been closest to Taylor in its religious sympathies. The Westfield Separates broke off from the main church in 1748, and in 1754 "Jedediah Dewey [was] set apart for a Teacher of the Separate company here." Dewey, a carpenter without formal education but imbued with the religious fervor that had characterized his ancestors, guided the small congregation of Separates for fifteen years in Westfield, and then organized their migration to Vermont, where he became the first pastor of the Bennington Separate church in 1763.[18]

In the secession and migration led by Jedediah Dewey, the vision of the church which Edward Taylor had brought with him to Westfield from his experience as a seventeenth-century English dissenter finally found fulfillment in New England. The New Light Separates in the post-Awakening era combined a particularly intense definition of the conversion experience with a desire to withdraw from the world into churches limited to those who shared this definition. But there were considerable differences between the English society which persecuted Edward Taylor and his fellow Puritans out of the churches and into dissent, and the world of eighteenth-century New England orthodoxy from which the Separates chose to secede. Many of the Separates were recent revival converts who ". . . lamented having practiced 'external duties' without, until this moment, experiencing the work of grace. Thus transformed, some of these lay people turned their new-found fervor against the half-way covenant, which they criticized for permitting unregenerate persons to enter the church."[19] However, in criticizing the traditional forms of piety and the institutions of church life offered by orthodox New England religious culture, separatists were rejecting the very preparatory experiences which had made their own conversions possible. They were denying the value of the "external duties" of practical piety which had taught them to comprehend their own ecstatic emotional reactions to evangelical preaching as a work of conversion. Without this preparation, they would never have responded to the messages of itinerant evangelists with such fervor.

In creating new churches with admission based strictly on the experience of the new birth, the Separates were, in effect, cutting off the image of their former selves from access to the church. The impulse that led these newly converted lay separatists to renounce their former experience as hypocrisy was a more extreme version of the same impulse that caused pro-revival ministers like Thomas Prince to discount the value of earlier revivals in the light of new and more powerful outpourings of God's grace upon their communities. Those Separates like Jedediah Dewey who withdrew from mainstream society and religious culture did so not because the culture of godliness was despised, as it had been in England in Taylor's day, but because in eighteenth-century New England it had become so routine, so widespread, and so all-encompassing as to include people not naturally inclined toward intense religious piety, as well as souls who had not yet experienced conversion for themselves. Westfield, unlike most of its neighbors in the Upper Connecticut Valley, suffered a separation in the aftermath of the revivals as a consequence of the form of its earlier preparation, as an outgrowth of the kind of religious community that had already been cultivated there.

⁂

In contrast to Westfield, a great deal of information exists about the Great Awakening in Boston. In fact, a subject so large deserves a book-length study of its own.[20] Given the attention that historians have lavished on many local communities in searching for the causes and consequences of the Great Awakening, it is remarkable that Boston has not received fuller treatment.[21] Yet in many ways, the best narrative account we have of the Great Awakening in Boston, despite the biases inherent in its promotional intent, is still Thomas Prince's "Some Account of the Late Revival of Religion in Boston," which he published in *The Christian History* in 1744.

Prince's account, which fills forty tightly crammed pages over the course of six issues of the weekly journal, reveals how the Third Church's long years of preparation for and anticipation of an outpouring of God's grace made the revival itself possible. It also demonstrates that Boston congregations were enormously receptive to the revivalist message, so much so that Boston became a magnet for every itinerant preacher. After the astonishing success of Whitefield in the fall of 1740, when he preached several times daily to audiences of as many as six thousand in the Old South Meetinghouse, and upwards of ten thousand on the Common (Whitefield claimed twenty thousand), Boston was flooded by Whitefield's followers and imitators over the course of the next several years.[22] Gilbert Tennent preached in Boston from December 1740 to March 1741, with overwhelming power in bringing people into "deep Concern about their Souls."[23] In the wake of Tennent's ministrations and with the continuing work of the Boston clergy to maintain the spiritual fervor, the rest of 1741 saw "the very Face of the Town . . . strangely altered." Even formerly irreligious people joined regular churchgoers in attending "religious societies." One of Boston's "worthy Gentlemen" expressed his amazement that his old practice of clearing the taverns of local revelers on Saturday evenings for the approaching Sabbath was no longer necessary, as "he found them empty of all but Lodgers."[24] After Tennent's labors, others like Andrew Croswell, John Cleaveland, and James Davenport brought their spiritual gifts to Boston, where they were received with varying degrees of responsiveness.[25]

That the revivals had an enormous impact in Boston is unquestioned. More significant is the fact that years of preparation in churches like the Old South, grounded in the evangelical vision articulated in the Halfway Covenant, made it possible for the community to experience the awakening as a relatively undisruptive continuation of an ongoing religious tradition, rather than a radical break from and critique of the past. Boston's orthodox churches saw relatively few separations. In the Third Church, calls for schism were limited to an extremely small number of radicals. Four men and two or three women out of the hundreds of Third Church members chose to follow James Davenport's and Andrew Croswell's call for separations.[26] The enthusiastic support which the Third Church's ministers, Joseph Sewall and Thomas Prince, gave to the cause of the revival makes it quite understandable that few New Lights would choose to leave.

Even more interesting is the absence of "conservative" or "Old Light" dissent from the Third Church's revivalistic tendencies. On the contrary, the traditional bastions of the Third Church, the "hedge" around the garden of the church made up of the leading lay people, embraced the revival with as much fervor as the average member, and in a markedly public and supportive manner.[27] Prior to Whitefield's arrival in September 1740, advance publicity had raised the expectations of Bostonians, due in part to the correspondence maintained between Whitefield and Josiah Willard, a Third Church member, the long-time secretary of the province and son of the late pastor Samuel Willard. When Whitefield arrived, Willard regularly entertained him and introduced the itinerant to the leading ministers and laymen in Boston.[28]

Among the latter was Jonathan Belcher, the Royal Governor of Massachusetts and member of the Third Church, whose response to Whitefield's message was striking. The son of one of Boston's most successful merchant families, Belcher can be seen as perhaps the most "anglicized" of all New Englanders. He lived abroad for many years, visited the courts of European heads of state, became Massachusetts' agent to the crown, and eventually, through his English connections, gained the appointment as Governor in 1730.[29] But despite his ties to English royal officialdom and his duty of occasionally occupying the Governor's pew at King's Chapel, Belcher's sympathies remained with orthodox Congregationalism and evangelical religion.[30] During the Awakening he made this abundantly clear. Before Whitefield's arrival, he sent his son with an advance party to meet the itinerant on the outskirts of Boston and escort him into town. While in Boston, Belcher became Whitefield's steady companion; he regularly drove him about in his coach, dined with him, prayed with him, and attended many of his sermons, where he was often visibly moved. In fact, in Whitefield's own view, the Governor's attendance seemed to inspire particularly soul-rending performances.

For Whitefield's farewell sermon, Belcher drove the preacher to the Boston Common in his coach and stayed with him throughout his address to the twenty-thousand people assembled there. With the Governor in his coach representing the trappings of state power and reinforcing the evangelist's message, the spectacle must have gained additional emotional force, lending the weight of Massachusetts' history as a holy commonwealth to the charisma of Whitefield himself. When Whitefield finally left Boston the next day for his tour of western New England, Belcher took him in his coach to the Charlestown ferry, where, wrote Whitefield, "he handed me into the boat, kissed me, and with tears bid me farewell." Yet the Governor could not bear to see Whitefield go. The next day Belcher galloped on horseback thirty miles west to Marlborough, where he met Whitefield and continued to escort him as far as Worcester. Belcher urged Whitefield to "go on stirring up the ministers, for . . . reformation must begin at the house of God," and he implored Whitefield: "do not spare rulers any more than ministers, no, not the chief of them." After listening to yet another of Whitefield's dramatic open-air sermons, Belcher finally took his last tearful leave, praying that "I may apply what has been said to my own heart," and asking Whitefield to "pray that I may hunger and thirst after righteousness."[31] The emotional impact of the Great Awakening has often been represented by examples like that of Nathan Cole, the semi-literate Connecticut farmer who dropped his plow and rode twelve miles in an hour to hear Whitefield preach in Middletown.[32] But the equally impassioned experience of Jonathan Belcher illustrates that the revival's appeal was not confined to the lowly. Even the most refined and sophisticated members of Boston society were prepared to respond with fervor to the message of the new birth.[33]

In a manner that had become a tradition in the Third Church, the Awakening was not merely embraced by the ministers and members, but improved upon and turned into yet another element in the widening means of grace intended to spread orthodox religious culture. Just as individual religious experiences like that of Elizabeth Butcher were transformed into exemplary models that might bring about further conversions,[34] so the Awakening was not understood simply as an end in itself, but was converted into a means for creating further revivals, both in Boston and elsewhere. In this way, the revival's continuity with earlier religious culture was firmly established, and the resources available to churches like the Old South were put to work in both traditional and innovative forms. In this vein, Joseph Sewall praised God for "spiritual Blessings already received in the remarkable Revival of his Work among us," and prayed that "it may go on and prosper, 'till the whole Land shall be filled with the blessed Fruits of the Spirit." To this end, he urged, "Let the success which God hath of late given to the Ministers of the Word above what we have known in Times past . . . animate us to labour more abundantly."[35]

The very sermon in which Sewall preached these words is evidence of the clergy's more abundant labors. It took place during a series of special days of prayer held sequentially in the Boston churches for the continuance of the revival. The means of grace which the Boston laity and clergy had cultivated over the decades now increased remarkably in quantity and diversity. New religious lectures were instituted on virtually every night of the week in many of the churches, and people seemed never to get enough preaching of "the sincere Milk of the Word." Devotional groups sprang up everywhere and filled to overflowing: "private Societies for religious Exercises, both of younger and elder Persons, both of Males and Females by themselves, in several Parts of the Town, now increased to a much greater Number than ever." The renewed interest in religion meant that "the People were constantly employing the Ministers to pray and preach at those Societies, as also at many private Houses where no form'd Society met." But Boston, with its dense religious culture and plenty of trained preachers and educated laymen, was well prepared to meet the demand, and the ministers made the most of it: "Some of our Ministers, to oblige the People, have sometimes preached in publick and private, at one House or another, even every Evening, except after Saturday, for a Week together. And the more we prayed and preached, the more enlarged were our Hearts . . . And O how many, how serious and attentive were our Hearers."[36] The result was a huge increase in the number of people concerned for their souls, convinced of their sins, and converted to a life of godliness in which they would need still further ministerial guidance.

As a consequence of this preaching-mania, the demand for pious books exploded during the revival, and here the resources of Boston's religious culture were again put to work. The traditional nature of the revivalistic piety and its continuity with the Puritan past is clear from the titles of the books that were suddenly popular. Thomas Prince noticed that "The People seem'd to have a renewed Taste for those old pious and experimental Writers, Mr.

Hooker, Shepard, . . . Dr. Owen, . . . as well as later, such as . . . Willard, Stoddard, Dr. Increase and Cotton Mather . . . ."[37] Part of this new taste for old books can be attributed to the fact that the clergy themselves saw the Awakening as a renewal of traditional religious belief, and part is due to the ministers' work, in conjunction with Boston's publishers and booksellers, to supply the people with reprinted editions of these older titles.[38] In fact, the very next issue of *The Christian History* included an advertisement for some of the treatises Prince had just mentioned. Thomas Shepard's *Sincere Convert* and *Sound Believer*, Samuel Willard's *Sacramental Meditations*, and Solomon Stoddard's *Safety of Appearing in the Righteousness of Christ* and *Guide to Christ* were all available at the bookstore of Daniel Henchman in Cornhill, just across the street from the Old South Meetinghouse.[39] The demand for this literature was fueled by the increased number of religious societies, lectures, and meetings and by the renewed intensity of personal devotion, for which these works were offered as indispensable guides.

Prince's magazine, *The Christian History*, was itself probably the most innovative means through which Boston's religious and cultural resources were employed to further the revival. Prince took advantage of the fact that Boston had become a hub of the transatlantic revival network to turn his magazine (actually edited by his son but firmly under his influence) into a clearinghouse for current revival narratives from New England and abroad.[40] *The Christian History* also became a place to print extracts from and advertisements for the "old writers" and descriptions of earlier revivals in New England history. It thus maintained a sense of continuity with the past and spread the message that traditional forms of New England piety were good models for understanding revivals of religion anywhere. Revival narratives, whether spread by word-of-mouth and private correspondence or printed in magazines and pamphlets, then triggered other similar revivals wherever communities had been primed to receive them.[41]

In putting their energy and resources to work for promoting further revivals in new places, the clergy and laity exceeded the traditional boundaries of the individual gathered church, just as they had increasingly done throughout the eighteenth century in their expanding charitable and missionary works. Indeed, through the Awakening and beyond, the Third Church continued to collect ever greater sums of money and earmark it for missionary preaching, poor relief, or the support of new churches in remote places like Dartmouth, Hull, and Nantucket.[42] By reaching out to other people beyond their own walls, the Old South Church had helped to prepare New England society at large for the Great Awakening. In that sense, it is almost inaccurate to say that there was a revival *in* the Third Church or *in* Boston, for the revival, like the earlier preparatory labors, was intentionally spread well beyond the local church and community. In former days, there had been spiritual harvests in individual churches, like the ones in John Cotton Jr.'s Plymouth Church after his arrival in the 1660s, in the Third Church after the covenant renewals of 1679, or periodically in Solomon Stoddard's Northampton church from the 1670s through the 1720s.[43] The steady development of a densely occupied, thoroughly prepared, and interconnected set of orthodox religious communities all across the New England landscape allowed these "harvests" within the nurturing gardens of local communities to become a unified Great Awakening, in which preaching tours conducted by itinerant evangelists could in a single season reap the rewards of a generation of patient sowing.[44] Throughout New England, as in Boston, this religious flowering manifested itself as an overwhelming increase in *demand*, in a desire for preaching, for prayer, for godly books and spiritual conversation, and for the feast of the Lord's Supper.

つ%%♪

In the late sixteenth and early seventeenth centuries, Puritanism had been centered in Britain—in the universities, especially Cambridge, in the market towns and surrounding countryside of East Anglia, in the West Country of Dorset, and among the merchant and professional classes of London, and it was fueled by strong connections, commercial and cultural, to the reformed capitals of the continent. It was also, to a certain degree, an exclusive movement—godly Puritans withdrew from their profane neighbors into private conventicles rather than seeking to convert them. When the first Puritan exiles reached Massachusetts, they were a remote outpost of a movement whose main body, centered in and focused on England, did not view their departure all that kindly. Out on the distant rim of the Atlantic, they had to import all their necessities, their ministers and godly books, and they worshipped in cold rude log hovels rather than the grand churches that some of them had left behind. In the American wilderness, the rich array of the means of grace that had nourished their faith back in England had been stripped down and thinned out to a bare minimum. But in the aftermath of the English civil wars, with the demise of the Protectorate and the Restoration of Charles II, the Puritan movement in England collapsed. Puritanism became dissent, a scattered, decentralized opposition without a clear focus or center, its clergy ejected from the universities and parish churches. So at this very same time, in the latter decades of the seventeenth century, Boston transformed itself from the recipient of the cultural resources of English Puritanism into the principal producer of the same, creating for itself and exporting out to its own hinterland, to its own cultural frontiers, the very same kinds of resources it had imported in an earlier generation. But in making this transformation, Bostonians developed an evangelical intensity, an urge to export its culture, that was something new.

This dramatic transformation in Boston's sense of identity and purpose can be traced by examining a series of documents from a genre which Cotton Mather labelled "ecclesiastical maps" of New England. From the very earliest days of settlement, religious leaders and historians of New England displayed a fondness for charting the extent of their culture's conquest of the wilderness. In 1631, less than a year after the arrival of the Winthrop fleet, Thomas Dudley began to define this genre in a letter to his English patron, the Countess of Lincoln, which described the half-dozen places around Massachusetts Bay that the immigrants had already settled. At this early date, Dudley feared that dispersal from a central location might expose the colonists to native attacks, and perhaps more dangerously, might snap the supply lines back to the source of Puritan culture in England.[45] By 1652, Edward Johnson described the settlement process more confidently in his *Wonder-Working Providence of Sion's Saviour in New England*, the first full-fledged history of Massachusetts Bay. Johnson carefully enumerated the "planting" of each of the thirty-some Massachusetts towns and churches as evidence of God's divine purpose in the colonizing enterprise.[46] But Johnson's text, like Dudley's, was intended to convince an English audience, still at the center of the Puritan enterprise, that these exiles were not wasting their time in the wilderness.

The next major entry in this genre represents a transitional moment. William Hubbard's *Present State of New England* was published twenty-five years later, in 1677, in the aftermath of King Philip's War. Hubbard included, for the first time, an actual graphic representation of New England's Puritan settlement, a rather primitive woodcut map that was folded into the original text. Expansion had been slowed by war, but there were now fifty Puritan settlements in New England, depicted as little buildings, possibly meant to be meetinghouses to represent churches, for some of them seem to have something like steeples on top. The map has many strange features—it grossly exaggerates the size of the Merrimack River and of the lake that is erroneously suggested to be its source, and north of that it fancifully, perhaps wishfully depicts the "Wine Hills." But to modern eyes, the oddest feature is its orientation. With north to the right, the Connecticut River at the top, and Cape Cod at the lower left instead of the lower right, the map looks all wrong to a modern viewer. This unfamiliar orientation suggests a view of New England for an observer still planted in the Old World—the projected reader of this map stands in England looking westward at a strange and distant land. Like Dudley and Johnson before him, Hubbard's map and text were anglocentric, but, at the same time, this map was the very first one actually printed by a press in Boston rather than in London. While Dudley and Johnson had sent their "maps" back to England for publication and consumption, Hubbard's map was published in Boston as part of the process of cultural production that was now shifting across the Atlantic to New England.[47]

Another quarter century after Hubbard, New England's settlements had doubled in number, and Cotton Mather concluded Book I of his *Magnalia Christi Americana* with a chapter entitled "Hecatompolis," or "having a hundred cities." He announced that "It is proper that I should now give the Reader an Ecclesiastical Map of the Country," which would demonstrate New England's growth to the year 1696, despite two decades of the "Blasting Strokes of Heaven." For each colony Mather systematically listed the churches and named the ministers who served them. For those very few towns, like Dartmouth in Bristol County, which lacked churches and ministers, Mather described their current condition as "perishing without vision."[48]

The eighteenth century saw enormous growth in the number of orthodox churches and congregants in New England. Thomas Prince, who attempted to record the annals of New England's history, was overwhelmed in trying to keep up with this expansion. At the time of his death in 1758, Prince was still sending out circular notices to towns, ". . . namely Newton, Groton, Chelmsford, Billerica . . ." and so on and on, asking earnestly for information from "records, gravestones, and ancient people."[49] It was left to Ezra Stiles, Prince's fellow historian and collector, to update Cotton Mather's enumeration, which he did in his *Discourse on the Christian Union* in 1761.[50] The Newport minister's version of New England's ecclesiastical map self-consciously followed Mather's plan, but the more ecumenically minded Stiles included separate lists of "Baptists, Friends, and Episcopalians" along with the Congregational churches. Nonetheless, the orthodox churches were still foremost in Stiles' estimation as well as in their numerical predominance in New England. They now numbered some 530 churches spread out across Massachusetts, Rhode Island, Connecticut, New Hampshire, and what is now Maine. From the roughly 20,000 English emigrants to New England in 1642, Stiles estimated, again following Mather, that the population had grown to 100,000 souls in 1696, and by 1760 there were 440,000 Congregationalists along with another 60,000 heterodox types.[51]

When we look at these "maps" of New England's religious development with respect to what we know of the nature and progress of the revivals, they begin to reveal a great deal about the course and timing of the Great Awakening and the evolution of New England's religious culture. If, for instance, we compare the religious landscape at the time of the Halfway Covenant with the period of the major revivals three quarters of a century later, we can see that much of the land which had been (in English eyes) vacant wilderness was now settled and organized into orthodox churches. The town of Dartmouth, "perishing without vision" in 1696, now had a minister supported by funds collected at the Old South Church. From areas that were vaguely described in 1677 as "Pequid Country," "Naraganset," and "Nipmuk" on the William Hubbard map, the native population had been largely driven out by Puritan colonists, who by 1740 had settled in dozens of neighboring towns closely connected by rivers and roads. Virtually every one of these towns maintained an orthodox minister, trained not in England but at Harvard or Yale College, a minister who preached the traditional doctrines of the Puritan churches.[52] The more remote areas of Plymouth Colony, Cape Cod, Martha's Vineyard, and Nantucket, along with the settlements reaching north and eastward into New Hampshire and Maine and the interior regions between the coast and the Connecticut Valley, had been filled up with towns and churches where few or none had existed in the 1660s. The "plenitude of means" with which the Third Church laity had attempted to saturate their own community had spread across the countryside as a whole, leaving few places where a person could travel very far without coming upon another utterly familiar religious community. In 1704 when Sarah Kemble Knight took her solitary journey by horseback from Boston to New York by way of New Haven, this blanketing of the landscape with Puritan communities was already becoming evident.[53] When George Whitefield passed through New England in 1740 on a similar tour, the importance of this gradual but profound development had become unmistakably clear.

Whitefield's first New England stop in September 1740 was the town of Newport, Rhode Island, an unlikely place for New England's Great Awakening to begin. At the time of the Halfway Covenant and indeed throughout the seventeenth century, Rhode Island had lacked any orthodox Congregational churches, and its dominant Quaker and Baptist congregations were among the denominations least receptive to Whitefield's brand of evangelical preaching. Yet by 1740, circumstances had changed through the efforts of churches like Boston's Third to sponsor orthodox religion throughout Rhode Island. When Whitefield arrived in Newport, he was entertained by an ancient minister, Nathaniel Clap, who made the strongest impression on Whitefield of anyone in the town. In Whitefield's eyes, Clap was "the most venerable man I ever saw in my life. He looked like a good old Puritan, and gave me an idea of what stamp those men were, who first settled in New England. . . . I could not but think, whilst at his table, that I was sitting with one of the patriarchs." Whitefield's enormous success in New England began in Newport at

Clap's church, thanks in no small part to the preparations that Clap and his clerical colleagues in Rhode Island had made over the years, preparations made possible by the material resources and moral support Boston had provided. When Whitefield moved on from Newport toward Boston, he found at every stop that "the people were apprised of my coming" in advance, and unexpectedly large crowds met him along the roads.[54]

After his first stay in Boston, Whitefield set out for country towns, riding circuits through the region, much as Samuel Sewall had once done as a judge, and in a way, to much the same purpose. He first headed north and eventually reached York, Maine, another outpost that had been wilderness half a century earlier, but was now served by yet another venerable Puritan minister. In Samuel Moody, Whitefield met Nathaniel Clap's equal, "a worthy, plain, and powerful minister of Jesus Christ," who "has lived by faith for many years, having no settled salary." Moody had no salary, but he did receive considerable support from people like Samuel Sewall, whose niece Moody had married, and from the resources donated by Boston churches and the Massachusetts General Court.[55] Like Clap, Moody had labored to plant another community on the ecclesiastical map of New England, and the revival engendered by Whitefield marked the flowering of his efforts. Whitefield claimed that just before he delivered a sermon in York, Moody assured him " 'that he believed I should preach to a hundred new creatures this morning in his congregation.' And, indeed,' added Whitefield, "I believe I did."[56] The aged minister knew the basis for his prediction of Whitefield's success, for he had laid the groundwork himself. The labors of Moody and others like him on the northern and eastern frontier had prepared this region to take part in the awakenings as well.[57]

Following his northern tour, Whitefield made a few shorter visits to Boston's neighboring towns before finally embarking on his westward journey. The route he took to the Connecticut Valley, the road along which Governor Belcher raced to catch up with his beloved itinerant in Marlborough, was virtually the same path that Edward Taylor had taken to Westfield in 1671. On Taylor's trip, the young minister had worried about the "way being unbeaten" or filled with snow. The traveling party got lost in the woods near "Quaubaug" (later to be settled as Brookfield), and they had to follow "markt trees" to find their way again and avoid "lying in the woods all night . . . 30 miles off from our Lodgen." But now, seventy years later, this route no longer constituted a "tedious and hazzardous" venture, "the desperatest journey that ever Connecticut men undertooke."[58] It had been reduced to an ordinary trip along the post road, broken up by villages every few miles. In each town where he stopped on his westward progress, in Concord, Sudbury, Marlborough, and Worcester, in Leicester, Brookfield, and Cold Spring, in Hadley, Northampton, Westfield, and beyond, Whitefield was met by hundreds if not thousands of people who had assembled to hear him repeat, in a forceful new style they had never before seen, a message that they already knew by heart. When Whitefield arrived in Westfield, he commented not on its wilderness aspect as Taylor had done seventy years earlier, but on the penetration of literate culture into the frontier. He "met with a little book, written by Dr. Cotton Mather, entitled 'The Ornaments of the Daughters of Zion,' which I would recommend to all, especially the Boston ladies." Here, and in York as well, Whitefield was impressed by the civilized aspect that religion had brought to remote settlements: "[I] could not but fancy myself in Old England. Surely God is keeping covenant."[59]

But it was the Puritans of New England, including the ladies and gentlemen of Boston, who had kept covenant. Their unremitting efforts to apply material wealth to the cultivation of religion had caused the spread of churches across the landscape and prepared the way for itinerant evangelists like Whitefield to draw such powerful responses from both a Nathan Cole and a Jonathan Belcher that they would chase across the countryside to listen to a stranger preach the gospel in "the old New England and puritanick way."[60] The proximity of New England's towns and villages allowed the Awakening to skip from church to church and allowed individuals to go "gadding after sermons" from one community to the next, so that revivals in one place would reinforce awakenings in another. In the eight decades after the Halfway Covenant, the countryside had been settled, orthodox churches had been gathered and maintained, and the population had learned to anticipate a work of grace in themselves and in their communities as the fulfillment of their religious experience, all of which encouraged the tendency within this religious culture toward local revivals to converge into a single overwhelming Great Awakening.

What made this convergence possible was the process of development described in the foregoing chapters on Boston and Westfield. Boston's Third Church and Edward Taylor's church in Westfield represented different types of New England communities, but both types were integral to the rise of a unified religious culture. Without the economic growth that was most obviously manifested in the expanding commercial economy of Boston, New England Puritanism would have stagnated. But the connection between economic and religious development was not automatic. Resources had to be consciously applied to the enhancement of godliness, and for this an inclusive, expansive, and activist vision, like that put forward in the Third Church under the Halfway Covenant, was a necessary element. Unless one believed that churches had a duty to gather in potential believers and spread the means of grace to all possible partakers, it made little sense to expend precious re-sources, whether material or spiritual, on those outside the church. With such a belief, the evangelical mission was unavoidable, and it became as much a part of the life of the church to broadcast the seeds of grace in the wilderness as to tend the plants in its own garden.

Westfield stood at the receiving end of this equation. As a community, it was chronically short of the resources, both spiritual and material, that Boston offered in abundance. Like many other rural towns that were barely able to meet their own needs, Westfield and its minister struggled over where the church's boundaries lay and what its responsibilities to the community were. In Westfield's case, this struggle was compounded by conflicting ideas about the nature of the church and religious experience held by the pastor and the laity. Consequently, a tendency toward conflict and schism that was always a part of the Puritan movement was built into the life of this community, and played itself out there over the years of Taylor's ministry. In the long run, the confluence of economic contention over scarce resources with disagreement over religious issues became inseparable. It was not that economic stress caused a decline in devotion to the church, or that particular religious beliefs were connected to diverging social classes. Rather, when the congregation fought over who should be included in the church or who should contribute to its support, when they argued with their minister over issues of doctrine and polity, they could not uncouple these issues from the mundane facts of where people lived, how much land they owned, what future they saw for their children, and whether or not they had the means and opportunity to learn and practice the traditional forms of Puritan piety. A separation like the one that occurred in Westfield in the wake of the Great Awakening, in which the seceding members of the church migrated to a new part of New England, was never simply a matter of doctrinal disagreement. It was also based on judgments about whether the present community's spiritual and material re-sources could satisfy the aspirations of the dissenters. But when gradually de-veloping land shortages contributed to the community's internal strife, exac-erbated its religious disagreements, and ended in separation and migration, the entire process contributed not to the decline but to the health of religious culture in the region as a whole.[61] Such decisions were not repudiations of the *ideals* of community, but evaluations of the declining relative value of a particular set of communal bonds in the face of immediate competition for scarce resources. In new communities under more favorable circumstances, the same emphasis on communal bonds could be restored, as exemplified in the gathering of the hundreds of new churches that filled the New England countryside in the eighteenth century.[62]

Towns like Westfield often experienced the internal pressures that divided communities and forced some members to leave for new and better
lands, bearing visions of new and better churches. Through this process, Westfield and other towns were unwittingly (and painfully) contributing to the
development of New England's religious culture. In Plymouth in the 1640s,
William Bradford had already identified this pattern, but he understood its
consequences only in part. From his point of view as an aging member of an
unusually intense version of this type of community, dispersal could only
mean decline, as it almost always appeared to those left behind by separation
or migration. But for anyone who could step back and view the process as a
whole, like the makers of New England's "ecclesiastical maps," the value of
the dispersal of the population and the replication of orthodox churches was
obvious. In their eyes, it turned a vacant and heathen wilderness into a Christian garden, and they willingly gave their surplus resources to support new
churches and settlements that opened up the wilderness to the means of grace.
In this way, Bradford's church in Plymouth, the Third Church in Boston, and
the church which Edward Taylor served in Westfield participated jointly in
the development of an integrated evangelical religious culture, a culture still
devoted to the original premises of its Puritan founders.

The Great Awakening stands as the crowning achievement of New England's long Puritan century. The revivals demonstrated above all that the
"Spirit of the Old Writers," the religious vision of the founding generation,
still held sway over the rapidly increasing population that Ezra Stiles so carefully calculated. But the Great Awakening forever altered New England's religious landscape as well. The gradual development of "linkages" between local
communities had made the astounding success of the Awakening possible.[63]
Revivals which had formerly been confined to local communities began to
occur simultaneously across the entire region. But the conflicts which had
long been endemic within individual churches were now likewise generalized and embodied in a permanent way throughout New England. Where
formerly individual churches had struggled with internal disputes over practical and doctrinal differences, after the Awakening there were identifiable
proto-denominations which embodied the different points of view once
contained within particular churches. This change is clear when one compares Ezra Stiles' ecclesiastical map of 1760, which recognizes and enumerates
the denominational competitors of Congregationalism, with Cotton Mather's
map of 1696 and its occasional off-hand reference to a heretical congregation
or two. The institutional development of these denominations and the accompanying diversification of society were by-products of the Great Awakening.

Both the remarkable waves of conversion and the bitter disputes that sometimes followed were significant aspects of the revivals, but in the subsequent historiography of the Great Awakening, the voices of contention have largely drowned out the more ecumenically minded. Yet there had always been members of this religious culture who were inclined to appreciate and enhance its unifying elements and minimize the significance of disagreement. From the lay people who founded the Third Church to the evangelical ministers like Samuel Willard and Thomas Prince who espoused its ecumenical mission, the desire to avoid divisive argument over inessentials for the sake of spreading the fundamental truths of Christian experience was carried forward into the era of the revivals. From their point of view, the contention that followed the Great Awakening and worked itself out in denominational forms was basically a squabble over who deserved credit for what was essentially God's work. In the midst of a dispute over whether unconverted ministers could act as the means to convert others, one clergyman reached for the garden metaphor to break through the irrelevant issues and insist that "I have planted, Mr. Whitefield has watered, but God has given the increase" to the seeds of faith.[64] What really mattered was that the garden of the church grew larger.

Promoters of this ecumenical vision of an expanding church cared less and less for the particular theological and ecclesiastical disputes that separated denominations, as long as orthodox evangelical communities continued to multiply. Ultimately, they foresaw a time when no matter where one might travel, the individual and communal experiences encouraged within New England's Puritan churches would be replicated in town after town, church after church. In May 1740, on the eve of the Great Awakening, Thomas Prince preached a sermon that outlined a remarkable vision of such a time. Prince imagined that "all the southern, western, and north-western parts of this new world, and Calefornia, will, in their times, be full of pure and pious churches," and that "the gospel will go round and conquer every nation in Japan and China, Tartary, India, Persia, Africa, and Egypt, until it return to Zion, where it rose." For this vision to be realized, Prince believed that the ministers must continue their traditional labors: "This we may promote in the various ways of praying, preaching, illustrious examples of our imitation of [Christ], recommending him to others, contributing to promote his kingdom (among the Heathen, or in poor parishes among ourselves and neighbors) and by innumerable other means, according to our various stations, situations, opportunities, and talents."[65]

Not be outdone when it came to grandiose visions, Ezra Stiles' *Discourse on the Christian Union* made predictions in numerical rather than geographical terms. Stiles estimated, based on then current figures and rates of growth, that by 1860 New England would have seven million Congregationalists and five thousand Congregational churches, with Baptists a poor second at only 352,000 members.[66] But for Stiles, whose *Discourse* argued for a loose union of all the Calvinist denominations into a single body, such denominational differences were of little lasting significance compared with the potential for spreading the gospel into new places. "It is truly important," he argued, "that this vine, which God hath planted with a mighty hand in this American wilderness should be cultivated into confirmed maturity." In Stiles' view, "differences and animosities" would "enervate and moulder down our cause," while "union and benevolence" would "strengthen and form it to defensible maturity." In order to promote this cause, Stiles believed that "It ought particularly to be inculcated upon our friends going from us to the settlement of new towns and provinces, to carry religion with them, to settle early in church order, and furnish themselves with a ministry of the word and ordinances, for the benefit of themselves and their children."[67]

Thomas Prince's vision of global orthodox Christianity and Ezra Stiles' straight-line projections for New England's Congregational population growth were bound to look foolish in hindsight. But despite their inflated rhetoric and extravagant claims, Prince and Stiles had each grasped something important about the development of New England's religious culture. If we were to follow Stiles' lead and draw an ecclesiastical map of greater New England a century later in 1860, and consider not just Congregational churches but, as Stiles imagined it, a union of the evangelical denominations, then the extent of New England's influence in matters of religion would have to reach at least as far as the "Burned Over District" in upstate New York.[68] It might go further, to the "Western Reserve" in Ohio and up into Michigan, where Edward Taylor's grandson, a Congregational minister, died in 1840 at the age of 78.[69] Perhaps its influence might extend as far as Kansas, where the New England Emigrant Aid Company transported settlers to fight the spread of slavery, or even to California, where descendants of the Puritans were gathering churches during the Gold Rush.[70] In 1852, on the anniversary of the Pilgrims' landing in Plymouth, Timothy Dwight Hunt addressed the New England Society of San Francisco in words that Ezra Stiles could have written, words that echo John Winthrop: "You are the representatives of a land which is the model for every other. You belong to a family whose dead are the pride of the living. Preserve your birth-right. . . . Here is our Colony. No higher ambition could urge us to noble deeds than, on the basis of the colony of Plymouth, TO MAKE CALIFORNIA THE MASSACHUSETTS OF THE PACIFIC."[71]

The "birthright" of greater New England, the inheritance that Hunt al-

luded to, was both a visionary ideal and a remembered experience, a combination of memory and prophecy bound together in the belief that community life should be a redemptive and exemplary process. A sense of declining
opportunity weakened the hold of *particular* New England communities on
their own expanding populations and encouraged families to migrate in
search of more and better land all across the northern stretches of the United
States. But in this movement, the migrants heeded Stiles' suggestion and carried with them their *imagined* communities, the social and religious aspirations which Boston's material resources had helped to produce and to satisfy,
aspirations which they had fought over in Westfield and in the hundreds of
towns like it that they left behind, and which they yet hoped to fulfill in their
new settlements. The demand for such communities was the driving force in
Puritan New England's extraordinarily dynamic spiritual economy. In the
generations following the Halfway Covenant, New England Puritanism did
not collapse in decay, but expanded and prospered until finally, in the triumph
of the Great Awakening, it outgrew the capacity of its institutional structure
to contain its powerful and sometimes contradictory impulses. In the aftermath of the Awakening, these impulses burst forth in the beginnings of a new
"dispensation," a new American spiritual economy, marked by continuing cy-
cles of revival among the nation's emerging religious denominations, as migrants from New England brought Puritan ideals of community, along with
practical knowledge of how to cultivate them, to the new towns and churches
they planted across the American landscape.

Reference Matter

Notes

For full forms of citations, see the Works Cited, pp. 297–317. The following special forms are used for frequently cited primary sources:

ET Chh. Recs.	Taylor, Edward. *Edward Taylor's "Church Records" and Related Sermons.*
ET Diary	Taylor, Edward. *The Diary of Edward Taylor.*
ET Poems	Taylor, Edward. *The Poems of Edward Taylor.*
ET "Town Recs."	Powell, Walter Louis, ed. "Edward Taylor's Westfield: An Edition of the Westfield 'Town Records.'"
OSC	Hill, Hamilton Andrews. *History of the Old South Church (Third Church), Boston, 1669–1884.*
SS Diary	Sewall, Samuel. *The Diary of Samuel Sewall, 1674–1729.*

Introduction

1. On the Great Migration, see Anderson, *New England's Generation*; Thompson, *Mobility and Migration*. Edward Johnson's *Wonder-Working Providence*, written in the early 1650s, details the first "planting" of New England's towns. Boston would not have a printing press until 1675, and although Cambridge, Massachusetts, had a press starting in 1638, its output was very small, amounting to no more than two or three titles per year, which consisted chiefly of almanacs, Harvard College commencement theses, and official publications like the 1638 "Freeman's Oath" or the colony's *Laws and Liberties* (1648). Not until 1652 did the Cambridge press print a New England minister's sermon series, Richard Mather's *Sermons upon Genesis 15:6*, and the practice would not become common in New England until the establishment of the Boston press. See Roden, *Cambridge Press*, pp. 145–49.

2. For population figures, see D. S. Smith, "Demographic History"; McCusker and Menard, *Economy of British America*, p. 103. For a contemporary estimate of the number of New England's churches, see Ezra Stiles, *Discourse on Christian Union*. On the popularity of seventeenth-century sermons during the Great Awakening, see Hambrick-Stowe, "Spirit of the Old Writers." On the publishing industry in Boston, see Franklin, ed., *Boston Printers*.

3. This definition is given by the *Oxford English Dictionary*, 2d ed., which cites a leading antagonist of the Puritans, Jeremy Taylor's *The Worthy Communicant* (1661), for an example of "economy" used in this sense, as well as similar usage by Milton, Hobbes, and Henry More, another Anglican theologian of the seventeenth century.

4. John Cotton, *Christ the Fountaine*, p. 17.

5. Cotton, *Christ the Fountaine*, p. 18.

6. For a similar argument, see Foster, "Godly in Transit," p. 238. Foster's perceptive essay deserves a place alongside Cotton's *Christ the Fountaine* as a more contemporary point of departure for this book.

7. By "myth," I do not intend to convey the "flat common sense of a false (often deliberately false) belief or account." Rather, I mean by this term the seemingly universal human tendency toward creative narration as a way to make sense of past experience. To recognize the presence of a myth-making impulse in the writing of history is not to impugn the motives or skill of the historian, but to acknowledge that the desire for structured forms of explanation, the need for particular kinds of stories, is a fundamental aspect of why people write history at all. On the range and complexity of uses for the word "myth," see Williams, *Keywords*, pp. 210–12. For a brief introduction to the literature on "why we need stories," see J. H. Miller, "Narrative."

8. Bradford, *Of Plymouth Plantation*, p. 334.

9. Throughout his account of the Plymouth colonists' exodus, Bradford consciously likens their struggles to those of the Hebrews, often to their own disadvantage. When they reached New England, Bradford, unlike Moses, could not "go up to the top of Pisgah to view from the wilderness a more goodly country to feed their hopes." The view from the *Mayflower* of the grey and sandy shores of Cape Cod in December offered nothing but a "hideous and desolate wilderness" of "wild and savage hue." Bradford, *Of Plymouth Plantation*, p. 62. For an extended discussion of Bradford's emotional response to the dispersal of the Plymouth settlers, see Peterson, "Plymouth Church," pp. 578–79; Sargent, "Bradford's 'Dialogue.'"

10. J. T. Adams, *Founding of New England*, pp. 253–77, describes the "Defeat of the Theocracy" in Massachusetts as a victory for liberal thought and toleration inspired by the growth of commercial interests. In essence, the structure of the declension narrative has remained largely the same, even when the dominant metaphors used by various authors have offered different interpretations of its meaning. A tragic mode was preferred by the Puritans themselves, who saw their own exalted hopes foiled by mankind's inherent sinfulness; nineteenth-century liberals gave a romantic reading to the story by emphasizing the triumph of reason, freedom, and commerce over Puritan superstition, intolerance, and restrictiveness; for twentieth-century scholars, an

ironic interpretation that sees the Puritans as subject to forces beyond their comprehension and control has been the most favored variation. For a discussion of metaphor and of emplotment in historical writing, see White, *Metahistory*, pp. 1-42.

11. There have been numerous studies of church membership in early New England, motivated at least in part by political historians' interest in the connection between church membership and the franchise, as well as by the declension argument, though the two issues are related: see Pope, *Halfway Covenant*; Moran, "The Puritan Saint"; Beales, "Halfway Covenant"; B. Katherine Brown, "Controversy over the Franchise." By contrast, there has been relatively little exploration of the numerical proliferation of New England's churches, mostly the work of historical demographers and cataloguers of church records; D. S. Smith, "Demographic History"; Worthley, *Inventory*.

12. Bradford, *Of Plymouth Plantation*, p. 254. On the weakness of church establishments in colonial America outside of New England, see Butler, *Awash in a Sea of Faith*, pp. 37-67; Bonomi, *Under the Cope of Heaven*. On the persistent claims for New England's religious decline, even in studies that survey the entire colonial spectrum of experience, see Greene, *Pursuits of Happiness*, pp. 55-80; Bailyn, *Peopling of British North America*, pp. 91-95.

13. The works by Miller that have given definitive form to the narrative of Puritan history are *Orthodoxy in Massachusetts, 1630-1650* (1933); *The New England Mind: The Seventeenth Century* (1939); and *The New England Mind: From Colony to Province* (1953). Also influential have been a number of Miller's essays, principally gathered in two collections: *Errand into the Wilderness* (1956) and *Nature's Nation* (1967). The bibliography supporting and challenging Miller's work is enormous; but for an introduction and overview of the scholarship on the declension paradigm, see Heimert and Delbanco, *Puritans in America*, pp. 415-21, and David D. Hall, "On Common Ground." My own analysis of the declension myth builds upon Robert Pope's essay "New England Versus the New England Mind."

14. Mary Beth Norton et al., *A People and a Nation*, pp. 41-43. For similar current textbook renditions of the declension argument, see Boyer et al., *Enduring Vision*, pp. 46-50; Berkin et al., *Making America*, pp. 52-55; Brinkley, *American History*, pp. 85-86. Brinkley's argument is more subtle than the others, and takes into consideration the rhetoric of Puritan self-perception, but nonetheless repeats the major touchstones of the declension narrative, linking the Halfway Covenant to the rise of commerce and worldliness.

15. Innes, *Creating the Commonwealth*, p. 274, italics added for emphasis. For another example of the same tendency, see Martin, *Profits in the Wilderness*. Martin makes a persuasive case that commercial impulses underlay the founding of New England towns from the very beginning, yet struggles with the notion that his argument undermines our sense that the founders were devoted Puritans. When Martin asserts that "one should not be led by the piety of [Samuel Sewall's] diaries to suppose him incapable of making a good deal" (p. 75), he shows the continuing power of the declension model and its clerical moral, which has taught us to believe that piety and pros-

perity are mutually exclusive. Even when its content is being directly challenged, the language and the explanatory assumptions of the reigning paradigm remain dominant.

16. One suspects that now, more than thirty years after Miller's death, in an era of shrinking course reading lists, some of the subtlety of Miller's work is also disappearing, as even graduate students receive condensed versions of his argument in essays like "Declension in a Bible Commonwealth" or "Errand into the Wilderness," rather than the full-blown versions of *Orthodoxy in Massachusetts* and *The New England Mind*.

17. For an introduction to the debate among historians of science on the nature of paradigm shifts, see Kuhn, *Structure of Scientific Revolutions*; Lakatos and Musgrave, eds., *Criticism and the Growth of Knowledge*. On the significance of Kuhn's work for the historical profession, see Hollinger, "T. S. Kuhn's Theory of Science."

18. In fact, the challenge of stepping outside Miller's paradigm (which he insisted was merely an elaboration of the Puritans' own worldview) was increased by Miller's defiant argument that it was intellectually untenable to adopt any other perspective, as though it were impossible to imagine a coherent historical narrative other than the one present to the minds of the Puritans themselves. For a revealing exchange on this point, see Bailyn, "Review of *The New England Mind*," and Miller, "Preface to the Beacon Press Edition."

19. Foster, *Long Argument*, pp. 1–4.

20. See Scobey, "Revising the Errand."

21. The organizational structure of Perry Miller's narrative of early New England reinforces this pattern more strongly than any other contribution to the scholarship. His first volume, *Orthodoxy in Massachusetts* (1933), chronicles the first generation's creation of the New England Way, while *The New England Mind: From Colony to Province* (1953), beginning with the elegiac farewell of an aging founder, traces the dissolution of this system from 1648 onwards. By sandwiching a static, analytical account of a stable and normative worldview—*The New England Mind: The Seventeenth Century* (1939)—between these two narrative volumes, the effect is further enhanced. Within the structure of Miller's work, orthodox Puritanism is what the first generation produced and later generations lost.

22. For a thorough treatment of this impulse in American Puritanism, see Bozeman, *To Live Ancient Lives*.

23. Foster, *Long Argument*, pp. 65–137, discusses this radicalizing process in detail and provides the necessary context for seeing American Puritanism as a stage in a larger movement.

24. See Janice Knight, *Orthodoxies in Massachusetts*, and Bremer, *Congregational Communion*, for two different perspectives on Davenport's early career.

25. Perry Miller, "Review of *The New Haven Colony*," p. 584. For more on Davenport's career, see Davenport, *Letters*, pp. 1–12. The idea that New Haven was the "most Puritan" colony still persists; see Cornelia Hughes Dayton, "Re-Examining the Most Puritan of Legal Regimes: New Haven Colony's Patriarchy," paper presented at "The Many Legalities of Early America" conference, sponsored by the Institute of Early American History and Culture, Williamsburg, Virginia, Nov. 22–24, 1996.

26. On the ongoing cultural warfare, see Collinson, *Religion of Protestants*, pp. 242–83. Contributers to the extensive literature on the social and religious composition of the Great Migration have argued over the question of the typicality of the social origins and religious beliefs of the migrants, but there seems little reason to believe that the migrants were not unusually committed to a godly way of life, as compared with the English population as a whole; see Breen and Foster, "Moving to the New World"; Anderson, "Migrants and Motives"; Cressy, *Coming Over*; Fischer, *Albion's Seed*; Thompson, *Mobility and Migration*.

27. John Winthrop, "A Modell of Christian Charity," p. 295. On the emotional experience of the Great Migration, see Caldwell, *Puritan Conversion Narrative*, pp. 119–34; Delbanco, *Puritan Ordeal*, pp. 81–117; Cressy, *Coming Over*; and Anderson, *New England's Generation*.

28. Innes, *Creating the Commonwealth*, pp. 197–98.

29. Bremer, *Congregational Communion*, pp. 123–201.

30. See Miller, *Orthodoxy in Massachusetts*; Morgan, *Visible Saints*.

31. Gura, *Glimpse of Sion's Glory*; Foster, *Long Argument*, pp. 138–74.

32. This sense of despair over the imminent destruction of the English church and English society is vividly expressed by Thomas Hooker's sermon "The Danger of Desertion" (1631), in *Writings in England and Holland*, pp. 228–46. See also Delbanco, *Puritan Ordeal*, pp. 41–80; Shepard, *Parable of the Ten Virgins*, 2:170; also see *Thomas Shepard's Confessions*, pp. 64, 66, 84.

33. Shepard, *Parable of the Ten Virgins*, 2:375, 377–78. Here the word "means" refers to the "means of grace," or the many forms through which Puritans believed that saving faith could be transmitted to the individual, including Bible-reading, preaching, prayer, devotional meetings, the reading of godly books, the counsel and teachings of ministers, parents, or other godly people, and the exercise of church discipline.

34. It is therefore no coincidence that the metaphor of New England settlement as an "errand into the wilderness" was a second-generation invention; see Perry Miller, *Errand Into the Wilderness*, p. 2, for a discussion of the origins of this phrase in Samuel Danforth's election sermon of 1670; see also Carroll, *Puritanism and the Wilderness*; and Karen Ordahl Kupperman, "Climate and Mastery of the Wilderness," which argues that only after a full generation did Puritan settlers comprehend how the reality of New England's climate differed from their expectations for it.

35. See R. R. Johnson, *Adjustment to Empire*.

36. See Innes, *Creating the Commonwealth*; Vickers, *Farmers and Fisherman*; Bailyn, *New England Merchants*.

37. On the founding of New England's colonies, the best general source remains Andrews, *Colonial Period*, vols. 1–3, "The Settlements." On the development of courts, see Haskins, *Law and Authority*; Konig, *Law and Society*; Mann, *Neighbors and Strangers*; and the Colonial Society of Massachusetts' 1984 conference volume, *Law in Colonial Massachusetts*.

38. Martin, *Profits in the Wilderness*; D. S. Smith, "Demographic History."

39. See Axtell, *School upon a Hill*; Morison, *Harvard in the Seventeenth Century*.

40. For the text of the Cambridge Platform, see Walker, *Creeds and Platforms*, pp. 194–237.

41. At its most basic level, the so-called Halfway Covenant, the result of the Massachusetts ecclesiastical synod of 1662, declared that the children of baptized church members were also eligible for baptism, regardless of whether the parents had "improved" upon their baptism and joined the church in full communion. This extended baptismal or "halfway" membership to the children of those who themselves were only "halfway" members. See Walker, *Creeds and Platforms*, pp. 313–14.

42. For a discussion of New England's origins myth that connects its creation to the writing of biographies of the founders, see Anderson, *New England's Generation*, pp. 201–8.

43. See Todd, "Puritan Self-Fashioning," and Knott, " 'Suffering People.' "

44. Bradford, *Of Plymouth Plantation*, p. 363. That Bradford saw Foxe's *Acts and Monuments* as a model for his own work is clear from his first chapter, which places the history of Bradford's separatist community within a context provided by Foxe.

45. John Norton, *Abel Being Dead Yet Speaketh* (1658), quoted in Heimert and Delbanco, *Puritans in America*, p. 217.

46. The original "Galeacius" to whom Mather compared Bradford was Galeazzo Carracioli, Marquis of Vico, who was converted to Protestantism by Peter Martyr in the sixteenth century, was exiled from Italy and forced to give up his title, and moved first to Germany and eventually to Geneva. In an English translation of Galeazzo's biography, the "Italian Convert" was also called a "Second Moses," making Mather's link to Bradford all the more obvious. See Cotton Mather, *Magnalia Christi Americana*, ed. Murdock, pp. 201, 213, 434n. On Winthrop as Mather's "American Nehemiah," see Bercovitch, *Puritan Origins*.

47. This quotation is a translation of the Latin epigraph from the title page of Book II, which reads in the original, "*Nondum haec, quae nunc tenet Saeculum, Negligentia Dei Venerat*"; Cotton Mather, *Magnalia*, ed. Murdock, pp. 197–98.

48. On the writing and reading of biographies as a form of devotional exercise, see Hambrick-Stowe, *Practice of Piety*, pp. 253–55.

49. Levin, *Cotton Mather*, p. xiii.

50. Cotton Mather biographies include Wendell, *Cotton Mather, Puritan Priest* (1891); Ralph and Louise Boas, *Cotton Mather, Keeper of the Puritan Conscience* (1928); Levin, *Cotton Mather: Young Life of the Lord's Remembrancer* (1978); Silverman, *Life and Times of Cotton Mather* (1984). Two of the better recent studies of more specialized subjects include Lovelace, *American Pietism of Cotton Mather* (1979), and Smolinski, ed., *Threefold Paradise of Cotton Mather* (1995), but these are only the tip of a very large iceberg.

51. Murdock, *Increase Mather, Foremost American Puritan* (1925); George Parker Winship, *A Representative Massachusetts Puritan, Increase Mather* (1931); Lowance, *Increase Mather* (1974); Michael G. Hall, *The Last American Puritan: The Life of Increase Mather* (1987). The titles of these works alone are indicative of their tendency to allow the individual life to stand for society as a whole. It was Cotton Mather who referred to his

father as "ever-memorable" in the subtitle of his own biography of Increase, *Parentator* (1724).

52. Twitchell, *John Winthrop: First Governor of Massachusetts* (1891); Morgan, *Puritan Dilemma* (1958); Schweninger, *John Winthrop* (1990); Mosely, *John Winthrop's World* (1992); Black, *The Younger John Winthrop* (1966). Francis Bremer of Millersville University is currently completing a study of the elder Winthrop's early life.

53. Dunn, *Puritans and Yankees* (1962); Middlekauff, *The Mathers* (1971).

54. See Rutman, *Winthrop's Boston*; Cotton Mather, *Magnalia Christi Americana*, ed. Murdock, p. 227, where, in his biography of Winthrop, Mather imagines the governor lamenting well before his death that "there remains not the appearance, not even the color, nor the way of life, and not the same aspect, of that which was before."

55. Peterson, "Plymouth Church."

56. Indeed, the most popular twentieth-century account of Plymouth Colony is enormously indebted to Bradford's text, so much so that it attempts to conceal Bradford's authorship of passages that make the "Pilgrims" seem either laughable or brutal; see Willison, *Saints and Strangers*, pp. 301, 329.

57. For a further discussion of this tendency in Puritan autobiographical writings, see Shea, *Spiritual Autobiography*, pp. 118–26.

58. In addition to the Mather and Winthrop biographies cited above, numerous other individuals have received careful scholarly attention, including John Cotton, Thomas Hooker, Anne Hutchinson, Anne Bradstreet, Samuel Willard, Samuel Sewall, and Jonathan Edwards, to name some of the leading figures. For citations, see Heimert and Delbanco, *Puritans in America*, pp. 421–432; Ammerman and Morgan, eds., *Books about Early America*, pp. 92–102. Many of these biographies also project the declension argument through the lives of their subjects, for example, Patricia Tracy, *Jonathan Edwards, Pastor*, and Van Dyken, *Samuel Willard*.

59. For a few excellent examples of these more general studies, see Cohen, *God's Caress*; Stout, *New England Soul*; Hambrick-Stowe, *Practice of Piety*; David Hall, *Worlds of Wonder*; Bozeman, *To Live Ancient Lives*.

60. Lockridge, *A New England Town*; other leading studies in this mode include Boyer and Nissenbaum, *Salem Possessed*; Rutman, *Winthrop's Boston*; Patricia Tracy, *Jonathan Edwards, Pastor*.

61. Innes, *Labor in a New Land*, pp. 123–50, especially pp. 124n, 129.

62. For the most recent and sophisticated discussion of the meaning of Winthrop's lay sermon, see Innes, *Creating the Commonwealth*, pp. 64–106. Here, Innes's position is substantially different from that of *Labor in a New Land*.

63. For a probing analysis of this historiography, see Bender, *Community and Social Change*, pp. 47–53. From the perspective of English Puritanism, this tendency is most peculiar, since many British scholars associate the rise of Puritanism with economic instability in an industrializing and commercializing economy, and locate the typical Puritan in thriving East Anglian market towns with cosmopolitan connections; see Spufford, *Contrasting Communities*, pp. 298–318; Collinson, *Religion of Protestants*, pp. 247–48; Fischer, *Albion's Seed*, pp. 42–49; Foster, *Long Argument*, pp. 15–16.

64. It should also be remembered that the first generation could be extraordinarily contentious. Some of the best known New England Puritan controversies took place in the first decade of settlement, and conflict often arose in communities made up of migrants who were strangers to one another. See Allen, *In English Ways*; also Anderson, *New England's Generation*.

65. Lake, "Defining Puritanism—Again?" pp. 14–16.

66. In fact, during his tenure at St. Botolph's, Cotton devised various strategies to avoid wearing priestly vestments and reading Common Prayer, but distanced himself from an act of iconoclastic vandalism committed by unknown parishioners in 1621, in which the church's stained glass windows were broken and its statuary destroyed; see Ziff, *John Cotton*, pp. 47–53.

67. See Harris, "Simplification of Europe Overseas"; also Greene, "Interpretive Frameworks."

68. See Moran and Vinovskis, *Religion, Family, and the Life Course*; Anne S. Brown, "Bound Up in a Bundle of Life."

69. For the formative influence of college experiences on the lives of English Puritan clergy, see Bremer, *Congregational Communion*, pp. 17–63; for examples of the scholarship beginning to address the difference between men's and women's spiritual lives, see Juster, *Disorderly Women*; Porterfield, *Female Piety*.

70. In fact, in Heyrman, *Commerce and Culture*, this challenge has already been taken on; Heyrman argues convincingly for two cases in which commercial development increased social harmony and encouraged religious revivals.

71. John Cotton, *Christ the Fountaine*, p. 16.

72. Bailyn, *New England Merchants*, p. 44.

73. See Peterson, "Plymouth Church."

Chapter 1

1. The peril in which the regicide judges of Charles I who fled to New England found themselves provides the most dramatic example of this; see Wilson, "Web of Secrecy."

2. For a general discussion of New England's reaction to the rise of British Imperial regulation, see Richard R. Johnson, *Adjustment to Empire*.

3. See Pope, *Halfway Covenant*; Anderson, *New England's Generation*, pp. 202–8.

4. On Boston's history in the first generation of settlement, see Rutman, *Winthrop's Boston*.

5. On the intentions of the First Church founders, see Winthrop, *History of New England*, 1:31–33; also Rutman, *Winthrop's Boston*, pp. 46–57, 108–15. On the innovation of the conversion relation and the movement of New England's churches toward a separatist position, see Foster, "English Puritanism"; also Morgan, *Visible Saints*, pp. 64–112; and Caldwell, *Puritan Conversion Narrative*, pp. 81–116. For an alternative reading of the institution of the conversion relation which nonetheless links it to the radicalism of the mid-1630s, see Ditmore, "Preparation and Confession."

6. On the transatlantic context of the Antinomian crisis, see Foster, "New En-

gland and the Challenge of Heresy." Cotton's evocative preaching style could spur his listeners toward spiritual enthusiasms that pushed beyond what Cotton himself would countenance, leaving him in an awkward bind during the Antinomian controversy, wanting neither to accept responsibility for all the doctrines Anne Hutchinson espoused nor deny the validity of some of her criticisms of the standing order. This ambidextrous quality made it possible for both sides in any number of New England's theological controversies to cite Cotton as an authority for their respective positions. See Ziff, *John Cotton*, pp. 106–48; DeLamotte, "John Cotton and the Rhetoric of Grace."

7. By "Independents," Winthrop meant those English Puritans pushing for the most complete separation of individual churches from any form of ecclesiastical authority; see Winthrop, *History of New England*, 2:269.

8. On the First Church's membership standards, see Pierce, ed., *Records of the First Church* 1:55–57. On Norton's views, see Simmons, "Founding of the Third Church," pp. 242–44; and Pope, *Halfway Covenant*, pp. 35–37, 48–49. See also David D. Hall, *Faithful Shepherd*, pp. 114, 118–19, 128, on Norton's clerical sacerdotalism.

9. John Norton, *Sion the Outcast*, pp. 10–11.

10. Simmons, "Founding of the Third Church," p. 245.

11. Lucas, "Colony or Commonwealth," pp. 92–93.

12. John Davenport to John Leverett, June 24, 1665, in Davenport, *Letters*, pp. 248–53.

13. Mr. [Humphrey?] Davie to John Davenport, undated, in "The Mather Papers," p. 204.

14. See editor's introduction in Davenport, *Letters*, pp. 2–7.

15. On his positions with respect to the early New England churches and the developments of the 1660s, see Davenport, *Letters*, pp. 8–10, 248.

16. On the second generation's invention of and veneration for the "ancient" ways of the founding generation, see Scobey, "Revising the Errand," p. 25.

17. This was the central point underlying the extended argument in the Elizabethan and Jacobean eras between those Puritans who remained within the Church of England and the "Brownists" or separatists who favored "reformation without tarrying for any"; see Miller, *Orthodoxy in Massachusetts*, and Morgan, *Visible Saints*, for discussions of this debate and of the "non-separating Congregationalism" that emerged from it.

18. John Norton, "The Epistle Dedicatory," in *Orthodox Evangelist*, no page.

19. Quoted in *OSC*, 1:9. In his "Preface" to the Result of the Synod of 1662, Mitchell wrote an extended defense of the "right middle way of Truth" as a means for determining proper church polity. Mitchell claimed that Christians should look for God to reveal his will to them in dealing with new situations, rather than cling in idolatrous fashion to the forms of the past: "The Lord's humble and faithfull Servants are not wont to be forward to think themselves perfect in their attainments, but desirous rather to make a progress in the knowledge and practise of God's holy Will." Just as the individual believer would continue to grow in grace after conversion, so

godly churches would evolve when confronted with new problems. See Mitchell, "Preface to the Christian Reader," in Walker, *Creeds and Platforms*, pp. 301–13, especially 304–5.

20. The dissenters' devotion to Mitchell is evident from the thoughts of John Hull, who commented on Mitchell's death in 1668 that "Rev. Mr. Mitchell died, the chief remaining pillar of our ministry." See Hull, "Diaries," p. 198.

21. Pierce, ed., *Records of the First Church*, 1:55–56.

22. These quotations are taken from the "Third Church Narrative," a document describing the events leading to the founding of Boston's Third Church, written in 1691 by four church members. Three of them, Jacob Eliot, Theophilus Frary, and Joshua Scottow, were founders of the church; the fourth, Samuel Sewall, was the son-in-law of another founder, John Hull. The "Third Church Narrative" must be seen as a biased account of these matters, since it was written twenty years after the event by members of the dissenting faction in an attempt to justify their behavior. However, much of the narrative actually consists of copies of significant letters, petitions, and other documents that were exchanged during the controversy. The veracity of many of these documents can be confirmed by the existence of independent copies, which lend support to the accuracy of the narrative's specific claims, if not to its overall interpretation of events. The "Third Church Narrative" is reprinted in full in *OSC*, 1:13–202; these quotations are at p. 17. In this text, the "Third Church Narrative" is interspersed with other primary documents from the period not included in the narrative, as well as with the compiler Hamilton Hill's own commentary. I have checked Hill's reproduction of the Third Church records in *OSC* against the microfilm copy of the church records in the Congregational Library, Boston, and save for minor spelling changes, Hill's transcription is accurate and complete. All subsequent citations to primary sources in *OSC* will specify the original document from which the citation is made.

23. Although the term "Halfway Covenant" does reflect something about its supporters' habits of thought, the use of the term is at best a convenient anachronism. The phrase was not in use in the 1660s—it was actually coined as a term of opprobrium roughly a century later, in yet another rehashing of the same controversy over membership and baptismal standards. During the 1660s, the two sides saw themselves as pro- and anti-Synod, a more accurate but also more awkward characterization; for a thorough discussion, see David D. Hall's introduction to Edwards, *Ecclesiastical Writings*.

24. Simmons, "Founding of the Third Church," pp. 244–45.

25. Hull, "Diaries," pp. 216–18.

26. "Third Church Narrative," in *OSC*, 1:16–18.

27. The specific sequence of events in this controversy, which lasted well over a year in its initial phase and which dragged on for over a decade in some of its lingering effects, has been fully documented in *OSC*, where much of the primary evidence can be found, but see also Simmons, "Founding of the Third Church"; Pope, *Halfway Covenant*; and David D. Hall, "Declension Politics," in *Faithful Shepherd*.

28. Miller, *From Colony to Province*, pp. 106–07.

29. On John Owen's place in Congregationalism and his connections with New England, see Owen, *Correspondence*, pp. 125–28, 135–36; on the First Church's calling of Owen, see "Third Church Narrative" in OSC, 1:14, 18.

30. "Third Church Narrative," in OSC, 1:15–18.

31. "Third Church Narrative," in OSC, 1:15–18, 23–24.

32. John Davenport to the First Church, Boston, October 28, 1667, in Davenport, *Letters*, pp. 271–73.

33. "Third Church Narrative" in OSC, 1:23; Hull, "Diaries," pp. 226–27.

34. Stout, *New England Soul*, p. 27.

35. "Third Church Narrative," in OSC, 1:24.

36. This position was strikingly similar in form to that of the Laudian program in the Church of England during the 1630s, which defined Anglican orthodoxy so narrowly as to assure the widespread existence of dissent, and yet also refused to tolerate dissent in any form as legitimate; see Lake, "Laudian Style."

37. "Third Church Narrative," in OSC, 1:28–29.

38. "Third Church Narrative," in OSC, 1:29–32.

39. "Third Church Narrative," in OSC, 1:32–42. See also Nicholas Street to Increase Mather[?], December 2, 1668, in OSC, 1:44–45, and fragment of letter from Nicholas Street to the First Church, Boston, October 12, 1668, Records of the Old South Church, Shelf 13.

40. Davenport's willingness to commit such a treacherous act for the sake of a cherished principle, even at the temporary expense of the principle itself, may have stemmed from his long-standing involvement with the escape and concealment of the regicide judges Whalley and Goffe, who fled crown retribution by hiding out in the Connecticut Valley. Throughout the 1660s, Davenport had come to see himself as the last of the founders, a remnant of spiritual fervor and righteousness in a declining world, and his willingness to defend his cause made him willing to lie, to defy authority, and to act in secret, first in concealing the regicide judges, but later in opposition to "enemies" like the First Church dissenters. See Hutchinson, ed., *Collection of Original Papers*, pp. 334–44; Davenport, *Letters*, pp. 198–201, 207–9.

41. On beliefs both popular and clerical regarding the dangers of partaking in communion, see David D. Hall, *Worlds of Wonder*, pp. 156–61; Holifield, *Covenant Sealed*, pp. 202–6.

42. In a treatise of 1654, John Norton emphasized this idea of the "judgment of charity" and the necessity for preaching to those not yet converted, the "preparatory" work that might lead to salvation; Norton, *The Orthodox Evangelist*, pp. 129ff.

43. "Third Church Narrative," in OSC, 1:42–47. Davenport's use of the sacrament as a "snare" or weapon only served to exacerbate the problem which the Halfway Covenant was intended to solve. Excessive anxiety over coming to the Lord's Supper for fear of damning oneself by partaking sinfully was a problem for many godly Protestants. Davenport's extremely strict view of the requirements for membership tended to encourage such fears, perhaps keeping many potential members out of the

church because of their excessive scrupulosity. While supporters of the Halfway Covenant sought ways to ease this hyper-scrupulosity by emphasizing the means of conversion offered to all within the covenant, Davenport's use of the sacrament as a "snare" could only reinforce popular beliefs about the dangers of risking church membership.

44. "Third Church Narrative," in *OSC*, 1:47–49.

45. "Third Church Narrative," in *OSC*, 1:49–53.

46. "Third Church Narrative," in *OSC*, 1:23–24.

47. "Third Church Narrative," in *OSC*, 1:25–27. The council was composed of clergy and laymen from the churches of Dorchester, Dedham, Roxbury, and Cambridge.

48. Deacon Eliot may have played the major role in organizing this council, for his brother John Eliot, minister of the Roxbury church, together with John Allin, minister at Dedham, composed a similar letter to the same three churches and asked them to send delegates to Charlestown in early April 1669, where a meeting would be held to discuss the issues; "Third Church Narrative," in *OSC*, 1:53–57.

49. "Third Church Narrative," in *OSC*, 1:59–60.

50. "Third Church Narrative," in *OSC*, 1:60–63. See also Hull, "Diaries," p. 229, where Hull raises the possibility that Davenport's rude treatment hastened the death of Richard Mather, which came only a week after Mather was forced to wait outside the Town House for the First Church's response.

51. Allin, "Brief History," 2:1–21; "Third Church Narrative," in *OSC*, 1:63–68.

52. "Third Church Narrative," in *OSC*, 1:72–76. Davenport had used similar language in describing the New Haven church's grudging acknowledgment that they could not prevent him from moving to the Boston church; see John Davenport to the First Church, Boston, October 28, 1667, in Davenport, *Letters*, pp. 271–73.

53. "Third Church Narrative," in *OSC*, 1:76.

54. See Pope, *Halfway Covenant*, pp. 152–84; Simmons, "Founding of the Third Church," pp. 241–52; and David D. Hall, *Faithful Shepherd*, pp. 233–37.

55. "Third Church Narrative," in *OSC*, 1:77.

56. In addition, the Charlestown minister, Thomas Shepard Jr., was one of the strongest supporters of the "dissenting brethren" and their cause; see David D. Hall, *Faithful Shepherd*, pp. 237–38.

57. "Third Church Narrative," in *OSC*, 1:78–80.

58. "The Covenant made by the Third Church in Boston, Gathred at Charlestown on 12th day of 3rd moneth 1669," in *OSC*, 1:127.

59. For a comparison with the Boston First Church covenant, see Pierce, ed., *Records of the First Church*, 1:10, 12. In the original First Church covenant of 1630, the members pledged to bind themselves to "the Rule of the Gospel" and "in mutual love, and respect to each other," but made no mention of future generations or of interchurch cooperation. The revised covenant of later years, written in the hand of James Allen, Davenport's colleague, altered the original language but maintained the same sense, and mentioned neither of the Third Church's innovative points. Similarly, the

covenant of Boston's Second Church, founded in the North End in 1649, called for the members to walk together "in all the ways of his worship, and of mutual love, and of special watchfulness one over another," but did not describe the church's responsibility to future generations or to other godly societies. See Robbins, *History of the Second Church*, pp. 209–10.

60. In this sermon, Davenport emphasized his personal role in the founding of the Massachusetts Bay Company, and restated his claim to embody the traditions of the colony; see Davenport, *A Sermon Preach'd*, pp. 12–15.

61. "Third Church Narrative," in *OSC*, 1:81–82, 84–89; John Davenport to the First Church, Boston, June 29, 1669, in Davenport, *Letters*, pp. 283–84. Increase Mather had shown his support for Davenport throughout the 1660s but turned against him and accepted the Halfway Covenant at this point. This suggests the effect of the controversy on many of the clergy who may have otherwise supported Davenport. See Increase Mather to John Davenport, in "The Mather Papers," pp. 205–6; also Mather, "An Apologetical Preface."

62. *OSC*, 1:128–29.

63. *OSC*, 1:129–32. Winthrop had been forced to give up much of this land in 1643 after an inept steward had mismanaged his estate, but the governor retained the portion on which he lived until his death; Morgan, *Puritan Dilemma*, pp. 174–76.

64. Winthrop, *History of New England*, 1:318.

65. "Mrs. Norton's Deed of Gift, 1669," in *OSC*, 1:133–35.

66. "Third Church Narrative," in *OSC*, 1:140–46.

67. "Third Church Narrative," in *OSC*, 1:145–46; Hull, "Diaries," p. 230.

68. In later years, this tradition would continue to be important. In 1714, when Samuel Sewall's son Joseph moved into the Third Church parsonage after his ordination as minister, the father visited and wished "... the Blessing of Winthrop, Norton, Willard, Pemberton to come upon him." *SS Diary*, 2:740–41.

69. See Cotton Mather, *Magnalia Christi Americana*, ed. Robbins, 1:236–37, on the 2nd "classis" of New England ministers who were educated in this fashion, of whom Thomas Thacher was one. This form of personal tutelage was the best method of instruction available in New England before Harvard College became well established.

70. *OSC*, 1:122–26. See Cotton Mather, *Magnalia Christi Americana*, ed. Robbins, 1:488–96, for his biography of Thacher.

71. For Thacher's admission to the First Church, see Pierce, ed., *First Church Records*, 1:62, 64.

72. At the time of Thacher's ordination in the Third Church, John Davenport complained that during the earlier controversies, Thacher had not stepped forward to join the dissenters, and that becoming their minister now was therefore somehow disingenuous; see "Third Church Narrative," in *OSC*, 1:156–57.

73. "Third Church Narrative," in *OSC*, 1:147, 152–53, 156–63.

74. The importance of this issue to the Third Church members can be seen even in the details of their ordinary business. For example, the early records noted that "Mrs. Blake widdow was admitted member of the third church by vertu of letter of

dismission from the church of Dorchester who in that act owned them to be a church of Christ." Similarly, their ongoing efforts to find an English clergyman to be Thacher's colleague were conducted through a correspondence that emphasized their commitment to the transatlantic dissenting community. See the "Third Church Narrative," in *OSC*, 1:147, 150, 165. See also Hull, "Diaries," pp. 159–60, 311–12.

75. See Morgan, *Puritan Family*, pp. 133–60; Hambrick-Stowe, *Practice of Piety*, pp. 136–37, 143–50.

76. "Third Church Narrative," in *OSC*, 1:165–70.

77. "Third Church Narrative," in *OSC*, 1:174–75, 180.

78. See *OSC*, 1:190–96. On Governor Bellingham's will, and the possibility that the will was tampered with by the Rev. James Allen of the First Church in a manner reminiscent of the Davenport dismissal letter, see Sewall, "Letter-Book," 1:99–105n. See also Oakes, *New England Pleaded With.*

79. "Third Church Narrative," in *OSC*, 1:199; Pierce, ed., *Records of the First Church*, 1:70–72. For the First Church's dealing with Sarah Pemberton, wife of Third Church founder James Pemberton, see Pierce, ed., *Records*, p. 66.

80. "Third Church Narrative," in *OSC*, 1:201–4.

81. For two very different discussions of the Synod of 1679, see Perry Miller, "Declension in a Bible Commonwealth," in *Nature's Nation*, pp. 24–33; Gildrie, *Profane, Civil, & Godly*, pp. 19–40.

82. Walker, *Creeds and Platforms*, pp. 409–39.

83. Pierce, ed., *Records of the First Church*, 1:75–76.

84. According the church records, 79 people came forward at this time; ". . . at least thirty were children of the founders," and "most of them in later years became members in full communion." *OSC*, 1:235.

85. See Willard, *Duty of a People*, the sermon Willard preached at the Third Church's covenant renewal ceremony, cited in Van Dyken, *Samuel Willard*, pp. 39–40. On the role of covenant renewal in the spiritual lives of the laity, see Stout, *New England Soul*, pp. 96–101.

86. The Third Church's covenant renewal of June 29, 1680, is reprinted in full in *OSC*, 1:240–41.

87. Chapter 13 concerned the "removall" of church members "from one Church to another, & letters of recomendation & dismission." In effect, the First Church wanted the Third Church to acknowledge the truth of the doctrine of the particular congregation's control over its members, even if they were willing to forgive this peculiar breach. Walker, *Creeds and Platforms*, pp. 224–26.

88. Pierce, ed., *Records of the First Church*, 1:79–80; *OSC*, 1:243–46.

89. The personal lives of the South Church clergy helped to bring about this reconciliation as well. In July 1679, Samuel Willard married Eunice Tyng, the daughter of Edward Tyng, a member of the First Church who had strongly opposed the dissenting brethren in the 1660s. See Van Dyken, *Samuel Willard*, pp. 37–38.

90. Several other Massachusetts Bay churches passed similar votes at about this time, including the churches at Charlestown, Cambridge, and Watertown; see David D. Hall, *Faithful Shepherd*, p. 205, and "Third Church Records," in *OSC*, 1:229.

91. For a prominent example of this argument, see Pope, *Halfway Covenant*, pp. 219-25.

92. On covenant renewal in the Third Church, see *OSC*, 1:235-36.

Chapter 2

1. Lockwood, *Westfield*, 1:52. On the role of the fur trade in the development of the Connecticut Valley, see McIntyre, *William Pynchon*; and McIntyre, "John Pynchon."

2. On the founding of the early Connecticut Valley towns, see Andrews, *River Towns*; for a discussion of early Windsor, see D. G. Allen, "Both Englands."

3. On John Pynchon's role in the development of the Connecticut Valley, see Bridenbaugh, ed., *Pynchon Papers*, 1: xxvii-xxxix; also Innes, *Labor in a New Land*, pp. 17-43. Numerous local histories provide details on the settlement of these towns, including Judd, *History of Hadley*, pp. 3ff; Trumbull, *History of Northampton*, 1:4-16; and more recently, Melvoin, *New England Outpost*, pp. 49-91. On the settlement of Westfield, see Lockwood, *Westfield*; and especially, W. L. Powell's introduction to ET "Town Recs.," pp. 1-131. For a general discussion of the role of entrepreneurial leadership in the founding of New England towns, see Martin, *Profits in the Wilderness*.

4. ET "Towns Recs.," p. 152.

5. Lucas, *Valley of Discord*, pp. 56, 73-86.

6. Lucas, pp. 38-40.

7. Lucas, pp. 62-63. See also Stiles, *Ancient Windsor*; and Bissell, "Family, Friends, and Neighbors."

8. Gura, *Glimpse of Sion's Glory*, pp. 311-12.

9. See Innes, *Labor in a New Land*, p. 16; Morison, *Builders of the Bay Colony*, p. 374.

10. In 1661, Pelatiah Glover settled as Springfield's new minister and remained until his death in 1692, but his tenure was also marked by frequent contention. He was involved in court cases concerning slander accusations, collection of his salary, and ownership of the town's ministerial lands; see Innes, *Labor in a New Land*, pp. 147-48.

11. Lucas, pp. 83-85, 111-14.

12. See Trumbull, *History of Northampton*, 1:77-80; Patricia Tracy, *Jonathan Edwards, Pastor*, pp. 21-22; Coffman, *Solomon Stoddard*, pp. 58-61.

13. ET *Chh. Recs.*, p. 99; Grabo, *Edward Taylor*, p. 3.

14. Edward Taylor, "The Lay-mans Lamentation . . . ," in *Minor Poetry*, pp. 13-18; see also Keller, *Example of Edward Taylor*, pp. 24-26.

15. Taylor brought letters of introduction addressed to Increase Mather and John Hull, written on his behalf by friends in England, suggestive of his connections with dissenting Congregationalists in England; *ET Diary*, p. 35. On the transatlantic connections between Puritan dissenters in the post-Restoration era, see Cressy, *Coming Over*, pp. 213-34; Bremer, *Congregational Communion*, pp. 202-52.

16. For biographical sketches of Taylor's classmates in the class of 1671, see Sibley, *Harvard Graduates*, 2:335-412.

17. Keller, *Example*, p. 18.

18. *ET Diary*, pp. 37-38.

19. See Sewall's autobiographical letter to his son, April 21–August 26, 1720, in *SS Diary*, 1:xxx-xxxi.

20. Michael G. Hall, *Last American Puritan*, pp. 41-48.

21. "Articles Objected by His Majesty's Commissioners for Causes Ecclesiastical against Charles Chauncey . . . ," in Demos, ed., *Remarkable Providences*, pp. 32-36. On Chauncy's English background and persecution, see Morison, *Founding of Harvard College*, pp. 89-91, 371; Bradford, *Of Plymouth Plantation*, pp. 313-14.

22. *ET Diary*, p. 39.

23. On this distinction, see Morgan, *Puritan Family*, pp. 161-86; also Morgan, *Visible Saints*, pp. 113-38.

24. Chauncy was the author of the major work opposing the results of the Synod of 1662, *Anti-Synodalia Scripta Americana*; on his New England career, see Morison, *Harvard in the Seventeenth Century*, 1:322-23; Miller, *From Colony to Province*, pp. 100-104.

25. By 1671, Taylor's last year at Harvard, Increase Mather changed his opinion on the Halfway Covenant, which may have influenced Taylor's own willingness to support broad baptismal standards in Westfield. See Grabo, *Edward Taylor*, p. 13; Middlekauff, *The Mathers*, pp. 85-86.

26. Words like "conservative" and "liberal" become problematic when describing early New England, given the Puritan movement's radical critique of English church polity. Perry Miller comments that Charles Chauncy and John Davenport can be called conservative only ". . . if we comprehend that they clung to what had been extreme radicalism in 1630, the principle of regenerate membership"; *From Colony to Province*, p. 101.

27. See Introduction, pp. 7-12.

28. This anxiety can be seen in the tension which pervades some of New England's later myth-making documents, most notably Cotton Mather's attempts to cover over or homogenize dissent in his *Magnalia Christi Americana*.

29. ET "Town Recs.," pp. 147-49. On the subsequent careers of John Holyoke and Moses Fiske, the two ministerial candidates who rejected Westfield's offers, see Sibley, *Harvard Graduates*, 2:102-3, 122-27.

30. *ET Chh. Recs.*, p. 4. Adams later accepted an offer from Dedham, Massachusetts, where he eventually settled; see Sibley, *Harvard Graduates*, 2:380-87.

31. *ET Diary*, p. 39.

32. *ET Diary*, p. 39.

33. ET "Town Recs.," pp. 169-72.

34. See Trumbull, *History of Northampton*, pp. 415-18; also *ET Chh. Recs.*, editors' note, p. 461.

35. *ET Chh. Recs.*, p. 161.

36. Taylor, Commonplace Book, Item no. 2.

37. Taylor, Commonplace Book, Item no. 3. Wilton was one of the group Eleazer Mather had recruited to Northampton a decade earlier. Here, the Westfield laymen describe the church as a "temple" rather than the "garden" metaphor more commonly

used by the founders of Boston's Third Church. Although this may well reflect their own vision of the church, it was strongly reinforced by Edward Taylor's preaching, as we shall see below in his foundation day sermon.

38. Taylor, Commonplace Book, Item no. 4.

39. Taylor, Commonplace Book, Item no. 5.

40. Edward Taylor, "Revised Foundation Day Sermon," in *ET Chh. Recs.*, p. 292.

41. *ET Chh. Recs.*, p. 4.

42. See Lockwood, *Westfield*, pp. 199-253, for an extensive discussion of Westfield's involvement in King Philip's War.

43. *ET Chh. Recs.*, p. 5.

44. Lockwood, *Westfield*, p. 97.

45. ET "Town Recs.," p. 179.

46. See the editor's introduction to ET "Town Recs.," pp. 27-29, for a description of Westfield's early geographical layout and the effects of the "new modelling" on the town.

47. ET "Town Recs.," p. 184.

48. ET "Town Recs.," p. 33.

49. ET "Town Recs.," pp. 182-91. On the difficulties Westfield (and other similar communities in New England) faced from absentee landowners and proprietors, see Martin, *Profits in the Wilderness*, pp. 44-45.

50. *ET Chh. Recs.*, p. 8.

51. *ET Chh. Recs.*, p. 7.

52. *ET Chh. Recs.*, pp. 7-8.

53. The subjects which Taylor chose merely to abbreviate in outline form and those which he chose to write out in full in his hastily drawn profession of faith are interesting in what they reveal about Taylor's religious beliefs. Taylor spent the most time discussing the nature and meaning of the sacraments, judgment day and the torments of hell, and the nature, varieties, and efficacy of prayer. See *ET Chh. Recs.*, pp. 10-96.

54. *ET Chh. Recs.*, p. 97. The contents of the founding members' conversion relations will be examined in chapter 4, where the religious lives of the Westfield laity are explored in greater detail.

55. This sermon is usually interpreted as a bold statement confronting Solomon Stoddard on the subject of more open church membership in New England. This may be true of the later revisions to the sermon which Taylor made in the 1690s, for by then, Stoddard had openly argued for his radical extension of membership privileges to virtually all well-behaved professing Christians, and Taylor had given much time and thought to counter-arguments. But as of 1679, Stoddard's position was still not fully formed and publicly expressed, and Taylor's foundation day sermon is more simply an expression of his understanding of the nature and function of a Christian church. Certainly the fact that his text was merely "in the Choice heads thereof gone over" due to the shortness of time on this busy day made the sermon seem more like a formality than a challenge. See *ET Chh. Recs.*, pp. xxiv-xxviii, 159.

56. *ET Chh. Recs.*, pp. 118–19.

57. *ET Chh. Recs.*, pp. 127–37. Taylor's discussion of this subject took up roughly one fourth of the entire sermon.

58. *OSC*, 1:127; see chapter 1, above.

59. See chapter 3.

60. *ET Chh. Recs.*, pp. 125–27.

61. *ET Chh. Recs.*, p. 159.

62. For studies of the "primitivist" impulse in Puritan theology and church polity, see Bozeman, *To Live Ancient Lives*; Coolidge, *Pauline Renaissance*.

63. *ET Chh. Recs.*, p. 160.

64. *ET Chh. Recs.*, p. 160.

Chapter 3

1. This was the prevailing metaphor which John Winthrop used in his 1630 lay sermon, "A Modell of Christian Charity"; see especially pp. 288–94.

2. This was the underlying argument conveyed by Thomas Shepard's use of the garden metaphor in his *Church-Membership of Children*, p. 8. Though written before his death in 1649, Shepard's text was published in 1662 by defenders of the Halfway Covenant Synod who sought to prove that the Synod fulfilled the desires of leading first-generation clergymen.

3. See for example, Willard, *Righteous Man's Death*, a funeral sermon preached for Thomas Savage. For an extended instance of clerical usage of the garden metaphor, see Willard, *Barren Fig Trees Doom*, a 300–page sermon series based on the parable of the fig tree in the vineyard. Among the founders, the most influential ministers, including John Cotton, Thomas Hooker, Richard Mather, and Thomas Shepard, all used garden imagery in defining the nature of the church; for a general discussion, see Carroll, *Puritanism and the Wilderness*, pp. 109–26.

4. See Selement, *Keepers of the Vineyard*; Plumstead, ed., *The Wall and the Garden*. For an interesting reading of the implications of this metaphor for relations with the native population and the development of a New England identity, see Stavely, "Roger Williams and the Enclosed Gardens of New England."

5. On the availability of this plenitude of means to godly Puritans in pre-migration England, and on its absence in the early years of New England settlement, see Foster, *Long Argument*, pp. 65–107, especially p. 88, and pp. 183–84. The phrase "plenitude of means" is borrowed from Foster, "Godly in Transit," p. 191. In general this reduction in the availability of the means of conversion in the rather primitive communities of early New England might be understood as an example of the simplification of European cultural forms among American colonists in the early stages of settlement. What I am describing in this chapter constitutes the colonists' awareness of and response to this stripping down of European culture, an attempt to reconstitute it in the New World; see Harris, "Simplification of Europe" and "European Beginnings"; also Greene, "Interpretive Frameworks," p. 519.

6. Among them were William Davis, an apothecary, Theodore Atkinson, Seth

Perry, and John Tappan in cloth trades, tailoring, and hat making, William Dawes, a mason and builder, Theophilus Frary, a cordwainer, Richard Trewsdale, a butcher, John Sanford, a schoolmaster, William Salter, a shoemaker, James Pemberton, a brewer, and John Alden, son of Plymouth's famous founder, a ship-master.

7. For information on the employment and wealth of the Third Church founders, see *OSC*, 1:113–20; also see the anonymous "Biographical sketches of ten of the church founders," in Records of the Old South Church and Congregation, Shelf 13.

8. Roberts, *Artillery Company*, 1:487–88.

9. See *OSC*, 1:113–20.

10. The 1687 tax list is reproduced in the *First Report of the Record Commissioners of the City of Boston*, pp. 91–133.

11. *SS Diary*, 1:30; 34, 42, 86.

12. Similarly, there were men like Elizur Holyoke and Gustavus Hamilton who contributed money to a fund raised by the church in 1693 for the benefit of the minister's family, yet whose names do not appear among the church records. This financial support was essential to the mission of the church, regardless of the formal church status of the contributors; see *OSC*, 1:295n, 298, and below, chapter 5.

13. Included are only those individuals for whom a positive identification can be made from the records of Hill and Bigelow, comps., *Historical Catalogue*. Consequently, many persons who may have been members of South Church families, but who cannot be confirmed as such, are excluded, which makes the above figure a somewhat conservative estimate of the total number of families in the South Church. One indication that this figure is a conservative estimate can be seen from the fact that there are individuals known to have joined the church in full communion, such as Samuel Sewall's daughter Hannah, who was accepted into the church on January 6, 1716/17, yet whose names do not appear in the official membership lists; see *SS Diary*, 2:843; *Historical Catalogue*, p. 27.

14. The list includes a ninth and tenth precinct, one at "Muddy River" in present-day Brookline, the other made up of the harbor islands and outlying regions that were technically part of the town of Boston and where Bostonians held lands. These two precincts were not included in the analysis of South Church members for two reasons. First, their geographical remoteness allowed for little participation in the ordinary life of the religious communities of Boston, and consequently, very few church affiliates actually lived in these regions. Of the 99 persons rated on these two precinct "sheets," only six can be identified as having any affiliation with the South Church. Second, the basis for taxation in these precincts was significantly different from the main part of Boston on Shawmut peninsula, which makes it difficult to find meaningful comparisons between these primarily agricultural outlying regions and the commercial economy of Boston proper. See *First Report of the Record Commissioners*, pp. 128–33.

15. Figures calculated from the Boston Tax List of 1687, in *First Report of the Record Commissioners*, pp. 91–133, along with Hill and Bigelow, *Historical Catalogue*.

16. See for example Richard R. Johnson, *John Nelson*, pp. 32, 118. Nelson was an English merchant who settled in Boston and played an important part in New England's commercial enterprises but remained aloof from Boston's social and cultural affairs and kept largely to himself.

17. See Bailyn, *New England Merchants*, pp. 192–95; and Bernard Bailyn and Lotte Bailyn, *Massachusetts Shipping*, pp. 74–76.

18. Bailyn and Bailyn, *Massachusetts Shipping*, pp. 20–21.

19. Women were, of course, essential to the life of the church—they would eventually constitute the majority of members in full communion, and their spirituality was vital to the internal sustenance of the church and to the continuity of family membership across generations. But their role with respect to public church leadership, especially in matters of financial support and control, was much less pronounced.

20. Willard, *Righteous Man's Death*, pp. 156–62.

21. See Introduction.

22. For a sample of sermons from this genre, see Bosco, ed., *New England Funeral Sermons*.

23. See, for instance, Samuel Willard, *High Esteem*, preached as a eulogy for John Hull; and Willard, *Sermon . . . upon Ezekiel*, a funeral oration for John Leverett.

24. On the class of 1671, of whom 7 out of 11 graduates became ministers, see Sibley, *Harvard Graduates*, 2:335–412; on Sewall's early life and calling, see *SS Diary*, 1:10–15.

25. See Bailyn, *New England Merchants*, pp. 134–35.

26. For brief accounts of the lives of these men, see Hill and Bigelow, *Historical Catalogue*, pp. 218–20, 313–14.

27. *SS Diary*, 1:368–69.

28. *SS Diary*, 2:723–24.

29. Scottow, *Old Men's Tears*.

30. See "Third Church Narrative" in *OSC*.

31. See Hambrick-Stowe, *Practice of Piety*, pp. 91–193, for an excellent discussion of the various forms of devotional practice.

32. Most of the surviving conversion narratives from early New England can be found in a few collections: Thomas Shepard, *Confessions*; John Fiske, *Notebook*; Michael Wigglesworth, *Diary*; and *ET Chh. Recs.*.

33. Savage, *Genealogical Dictionary*, 1:258–59; Hill and Bigelow, *Historical Catalogue*, p. 313.

34. *First Report of the Record Commissioners*, p. 122.

35. Bromfield, Sermon Notes, vol. 6, sermon no. 12, July 10, 1692, leaf 2. For a discussion of the significance of these Boston sermons during the Salem witchcraft crisis, see Peterson, "Ordinary Preaching."

36. See Stout, *New England Soul*, pp. 91–95.

37. Hill and Bigelow, *Historical Catalogue*, p. 20.

38. Pierce, ed., *First Church Records*, 1:51. Mary Rock's one surviving notebook contains 31 sermons, and covers the period from July 28 to October 7, 1687. It seems

likely that Mary Rock attended regularly at the South Church, since Samuel Willard is the regular preacher of the sermons recorded, with intermittent guest sermons by visiting ministers. Mary Rock's case is further evidence that formal records for full membership are unreliable indicators of the extent of participation in the life of a particular church.

39. Bromfield, Sermon Notes, [Mary Rock] vol. 1, sermon no. 14, 28 August 1687, leaf 66; [Edward Bromfield Jr.] vol. 10, Sermon no. 3, 7 February 1719/20, leaf 12.

40. Hill and Bigelow, *Historical Catalogue*, p. 35.

41. Further evidence of Mary Rock's efforts along these lines may be found in another collection of sermon notebooks, attributed to her son John Danforth, minister of Roxbury and colleague of John Eliot, but which may be in her hand as well. See Danforth, Notes of Sermons.

42. On the general practice of private devotional meetings, see Hambrick-Stowe, *Practice of Piety*, pp. 137–43.

43. *SS Diary*, 1:603.

44. Willard, *Barren Fig Trees Doom*, pp. 183–200.

45. See David D. Hall, "The Uses of Literacy," in *Worlds of Wonder*, pp. 21–71; Richard D. Brown, *Knowledge is Power*.

46. *SS Diary*, 2:653; the sermon cited by Sewall was from Thomas Shepard, *Parable of the Ten Virgins*, and was probably either a reprint edition issued in the Netherlands in 1695 or the Cambridge, Massachusetts, edition of 1659. Given the fact that a modern edition of this work runs to more than 600 pages, the book was probably rather expensive; by owning a copy and sharing its contents in a devotional meeting, Sewall was sharing his wealth in an evangelical fashion.

47. The titles borne by these men, ranging from "Captain" to "Mr." to "Goodman," indicate variations in the social status and wealth of the men who provided religious instruction and nurture to the young Sewall, and suggest that status within the church did not always follow secular standards; see *SS Diary*, 1:29.

48. *SS Diary*, 1:35–41.

49. For Sewall's anxious first communion, see *SS Diary* 1:40; on popular concern among New England Puritans that the Lord's Supper was a "zone of danger," see David D. Hall, *Worlds of Wonder*, pp. 156–61, 226–27.

50. Hambrick-Stowe, *Practice of Piety*, 125–26. Even during his anxious first communion, Sewall looked forward to the next sacrament when he hoped to "do better" and gain a "glimpse" of Christ; *SS Diary*, 1:40.

51. Some New England churches excluded all but full members from the meetinghouse during the Lord's Supper, but as early as 1642, Boston's First Church allowed non-members to observe the administration of the sacrament. The Third Church founders' support of the Halfway Covenant and their generally inclusive approach toward non-members make it likely that they retained this practice in their own church; see Lechford, *Plain Dealing*, pp. 16–17.

52. *SS Diary*, 1:528.

53. Davies, *Worship of the American Puritans*, pp. 164–68.

54. *SS Diary*, 2:757.

55. For an extended discussion of the spiritual value of communion silver in early New England, see Peterson, "Puritanism and Gentility."

56. See Morison, *Builders of the Bay Colony*, pp. 153–57; Roe and Trent, "Robert Sanderson"; Peterson, "Puritanism and Gentility."

57. "Third Church Records," October 26, 1685, in *OSC*, 1:253–54.

58. This occurred in 1713, when the membership voted it "convenient to appoint one of the congregation," that is, not a full member, to be an overseer of the seats; *SS Diary*, 2:713.

59. My use of the term "tribal" in this case follows that of Morgan, *Puritan Family*, pp. 90–104, and *Visible Saints*, p. 138–39, where he writes that the Halfway Covenant "was a narrow tribal way of recruiting saints, for it wholly neglected the church's evangelical mission to perishing sinners outside the families of its members." However, Puritan "tribalism" was in actual practice not necessarily very exclusive, and could often encourage growth in church membership; see Moran, "Religious Renewal."

60. For a general discussion of New England practices, see Dinkin, "Seating the Meetinghouse."

61. Collinson, *English Puritanism*, pp. 16–18; Morgan, *Visible Saints*, pp. 9–12.

62. Willard, *Barren Fig Trees Doom*, pp. 281–300.

63. *SS Diary*, 1:170.

64. For details of the Judd case, see "Third Church Records," Jan. 22, 1698/9, in *OSC*, 1:305–7.

65. For one example of this kind of informal resolution to conflict within the church, see the May 13, 1696, entry in *SS Diary*, 1:350, in which a private meeting among various laymen at Sewall's home resolves a difference between Third Church members Theophilus Frary and Seth Perry. It is possible that the scarcity of disciplinary cases among the church records is simply a reflection of poor record-keeping, but given the high quality of the records for other aspects of church life, this seems unlikely.

66. *SS Diary*, 2:627.

67. *SS Diary*, 1:600.

68. This "7th Comp." may correspond to one of the precinct divisions on the 1687 tax list; see *SS Diary*, 1:588.

69. Similarly, on the night of August 8, 1715, Sewall set out "at night on Horseback" with fellow church member Thomas Wallis "to inspect the order of the Town." During their rounds, they "dissipated the players at Nine Pins at Mount-Whoredom," [that is, Mt. Vernon], they "Reproved Thomas Messenger for entertaining them," and "between 2 and three [A.M.] took up Peter Griffis the notorious Burglarer, and committed him to Prison." *SS Diary*, 2:795–96. The peace and order of the town was a secular as much as it was a religious matter, but men like Sewall, Daniel Oliver, and Thomas Wallis brought their religious concerns to bear on the preservation of a moral environment.

70. *SS Diary*, 2:637–38.

71. *SS Diary*, 2:645–49.

72. For an excellent discussion of the way divided authority within small rural towns could lead to community fragmentation, see Bushman, *From Puritan to Yankee*, pp. 155–63.

73. For an overview of Williams's career, see Shipton, *Sibley's Harvard Graduates*, 4: 182–86.

74. See *SS Diary*, 1:522, 583, 602; 2:1009, 1052, 1019, 1022.

75. *Eighth Report of the Record Commissioners*, p. 65.

76. Shipton, *Sibley Harvard Graduates*, 4:185; and Franklin B. Dexter, *Documentary History of Yale University*, pp. 239–40.

77. Prince, *Funeral Sermon on Nathaniel Williams*, pp. 25–30.

78. *SS Diary*, 1:611.

79. *SS Diary*, 1:495. On Phillips, Buttolph, Elliot, and Boone, Boston booksellers of the eighteenth century, see Goddard, "Press and Literature of the Provincial Period," 2:433.

80. *SS Diary*, 2:958–61.

81. *SS Diary*, 2:1047. For a discussion of print culture in early New England and of Samuel Sewall's use of books, see David D. Hall, *Worlds of Wonder*, pp. 45–58, 234–38.

82. Peters, *Dying Father's Legacy*; see also Stearns, *Strenuous Puritan*, pp. 416, 419–24.

83. See *SS Diary*, 2:1107.

84. On the posthumous publication of Willard's work, see Joseph Sewall and Thomas Prince, "The Preface," to Willard, *Compleat Body of Divinity*, pp. i–iv; Goddard, "Press and Literature of the Provincial Period," 2: 434. On Daniel Henchman's career, see Silver, "Publishing in Boston"; Nance, "Daniel Henchman." A number of prominent Boston publishers, printers, and booksellers were members or congregants of the Third Church and helped in the distribution of pious books and pamphlets, including Henchman, Bartholomew Green, Benjamin Eliot, Samuel Gerrish, and Nicholas Boone; see Franklin, ed., *Boston Printers*, pp. 46–51, 145–49, 200–204.

85. This particular concern was common to devout Puritans struggling for a sense of assurance in salvation. Samuel Sewall's daughter Betty suffered through an extended crisis of self-doubt expressed in similar terms. She told Sewall ". . . of the various Temptations she had; as that [she] was a Reprobat, Loved not God's people as she should," or that she ". . . was afraid [she] should go to Hell, was like Spira, not Elected." *SS Diary*, 1:359, 348. For a discussion of these experiences as a part of popular religious culture in Puritan New England, see David D. Hall, *Worlds of Wonder*, pp. 131–36.

86. *SS Diary*, 2:927–28.

87. On the printing history of this pamphlet, see Shipton and Mooney, *American Imprints*, 2:772.

Chapter 4

1. Taylor, Commonplace Book, Item no. 22.

2. A review of *Sibley's Harvard Graduates* and Dexter's *Annals of Yale College* shows that no Westfield resident received any college training during Taylor's tenure. The sole exception was Ezekiel Lewis, Harvard Class of 1695, who was not a Westfield native but was hired in the late 1690s to serve as the town's schoolmaster. However, Lewis left Westfield shortly thereafter, moved to Boston to take up a career in trade and the law, and became an active member of the Old South Church; see Shipton, *Sibley's Harvard Graduates*, 4:242–45. In the 1720s, when illness and age had enfeebled Taylor, two Yale graduates were brought in as potential replacements for Taylor; see Franklin B. Dexter, *Annals of Yale College*, 1:264–67, 279–80.

3. Lockwood, *Westfield*, p. 79.

4. W. L. Powell, "Introduction," in ET "Town Recs.," pp. 55–70; on the severe weather of the 1690s, see Kupperman, "Climate and Mastery of the Wilderness," pp. 30–37.

5. Powell, "Introduction," in ET "Town Recs.," p. 69.

6. See Melvoin, *New England Outpost*; Demos, *Unredeemed Captive*.

7. These figures are compiled from the "List of Inhabitants, Town of Westfield: 1679, 1689, 1699, 1729," Appendix B in ET "Town Recs.," pp. 401–22.

8. ET "Town Recs.," pp. 61, 401–22.

9. This phrase is borrowed from Lockridge, *New England Town*, who suggests that closed, corporate communities, as he describes the early years of Dedham, Massachusetts, were ideal "peasant utopias" for fostering a communal spirit that nurtured Puritan religious faith. The experience of Westfield challenges this argument; similarly, Christine Heyrman in her study of Gloucester and Marblehead shows that the growth of urban commercial economies in some cases actually increased communal solidarity and helped these towns foster their commitment to traditional Puritan religious beliefs; see Heyrman, *Commerce and Culture*.

10. ET "Town Recs.," p. 213.

11. "The farms" became something of an independent village within the town, and the core of what was eventually incorporated as the town of Southwick, Massachusetts. Population figures compiled from ET "Town Recs.," pp. 410–22. The number of settlers at Pochassic and "the farms" was probably higher than these figures indicate, for the residence of many people listed as inhabitants in the 1729 town records is unknown, and it seems unlikely that inhabitants of unknown residence lived near the town center.

12. For an argument that nucleated villages built around a single center were not necessary for creating "community" bonds, see Wood, "Village and Community."

13. Daniel Vickers has defined "competency" as the "degree of well-being that was both desirable and morally legitimate" to early modern English people; see Vickers, "Competency and Competition."

14. ET "Town Recs.," pp. 157ff.

15. ET "Town Recs.," pp. 204–5. Indeed, the agricultural economy of Westfield was among the most diverse in seventeenth-century Hampshire County, the western-most county in Massachusetts. Probate inventories from Westfield's citizens show a wider range of crops being grown by the town's farmers than in most other Hampshire towns; see Mark William Taylor, "Regional Diversity," pp. 12–13.

16. See, for example, ET "Town Recs.," pp. 215–19.

17. See Powell, "Introduction," in ET "Town Recs.," p. 48; Adams and Stiles, *Ancient Wethersfield*, 2:623.

18. ET "Town Recs.," p. 164.

19. See "Brother Thomas Dewy's Case," and "Brother Joseph Pomeries Case as to the Mill matters," in *ET Chh. Recs.*, pp. 179–85.

20. See "The West Indies Trade," in Bridenbaugh, ed., *Pynchon Papers* 2:147–94, especially pp. 147–48.

21. ET "Town Recs.," p. 224; Bridenbaugh, ed., *Pynchon Papers*, 2:211–12, 238–52.

22. ET "Town Recs.," pp. 266–67. The exploitation of trees on common lands for the purpose of tar-making was also a recurring problem.

23. ET "Town Recs.," pp. 219–20.

24. See Pruitt, "Self-Sufficiency."

25. At his death in 1683, the estate of John Hull, the Boston merchant and mint-master, was valued at roughly £8,000, more than ten times as large as Thomas Dewey's; see Morison, *Builders of the Bay Colony*, p. 181; Mark William Taylor, "Regional Diversity," Appendix 3. Taylor's research in probate records suggests that Westfield's farmers may have been relatively prosperous by Hampshire County standards, although the unusually low number of inventories probated in seventeenth-century Westfield may skew these figures by over-representing the town's wealthier residents. Only twelve estate inventories were probated in Westfield between 1660 and 1692, compared with more than fifty each from Springfield, Northampton, and Hadley, and twenty-one from Suffield, a town founded after Westfield was already established. Yet even if Westfield was relatively prosperous within Hampshire County, the contrast with Boston, especially in terms of the cultural expression of wealth, remains rather stark.

26. As Vickers argues, the struggle for individual families to maintain a competency almost inevitably created conflict among pre-industrial Americans. The communal institutions and communitarian spirit we think of as characteristic of early American economic life were necessary to resolve the deep social tensions engendered by the universal desire for competency. According to this argument, then, contention and cooperation were the "flip-sides" of the same coin, necessary parts of the basic conditions and values of economic life in pre-industrial America; see Vickers, "Competency and Competition," pp. 4, 28–29.

27. See Joseph H. Smith, ed., *Colonial Justice*, pp. 318, 320, 326–28, 344–45, and 368–69 for King's appearances; pp. 301, 313–14, 320, 337, and 361 for the Deweys.

28. Stephen Innes has argued that the levels of contention and the aggressive, individualistic economic behavior that characterized seventeenth-century Springfield,

Westfield's immediate neighbor to the east, indicate that Springfield as a community was "generally non-Puritan"; Innes, *Labor in a New Land*, pp. 129, 123–50. But Springfield's church records from the seventeenth century no longer exist, which makes it impossible to say much about the nature of religious culture in this community. The simple fact of contention or litigiousness should not be assumed to imply an absence of devout religious belief or a commitment to the Puritan church. John Hull, one of the founders of Boston's Third Church, is a convenient counterexample; Hull was forced to compete aggressively in the Atlantic mercantile economy, yet maintained a lifelong devotion to Puritan piety of the most traditional kind. See Hull, "Diaries," pp. 123–38. In many cases, the inevitability of social tension in a commercial economy led individuals to believe all the more strongly in the need for communal bonds that institutions like the church could reinforce or maintain.

29. ET "Town Recs.," pp. 173–74.

30. ET "Town Recs.," pp. 373–79.

31. ET "Town Recs.," p. 253.

32. ET "Town Recs.," p. 248.

33. Compiled from the "List of Inhabitants" in ET "Town Recs.," pp. 401–22.

34. ET "Town Recs.," p. 268. The decision to make the Westfield school a "moving school" followed the pattern that was evolving in towns all across New England during this period; see Updegraff, *Origins of the Moving School*, pp. 94–106.

35. Powell, "Introduction," in ET "Town Recs.," p. 81.

36. For an extended exploration of the concept of the town meeting as a consensus producing body, see Zuckerman, *Peaceable Kingdoms*, pp. 154–86.

37. ET "Town Recs.," pp. 305–09.

38. See Smith, ed., *Colonial Justice*, pp. 65–88, for an overview of the Massachusetts judicial system. On the increasing complexity of legal pleadings in eighteenth-century New England, see Mann, *Neighbors and Strangers*, pp. 67–100. For comparable developments in another frontier region, see Neal W. Allen Jr., "Law and Authority to the Eastward." Also see Murrin, "Legal Transformation."

39. On Pomery, see *ET Chh. Recs.*, editors' note, p. 471; for comparable developments in Connecticut, see Mann, *Neighbors and Strangers*, pp. 93–100.

40. In Westfield, this pressure would eventually become a disturbing force in the church's disciplinary proceedings, which are examined in chapter 8.

41. See, for example, the price determinations for the year 1689/90, in ET "Town Recs.," pp. 210–11.

42. See "The West Indies Trade," in Bridenbaugh, ed., *Pynchon Papers*, 2:147–94. A vivid and colorful description of the use of "country pay" in New Haven, Connecticut, that reveals how quaint this rustic custom appeared to a cosmopolitan Bostonian can be found in Sarah Kemble Knight, "The Journal of Madam Knight," 2:438.

43. ET "Town Recs.," pp. 289, 313.

44. ET "Town Recs.," pp. 346, 355, 367.

45. Miller, *From Colony to Province*, pp. 305–23.

46. Perry Miller saw the contention that arose in New England over the need to

solve colonial monetary troubles as the beginnings of a "Splintering of Society" ruin-
ous to the coherence of the New England Mind. For other examples, see Rutman,
Winthrop's Boston; Bushman, *From Puritan to Yankee*; Innes, *Labor in a New Land*. More
recently, John Frederick Martin repeats some of these same assumptions in his discussion of the entrepreneurs who founded New England towns, but the overall thrust of
his argument puts the relationship between commercial development and Puritan
piety in a new light. Martin places the entrepreneurial motive together with religious
idealism at the very beginnings of New England settlement, rather than arguing that
later commercial development undermined an original commitment to communal
peasant utopias. See Martin, *Profits in the Wilderness*, especially pp. 111–28.

47. Powell, "Introduction," in ET "Town Recs.," pp. 121–28. For a sophisticated
discussion of varieties of individualism and their impact on the culture of early New
England, see Gildrie, *Profane, Civil, & Godly*.

48. This point is convincingly demonstrated by Christine Heyrman in her description of the response of the people of Gloucester, Massachusetts, to commercial
development and religious revivalism; see *Commerce and Culture*, pp. 182–204.

49. Figures on church admissions and population here and in the following para-
graph have been compiled from the "List of Inhabitants" in ET "Town Recs.," pp.
401–22, and from the "The Admissions Records," in *ET Chh. Recs.*, pp. 162–72.

50. This pattern of church admissions in Westfield corresponds closely to patterns
found in similar towns in western New England; see for example Moran, "Religious
Renewal."

51. These figures are consistent with conditions in most New England Puritan
churches in the later decades of the seventeenth century; see Moran and Vinovskis,
" 'Sisters' in Christ," in *Religion, Family, and the Life Course*, pp. 85–108.

52. Figures compiled from "List of Inhabitants," in ET "Town Recs.," pp. 401–22,
and from "Baptismal Records," in *ET's Chh. Recs.*, pp. 243–74.

53. For a discussion of popular perceptions of the Lord's Table as a "zone of danger" compared to the protective and nurturing qualities of baptism, see David D.
Hall, *Worlds of Wonder*, pp. 147–62; Holifield, *Covenant Sealed*, pp. 186–93. The emphasis that Taylor gave to the requirements for taking communion had the opposite
effect of the more charitable policies implemented by John Cotton Jr. in Plymouth;
see Peterson, "Plymouth Church," pp. 584–86.

54. For a discussion of Taylor's disagreement with Stoddard on membership standards, see Taylor, *Taylor vs. Stoddard*, pp. 1–57; Taylor, Commonplace Book, Items no.
14–15. While Taylor's dispute with Stoddard over the requirements for participation
in the Lord's Supper is well known, Taylor's relative isolation in this position with respect to his fellow Connecticut Valley ministers has been more recently uncovered;
see Gura, "Going Mr. Stoddard's Way." Taylor's motivations and the effects his control
over admission to the Lord's Table had on the community will be considered in
chapter 6.

55. *ET Chh. Recs.*, p. 161.

56. For further discussion of this issue in other early New England contexts, see

Moran and Vinovskis, " 'Sisters' in Christ," in *Religion, Family, and the Life Course*, pp. 85–108; David D. Hall, *Worlds of Wonder*, pp. 154–55; Porterfield, *Female Piety*; Anne S. Brown, "Bound Up in a Bundle of Life."

57. Taylor frequently refers to these men by their militia titles in his church records, a fact which highlights the social significance of military service on the early New England frontier.

58. This variation in quality and style among conversion relations is not unusual. The relations which Thomas Shepard recorded from his Cambridge congregation in the 1630s through the 1650s are similarly uneven; see *Thomas Shepard's Confessions*.

59. "Relation of Ensign Samuel Loomis," in *ET Chh. Recs.*, p. 107.

60. "Relation of Brother John Root," in *ET Chh. Recs.*, p. 112.

61. "Relation of Lt. John Mawdsley," in *ET Chh. Recs.*, p. 107.

62. For example, Ensign Loomis recounts the influence of his parents, the preaching of three different ministers, the "discourses" of friends, and the support of the ruling elder of his former church in the space of the four paragraphs of his brief relation; *ET Chh Recs.*, pp. 107–8.

63. "The Relation" in *ET Chh Recs.*, pp. 97–104. See also Shea, *Spiritual Autobiography*, pp. 92–100.

64. On the "American" or at least "New England" qualities of the Puritan conversion narratives delivered on this side of the Atlantic, see Caldwell, *Puritan Conversion Narrative*. Caldwell focuses on the narratives of the immigrant generation, and her claims for an "American morphology of conversion" are based on the immigrants' search for new religious feelings in a new world, feelings that shaped the spiritual development of the first generation. In contrast, the Westfield founders' and their descendants' "New England" spirituality is, in my reading, a product of their experience as members of a society officially and thoroughly devoted to godliness, in which some level of commitment to the Puritan church was assumed for the great majority of the population. What gives Westfield's lay founders' relations an "American" character, in contrast to Taylor's, is the extent to which their spiritual lives were the products of these conditions in New England, while his was formed in the much different environment of England's turbulent religious politics.

65. See David D. Hall, *Worlds of Wonder*, pp. 239–45; Moran and Vinovskis, *Religion, Family, and the Life Course*, pp. 109–208; Greven, *Protestant Temperament*, pp. 21–148.

66. *ET Chh. Recs.*, pp. 105–6, and see Josiah Dewey's relation, p. 112, for similar evidence. Mawdsley's account is not unlike the story of Elizabeth Butcher in *Early Piety, Exemplified*, discussed in chapter 3.

67. My use of the passive voice here is meant to acknowledge our changing understanding of the concept of preparation in Puritan religious culture. It is now generally accepted that although Puritan New England orthodoxy emphasized preparation for conversion, this emphasis was not a legalistic subversion of the Calvinist doctrine of predestination. Those who preached preparation (literally, pre-paring, cutting the individual off from the love of sin and the world) understood that the effectual work of preparation was not performed by the striving individual, but by God. "The cumulative effect of all the disciplines practiced by the believer was the

advancing of God's own preparation of the heart for salvation"; Hambrick-Stowe, *Practice of Piety*, p. 241, and more generally, pp. 197–241. However, while this was how early New Englanders understood the process, the cultivation of a godly sensibility can also be understood as the "work" done by the religious culture on the individual.

68. *ET Chh. Recs.*, p. 106.

69. *ET Chh. Recs.*, p. 107.

70. The development of John Mawdsley's religious sensibility, his growing need for the ordinances of the church, bears an interesting similarity to the patterns of desire which cultural historians have identified as a distinctive feature of modern consumer culture. New products "educate" consumers to develop more and more needs, needs which still more new products then attempt to meet, though never to final satisfaction, leaving the consumer in unending pursuit of the momentary satisfactions conveyed in the act of purchasing. In a sense, we can see the sensibility which Edward Taylor attempted to cultivate in his flock as a highly abstract precursor to the commodity fetishism of a later era; in Puritan culture, the *experience* of divine connection was the great object of desire, but physical objects and cultural products, the bearers of the means of grace, were essential mediators in the process of seeking a satisfying experience of grace. For a review of recent scholarship on consumer culture, including a discussion of its moral dimensions, see Agnew, "Coming Up for Air." See also Peterson, "Puritanism and Gentility."

71. *ET Chh. Recs.*, pp. 109–12.

72. In many New England churches, like John Cotton Jr.'s church in Plymouth or the Third Church of Boston, the insecurity of potential saints was eased by ministers who encouraged their congregations to judge themselves charitably in searching for signs of grace; see Peterson, "Plymouth Church," and chapter 5, below. The extent to which Taylor was able to perform such a role for his congregation is discussed in chapter 6.

73. *ET Chh. Recs.*, p. 106.

74. For examples of this temptation and how these founders fought against it, see the relations of Mawdsley, Dewey, Phelps, and Ingerson, *ET Chh. Recs.*, pp. 106, 109, 114, 116. Recently, Jon Butler's *Awash in a Sea of Faith* has argued that an alternative to Protestant religious culture existed in early America in the form of occult and magical beliefs and practices. However, it might better be said that belief in the occult existed within the Christian framework and contributed to the religious mentality of early New Englanders; that to posit the existence of a doctrinal Christianity free of occult influences is to hold up an ideal standard that never existed in reality. In some sense, witchcraft, hermeticism, and occult traditions were not absolute alternatives to but rather elements within Puritan religious culture. To the extent that they were alternatives, they were fragmented and undernourished competitors with respect to their institutional, intellectual, and cultural power; see David D. Hall, *Worlds of Wonder*, pp. 71–116; Godbeer, *Devil's Dominion*; Brooke, *Refiner's Fire*.

75. See Edward Taylor to Solomon Stoddard, April 6, 1710, in Taylor, Commonplace Book, Item no. 24; *ET Chh. Recs.*, pp. 467–68.

76. Powell, "Introduction," in ET "Town Recs.," pp. 53–54.

77. Powell, "Introduction," in ET "Town Recs.," pp. 101–11; for a full discussion of the meetinghouse controversy, see below, chapter 8.

78. See E. Alfred Jones, *Old Silver of American Churches*.

79. See Mark William Taylor, "Regional Diversity."

80. See Peterson, "Puritanism and Gentility," and above, chapter 3.

81. Taylor, Commonplace Book, Item no. 13.

82. *ET Poems*, pp. 130–31.

83. Taylor, Commonplace Book, Item no. 13.

84. *SS Diary*, 1:39.

85. Gerald Moran has rightly pointed out that these "tribal" practices, which Edmund Morgan originally identified as a cause for decline in the Puritan churches of rural New England, did not actually create a diminishing membership, and that family lineage worked quite well as a source for membership recruitment. Nevertheless, the fact of this "tribalism" had negative effects on the church's evangelical mission, its ability to reach out to strangers or newcomers, in those rural villages like Westfield where virtually everyone was included under the covenant. This would become a more significant problem as the population of New England in the eighteenth century became more mobile and less homogeneous. When more people began to slip through the cracks of covenanted membership, the appeal of alternative religious cultures that were more evangelical in their approach would grow. See Moran, "Religious Renewal"; Morgan, *Puritan Family*, pp. 161–86.

86. Taylor, "Elegy on David Dewey," p. 79.

87. Taylor, "Elegy," p. 82.

88. As such, Taylor's elegy may be a more successful literary creation by modern critical standards, but less effective as an evangelical device in early eighteenth-century Puritan society; see Taylor, "Elegy," p. 80.

89. Taylor, "Elegy," pp. 75–76.

Chapter 5

1. See John Norton, *Orthodox Evangelist*. Here and in his other publications, and in his role as pastor of Boston's First Church before his untimely death in 1664, Norton had been the inspiration to many of the lay people who broke off from the First Church and founded the Third Church. In addition, Norton was one of the leading exponents among the first-generation clergy of the reforms ushered in by the Half-way Covenant synod; see chapter 1, above.

2. Walker, *Creeds and Platforms*, pp. 210–13.

3. The difficulties faced by a poor rural village in maintaining a minister can be seen in Edward Taylor's church in Westfield; see chapters 6 and 8, below. See also David D. Hall, *Faithful Shepherd*, for a general discussion of the seventeenth-century minister's role and relationship with the laity.

4. *OSC*, 1:114–15, 160.

5. See *OSC*, 1:241–42, and above, chapter 3, for a discussion of the laity's unofficial leadership activities. In addition, it might be argued that the existence of the of-

fice of ruling elder did not fit very comfortably with the sacerdotal view of the clergy which John Norton and his followers in the Third Church were trying to promote. However, in the early eighteenth century, the Third Church's ministers considered re-establishing the office as an intermediary between the clergy and the congregation; see Harlan, *Clergy and the Great Awakening*, p. 44.

6. For a full account of Hoar's presidency, see Morison, *Harvard in the Seventeenth Century*, 2:390–414.

7. On Simon Willard, father of the minister, see Martin, *Profits in the Wilderness*, pp. 19–20, 126.

8. For example, during a three-month span in 1692, Samuel Willard was assisted by John Bailey, who preached three sermons, and by four other visiting ministers who preached on single occasions; see Bromfield, Sermon Notes, vol. 6.

9. David D. Hall, *Faithful Shepherd*, pp. 145–49, 182–94; on the early eighteenth century, see Youngs, *God's Messengers*, pp. 102–8.

10. "Third Church Records" in *OSC*, 1:228n. A leading Boston minister required money for entertaining at the annual elections in May because ministers from all over the colony congregated in Boston to hear the election sermon and depended on colleagues like Willard for hospitality during their stay.

11. "Third Church Records" in *OSC*, 1:295. Twenty-four years later, Joseph Sewall was similarly favored when the congregation raised £287 for "an Annuity towards the better Support of his Wife and Family"; *OSC*, 1:387–88.

12. Edward Taylor, for example, had to apprentice one of his sons to a shopkeeper in Ipswich, in an arrangement undertaken by Taylor's old college classmate, Samuel Sewall; see *SS Diary*, 1:279.

13. Much of the recent scholarship on Puritanism has affirmed that the Puritan understanding of the conversion experience was rarely the sudden and complete transformation of the individual, the ravishing of the soul, that has become something of a stereotype. Rather, conversion was seen as a gradual process, involving much progress and backsliding, and requiring a lifetime of introspection and pious practice; see Cohen, *God's Caress*; Hambrick-Stowe, *Practice of Piety*. In effect, this definition of conversion required that the pastor serve as a steady spiritual guide and counselor to those full members who were, in theory, fully "regenerate," for the experience of conversion was never one of full and easy assurance, and the life of the saint was still a life in which faith was constantly being tried and tested; see also Shepard, *God's Plot*. For a general review of this trend in scholarship on the nature of Puritan piety and conversion, see David D. Hall, "On Common Ground," pp. 215–21.

14. Thomas Thacher's sons also passed this concern for family religion on to their offspring and created a Thacher "line" among the clergy of New England which spanned several generations; see Weis, *Colonial Clergy*; also Hamilton, ed., "Diary of Peter Thacher."

15. Cotton Mather, *Magnalia Christi Americana*, ed. Robbins, 1:488–92.

16. More recent work has begun to rectify this imbalance, notably Hambrick-Stowe, *Practice of Piety*; also Selement, *Keepers of the Vineyard*.

17. *SS Diary*, 1:38.

18. *SS Diary*, 2:1049.

19. *SS Diary*, 1:346–47, 181, 297, 412.

20. In addition to Perry Miller's frequent references to Willard's writings in *The New England Mind: The Seventeenth Century*, the two book-length studies of Willard both focus on his intellectual and theological positions. See Lowrie, *Shape of the Puritan Mind*; Van Dyken, *Samuel Willard*. On Miller's use of Willard, see Hoopes, ed., *Sources for 'The New England Mind.'*

21. Lowrie, *Shape of the Puritan Mind*, p. 3. David Hall describes Willard's *Compleat Body* as primarily a written work of theology which expressed the minister's "private interests" rather than a useful and popular lecture series preached in public to his congregation; see *Faithful Shepherd*, p. 258n.

22. Prince and Sewall, "Preface," to Willard, *Compleat Body*, p. i.

23. *SS Diary*, 1:419, 518.

24. *SS Diary*, 1:455.

25. *SS Diary*, 2:735.

26. See Selement, *Keepers of the Vineyard*, pp. 13–43.

27. *OSC*, 1:398n.

28. Prince, "Diary."

29. For comparisons, see Fiske, *Notebook*, pp. 219–22, which discusses the economic constraints that prevented the rural town of Chelmsford from hiring a second minister; see also pp. xxxvi–xxxviii on Fiske's economic concerns. For a later example, see Jedrey, *World of John Cleaveland*, pp. 58–70, 84–94. Yet another comparison can be made with the economic life of Ralph Josselin, a Puritan minister in Earls Colne in the English county of Essex, in MacFarlane, *Family Life of Ralph Josselin*, pp. 33–80. These and many other examples show the constraints that economic worries placed upon these country ministers' ability to fulfill their pastoral roles; for a general discussion of this issue, see Youngs, *God's Messengers*, pp. 40–46.

30. *SS Diary*, 2:762.

31. On Pemberton's library, see *MHSP*, 2d ser., 10 (1895–96): 540–41; also Shipton, *Sibley's Harvard Graduates*, 4:111.

32. *SS Diary*, 2:905.

33. For a discussion of parallel developments in Boston's Old North Church, see Lovelace, *American Pietism of Cotton Mather*, pp. 110–281.

34. See Collinson, *English Puritanism*, pp. 10–11.

35. In fact, it could well be argued that the theological controversies of early New England all centered around the question of who the proper audience of Puritan preaching should be, with the antinomians, for example, defending the most rarefied group of the elect as the proper object of the clergy's attention; for a version of this argument, see Stout, *New England Soul*, pp. 24–25.

36. This theme is most fully developed in Gura, *A Glimpse of Sion's Glory*.

37. David Hall has described this complacency, and the means by which some people maintained a distance from though not an opposition to the culture of godliness; see *Worlds of Wonder*, pp. 14–18, 147–65; see also Gildrie, *Profane, Civil, & Godly*; and chapter 4, above.

38. Hutchinson, ed., *Collection of Original Papers*, pp. 531–33.

39. Willard, *Ne Sutor Ultra Crepidam*; Willard, *Covenant Keeping*. For a full discussion of Willard's opposition to the restricted views on church polity of the Particular Baptists, see Van Dyken, *Samuel Willard*, pp. 135–55. The Baptists' vehement opposition to Willard might be another explanation of Randolph's statement that Willard was hated for his baptismal practices.

40. Willard, *Barren Fig Trees Doom*, pp. 32–33.

41. "Third Church Records," February 14, 1678, in *OSC*, 1:229.

42. For similar developments in John Cotton Jr.'s church in Plymouth, see *Plymouth Church Records*, 1:163, and Peterson, "The Plymouth Church," pp. 585–86.

43. Willard, *Barren Fig Trees Doom*, pp. 74, 171.

44. Willard, *Barren Fig Trees Doom*, pp. 171–85, 242, 245–46, 250–60.

45. Willard, *Barren Fig Trees Doom*, pp. 292, 281.

46. See Holifield, *Covenant Sealed*, pp. 200–206.

47. Willard, *Morality Not to be Relied on for Life*, pp. 1, 23. This discussion of Willard's position on the nature of the sacraments and their relation to conversion is informed by Holifield, *Covenant Sealed*, pp. 200–224; and Lowrie, *Shape of the Puritan Mind*, pp. 160–85, especially 175–85. For more on Willard's ecclesiastical positions and preaching, especially regarding his *Barren Fig Trees Doom* series, see David D. Hall, *Faithful Shepherd*, pp. 253–66. I am indebted to Hall's discussion of the "mingling of themes" in Willard's sermons, though I differ on the matter of Willard's "moralistic legalism"; see pp. 254, 258. However, see Hall's review of recent scholarship on legalism and conditionality in "On Common Ground."

48. Willard, *Impenitent Sinners Warned*, pp. 23–29. In effect, a sermon like this one stood at the opposite end of the spectrum of religious instruction from the life of Elizabeth Butcher described in the pamphlet *Early Piety, Exemplified*. While the events in each case were radically different, the message of both was the same, that children of the church were obliged to "bear fruit," to take advantage of the blessing of baptism and godly nurture, or else they would be damned for their sins.

49. Stout, *New England Soul*, pp. 94–95; Willard quotation cited in Stout, p. 94. For a more extensive theological discussion of Willard's conversionist preaching see Lowrie, *Shape of the Puritan Mind*, pp. 160–85.

50. Pemberton, "The Author's Character," in Willard, *Compleat Body*, p. 2.

51. Pemberton, "The Author's Character," in Willard, *Compleat Body*, p. 2.

52. See Joseph Sewall, "Precious Treasure," in Pemberton, *Sermons and Discourses*, p. 308.

53. Stout, *New England Soul*, p. 104.

54. Pemberton, "A Christian Fixed in His Post," and "Advice to a Son," in *Sermons and Discourses*, pp. 29–53, 55. Even the "moralism" of the former sermon is tempered by Pemberton's assertion that mere "pagan" morality will not bring about a reformation of society or man's salvation, but that individuals must "seek first the Kingdom of God and the righteousness thereof, for this is the one thing needful," p. 37.

55. Benjamin Colman, "Precious Treasure" in Pemberton, *Sermons and Discourses*, pp. 297, 303.

56. Cotton Mather, who was often a great friend and supporter of Sewall and an admirer of his piety, seems to have shared Pemberton's rather low opinion of Sewall's scholarship and intellect; see *Diary of Cotton Mather*, 2:748.

57. Shipton, *Sibley's Harvard Graduates*, 5:376–93, 387.

58. John Eliot, *Biographical Dictionary*, pp. 422–23, cited in Shipton, *Sibley's Harvard Graduates*, 5:383–84.

59. *Diary of Cotton Mather*, 2:685.

60. Joseph Sewall, *Holy Spirit the Gift of God*, p. 14.

61. Further evidence of the continuity in the preaching of conversion as the undeserved gift of God's grace is evident in the Bromfield family sermon notebooks, in which grandmother and grandson cite the same message preached by two generations of Third Church ministers; see chapter 3.

62. Prince, *Ordination Sermon*, p. iv.

63. Shipton, *Sibley's Harvard Graduates*, 5:344–45.

64. Joseph Sewall, *Duty, Character and Reward*, pp. 12–14.

65. See Middlekauff, *The Mathers*, pp. 84–85.

66. Joseph Sewall and Thomas Prince, "The Preface," in Willard, *Compleat Body*, pp. iii–iv.

67. Samuel Willard, *Duty of a People*; also Willard, *Necessity of Sincerity*; and Willard, *Covenant-Keeping*.

68. Hambrick-Stowe, *Practice of Piety*, pp. 130–32.

69. *OSC*, 1:235–36, 240–41. Although there is no evidence of direct influence on the Third Church ministers at this early date from Scottish sources, there is nonetheless a similarity between the development of the ritual of covenant renewal in New England and the "sacramental occasions" that were a characteristic part of Scottish Presbyterian religious practice. The celebration of the eucharist in mass meetings designed to remind lay people of the tenets and obligations of their faith served as a form of "visible gospel," where the word of God was as much "performed" as it was preached. The ritual of covenant renewal, in which the laity were led in rededicating themselves to partaking in the "body of Christ" in the form of the church, was also a ritual performance of the message that they heard in ordinary preaching, an acting out of the "preparation" that an individual went through in the process of conversion, as well as a preparation of the entire community for a general revival of religion. See Schmidt, *Holy Fairs*, pp. 69–114; and Crawford, *Seasons of Grace*. Later the Scots connection would become a reality, when Joseph Sewall and Thomas Prince would cultivate relationships with Scottish evangelicals and draw explicit parallels between Scottish and American revivals.

70. Walker, *Creeds and Platforms*, pp. 411–19.

71. Peterson, "Plymouth Church," pp. 588–89.

72. Selement, "Publication and the Puritan Minister," p. 225.

73. Selement defines as "prolific" those authors who published ten or more works in their lifetime. At the time of his death at the age of 45, Pemberton had published nine times; see Selement, "Publication and the Puritan Minister," pp. 225–26, 228–30.

For a list of Pemberton's works, see *OSC*, 2:608–10; Shipton, *Sibley's Harvard Graduates*, 4:112–13.

74. The street known as "Cornhill," running from King Street to the corner of Milk Street where the South Church stood, was the center of Boston publishing and remained so until the twentieth century, when the last of the major metropolitan newspapers moved out; see Whitehill, *Boston: A Topographical History*; Thwing, *Crooked and Narrow Streets*, pp. 97, 171.

75. Selement, "Publication and the Puritan Minister," pp. 225–26.

76. See Levin, *Cotton Mather*, pp. 250–69.

77. Prince, *People of New England Put in Mind of the Righteous Acts of the Lord*, in Plumstead, ed., *Wall and the Garden*, pp. 183–220.

78. For the reception of Prince's *Chronological History*, see Shipton, *Sibley's Harvard Graduates*, 5:354–55.

79. See above, chapter 3; also Tucker, "Reinvention of New England."

80. Prince, "Some Account of the Revival," 2:375. These sermons were published in 1721 under the title *A Course of Sermons on Early Piety, By . . . Eight Ministers.*

81. Prince, "Some Account of the Revival," 2:377–78.

82. Prince's own sermon on the earthquake was published in 1727 under the title *Earthquakes the Works of God and Tokens of his Just Displeasure*, and was popular enough to require two editions in that year.

83. Hill and Bigelow, *Historical Catalogue*, pp. 32–35.

84. The publication of *The Christian History* by Prince and his son was yet another innovation within New England's religious culture, the first religious periodical produced in America.

85. For a similar argument, see Youngs, *God's Messengers*, pp. 112–19.

Chapter 6

1. Taylor, *Diary*, pp. 39–40.

2. *ET Chh. Recs.*, p. 4.

3. See "Edward Taylor's Lands in Westfield," Appendix D in ET "Town Recs.," pp. 425–28.

4. ET "Town Recs.," p. 215. At this time, New Englanders were suffering under heavy taxation to pay for military expeditions against French Canada; see Breen, "War, Taxes, and Political Brokers."

5. ET "Town Recs.," p. 378.

6. ET "Town Recs.," pp. 73–76, 232.

7. ET "Town Recs.," p. 237. Coincidentally, Taylor's conflict with the Westfield taxpayers was taking place at roughly the same time that the Third Church of Boston was rewarding Samuel Willard with a gift of £336; see above, chapter 5.

8. Taylor had eight children by his first wife, Elizabeth Fitch, though five of these died during their fifteen-year marriage. After Elizabeth's death in 1689, Taylor remarried in 1692, and fathered six more children by his second wife, Ruth Wyllys; see Keller, *Example*, pp. 44–48.

9. Powell, "Introduction," in ET "Town Recs.," pp. 48–49. Among the items listed in the probate inventory taken at Taylor's death in 1729 were three cows, three heifers, two sows, a beehive, and several plows, hoes, plow irons, and other farm implements. I am grateful to Professor Kevin Sweeney of Amherst College for bringing this information to my attention.

10. See Keller, *Example*, pp. 56, 60–69.

11. In his "Church Records," Taylor described his usual practice in a particular case: "Now I being Calld to him I applied myself to him as I was used to do to sick persons, to looke over his life past to see what was amiss therein & so renew Repentance & so to go humbly to Christ by Faith;" *ET Chh. Recs.*, p. 216.

12. Taylor, *Lord's Supper*, pp. 153–54.

13. *ET Chh. Recs.*, p. 169; Powell, "Introduction," in ET "Town Recs.," pp. 71–72.

14. Powell, "Introduction," in ET "Town Recs.," p. 36.

15. Like Samuel Willard and Joseph Sewall of the Third Church, Stoddard enjoyed the advantages of being related to a wealthy Boston mercantile family; see Coffman, *Solomon Stoddard*, p. 59; Miller, *From Colony to Province*, p. 229.

16. ET "Town Recs.," p. 395.

17. See Morison's description of the "typical Harvard alumnus" of 1700 in *Harvard in the Seventeenth-Century*, 2:564; for a comparison with English conditions, see MacFarlane, *Ralph Josselin*.

18. For descriptions of existing Taylor manuscripts, see *ET Poems*, pp. 499–521; also Taylor, *Unpublished Writings* and *Upon the Types of the Old Testament*.

19. Karl Keller refers to the image we have of Taylor from the available biographical information as "something very wooden—something like a wooden Indian in Harvard clothes that stands outside the door to the storehouse of early American culture"; see Keller, *Example*, p. 13.

20. *ET Poems*, p. 467.

21. See Louis L. Martz, "Foreword" in *ET Poems*, pp. xxix-xxxvii; Lewalski, *Protestant Poetics*.

22. For the influence of Taylor's family life upon his poetry, see Hambrick-Stowe, *Meditative Poetry*, pp. 38–61.

23. In fact, it seems likely that Taylor's strong feelings on these matters were carried over from the impact of mid-seventeenth-century English politics on his early life, rather than an outgrowth of any direct involvement in New England political life; see Stanford, "Introduction," in *ET Poems*, pp. xlvi-xlvii.

24. *ET Chh. Recs.*, pp. 4–5.

25. Here, Taylor's interests and experience stand in sharp contrast to a contemporary like John Cotton Jr. of Plymouth; see Peterson, "Plymouth Church."

26. *ET Poems*, pp. 458–59.

27. Taylor's series of sermons on typology was discovered in a collection of family papers given to the University of Nebraska in 1977, and has now been published; see Taylor, *Upon the Types of the Old Testament*; see also Rowe, *Saint and Singer*, pp. xi-xii.

28. See Grabo, *Edward Taylor*, p. 2; Keller, *Example*, p. 11; *ET Poems*, p. xlvi. An ex-

ception is Davis, *A Reading*, which attempts to integrate the progress of Taylor's poetical development with the course of events in his life.

29. Many critics have noted the generally inward or introspective nature of Taylor's poetical works and the sense of isolation Taylor felt in Westfield, but few have commented on the potential effects that Taylor's solitary temperament may have had on his work as a rural minister; see for example, Hambrick-Stowe's observation that Taylor "ironically . . . sought to overcome isolation by isolation," in *Meditative Poetry*, p. 41. Isolation, however, is as much a mental predisposition as it is a fact of geography. Cotton Mather often felt isolated in the dense bustle of Boston's North End, while Solomon Stoddard, Taylor's frontier neighbor, was tightly "networked" among his Connecticut Valley relatives and in the metropolis as well.

30. See Selement, "Publication and the Puritan Minister."

31. The existing scholarship on Taylor's poetry, often focused chiefly on the "Preparatory Meditations," is quite extensive. Among the major works are Donald E. Stanford's introduction to *ET Poems*; Grabo, *Edward Taylor*; Sheick, *Will and Word*; Keller, *Example*; Rowe, *Saint and Singer*; Hambrick-Stowe, *Meditative Poetry*; Gatta, *Gracious Laughter*; Davis, *A Reading*. Davis's work makes the strongest case that the sacrament's significance for Taylor's spiritual life and for his understanding of church membership grew stronger over time, beginning in the 1680s.

32. *ET Poems*, p. 169.

33. *ET Poems*, pp. 129, 480.

34. See above, chapter 5.

35. This attitude is particularly clear in Taylor's later meditations from the 1710s and 1720s, focused on the Book of Canticles, which served "to provide a meditative retreat from a world which he found increasingly disruptive, even puzzling"; Davis, *A Reading*, p. 174.

36. Taylor, *Lord's Supper*, p. 48.

37. In this poem, Taylor dealt only with the various ways in which the elect, those predestined by God for salvation, made their way into church fellowship. For the best estimate of a precise date for "Gods Determinations," see Davis, *A Reading*, pp. 27−28, which suggests that the poem was probably composed in the years between 1678 and 1681.

38. For the full text of "Gods Determinations," see *ET Poems*, pp. 385−459. My discussion of Taylor's intentions regarding the unconverted in this poem follows Colacurcio, "Gods Determinations"; Keller, *Example*, pp. 129−38; Davis, *A Reading*, pp. 32−47.

39. *ET Poems*, p. 454.

40. *ET Poems*, p. 454.

41. *ET Poems*, p. 458.

42. Indirect evidence for this emerges in an incident in the life of one of Taylor's successors in the pulpit. In 1743, the newly ordained Rev. John Ballantine married a woman from Dedham, Massachusetts, and brought her home to Westfield in a "Chair," a wheeled vehicle without a top for which he bargained with a "Mr.

Trescott" of Boston. Their arrival caused quite a stir in Westfield, as apparently it was the first such vehicle ever seen in the town; Lockwood, *Westfield*, pp. 379–80.

43. *ET Poems*, pp. 235–36.

44. Keller, *Example*, p. 138.

45. David Hall refers to the individuals who occupied the margins of New England church life as " 'horseshed' Christians . . . who hung back from the Lord's Table, . . . went to church and between services talked animatedly of 'their Farms, their Horses, their Cows' "; Hall, *Worlds of Wonder*, p. 138.

46. It has been speculated that the difference of opinion between Hooker and Cotton on the aim of the church led Hooker and his Newtowne congregation to migrate to Connecticut, where many of the early settlements experimented with more charitable, less rigorous approaches to church admissions; see Lucas, *Valley of Discord*, pp. 25–30, on Hooker's beliefs and practices in Hartford; see also Perry Miller, "Thomas Hooker and the Democracy of Connecticut," in *Errand*, pp. 31–33.

47. See Lucas, *Valley of Discord*, pp. 36, 38–40; and above, chapter 2.

48. *ET Chh. Recs.*, pp. 107, 113, 115.

49. These "harvests" took place in 1679, 1683, 1696, 1712, and 1718; see Coffman, *Solomon Stoddard*, pp. 18–21.

50. Of the numerous accounts of the Stoddard-Mather debate, the most recent and thorough can be found in *Edward Taylor vs. Solomon Stoddard*, pp. 1–49; but see also Miller, *From Colony to Province*, pp. 226–47; Lucas, *Valley of Discord*, pp. 143–87; Coffman, *Solomon Stoddard*, pp. 48–140; Middlekauff, *The Mathers*, pp. 113–38.

51. On Stoddard's importance and connections in Boston, see Miller, *From Colony to Province*, pp. 228–31.

52. For the most complete and accurate discussion of Taylor's part in these matters, as well as editions of the significant documents, see *Edward Taylor vs. Solomon Stoddard*; see also Schuldiner, "Rise of Consciousness," pp. 107–39.

53. Taylor, *Lord's Supper*, p. 68.

54. Grabo, *Edward Taylor*, pp. 16–17.

55. Taylor, *Lord's Supper*, p. 59. The sermon in which Taylor explains this doctrine and denounces the notion of the Lord's Supper as a converting ordinance is by far the longest in the treatise; see pp. 59–146; also Davis, *A Reading*, p. 65.

56. On the increasing prevalence of "Stoddardeanism" in the Connecticut Valley, see Gura, "Going Mr. Stoddard's Way."

57. For the private writings of Taylor that accompanied his *Treatise Concerning the Lord's Supper*, see *Edward Taylor vs. Solomon Stoddard*, which includes Taylor's "Animadversions" and his "Anti-Stoddard Syllogisms" along with "The *Appeale* Tried."

58. Keller, *Example*, p. 142.

59. For a more extensive discussion of the *Metrical History*, see Keller, *Example*, pp. 139–59; also Davis, *A Reading*, pp. 139–40.

60. Keller, *Example*, pp. 158–59.

61. On the date of the *Metrical History*, see Davis, *A Reading*, pp. 139–40. Davis describes these poems as "mechanical, labored, and—with very few exceptions—unre-

deemable doggerel," while Keller calls them "embarrassing," "an almost completely botched work," and "annoyingly antihumanistic"; *Example*, p. 159. Even John Gatta's *Gracious Laughter*, which emphasizes Taylor's "meditative wit" and the "comic design" of his work, dismisses the *Metrical History* as "repellent," p. 105.

62. Taylor, *Upon the Types of the Old Testament*. For a recent review of varying typological practices among early New England writers, see Smolinski, *Threefold Paradise*; also Mares, "Cotton Mather's 'Problema Theologicum.' "

63. See Rowe, *Saint and Singer*, pp. 53–89, especially 88–89. See also Charles W. Mignon's "Introduction," in Taylor, *Upon the Types of the Old Testament*, pp. xxxiv–xxxv, which makes this distinction somewhat differently. Mignon suggests that Taylor limited himself to "biblical typology," which examines Old Testament prefigurements of the coming of Christ, and avoided "historical typology" which "centered on the contemporary experience of the community" as a latter-day fulfillment of Old Testament foreshadowings.

64. See above, chapter 5.

65. *ET Poems*, pp. 236, 235.

66. Keller, *Example*, p. 159.

67. See Taylor, Commonplace Book, Item no. 40, and Taylor, "The Great Bones Dug Up at Claverack," in *Minor Poetry*, pp. 211–16.

68. On Taylor as physician, see Keller, *Example*, pp. 60–69; on his role in church councils, see Taylor, Commonplace Book, Items no. 7, 8, 12.

Chapter 7

1. "The Covenant made by the Third Church in Boston," in *OSC*, 1:127.

2. Thacher, Draft Reply to Letter from John Davenport and the First Church in Boston, *OSC*, 1:157n.

3. Shepard, *Eye-Salve*, pp. 15–16, 22–23, 30.

4. Thacher, "Preface," in Shepard, *Eye-Salve*, p. ii.

5. Thacher, "Essay for Accommodation," in *OSC*, 1:174.

6. The lay representatives were Edward Rainsford, John Hull, Thomas Savage, and Peter Thacher, the son of the first minister; *OSC*, 1:234n.

7. See Pierce, ed., *First Church Records*, 1:75–78.

8. *SS Diary*, 1:103–6.

9. *SS Diary*, 2:1010.

10. *SS Diary*, 1:600.

11. In the early 1670s, the First Church had demonstrated the extent of its hostility to inter-church fellowship when it opposed a government order allowing ministers from other Boston churches to share in the preaching of the Boston Thursday lecture in the First Church meetinghouse, for fear that it tended "to the infringement of Church Libertie"; see Pierce, ed., *First Church Records*, 1:76–77. Similarly, the First Church had refused to let outsiders participate in the funeral of John Davenport in 1670; see above, chapter 1.

12. The story of Eunice Williams, taken captive in the raid on Deerfield in 1704,

illuminates this point; see Demos, *Unredeemed Captive*. But Mary Rowlandson's own sensitivity to the spiritual impact of English Puritan cultural resources can be charted through her dramatic narrative. Her growing acclimation to Indian food, for instance, was necessary to her survival, but also marked her movement away from English society. The fear that she had "gone native" lingered; it kept her awake at night long after her "redemption" and expressed itself most vehemently in her extreme hostility toward those former praying Indians who had gone over to fight with King Philip against the English. Rowlandson recounts obsessively the atrocities committed by these turncoats, and lingers on one dramatic instance when she encountered a former praying Indian in post-war Boston who had threatened her life during her captivity. In the image of this man, Rowlandson sees something of herself, a person who has crossed the cultural barrier between the garden and the wilderness, between godliness and deviltry, and whose loyalties and true spiritual condition are therefore suspect. Despite theoretical acknowledgements that an omnipotent God could convert anyone, anywhere, Puritans knew in their souls that salvation came within the confines of godly English society, and looked to Boston for the resources to sustain it. See Rowlandson, "Sovereignty and Goodness," pp. 51, 59–60, 74–75.

13. Rowlandson, "Sovereignty and Goodness," p. 71. Twenty pounds would have been roughly a third to a fourth of a year's salary for Joseph Rowlandson, minister of Lancaster, and as frontier ministers were often paid in kind—grain, livestock, firewood—it seems unlikely that he could have raised the money to ransom his wife without the assistance of Boston's merchant class.

14. Mary and Joseph Rowlandson had been staying with Thomas Shepard Jr., the minister of Charlestown and ally of the South Church during its founding crisis, but the Shepard home was not big enough to contain the Rowlandson family; Rowlandson, "Sovereignty and Goodness," p. 71. Hill and Bigelow, *Historical Catalogue*, p. 329, lists James Whetcomb, the owner of this house, as a member of the Third Church under the Halfway Covenant.

15. Rowlandson, "Sovereignty and Goodness," pp. 71, 74.

16. Bynner, "Topography and Landmarks of the Provincial Period," in Justin Winsor, ed., *Memorial History of Boston*, 2:504–5.

17. *SS Diary*, 2:669; Pierce, ed., *First Church Records*, 1:122–25.

18. Examples of works that focus on the deterioration of orthodox solidarity in this period are numerous, and range from Jones, *Shattered Synthesis*, to Miller, *From Colony to Province*.

19. See above, chapter 3.

20. The historical literature on the "New Learning" or the development of "liberal" thought at Harvard is extensive, but see Stout, *New England Soul*, pp. 131–37; also Fiering, "First American Enlightenment."

21. Michael Hall, *Last American Puritan*, pp. 292–301, provides an account sympathetic to Mather's point of view. See Increase Mather, *Order of the Gospel*; Colman et al., *Gospel Order Revived*; Stoddard, *Instituted Churches*.

22. Mather played a significant role in an attempt at reconciliation between these

two branches of English nonconformity in 1691, which culminated in the signing of the "Heads of Agreement of the United Ministers" of London; see Michael Hall, *Last American Puritan*, pp. 238–40; Walker, *Creeds and Platforms*, pp. 440–62.

23. *SS Diary*, 1:420–21.

24. Additionally, the fact that the religious faith professed and practiced by Colman, Leverett, and the Brattles was ultimately not very different from that of the Mathers and other more conservative clergy and laymen eventually helped to smooth over the tensions present at the Brattle Church's founding; see Stout on "The Limits of the New Learning," in *New England Soul*, pp. 135–37.

25. *SS Diary*, 1:418–21.

26. On Colman's preaching, see Toulouse, *Art of Prophesying*, pp. 46–74; on the Brattle Street Church's incorporation into orthodox religious culture, see Stout, *New England Soul*, p. 143.

27. For instance, the class of 1707, which contained nineteen members, saw twelve of its graduates enter the ministry. These twelve, headed by Joseph Sewall and Thomas Prince, Willard's successors at the Third Church, maintained close ties to one another throughout their lives and encouraged a movement toward clerical solidarity in the eighteenth century; see Van De Wetering, "Thomas Prince," p. 36. By way of contrast, the leaders of the "liberal" religious movement which Increase Mather so strongly opposed were all trained at Harvard during Mather's tenure as president. Although Mather may not have condoned the "liberal mode of philosophizing" that took hold at the college in the 1690s, the changes made by Leverett and Brattle were possible because of Mather's inattention to the college's daily life and instruction; Morison, *Harvard in the Seventeenth Century*, 2:503. Stephen Foster has suggested that as tutors, Brattle and Leverett "had virtually run Harvard in the 1690s"; Foster, *Long Argument*, p. 281.

28. This, at least, was Increase Mather's defense of the new charter against those who attacked it as an abdication of the first charter's protection of New England religion. see Michael Hall, *Last American Puritan*; Stout, *New England Soul*, pp. 118–22, 128–31.

29. See "The Massachusetts Charter of 1691," in Hall, Leder, and Kammen, eds., *Glorious Revolution*, pp. 76–79.

30. Richard Baxter attempted to form one such voluntary association of Congregational ministers in England; see Cross, "Church in England," pp. 117–20; Hill, *World Turned Upside Down*, pp. 278–91; Walker, *Creeds and Platforms*, pp. 442, 470.

31. In the early years of Massachusetts settlement, it had been common for ministers to meet independently of their churches to discuss matters of importance. These meetings were viewed with suspicion by the more "independent" members of the clergy, which was only natural given their recent escape from episcopal authority. Ministerial associations carried a hint of prelacy, and New England's early settlers were careful to avoid this danger. Independent clerical bodies were never granted coercive authority, and the Cambridge Platform made certain that inter-church councils and synods always included laymen as well as ministers. By the middle of the seven-

teenth century, several New England ministers took an extreme position against such ministerial meetings, and the practice fell into disuse, just as it was coming into prominence among English Independents.

32. Although the timing of this New England movement toward ministerial associations was based on local political changes, its particular form was of English origin. In 1686, Charles Morton, a member of the first Congregational ministerial association in Cornwall, emigrated to Massachusetts and was installed as pastor of Charlestown. When the Boston area ministers formed an association in 1690, they organized themselves on the model of the Cornwall association and even kept their records in the Cornwall record book, which Morton had brought to the New World. The ministers in the Cambridge Association (so-called because they met at Harvard College) deliberated on cases proposed by churches or private persons, and believed that their recommendations should be decisive in settling conflicts about church polity or discipline; see Walker, *Creeds and Platforms*, pp. 470–72.

33. "Proposals of 1705," in Walker, *Creeds and Platforms*, pp. 486–88.

34. However, any individuals within an offending church who "do not justifie their Disorders, but suitably testifie against them" would be eligible for reception into some other church in the consociation; Walker, *Creeds and Platforms*, pp. 488–90.

35. See Wise, *Churches Quarrel*; and Wise, *Vindication*. The failure of the Proposals to gain the approval of the General Court has been attributed to Mather's opposition and to Wise's pamphlets. However, a more likely explanation for this failure is that the religious establishment under the Massachusetts provincial government discouraged the ratification of these proposals. The new charter guaranteed the protection of all Protestant churches in Massachusetts, and although the Proposals were intended only for the orthodox Congregational churches, the Anglican, Baptist, and Quaker communities in Massachusetts feared an increase in clerical authority sanctioned by law, as did some of the more independent Congregationalists like Wise and Mather. In Connecticut, where the charter government continued to lend state support for the Congregational churches, the Proposals of 1705 did succeed as the basis for the Saybrook Platform, which lends weight to the importance of the political context in which the Proposals were received; Walker, *Creeds and Platforms*, pp. 491–94.

36. Youngs, *God's Messengers*, pp. 72–76. David Harlan has argued that Youngs overstates the power of the clerical associations over ecclesiastical affairs in the eighteenth century. While this may be true, the point here is not so much a question of the clergy's relative power over the laity, but the success of the associational movement in creating unity and cooperation among the churches through the agency of the ministers; see Harlan, *Clergy and Great Awakening*, pp. 11–30.

37. *SS Diary*, 2:779.

38. *SS Diary*, 1:528; Davies, *Worship of American Puritans*, pp. 178–79.

39. Murrin, "Anglicizing an American Colony."

40. See Gura, *Glimpse of Sion's Glory*.

41. In contrast, proponents of a strict congregationalism who opposed the Halfway Covenant, like the First Church majority who called John Davenport to the pul-

pit, tended to be sympathetic to radical dissenters, and especially to the separate Baptists, whose ideas on church polity were rather close to their own. First Church members like Governor John Leverett were among the allies of the Baptists within the Massachusetts government. See Foster, *Long Argument*, pp. 176–78, 203–5.

42. See Cotton Mather, *Magnalia Christi Americana*, ed. Robbins, 1:488–96.

43. This discussion clarifies the position that the supporters of the Halfway Covenant took with respect to accommodation of the Restoration government. They have tended to be included among the "moderates" in their willingness to agree to modifications in the terms of the Massachusetts Bay charter, but this moderation was not based on an indifference to religious traditions. Rather, they felt the best way to preserve their distinctive religious heritage was to cooperate with the crown on those governmental issues where they felt the crown had a right to intervene. But when it came to matters of religious belief, they were willing to follow their consciences and "trust God" with the outcome, even if it meant offending imperial authority.

44. *SS Diary*, 1:29–30, 600.

45. On the ongoing concern over Quaker influences on New England orthodox society, see Heyrman, *Commerce and Culture*, 96–142.

46. New England Puritans believed that challenges from radicals and from Anglicans were all of a piece, and opposed both with equal vigor. This view was confirmed by the strange career of a dissenter named George Keith. In the 1680s, Keith, then a radical Quaker, caused a disturbance in Boston by insisting on debating the orthodox ministers. In 1702, Keith again passed through Boston and was seen as a menace by the Puritan clergy, but now as an ordained minister of the Church of England and one of the first missionaries of the Anglican Society for the Propagation of the Gospel. See Van Dyken, *Samuel Willard*, pp. 104–7, 158–60.

47. Van Dyken, *Samuel Willard*, pp. 50–55; quotation from Willard, *All Plots Detected*, cited in Van Dyken, p. 55.

48. On the events leading to the writ of *quo warranto*, see Michael Hall, *Edward Randolph*, pp. 53–83.

49. Diary of Peter Thacher, November 9, 1683, cited in *OSC*, 1:250.

50. Increase Mather, "Autobiography," pp. 307–8.

51. Michael Hall, *Edward Randolph*, pp. 82–83; also Lovejoy, *Glorious Revolution*, pp. 143–59.

52. *OSC*, 1:265–68; see also *SS Diary*, 1:135–36.

53. Willard, "Brief Discourse"; see also Van Dyken, *Samuel Willard*, pp. 67–69.

54. *SS Diary*, 1:167–68.

55. The catechetical lectures were begun on January 31, 1687/8; see Willard, *Compleat Body of Divinity*, "The Preface," and pp. 52–55.

56. Increase Mather, "Vindication of New England," 2:44.

57. *SS Diary*, 1:162–63, 171.

58. Increase Mather, "Vindication of New England," 2:65; see also Joshua Moody to Increase Mather, in "The Mather Papers," pp. 369–71.

59. Shortly after the arrest of Andros and his supporters, Willard and four other

Boston ministers were called in to help decide how best to deal with the tyrants; Edward Randolph to the Committee of Public Safety, May 29, 1689, cited in *OSC*, 1:279.

60. Willard, *Sinfulness*; see also Van Dyken, pp. 72—75.

61. See Dunn, *Puritans and Yankees*.

62. As David Lovejoy points out, the 1691 trial and execution of Jacob Leisler in New York, before the arrival of the new Massachusetts charter, must have created a great deal of anxiety among the Bostonians who overthrew Andros; see Lovejoy, *Glorious Revolution*, pp. 354—58.

63. Peter Sergeant joined on July 28, 1689, and Wait Winthrop on August 25; see Hill and Bigelow, *Historical Catalogue*, pp. 15, 288, 290.

64. Collinson, *Religion of Protestants*; Foster, *Long Argument*, pp. 11—13.

65. Foote, *Annals of King's Chapel*, 2:183—84.

66. *SS Diary*, 1:601—2.

67. See also July 15, 1698, where Sewall refuses to attend the funeral of John Ive, "a very debauched, atheistical man." In Sewall's words, "the knowledge of his notoriously wicked life made me sick of going," and so he stayed at home and conversed with Increase Mather, which to Sewall's mind was the more godly thing to do; *SS Diary*, 1:396.

68. *SS Diary*, 1:518.

69. *SS Diary*, 2:741—45.

70. Joshua Moody to Increase Mather, in "The Mather Papers," p. 371.

71. *SS Diary*, 1:384.

72. *SS Diary*. 1:780; for general accounts of this practice in early New England, see Restad, *Christmas in America*; Schmidt, *Consumer Rites*; Spencer, "Christmas, the Upstart."

73. See above, chapter 5.

74. *SS Diary*, 2:1018.

75. *SS Diary*, 2:838. Even New Englanders who were, often because of disputes within their own churches, temporarily attracted to Anglican churches found it difficult to give up their Puritan biases. As John Murrin describes it, "the Anglicans learned that disgruntled Congregationalists did not cease to be Puritans just because they welcomed an Anglican minister. The struggle between Anglican and Puritan could go on within the Church as well as outside"; Murrin, "Anglicizing an American Colony," p. 30.

76. Sewall commented that "pretty much blood was shed by means of this blody Cross, and the poor Dog a sufferer." *SS Diary*, 1:545.

77. *SS Diary*, 1:411; 2:680, 843.

78. On the origins of the New England Company and its support of missionary work in the seventeenth century, see Kellaway, *New England Company*, pp. 1—165; see pp. 32—33 for Eliot's solicitation of independent contributions. See also Ford, ed., *Correspondence*.

79. Sewall's records can be found in the New England Company Ledger, Massachusetts Historical Society.

80. On Sergeant, see Ford, *Correspondence*, p. xxvi; on Oliver and Stoddard, see Kellaway, *New England Company*, pp. 238, 299, 301; on Stoddard, see Shipton, *Sibley's Harvard Graduates*, 4:383–85. For Sewall's role and a near-disaster regarding the New England Company's paper, see *SS Diary* 2:621–22; Kellaway, 205–6.

81. "Third Church Records," 24 March 1725/6, in *OSC*, 1:418–19.

82. *New England Historic and Genealogical Register*, 15 (1861): 309–13; Shipton, *Sibley's Harvard Graduates*, 9: 87; "Third Church Records," in *OSC*, 1:432.

83. *MHSC*, 6th ser., 6 (1893): 103.

84. Joseph Sewall, *Christ Victorious*; see also *OSC*, 1:464–66.

85. Shipton, *Sibley's Harvard Graduates*, 9:87–92.

86. Thomas Smith, a near contemporary of Seccombe, had a similar career. He too was the son of a Third Church family, went to Harvard College, and took up missionary preaching on the eastern frontier in what was then Falmouth, now Portland, Maine; see Shipton, *Sibley's Harvard Graduates*, 6: 400–410.

87. Withey, *Urban Growth*, pp. 13–32.

88. "Third Church Records," in *OSC*, 1:418–19.

89. "Third Church Records," in *OSC*, 1:428, 457, 485, 495–97.

90. Shipton, *Sibley's Harvard Graduates*, 4:36. The members of the First Congregational Church gathered in Newport in 1725 were all originally immigrants to Rhode Island from Massachusetts or England; see Second Congregational Church, Record Book, Ms. Vol. 836E.

91. *SS Diary*, 2:668.

92. See Second Congregational Church Records, 1728, Ms. Vol. 838B. The Second Congregational Church was formed by the disgruntled members of Clap's church, who charged Clap with neglecting communion, which the members seemed urgently to desire. See also Shipton, *Sibley's Harvard Graduates*, 4:36–37.

93. "Third Church Records," in *OSC*, 1:428.

94. Shipton, *Sibley's Harvard Graduates*, 7:50–52; "Third Church Records," in *OSC*, 1:428.

95. Diary of Joseph Sewall, May 11–14, 1732, cited in *OSC*, 1:498–99.

96. See *OSC*, 1:488–90; Foote, *Annals of King's Chapel*, 1:466–67; Updike, *Episcopal Church in Narragansett*, pp. 68–83.

97. The first American edition of Bunyan's *Pilgrim's Progress* was printed under the direction of Samuel Sewall in 1681, shortly after Sewall was appointed by the General Court to undertake the management of the Boston printing press; see *SS Diary*, 2:1107.

Chapter 8

1. Such was obviously the case in the crisis within Boston's First Church in the 1660s, which ultimately led to schism and the founding of the Third Church; see above, chapter 1. The subject of church discipline has been carefully examined in Oberholzer, *Delinquent Saints*, which deals largely with the more legalistic aspects of church discipline and its relationship to society and to civil law. For a discussion of

the spiritual and devotional purposes of church discipline, see Hambrick-Stowe, *Practice of Piety*, pp. 93–94.

2. *ET Chh. Recs.*, p. 174.

3. As a source of information, Taylor's records of the church disciplinary cases are by nature biased and partial. Nonetheless, Taylor does seem to have been reasonably accurate in his description of events. Where his biases come into play, they are often quite obviously put forward, and do not always show Taylor in the best of lights. In addition, Taylor often recorded events in great detail and quoted bits of dialogue which give quite a vivid portrayal of the beliefs and attitudes of individual church members. The disciplinary records also include verbatim quotations from pertinent documents, lending a further sense of authenticity to Taylor's reporting. In sum, it would be fair to say that these disciplinary records, if read with care and with an eye for Taylor's biases, can convey a reliable if one-sided sense of the relationship between the minister and the members of the Westfield church during the course of Edward Taylor's tenure.

4. *ET Chh. Recs.*, p. 177.

5. *ET Chh. Recs.*, pp. 174–79.

6. *ET Chh. Recs.*, pp. 179–80.

7. *ET Chh. Recs.*, pp. 180–85.

8. *ET Chh. Recs.*, pp. 185–89.

9. In these cases, the process of church discipline conducted in the Westfield church compares favorably with that of Boston's Third Church under Samuel Willard, where Willard allowed the laity to conduct most of the disciplinary action necessary to maintain peace and order within the church, which prevented all but a very few cases from reaching the stage where formal church disciplinary action was even required; see above, chapter 3.

10. On Taylor's family life, see Keller, *Example*, pp. 43–51, and above, chapter 6.

11. Powell, "Introduction," in ET "Town Recs.," pp. 68–75.

12. See *Edward Taylor vs. Solomon Stoddard*, p. 30.

13. *ET Poems*, p. 83; Davis, *A Reading*, pp. 134–45.

14. Taylor, Commonplace Book, Item no.22.

15. For a brief biography of Benjamin Ruggles, see Shipton, *Sibley's Harvard Graduates*, 4:171–72. For Taylor's record of the Suffield Concerns, see *ET Chh. Recs.*, pp. 189–96. On Stoddard's *Doctrine of Instituted Churches*, see Miller, *From Colony to Province*, pp. 256–58. In Connecticut, the entire body of the colony's Congregational church establishment would soon take on a more "presbyterian" form with the passage of the Saybrook Platform in 1708, which essentially enacted the Massachusetts clergy's "Proposals" of 1705 as the colony's official platform of church polity; see Walker, *Creeds and Platforms*, pp. 495–523.

16. *ET Chh. Recs.*, p. 191.

17. In fact, Taylor's position here is quite similar to that taken thirty years earlier by John Davenport in the controversy over the First Church in Boston; like Davenport, Taylor tended to reify the first-generation's congregational polity into an unal-

terable standard of orthodoxy, and to create a link between the first generation's sufferings and the sanctity of the particular ecclesiastical forms they chose to promote in
the New World; see above, Introduction and chapter 1.

18. For a full account of this case, see *ET Chh. Recs.*, pp. 189–96; also see Stanford,
" 'Young Cockerill.' "

19. The extent to which the Connecticut Valley clergy were suffering financial
hardship in the later 1690s is evident from the detailed contract for payment that
Benjamin Ruggles drew up in 1697 when he was negotiating the terms of his employment with the town of Suffield. In this document, Ruggles carefully specified
not only the amount of his salary but the percentages of the various forms of payment he would accept for each of the next five years; see Shipton, *Sibley's Harvard
Graduates*, 4:172.

20. See *ET Chh. Recs.*, pp. 463–65; ET "Town Recs.," p. 237; and above, chapter 6.

21. This was Taylor's first reference to Ebenezer Pomery, the nephew of a Westfield man, who became sheriff of Hampshire County and "His Majesties Council" for
the district. Pomery becomes a prominent figure in the later disciplinary cases, and his
legal training becomes a focus of Taylor's resentment; see *ET Chh. Recs.*, p. 471.

22. This, of course, was a very traditional position to take; the similarities to
William Bradford's account of the dispersal of population in early Plymouth hardly
need mentioning.

23. For Taylor's narrative of the "Pochassuck Matters," see *ET Chh. Recs.*, pp.
197–99.

24. This extended gap in Taylor's records may indicate an absence of disciplinary
cases for this period, but there is also evidence that suggests some disciplinary cases
went unrecorded; see *ET Chh. Recs.*, p. 468.

25. Lucas, *Valley of Discord*, pp. 196–97; Coffman, *Solomon Stoddard*, pp. 109–12.

26. See *ET Chh. Recs.*, pp. 201–3, 466–68.

27. On the fusion of "theological rigor" with a "popular orientation" in the evangelical preaching of the eighteenth century, see Stout, *New England Soul*, pp. 179–
81, 228–31. For an example of a clergyman's expression of this desire, see Samuel
Wigglesworth, "Essay for Reviving Religion."

28. On the suspension of lecture days, see chapter 4, above. Along with these possible explanations, Ensign Kellogg's later problem with alcoholism, which appears
frequently in the church records, does not clarify matters any. See *ET Chh. Recs.*, pp.
205–6, 236, 241–42.

29. ET "Town Recs.," pp. 285–88.

30. *Edward Taylor vs. Solomon Stoddard*, pp. 43–44, 47, 187–216.

31. Powell, "Introduction," in ET "Town Recs.," pp. 88–95.

32. *ET Chh. Recs.*, pp. 173, 278; Taylor, "Elegy on David Dewey," pp. 78–82; also
see above, chapter 4.

33. *ET Chh. Recs.*, p. 209. Subsequent citations to Taylor's "Church Records" for
the following account of the Walter Lee/Benjamin Smith case will appear parenthet-
ically in the text.

34. Actually, Walter Lee seems to have had yet a third brief marriage after Hepzibah's death; the name of his third wife is unrecorded, and she died before 1711 as well; see *ET Chh. Recs.*, p. 209.

35. Taylor's own advancing age may well have shaped his opinion of the "unrighteousness" of putting Walter Lee "out of the law."

36. The similarity is striking between Taylor's position on this matter and that of John Davenport during the controversy that led to the founding of Boston's Third Church; see above, chapter 1.

37. At Smith's urging, Woodbridge had shown this correspondence to Daniel Brewer, the Springfield minister, who took Smith's side in opposition to Taylor; *ET Chh. Recs.*, pp. 220–21.

38. In Hebrews 13:17, Paul instructs the churches to "Obey them that have the rule over you, and submit yourselves," while 1 Peter 5:2–3 directs church elders to "Feed the flock of God which is among you, taking the oversight thereof, not by constraint but willingly, . . . neither as being lords over God's heritage, but being ensamples to the flock."

39. Both men were arguing from the basic premises of the Cambridge Platform, but Taylor's interpretation was probably more consistent with the letter of the law, if not the spirit; see editors' note in *ET Chh. Recs.*, p. 474; see also Walker, *Creeds and Platforms*, p. 218.

40. Evidence for the duration of the suspension comes from Taylor's "Preparatory Meditations," which at this stage in Taylor's career seem to have been written in preparation for the sacrament. There is a lengthy gap in the series in the middle of the year 1713, implying that Taylor did not offer communion during this period; see *ET Poems*, pp. 288–90.

41. *ET Chh. Recs.*, p. 213.

42. *ET Chh. Recs.*, pp. 214, 223; ET "Town Recs.," p. 305.

43. *ET Chh. Recs.*, p. 216.

44. See *ET Chh. Recs.*, p. 225, where Taylor names Stoddard as a source of "Greate Encouragement to Smith in this his Evil Case."

45. *ET Chh. Recs.*, pp. 218–19.

46. *ET Chh. Recs.*, p. 225.

47. The sermons were preached on two verses from the New Testament, Matthew 18:17–18, in which Jesus states that those who disobey the church shall be treated "as an heathen man and a publican," and that a soul cut loose from the church on earth will also "be loosed in heaven." See *ET Chh. Recs.*, pp. 375–446.

48. For the Sewall-Pemberton dispute, see above, chapter 3.

49. *ET Chh. Recs.*, pp. 236–42.

50. The new bell cost the town £50, more than half Taylor's annual salary.

51. ET "Town Recs.," p. 345.

52. ET "Town Recs.," p. 347.

53. Lockwood, *Westfield*, 1:319. For an account of the entire controversy, see ET "Town Recs.," pp. 101–15, 320–52.

54. See Taylor, *Minor Poetry*, pp. 217–41, especially pp. 220, 223–24.

55. ET "Town Recs.," p. 353.

56. ET "Town Recs.," p. 349.

57. ET "Town Recs.," pp. 365–67.

58. Franklin B. Dexter, *Annals of Yale College*, 1:264–67, 279–80.

59. ET "Town Recs.," p. 384.

60. See *ET Chh. Recs.*, p. 464; ET "Town Recs.," p. 395.

61. Lockwood, *Westfield* p. 333.

62. Richard Hooker, *Laws of Ecclesiastical Polity*, 1:242–63.

63. See Lockwood, *Westfield*, pp. 329–30; for comparison with admissions in Taylor's tenure, see *ET Chh. Recs.*, pp. 162–72.

64. *ET Chh. Recs.*, pp. 224, 474.

65. See Patricia Tracy, *Jonathan Edwards, Pastor*, pp. 171–94; David D. Hall, "Editor's Introduction," in Edwards, *Ecclesiastical Writings*.

Conclusion

1. As Michael J. Crawford has argued, "Conversion of a large number of unassociated individuals did not constitute a revival of religion. Revival meant the transformation by grace of a community, a group of people bound together as a single moral entity"; see Crawford, *Seasons of Grace*, p. 180.

2. Lockwood, *Westfield*, 1:329–30.

3. Edwards, *Great Awakening*, pp. 119, 153.

4. Edwards, *Great Awakening*, p. 102; italics added for emphasis.

5. Perhaps the scoffers were Mawdsley, Kellogg, and the other opponents of Taylor from the controversies of the 1710s and 1720s?

6. Edwards, *Great Awakening*, p. 143. The events surrounding the revivals in Westfield are less well known than in many other New England communities. No revival narratives exist, partly because of the irregular tenures of the Westfield ministers in the 1730s and 1740s. Through indirect forms of evidence like Edwards' *Narrative*, the circumstances of the revivals can be pieced together to reveal the significance of local religious history for understanding Westfield's response to the awakenings.

7. Before his death, Bull was troubled by the same kinds of salary disputes that had recurred throughout Taylor's tenure, but these seem to have had little impact on the religious community or its response to the revival; Lockwood, *Westfield*, 1:335–36.

8. Whitefield, *Journals*, pp. 477–78.

9. Lockwood, *Westfield*, 1:329–30.

10. Whitefield, *Journals*, pp. 475–76.

11. For a further discussion of the significance of local ministers in preparing the groundwork for revivals, see Gura, "Sowing for the Harvest"; Nordbeck, "Almost Awakened." Whitefield's awareness of the revival history of New England communities like Northampton, and his careful preparations for taking advantage of this "New Religious History" are discussed in Stout, *Divine Dramatist*, pp. 113–32.

12. In Northampton, Edwards reported that after Whitefield's visit, "in about a

month there was a great alteration in the town." The time delay indicates that Edwards must have added his own efforts to those of Whitefield in bringing about the Awakening; Stout, *Divine Dramatist*, p. 126. For a series of examples of this pattern in local revivals, see Joseph Tracy, *Great Awakening*, pp. 114–203. Numerous examples abound in case studies and narratives from individual New England churches; see Beales, "Solomon Prentice's Narrative"; Harper, "Clericalism and Revival"; Nordbeck, "Almost Awakened."

13. Lockwood, *Westfield*, 1:369–78.

14. Before he moved to Westfield, Ballantine had been a member of Benjamin Colman's Brattle Street Church, where the revivals had been strongly supported and Whitefield's preaching had been particularly effective. Ballantine was born into a prominent Boston mercantile family that had long been associated with the Brattle Street Church, he was educated by Nathaniel Williams at the Boston Latin School, and graduated from Harvard College in 1735; Shipton, *Sibley's Harvard Graduates*, 9:468–72.

15. See Lockwood, *Westfield*, 1:374–78, on Ballantine's ordination. For a discussion of the Breck affair and its impact on Connecticut Valley religious politics, see David D. Hall, "Editor's Introduction," in Edwards, *Ecclesiastical Writings*, pp. 4–16.

16. In commenting on a dispute between Separate Baptists and an orthodox church in 1760, Ballantine expressed his pleasure at "a rare instance of Catholicism. . . . It appears to me quite reasonable that we should hold communion with those with whom we hope to live in heaven, though they differ from us in some non-essentials, as the subjects and mode of baptism. All true Christians are members of Christ." See the "Journal of John Ballantine," cited in Lockwood, *Westfield*, 1:392. This position linked Ballantine with others raised in Boston's more "catholick" and ecumenical Congregationalism of the early eighteenth century; see John Corrigan, *Prism of Piety*.

17. On the remarkable absence of separatist schisms in the Upper Connecticut Valley where "Stoddardeanism" had its strongest impact, see the map of "The Extent of Separatism" in Goen, *Revivalism and Separatism*, following p. 114. Of the Massachusetts towns in the Connecticut Valley, only Westfield, where Taylor had opposed Stoddard's approach, and Sunderland, a recently settled town, experienced separatist schisms during the revival era.

18. "Journal of John Ballantine," in Lockwood, *Westfield*, 1:383; Goen, *Revivalism and Separatism*, p. 108.

19. David D. Hall, "Editor's Introduction," in Edwards, *Ecclesiastical Writings*, p. 46.

20. Except for the attention paid to Boston in monographs on the revivals such as Gaustad, *Great Awakening*; Goen, *Revivalism and Separatism*; and Crawford, *Seasons of Grace*; there are relatively few specialized treatments of the Great Awakening in Boston. Among them are Harper, "Clericalism and Revival," and Schmidt, "'Second and Glorious Reformation.'" In Nash, *Urban Crucible*, pp. 198–219, the Boston revival is described more as a symptom of economic change and social upheaval than as a meaningful event in New England's religious culture.

21. Among the many studies of local communities elsewhere in New England during the Great Awakening are Bushman, *From Puritan to Yankee*; Patricia Tracy,

Jonathan Edwards, Pastor; Heyrman, *Commerce and Culture*; Nordbeck, "Almost Awakened"; Jeffries, "Separation in Canterbury"; Walsh, "Great Awakening in Woodbury"; Bumsted, "Revivalism and Separatism"; Bumsted, "Religion, Finance, and Democracy"; Willingham, "Religious Conversion in Windham"; Onuf, "New Lights in New London"; Stout and Onuf, "James Davenport."

22. Whitefield, *Journals*, pp. 457–72.

23. Prince, "Account of the Revival," 2:391.

24. Prince, "Account of the Revival," 2:397. This passage indicates that the practice of policing the morality of the town was not unique to Sewall and Bromfield's time, as discussed in chapter 3, but was continued in this later era.

25. In general, it seems that the more controversial and divisive the itinerants became, the less successful their preaching was in creating lasting conversions. The exception may be Andrew Croswell, who eventually gathered the only Separate church to emerge from the revival in Boston, but even this society was sparsely attended and did not survive Croswell's death; see Schmidt, "Second and Glorious Reformation," pp. 221–26. See also Jedrey, *World of John Cleaveland*.

26. Prince, "Account of the Revival," 2:408. Of the four men who separated, three were quite recent converts; one became a full member in 1738 and two had just joined in 1741. Of these, the most prominent, Nathaniel Wardell, was later excommunicated, not for his desire for separation, but for his "frequent and profane cursing and swearing, and a course of Drunkenness." The separation of Wardell and friends was clearly not a major controversy or division within the church; see *OSC*, 1:539–42, 587–88.

27. Among the new members who joined in full communion in 1741, the year of the great "alteration," were the sons of leading mercantile families like Samuel Fayerweather, Joshua Hemmenway, and a third-generation Edward Bromfield, as well as tradesmen like Jeremiah Belknap, a maker of leather breeches, and also slaves or other people so obscure that their full names are unknown, "Scipio," "Ann," and "Cornwall"; Hill and Bigelow, *Historical Catalogue*, pp. 40–42.

28. *OSC*, 1: 504–5; Whitefield, *Journals*, pp. 457, 461, 504. At the time of his death in 1756, Willard's loss was much lamented by the community and he was praised for his piety and public service. The traditional rhetoric of the "gap in the hedge" was once more used by his eulogists: "Where is the Man to be found among you to stand in the Gap?" See Shipton, *Sibley's Harvard Graduates*, 4:425–32.

29. *OSC*, 1:453; Shipton, *Sibley's Harvard Graduates*, 4: 434–49.

30. The English Nonconformist community strongly supported Belcher's appointment, and Isaac Watts wrote an ode in his honor celebrating the news. Belcher himself vehemently opposed the notion of his daughter marrying a "churchman," and demanded that her suitor "promise he would never more go to the Church of England." His own children remained devoted to the South Church in later years, and Belcher was an avid supporter of the orthodox college at Princeton after he became Governor of New Jersey in 1747; *OSC*, 1:453–56; Shipton, *Sibley's Harvard Graduates*, 4:439–48.

31. Whitefield, *Journals*, pp. 456–57, 464, 469–70, 472, 474–75. Shipton's bio-

graphical sketch of Belcher tends to perpetuate the image of the governor as a thoroughly anglicized politician and discredits his religious beliefs as the hypocritical cant of "the successful politician . . . harp[ing] on worn-out political phrases which sound familiar to the voters and have the sanction of tradition"; Shipton, *Sibley's Harvard Graduates*, 4:448. However, Shipton omits from his sketch any discussion of Belcher's response to George Whitefield and the Great Awakening, and of the genuine expressions of religious conviction expressed in Belcher's private correspondence; see for example Belcher to Madam Partridge, November 15, 1736, and Belcher to Mrs. Allen, November 15, 1736, Jonathan Belcher Letterbooks, Vol. 5, leaves 36–39.

32. On Nathan Cole, see Crawford, "Spiritual Travels."

33. The same was true in Benjamin Colman's church in Brattle Street; Colman reported to Prince that among the converts in the *annus mirabilis* 1741 "were many of the rich and polite of our Sons and Daughters"; see Prince, "Account of the Revival," 2:397.

34. See above, chapter 3.

35. Prince, "Account of the Revival," 2:399. Sewall's sermon was preached on January 11, 1741/2, at the height of the Awakening.

36. Prince, "Account of the Revival," 2:398–99, 395.

37. Prince, "Account of the Revival," 2:392.

38. For a discussion of this phenomenon, see Hambrick-Stowe, "Spirit of the Old Writers"; also O'Brien, "Transatlantic Community," pp. 819–20.

39. Prince, "Account of the Revival," 2:400. For a discussion of Daniel Henchman and the other Third Church members involved in publishing godly books, see above, chapters 3 and 5; also O'Brien, "Transatlantic Community," pp. 819–20. It is notable that the authors of particular popularity during the revivals were those like Hooker, Shepard, Willard, and Stoddard who had championed the cause of a more inclusive church and more evangelical preaching styles within the context of New England's traditional debates over the scope of the church and its relationship to the larger world; John Davenport had little to do with this revival tradition.

40. Of the revival narratives from non-New England sources that appeared in *The Christian History*, the most famous were probably those at Cambuslang and Kilsyth in Scotland in 1742; see Stout, *Divine Dramatist*, pp. 148–55; Crawford, *Seasons of Grace*, pp. 156–66.

41. For discussions of "Letter Days" organized by clergymen to use correspondence between churches to foster further revivals, see O'Brien, "Transatlantic Community," pp. 823–25; Crawford, *Seasons of Grace*, pp. 164–66, 172–74; Hambrick-Stowe, "The Spirit of the Old Writers."

42. For just one of many examples, see the church and congregation vote of November 2, 1740, which allotted £46 for charity to the local poor, £10 for the Rev. Richard Pierce at Dartmouth, £10 for the Rev. Timothy White at Nantucket, £5 for the Rev. Ezra Carpenter in Hull, and the remaining £5.9.5 for "Books of Piety" to be distributed by the ministers to "proper objects of such a Charity"; OSC, 1:514–15.

43. Other examples can be found in abundance from the local records of New England churches and towns; see Crawford, *Seasons of Grace*, pp. 104–14.

44. Jon Butler has objected to the categorization and interpretation of eighteenth-century American revivals as a single event, and has called attention to the need to understand the local and particular causes of revivals. Though Butler distinguishes among revival movements, he concedes that a "Great Awakening" can be usefully identified as a single unified event in the New England colonies in the 1740s; see Butler, "Enthusiasm Described," p. 309.

45. Dudley, *Letter to the Countess of Lincoln*, pp. 8–9, 15.

46. Edward Johnson, *Wonder-Working Providence*. For a different interpretation of the tone of Johnson's work, see Delbanco, *Puritan Ordeal*, pp. 189–93.

47. Outlying settlements beyond the Piscataqua River in Maine are numbered on the map but not supplied with names or images of buildings, as no churches had yet been gathered there; Hubbard, *Present State*, frontispiece and following p. 131. See also Lincoln A. Dexter, ed., *Maps of Early Massachusetts*.

48. Cotton Mather, *Magnalia Christi Americana*, Murdock, ed., pp. 172–79.

49. Prince, *Chronological History*, pp. 438–39.

50. Ezra Stiles, *Discourse*. Stiles' enlarged text was based on a sermon he had preached to the Rhode Island convention of Congregational ministers in 1760.

51. Ezra Stiles, *Discourse*, pp. 102–3, 108–15, 129–39.

52. In fact, many of the eighteenth-century towns examined in recent community studies of the Great Awakening were located in places where English settlement was fairly recent, where there had been no towns or churches at the time of the Halfway Covenant; see Bumsted, "Religion, Finance, and Democracy," pp. 818–19; Jeffries, "Separation in Canterbury," p. 525; Walsh, "Great Awakening in Woodbury," pp. 544–45; Willingham, "Religious Conversion in Windham," pp. 109–10; Nordbeck, "Almost Awakened"; and Beales, "Solomon Prentice's Narrative," 132–33. Many of the towns examined by Bushman in *From Puritan to Yankee*, and the town of Marblehead studied by Heyrman in *Commerce and Culture*, were only recently established as orthodox communities at the time of the awakening.

53. The customs of life in New Haven were slightly different yet still quite familiar to this traveler from Boston; see Sarah Kemble Knight, "Journal," 2:436–39.

54. Whitefield, *Journals*, pp. 451–56; Shipton, *Sibley's Harvard Graduates*, 4:36–40.

55. Sewall provided his "Cousin Moodey" with everything from Hebrew lexicons to folios of "Calvin's Exposition" to pairs of "new Slippers," and also helped to publish and distribute some of Moody's sermons; *SS Diary*, 1:461, 526, 564.

56. Whitefield, *Journals*, pp. 466–67; Shipton, *Sibley's Harvard Graduates*, 4:356–65.

57. Nordbeck, "Almost Awakened," pp. 33–35, cites Moody as one of the ministers who helped to create a "psychological receptivity" and an "experiential knowledge of the strange and surprising ways" of God among the northern population in advance of Whitefield's revivals. When Whitefield returned to New England for another tour in 1744, he chose to begin his itinerary by visiting Moody in York; see Whitefield, *Journals*, pp. 516–19.

58. *ET Diary*, p. 39.

59. Whitefield, *Journal*, pp. 466, 474–77.

60. "Diary of Henry Flynt," 2:1453–54.

61. This general pattern, which underlay the controversies that plagued the West-field church in the eighteenth century, has also been described in Greven, *Four Generations*; Bumsted, "Religion, Finance, and Democracy"; Walsh, "Great Awakening in Woodbury"; and Willingham, "Religious Conversion in Windham." But while these studies tend to see the controversies as signs of Puritan declension, I would argue that in the larger context of New England's development, these conflicts were signs of vitality and engines of cultural expansion.

62. Zuckerman, *Peaceable Kingdoms*.

63. On the concept of "linkage" as a way to describe the "incorporation of one place into an integrated system of places," see Rutman, "Assessing the Little Communities," pp. 175–78.

64. Appleton, *God, and Not Ministers*, p. 21.

65. Prince, "Endless Increase," pp. 27, 38. The sermon was preached before the Massachusetts clergy at their annual convention in Boston.

66. Ezra Stiles, *Discourse*, pp. 114–15. For a discussion of some of Stiles' more extravagant notions, see Morgan, *Gentle Puritan*, pp. 158–66.

67. Ezra Stiles, *Discourse*, pp. 102, 116.

68. For a fascinating discussion of one version of this process, see Bushman, *Joseph Smith*.

69. Remarkably, in just three generations, Taylor's, his son's, and his grandson's lives spanned two centuries, from Edward Taylor's birth in Leicestershire in 1642, to John Taylor's death in Bruce, Michigan, in 1840; Lockwood, *Westfield*, 1:165–66.

70. Thayer, *New England Emigrant Aid Company*.

71. Cited in Starr, *Americans and the California Dream*, p. 86; see pp. 85–109 for a general discussion of New England's influence on the settlement of California.

Works Cited

The following abbreviations are used in the Works Cited:

AASP	*American Antiquarian Society Proceedings*
MHSC	*Massachusetts Historical Society Collections*
MHSP	*Massachusetts Historical Society Proceedings*
NEQ	*New England Quarterly*
WMQ	*William and Mary Quarterly*, Third Series

Adams, James Truslow. *The Founding of New England.* Boston: Atlantic Monthly Press, 1921.

Adams, Sherman W., and Henry R. Stiles. *The History of Ancient Wethersfield.* 2 vols. New York: Grafton Press, 1904.

Agnew, Jean-Christophe. "Coming Up for Air: Consumer Culture in Historical Perspective." In John Brewer and Roy Porter, eds., *Consumption and the World of Goods*, pp. 19–39. New York: Routledge, 1994.

Allen, David Grayson. "Both Englands." In David D. Hall and David Grayson Allen, eds., *Seventeenth-Century New England*, pp. 55–82. Colonial Society of Massachusetts Publications, vol. 63. Boston, 1984.

———. *In English Ways: The Movement of Societies and the Transferal of English Local Law and Custom to Massachusetts Bay in the Seventeenth Century.* Chapel Hill: University of North Carolina Press, 1981.

Allen, Neal W., Jr. "Law and Authority to the Eastward: Maine Courts, Magistrates, and Lawyers, 1690–1730." In *Law in Colonial Massachusetts, 1630–1800*, pp. 273–312. Colonial Society of Massachusetts Publications, vol. 62. Boston, 1984.

Allin, John. "Brief History of the Church of Christ . . . at Dedham in New England." In *Early Records of the Town of Dedham*. 6 vols. Dedham, Mass., 1886–1936.

Ammerman, David, and Philip Morgan, eds. *Books About Early America*. Williamsburg, Va.: Institute of Early American History and Culture, 1989.

Anderson, Virginia DeJohn. "Migrants and Motives: Religion and the Settlement of New England, 1630–1640." *NEQ* 58 (1985): 339–83.

———. *New England's Generation: The Great Migration and the Formation of Society and Culture in the Seventeenth Century*. Cambridge: Cambridge University Press, 1991.

Andrews, Charles McLean. *The Colonial Period of American History*. 4 vols. New Haven: Yale University Press, 1934–38.

———. *The River Towns of Connecticut*. Johns Hopkins University Studies in Historical and Political Science, 7th ser., 7–9. Baltimore, 1889.

Appleton, Nathanael. *God, and Not Ministers to Have the Glory of the Success Given to the Preached Gospel*. Boston, 1741.

Axtell, James. *The School upon a Hill: Education and Society in Colonial New England*. New Haven: Yale University Press, 1974.

Bailyn, Bernard. *The New England Merchants in the Seventeenth Century*. Cambridge, Mass.: Harvard University Press, 1955.

———. *The Peopling of British North America: An Introduction*. New York: Knopf, 1986.

———. "Review of *The New England Mind: From Colony to Province*, by Perry Miller." *NEQ* 27 (1954): 112.

Bailyn, Bernard, and Lotte Bailyn. *Massachusetts Shipping, 1697–1714*. Cambridge, Mass.: Harvard University Press, 1959.

Beales, Ross W. "The Halfway Covenant and Religious Scrupulosity: The First Church of Dorchester as a Test Case." *WMQ* 31 (1974): 465–80.

Beales, Ross W., ed. "Solomon Prentice's Narrative of the Great Awakening." *MHSP* 83 (1972): 130–47.

Belcher, Jonathan. Letterbooks. Massachusetts Historical Society, Boston, Massachusetts. [Microfilm copy, Harvard University].

Bellamy, Joseph. *The Half-way Covenant: A Dialogue*. Boston, 1769.

Bender, Thomas. *Community and Social Change in America*. New Brunswick, N.J.: Rutgers University Press, 1978.

Benes, Peter, and Phillip D. Zimmerman, eds. *New England Meetinghouse and Church: 1630–1850*. Boston: Boston University and the Currier Gallery of Art, 1979.

Bercovitch, Sacvan. *The American Jeremiad*. Madison: University of Wisconsin Press, 1978.

———. *The Puritan Origins of the American Self*. New Haven: Yale University Press, 1975.

Berkin, Carol, Christopher L. Miller, Robert W. Cherny, and James L. Gormly. *Making America: A History of the United States*. Boston: Houghton Mifflin, 1995.

"Biographical Sketches of Ten Founders of the Third Church." Records of the Old South Church (Third Church), Boston. Shelf 13, Congregational Library. Boston, Massachusetts.

Bissell, Linda A. "Family, Friends, and Neighbors: Social Interaction in Seventeenth-Century Windsor." Ph.D. diss., Brandeis University, 1973.

Black, Robert C. *The Younger John Winthrop*. New York: Columbia University Press, 1966.

Boas, Ralph, and Louise Boas. *Cotton Mather: Keeper of the Puritan Conscience*. New York: Harper, 1928.

Bonomi, Patricia U. *Under the Cope of Heaven: Religion, Society, and Politics in Colonial America*. New York: Oxford University Press, 1986.

Bosco, Ronald E., ed. *New England Funeral Sermons*. Vol. 4 of *The Puritan Sermon in America, 1630–1750*. Delmar, N.Y.: Scholars Facsimiles and Reprints, 1978.

Boyer, Paul S., and Stephen Nissenbaum. *Salem Possessed: The Social Origins of Witchcraft*. Cambridge, Mass.: Harvard University Press, 1972.

Boyer, Paul S., Clifford E. Clark, Jr., Sandra McNair Hawley, Joseph F. Kett, Neal Salisbury, Harvard Sitkoff, and Nancy Woloch. *The Enduring Vision: A History of the American People*. Concise 2d ed. Lexington, Mass.: D.C. Heath, 1995.

Bozeman, Theodore Dwight. *To Live Ancient Lives: The Primitivist Dimension in Puritanism*. Chapel Hill: University of North Carolina Press, 1988.

Bradford, William. *Of Plymouth Plantation, 1620–1647*. Ed. Samuel Eliot Morison. New York: Knopf, 1952.

Breen, T. H. *Puritans and Adventurers: Change and Persistence in Early America*. New York: Oxford University Press, 1980.

Breen, T. H., and Stephen Foster. "Moving to the New World: The Character of Early Massachusetts Migration." *WMQ* 30 (1973): 189–222.

Bremer, Francis J. *Congregational Communion: Clerical Friendship in the Anglo-American Puritan Community, 1610–1692*. Boston: Northeastern University Press, 1994.

———. "Increase Mather's Friends: the Trans-Atlantic Congregational Network of the Seventeenth Century." *AASP* 94 (1984): 59–96.

Bridenbaugh, Carl. *Cities in the Wilderness: The First Century of Urban Life in America, 1625–1742*. New York: Oxford University Press, 1938.

Bridenbaugh, Carl, ed. *The Pynchon Papers*. 2 vols. Colonial Society of Massachusetts Publications, vols. 60–61. Boston, 1982–85.

Brinkley, Alan. *American History: A Survey*. 9th ed. New York: McGraw Hill, 1995.

Bromfield, Edward, Mary Rock, and Edward Bromfield, Jr. Notes of Sermons by Boston Ministers, 1682 to 1721. Bromfield Collection. Massachusetts Historical Society. Boston, Massachusetts.

Brooke, John L. *The Refiner's Fire: The Making of Mormon Cosmology, 1644–1844*. Cambridge: Cambridge University Press, 1994.

Brown, Anne S. "'Bound Up in a Bundle of Life': The Social Meaning of Religious Practice in Northeastern Massachusetts, 1700–1765." Ph.D. diss., Boston University, 1995.

Brown, B. Katherine. "The Controversy over the Franchise in Puritan Massachusetts, 1954 to 1974." *WMQ* 33 (1976): 212–41.

Brown, Richard D. *Knowledge is Power: The Diffusion of Information in Early America, 1700–1865*. New York: Oxford University Press, 1989.

Bumsted, J. M. "A Caution to Erring Christians: Ecclesiastical Disorder on Cape Cod, 1717 to 1738." *WMQ* 28 (1971): 413–38.

———. *The Pilgrim's Progress: The Ecclesiastical History of the Old Colony, 1620–1775.* New York: Garland Publishing, 1989.

———. "Religion, Finance, and Democracy in Massachusetts: The Town of Norton as a Case Study." *Journal of American History* 57 (1971): 817–31.

———. "Revivalism and Separatism in New England: The First Society of Norwich, Connecticut as a Case Study." *WMQ* 24 (1967): 588–612.

Bunyan, John. *The Pilgrim's Progress.* Ed. Roger Sharrock. London: Penguin Books, 1965.

Bushman, Richard L. *From Puritan to Yankee: Character and the Social Order in Connecticut, 1690–1765.* Cambridge, Mass.: Harvard University Press, 1967.

———. *Joseph Smith and the Beginnings of Mormonism.* Urbana: University of Illinois Press, 1984.

———. *The Refinement of America: Persons, Houses, Cities.* New York: Knopf, 1992.

Butler, Jon. *Awash in a Sea of Faith: Christianizing the American People.* Cambridge, Mass.: Harvard University Press, 1990.

———. "Enthusiasm Described and Decried: The Great Awakening as Interpretive Fiction." *Journal of American History* 70 (1982): 305–25.

Caldwell, Patricia. *The Puritan Conversion Narrative: The Beginnings of American Expression.* Cambridge: Cambridge University Press, 1983.

Carroll, Peter N. *Puritanism and the Wilderness: The Intellectual Significance of the New England Frontier, 1629–1700.* New York: Columbia University Press, 1969.

Chauncy, Charles. *Anti-Synodalia Scripta Americana: Propositions Concerning the Subject of Baptism and Consociation of Churches.* [London?], 1662.

Coffman, Ralph J. *Solomon Stoddard.* Boston: Twayne Publishers, 1978.

Cohen, Charles L. *God's Caress: The Psychology of Puritan Religious Experience.* New York: Oxford University Press, 1986.

Colacurcio, Michael J. "Gods Determinations Touching Half-Way Membership: Occasion and Audience in Edward Taylor." *American Literature* 39, no. 3 (1967): 298–314.

Collinson, Patrick. *English Puritanism.* London: The Historical Association, 1983.

———. *The Religion of Protestants: The Church in English Society.* Oxford: Clarendon Press, 1982.

Colman, Benjamin, et al. *The Gospel Order Revived.* [New York], 1700.

Cook, Edward M., Jr. *The Fathers of the Towns: Leadership and Community Structure in Eighteenth-Century New England.* Baltimore: Johns Hopkins University Press, 1976.

Coolidge, John S. *The Pauline Renaissance in England: Puritanism and the Bible.* Oxford: Clarendon Press, 1970.

Corrigan, John. *The Prism of Piety: Catholick Congregational Clergy at the Beginning of the Enlightenment.* New York: Oxford University Press, 1991.

Cotton, John. *Christ the Fountaine of Life.* London, 1651. Reprint. New York: Arno Press, 1972.

Cotton, John [of Halifax]. *The General Practice of the Churches of New England, Relating to Baptism, Vindicated.* Boston, 1772.

————. *The General Practice . . . Further Vindicated*. Boston, 1773.

Cotton, John, IV. "An Account of the Church of Christ in Plymouth, the First Church in New England, from its Establishment to the Present Day." *MHSC* 1st ser., 4 (1795).

Cotton, Josiah. "Account of the Cotton Family, 1727–1755." Houghton Library, Harvard University. Cambridge, Massachusetts.

A Course of Sermons on Early Piety, By . . . Eight Ministers. Boston, 1721.

Crawford, Michael J. *Seasons of Grace: Colonial New England's Revival Tradition in Its British Context*. New York: Oxford University Press, 1991.

————. "The Spiritual Travels of Nathan Cole." *WMQ* 33 (1976): 89–126.

Cressy, David. *Coming Over: Migration and Communication Between England and New England in the Seventeenth Century*. Cambridge: Cambridge University Press, 1987.

Cross, Claire. "The Church in England, 1646–1660." In G. E. Aylmer, ed., *The Interregnum: The Quest for Settlement, 1646–1660*, pp. 99–120. London: Macmillan, 1972.

Cushman, Robert. "Reasons and Considerations Touching the Lawfulness of Removing out of England into the Parts of America" (1621). In Alexander Young, ed., *Chronicles of the Pilgrim Fathers*, pp. 239–49. Boston: Little, Brown, 1841.

Danforth, John [and Mary Rock?]. Notes of Sermons given by John Eliot et al., 1675–1680. 2 cases. John Eliot Collection. Massachusetts Historical Society. Boston, Massachusetts.

Davenport, John. *Letters of John Davenport, Puritan Divine*. Ed. Isabel M. Calder. New Haven: Yale University Press, 1937.

————. *A Sermon Preach'd at the Election of the Governour at Boston in New England, May 19th, 1669*. [Cambridge, Mass.], 1670.

Davies, Horton. *The Worship of the American Puritans, 1629–1730*. New York: Peter Lang, 1990.

Davis, Thomas M. *A Reading of Edward Taylor*. Newark: University of Delaware Press, 1992.

DeLamotte, Eugenia. "John Cotton and the Rhetoric of Grace." *Early American Literature* 21 (1986): 49–74.

Delbanco, Andrew. *The Puritan Ordeal*. Cambridge, Mass.: Harvard University Press, 1989.

Demos, John. *A Little Commonwealth: Family Life in Plymouth Colony*. New York: Oxford University Press, 1970.

————. *The Unredeemed Captive: A Family Story from Early America*. New York: Knopf, 1994.

Demos, John, ed. *Remarkable Providences, 1600–1760*. New York: George Braziller, 1972.

Dexter, Franklin B. *Biographical Sketches of the Graduates of Yale College with Annals of the College History*. 6 vols. New York: H. Holt, 1885.

————. *Documentary History of Yale University under the Original Charter, 1701–1745*. New Haven: Yale University Press, 1916.

Dexter, Henry M., and Morton Dexter. *The England and Holland of the Pilgrims*. Cambridge, Mass.: Houghton Mifflin, 1905.

Dexter, Lincoln A., ed. *Maps of Early Massachusetts*. Rev. ed. Brookfield, Mass., 1984.

Dinkin, Robert J. "Seating the Meetinghouse in Early Massachusetts." In Robert Blair St. George, ed., *Material Life in America, 1600–1860*, pp. 407–18. Boston: Northeastern University Press, 1988.

Ditmore, Michael G. "Preparation and Confession: Reconsidering Edmund S. Morgan's *Visible Saints*." *NEQ* 67 (1994): 298–319.

Dudley, Thomas. *Gov. Thomas Dudley's Letter to the Countess of Lincoln, March, 1631*. In Peter Force, ed., *Force's Tracts*, 2: Item no. IV. 3 vols. Washington, D.C., 1838. Reprint. Gloucester, Mass.: Peter Smith, 1947.

Dunn, Richard S. *Puritans and Yankees: The Winthrop Dynasty of New England, 1630–1717*. Princeton, N.J.: Princeton University Press, 1962.

Early Piety; Exemplified in Elizabeth Butcher of Boston. Boston, 1718.

Edwards, Jonathan. *Ecclesiastical Writings*. Ed. David D. Hall. Vol. 12 of *The Works of Jonathan Edwards*. New Haven: Yale University Press, 1994.

————. *The Great Awakening*. Ed. C. C. Goen. Vol. 4 of *The Works of Jonathan Edwards*. New Haven: Yale University Press, 1972.

Eighth Report of the Record Commissioners of the City of Boston, Containing the Boston Records from 1700 to 1728. Boston, 1883.

Eliot, John. *John Eliot's Indian Dialogues: A Study in Cultural Interaction*. Ed. Henry W. Bowden and James P. Ronda. Westport, Conn.: Greenwood Press, 1980.

Fiering, Norman. "The First American Enlightenment: Tillotson, Leverett, and Philosophical Anglicanism." *NEQ* 44 (1981): 307–44.

First Report of the Record Commissioners of the City of Boston. Boston, 1876.

Fischer, David Hackett. *Albion's Seed: Four British Folkways in America*. New York: Oxford University Press, 1989.

Fiske, John. *The Notebook of the Reverend John Fiske, 1644–1675*. Ed. Robert G. Pope. Colonial Society of Massachusetts Publications, vol. 47. Boston, 1974.

Flynt, Henry. "Diary of Henry Flynt, 1675–1760." 2 vols. Ed. Edward T. Dunn. Ph.D. diss., State University of New York at Buffalo, 1978.

Foote, Henry Wilder. *Annals of King's Chapel*. 2 vols. Boston: Little, Brown, 1882.

Ford, John W., ed. *Correspondence of the New England Company* (1896). Reprint. New York: Burt Franklin, 1970.

Foster, Stephen. "English Puritanism and the Progress of New England Institutions, 1630–1660." In David D. Hall, John M. Murrin, and Thad W. Tate, eds., *Saints and Revolutionaries: Essays on Early American History*, pp. 1–37. New York: Norton, 1984.

————. "The Godly in Transit: English Popular Protestantism and the Creation of a Puritan Establishment in America." In David D. Hall and David Grayson Allen, eds., *Seventeenth-Century New England*, pp. 185–238. Colonial Society of Massachusetts Publications, vol. 63. Boston, 1984.

————. *The Long Argument: English Puritanism and the Shaping of New England Culture, 1570–1700*. Chapel Hill: University of North Carolina Press, 1991.

————. "New England and the Challenge of Heresy, 1630–1660: The Puritan Crisis in Transatlantic Perspective." *WMQ* 38 (1981): 624–60.

Gatta, John. *Gracious Laughter: The Meditative Wit of Edward Taylor.* Columbia: University of Missouri Press, 1989.

Gaustad, Edwin. *The Great Awakening in New England.* New York: Harper, 1957.

Gildrie, Richard P. *The Profane, the Civil, and the Godly: The Reformation of Manners in Orthodox New England, 1679–1749.* University Park: Penn State University Press, 1994.

Godbeer, Richard. *The Devil's Dominion: Magic and Religion in Early New England.* Cambridge: Cambridge University Press, 1992.

Goddard, Delano A. "The Press and Literature of the Provincial Period, 1692–1770." In Justin Winsor, ed., *The Memorial History of Boston,* 2:387–436. 4 vols. Boston, 1880–81.

Goen, C. C. *Revivalism and Separatism in New England, 1740–1800: Strict Congregationalists and Separate Baptists in the Great Awakening.* Rev. ed. Middletown, Conn.: Wesleyan University Press, 1987.

Grabo, Norman. *Edward Taylor.* Rev. ed. Boston: Twayne Publishers, 1988.

Green, Samuel A. "An Early Book-catalogue Printed in Boston." *MHSP* 2d ser., 10 (1895–96): 540–41.

Greene, Jack P. "Interpretive Frameworks: The Quest for Intellectual Order in Early American History." *WMQ* 48 (1991): 515–30.

———. *Pursuits of Happiness: The Social Development of Early Modern British Colonies and the Formation of American Culture.* Chapel Hill: University of North Carolina Press, 1988.

Greven, Philip J., Jr. *Four Generations: Population, Land, and Family in Colonial Andover, Massachusetts.* Ithaca, N.Y.: Cornell University Press, 1970.

———. *The Protestant Temperament: Patterns of Child-Rearing, Religious Experience, and the Self in Early America.* Chicago: University of Chicago Press, 1977.

Gura, Philip F. *A Glimpse of Sion's Glory: Puritan Radicalism in New England, 1620–1660.* Middletown, Conn.: Wesleyan University Press, 1984.

———. "Going Mr. Stoddard's Way: William Williams on Church Privileges, 1693." *WMQ* 45 (1988): 489–98.

———. "Sowing for the Harvest: William Williams and the Great Awakening." *Journal of Presbyterian History* 56 (1978): 326–41.

Hall, David D. *The Faithful Shepherd: A History of the New England Ministry in the Seventeenth Century.* Chapel Hill: University of North Carolina Press, 1972.

———. "On Common Ground: The Coherence of American Puritan Studies." *WMQ* 44 (1987): 193–229.

———. *Worlds of Wonder, Days of Judgment: Popular Religious Belief in Early New England.* New York: Knopf, 1989.

Hall, David D., ed. *The Antinomian Controversy, 1636–1638: A Documentary History.* 2d ed. Durham, N.C.: Duke University Press, 1990.

Hall, David D., and David Grayson Allen, eds. *Seventeenth-Century New England.* Colonial Society of Massachusetts Publications, vol. 63. Boston, 1984.

Hall, Michael G. *Edward Randolph and the American Colonies, 1676–1703.* Chapel Hill: University of North Carolina Press, 1960.

———. *The Last American Puritan: The Life of Increase Mather*. Middletown, Conn.: Wesleyan University Press, 1987.

Hall, Michael G., Lawrence Leder, and Michael Kammen, eds. *The Glorious Revolution in America: Documents on the Colonial Crisis of 1689*. New York: Norton, 1964.

Hambrick-Stowe, Charles E. *Early New England Meditative Poetry: Anne Bradstreet and Edward Taylor*. New York: Paulist Press, 1988.

———. *The Practice of Piety: Puritan Devotional Disciplines in Seventeenth-Century New England*. Chapel Hill: University of North Carolina Press, 1982.

———. "The Spirit of the Old Writers: The Great Awakening and the Persistence of Puritan Piety." In Francis J. Bremer, ed., *Puritanism: Transatlantic Perspectives on a Seventeenth-Century Anglo-American Faith*, pp. 277–91. Boston: Massachusetts Historical Society, 1993.

Hamilton, Edward Pierce, ed. "The Diary of a Colonial Clergyman, Peter Thacher of Milton." *MHSP* 71 (1959): 50–63.

Harlan, David. *The Clergy and the Great Awakening in New England*. Ann Arbor, Mich.: UMI Research Press, 1980.

Harper, George W. "Clericalism and Revival: The Great Awakening in Boston as a Pastoral Phenomenon." *NEQ* 57 (1984): 554–66.

Harris, Cole. "European Beginnings in the Northwest Atlantic: A Comparative View." In David D. Hall and David Grayson Allen, eds., *Seventeenth-Century New England*, pp. 119–52. Colonial Society of Massachusetts Publications, Vol. 63. Boston, 1984.

———. "The Simplification of Europe Overseas." *Annals of the Association of American Geographers* 67 (1977): 469–83.

Haskins, George Lee. *Law and Authority in Early Massachusetts: A Study in Tradition and Design*. New York: Macmillan, 1960.

Heimert, Alan, and Andrew Delbanco, eds. *The Puritans in America: A Narrative Anthology*. Cambridge, Mass.: Harvard University Press, 1985.

Heimert, Alan, and Perry Miller, eds. *The Great Awakening: Documents Illustrating the Crisis and Its Consequences*. Indianapolis: Bobbs-Merrill, 1967.

Heyrman, Christine Leigh. *Commerce and Culture: The Maritime Communities of Colonial Massachusetts, 1690–1750*. New York: Norton, 1984.

Hill, Christopher. *The World Turned Upside Down: Radical Ideas During the English Revolution*. New York: Viking, 1972.

Hill, Hamilton Andrews. *History of the Old South Church (Third Church), Boston, 1669–1884*. 2 Vols. Boston: Houghton Mifflin, 1890.

Hill, Hamilton Andrews, and George Frederick Bigelow, comps. *An Historical Catalogue of the Old South Church (Third Church), Boston*. Boston: privately printed, 1883.

Holifield, E. Brooks. *The Covenant Sealed: The Development of Puritan Sacramental Theology in Old and New England, 1570–1720*. New Haven: Yale University Press, 1974.

Hollinger, David A. "T. S. Kuhn's Theory of Science and Its Implications for History." *American Historical Review* 78 (1973): 370–93.

Hooker, Richard. *The Laws of Ecclesiastical Polity* (1593). Ed. Ernest Rhys. 2 vols. London: Everyman, 1925.

Hooker, Thomas. *Thomas Hooker: Writings in England and Holland, 1626–1633.* Ed. George H. Williams. Cambridge, Mass.: Harvard University Press, 1975.

Hoopes, James, ed. *Sources for 'The New England Mind: The Seventeenth Century' by Perry Miller.* Williamsburg, Virginia: Institute of Early American History and Culture, 1981.

Hubbard, William. *The Present State of New-England* (1677). Reprint. Introd. Cecelia Tichi. Bainbridge, N.Y.: York Mail-Print, 1972.

Hull, John. "The Diaries of John Hull, Mint-Master and Treasurer of the Colony of Massachusetts Bay." *Transactions and Collections of the American Antiquarian Society* 3 (1857): 109–316.

Hutchinson, Thomas, ed. *A Collection of Original Papers Relative to the History of the Colony of Massachusets-Bay.* Boston, 1769.

Innes, Stephen. *Creating the Commonwealth: The Economic Culture of Puritan New England.* New York: Norton, 1995.

———. *Labor in a New Land: Economy and Society in Seventeenth-Century Springfield.* Princeton, N.J.: Princeton University Press, 1983.

Jedrey, Christopher M. *The World of John Cleaveland: Family and Community in Eighteenth-Century New England.* New York: Norton, 1979.

Jeffries, John W. "The Separation in the Canterbury Church: Religion, Family, and Politics in a Connecticut Town." *NEQ* 52 (1979): 522–49.

Johnson, Edward. *Johnson's Wonder-Working Providence, 1628–1651.* Ed. J. Franklin Jameson. Original Narratives of Early American History. New York: Scribner's, 1910.

Johnson, Richard R. *Adjustment to Empire: The New England Colonies, 1675–1715.* New Brunswick, N.J.: Rutgers University Press, 1981.

———. *John Nelson, Merchant Adventurer: A Life Between Empires.* New York: Oxford University Press, 1991.

Jones, E. Alfred. *The Old Silver of American Churches.* Letchworth, England: privately printed for the National Society of Colonial Dames at Arden Press, 1913.

Jones, James W. *The Shattered Synthesis: New England Puritanism Before the Great Awakening.* New Haven: Yale University Press, 1973.

Judd, Sylvester. *History of Hadley: Including the Early History of Hatfield, South Hadley, Amherst and Granby, Massachusetts.* Northampton, Mass.: Metcalf, 1863.

Juster, Susan. *Disorderly Women: Sexual Politics and Evangelicalism in Revolutionary New England.* Ithaca: Cornell University Press, 1994.

Kellaway, William. *The New England Company, 1649–1776.* London: Longmans, 1961.

Keller, Karl. *The Example of Edward Taylor.* Amherst: University of Massachusetts Press, 1975.

Knight, Janice. *Orthodoxies in Massachusetts: Rereading American Puritanism.* Cambridge, Mass.: Harvard University Press, 1994.

Knight, Sarah Kemble. "The Journal of Madam Knight" (1704). In Perry Miller and Thomas Johnson, eds., *The Puritans,* 2:425–47. 2 vols. Rev. ed. New York: Harper & Row, 1963.

Knott, John R. " 'A Suffering People': Bunyan and the Language of Martyrdom." In Francis J. Bremer, ed., *Puritanism: Transatlantic Perspectives on a Seventeenth-Century Anglo-American Faith*, pp. 88–123. Boston: Massachusetts Historical Society, 1993.

Konig, David T. *Law and Society in Puritan Massachusetts: Essex County, 1629–1692*. Chapel Hill: University of North Carolina Press, 1979.

Kuhn, Thomas S. *The Structure of Scientific Revolutions*. 2d ed. Chicago: University of Chicago Press, 1970.

Kupperman, Karen Ordahl. "Climate and Mastery of the Wilderness in Seventeenth-Century New England." In David D. Hall and David Grayson Allen, eds., *Seventeenth-Century New England*, pp. 3–38. Colonial Society of Massachusetts Publications, vol. 63. Boston, 1984.

Lakatos, Imre, and Alan Musgrave, eds. *Criticism and the Growth of Knowledge*. Cambridge: Cambridge University Press, 1970.

Lake, Peter. "Defining Puritanism—Again?" In Francis J. Bremer, ed., *Puritanism: Transatlantic Perspectives on a Seventeenth-Century Anglo-American Faith*, pp. 3–29. Boston: Massachusetts Historical Society, 1993.

———. "The Laudian Style in the Church of England." Paper presented at the British History Workshop, Harvard University, October 22, 1991.

Langdon, George D., Jr. *Pilgrim Colony: A History of New Plymouth, 1620–1691*. New Haven: Yale University Press, 1966.

Lechford, Thomas. *Plain Dealing; or, News from New England*. London, 1642.

Leonard, Nathaniel. "A Brief Account of the Late Revival of Religion in Plymouth; the First Settled Town in New-England." *The Christian History* 2 (Boston, 1745): 313–17.

Levin, David. *Cotton Mather: The Young Life of the Lord's Remembrancer, 1663–1703*. Cambridge, Mass.: Harvard University Press, 1978.

Lewalski, Barbara Kiefer. *Protestant Poetics and the Seventeenth-Century Lyric*. Princeton, N.J.: Princeton University Press, 1979.

Lockridge, Kenneth A. *A New England Town, the First Hundred Years: Dedham, Massachusetts, 1636–1736*. New York: Norton, 1970.

Lockwood, John H. *Westfield and Its Historic Influences, 1669–1919*. 2 vols. Springfield, Mass.: privately printed, 1922.

Lord, Arthur. "Remarks . . . on Certain Charges Against the Rev. John Cotton of Plymouth." Colonial Society of Massachusetts Publications, vol. 26 (1927): 79–81.

Lovejoy, David S. *The Glorious Revolution in America*. Rev. ed. Middletown, Conn.: Wesleyan University Press, 1987.

Lovelace, Richard F. *The American Pietism of Cotton Mather: Origins of American Evangelicalism*. Grand Rapids, Mich.: Wm. B. Eerdmans, 1979.

Lowance, Mason I., Jr. *Increase Mather*. New York: Twayne, 1974.

Lowrie, Ernest Benson. *The Shape of the Puritan Mind: The Thought of Samuel Willard*. New Haven: Yale University Press, 1974.

Lucas, Paul R. *Valley of Discord: Church and Society along the Connecticut River, 1636–1725*. Hanover, N.H.: University Press of New England, 1976.

————. "Colony or Commonwealth: Massachusetts Bay, 1661–1666." *WMQ* 24 (1967): 88–107.

MacFarlane, Alan. *The Family Life of Ralph Josselin, a Seventeenth-Century Clergyman.* Cambridge: Cambridge University Press, 1970.

Mann, Bruce H. *Neighbors and Strangers: Law and Community in Early Connecticut.* Chapel Hill: University of North Carolina Press, 1987.

Mares, Jeffrey Scott. "Cotton Mather's 'Problema Theologicum': An Authoritative Edition." *AASP* 104, part 2 (1994): 333–440.

Martin, John Frederick. *Profits in the Wilderness: Entrepreneurship and the Founding of New England Towns in the Seventeenth Century.* Chapel Hill: University of North Carolina Press, 1991.

Mather, Cotton. *The Diary of Cotton Mather*, 2 vols. *MHSC*, 7th ser., 7–8 (1911–1912). Reprint. New York: Frederick Ungar, [1957].

————. *Magnalia Christi Americana, or the Ecclesiastical History of New England* (1702). Ed. Thomas Robbins. 2 vols. Hartford, Conn., 1853.

————. *Magnalia Christi Americana, Books I-II.* Ed. Kenneth B. Murdock. Cambridge, Mass.: Harvard University Press, 1977.

————. *Parentator: Memories of Remarkables in the Life and Death of the Ever-Memorable Dr. Increase Mather.* Boston, 1724.

Mather, Increase. "An Apologetical Preface." In John Davenport, *Another Essay for the Investigation of the Truth.* Cambridge, Mass., 1663.

————. "Autobiography of Increase Mather." Ed. Michael G. Hall. *AASP* 71, part 2 (1961): 271–360.

————. *The Order of the Gospel, Professed and Practised by the Churches of Christ in New England.* Boston, 1700.

————. "A Vindication of New England." In W. H. Whitmore, ed., *The Andros Tracts,* 2:19–78. 3 vols. Prince Society Publications, 5–7. Boston, 1868–74.

"The Mather Papers." *MHSC*, 4th ser., 8 (1868).

McIntyre, Ruth A. "John Pynchon and the New England Fur Trade, 1652–1676." In Carl Bridenbaugh, ed., *The Pynchon Papers,* 2:3–70. 2 vols. Colonial Society of Massachusetts Publications, vols. 60–61. Boston, 1985.

————. *William Pynchon: Merchant and Colonizer, 1590–1662.* Springfield, Mass.: Connecticut Valley Historical Museum, 1961.

Melvoin, Richard I. *New England Outpost: War and Society in Colonial Deerfield.* New York: Norton, 1989.

Middlekauff, Robert. *The Mathers: Three Generations of Puritan Intellectuals, 1596–1728.* New York: Oxford University Press, 1971.

Miller, J. Hillis. "Narrative." In Frank Lentricchia and Thomas McLaughlin, eds., *Critical Terms for Literary Study*, pp. 66–79. Chicago: University of Chicago Press, 1990.

Miller, Perry. *Errand Into the Wilderness.* Cambridge, Mass.: Harvard University Press, 1956.

————. *Nature's Nation.* Cambridge, Mass.: Harvard University Press, 1967.

————. *The New England Mind: From Colony to Province*. Cambridge, Mass.: Harvard University Press, 1953.

————. *The New England Mind: The Seventeenth Century*. Cambridge, Mass.: Harvard University Press, 1939.

————. *Orthodoxy in Massachusetts, 1630–1650*. Cambridge, Mass.: Harvard University Press, 1933.

————. "Preface to the Beacon Press Edition." In *The New England Mind: From Colony to Province*. Boston: Beacon Press, 1961.

————. "Review of *The New Haven Colony*, by Isabel M. Calder." *NEQ* 8 (1935): 582–84.

Moran, Gerald F. "The Puritan Saint: Religious Experience, Church Membership, and Piety in Connecticut, 1636–1776." Ph.D. diss., Rutgers University, 1974.

————. "Religious Renewal, Puritan Tribalism, and the Family in Seventeenth-Century Milford, Connecticut." *WMQ* 36 (1979): 236–54.

Moran, Gerald F., and Maris A. Vinovskis. *Religion, Family, and the Life Course: Explorations in the Social History of Early America*. Ann Arbor: University of Michigan Press, 1992.

Morgan, Edmund S. *The Gentle Puritan: A Life of Ezra Stiles, 1727–1795*. Chapel Hill: University of North Carolina Press, 1962.

————. *The Puritan Dilemma: The Story of John Winthrop*. Boston: Little, Brown, 1958.

————. *The Puritan Family: Religion and Domestic Relations in Seventeenth-Century New England*. Rev. ed. New York: Harper & Row, 1966.

————. *Visible Saints: The History of a Puritan Idea*. New York: New York University Press, 1963.

Morison, Samuel Eliot. *Builders of the Bay Colony*. Rev. ed. Boston: Houghton Mifflin, 1958.

————. *The Founding of Harvard College*. Vol. 1 of *The Tercentennial History of Harvard College and University, 1636–1936*. Cambridge, Mass.: Harvard University Press, 1935.

————. *Harvard College in the Seventeenth Century*. Vols. 2 and 3 of *The Tercentennial History of Harvard College and University, 1636–1936*. Cambridge, Mass.: Harvard University Press, 1936.

————. "New Light Wanted on the Old Colony." *WMQ* 15 (1958): 359–64.

Mosely, James G. *John Winthrop's World*. Madison: University of Wisconsin Press, 1992.

Murdock, Kenneth B. *Increase Mather, the Foremost American Puritan*. Cambridge, Mass.: Harvard University Press, 1925.

Murrin, John M. "Anglicizing an American Colony: The Transformation of Provincial Massachusetts." Ph.D. diss., Yale University, 1966.

————. "The Legal Transformation: The Bench and Bar of Eighteenth-Century Massachusetts." In Stanley N. Katz, ed., *Colonial America: Essays in Politics and Social Development*, 415–49. Boston: Little, Brown, 1971.

Naeher, Robert James. "Dialogue in the Wilderness: John Eliot and the Indian Exploration of Puritanism as a Source of Meaning, Comfort, and Ethnic Survival." *NEQ* 62 (1989): 346–68.

Nance, Donna. "Daniel Henchman." In Benjamin Franklin V, ed., *Boston Printers, Publishers, and Booksellers: 1640–1800*, pp. 284–91. Boston: G.K. Hall, 1980.

Nash, Gary B. *The Urban Crucible: Social Change, Political Consciousness, and the Origins of the American Revolution.* Cambridge, Mass.: Harvard University Press, 1979.

Nelson, William E. *Dispute and Conflict Resolution in Plymouth County, Massachusetts, 1725–1825.* Chapel Hill: University of North Carolina Press, 1981.

New England Company Ledger. Massachusetts Historical Society. Boston, Massachusetts.

Nordbeck, Elizabeth C. "Almost Awakened: The Great Revival in New Hampshire and Maine, 1727–1748." *Historical New Hampshire* 35 (1980): 23–58.

Norton, John. *Abel Being Dead, Yet Speaketh* (1658). Reprint. Introd. Edward J. Gallagher. Delmar, N.Y.: Scholars' Facsimiles and Reprints, 1978.

————. *The Orthodox Evangelist* (1654). Reprint. Library of American Puritan Writings, ed. Sacvan Bercovitch. Vol. 11. New York: AMS Press, 1982.

————. *Sion the Outcast Healed of Her Wounds* (1661). In *Three Choice and Profitable Sermons.* Cambridge, Mass., 1663.

Norton, Mary Beth, David M. Katzman, Paul D. Escott, Howard P. Chudacoff, Thomas G. Paterson, William M. Tuttle Jr., and William J. Brophy. *A People and a Nation: A History of the United States.* Brief ed. Boston: Houghton Mifflin, 1991.

Oakes, Urian. *New England Pleaded With, and Pressed to Consider the Things Which Concern Her Peace.* Cambridge, Mass., 1673.

Oberholzer, Emil, Jr. *Delinquent Saints: Disciplinary Action in the Early Congregational Churches of Massachusetts.* New York: Columbia University Press, 1956.

O'Brien, Susan. "A Transatlantic Community of Saints: The Great Awakening and the First Evangelical Network, 1735–1755." *American Historical Review* 91 (1986): 811–32.

Onuf, Peter S. "New Lights in New London: A Group Portrait of the Separatists." *WMQ* 37 (1980): 627–43.

Owen, John. *The Correspondence of John Owen (1616–1683), with an Account of His Life and Work.* Ed. Peter Toon. Cambridge: James Clarke, 1970.

Paine, Gustavus Swift. "Ungodly Carriages on Cape Cod." *NEQ* 25 (1952): 181–98.

Pemberton, Ebenezer. *Sermons and Discourses on Several Occasions.* London, 1727.

Pestana, Carla Gardina. *Quakers and Baptists in Colonial Massachusetts.* Cambridge: Cambridge University Press, 1991.

Peters, Hugh. *A Dying Father's Last Legacy to an Only Child* (1649). Reprint. Boston, 1717.

Peterson, Mark A. "Ordinary Preaching and the Interpretation of the Salem Witchcraft Crisis by the Boston Clergy." *Essex Institute Historical Collections* 129 (1993): 84–102.

————. "The Plymouth Church and the Evolution of Puritan Religious Culture." *NEQ* 66 (1993): 570–93.

————. "Puritanism and Gentility in Early New England: Reflections on Communion Silver." In *Silver and Silversmithing in Colonial New England.* Colonial Society of Massachusetts Publications. Boston, forthcoming.

Pettit, Norman. *The Heart Prepared: Grace and Conversion in Puritan Spiritual Life*. New Haven: Yale University Press, 1966.

Pierce, Richard D., ed. *The Records of the First Church in Boston, 1630–1868*. 3 vols. Colonial Society of Massachusetts Publications, vols. 39–41. Boston, 1961.

Plooij, Daniel. *The Pilgrim Fathers from a Dutch Point of View*. New York: New York University Press, 1932.

Plumstead, A.W., ed. *The Wall and the Garden: Selected Massachusetts Election Sermons, 1670– 1775*. Minneapolis: University of Minnesota Press, 1968.

Plymouth Church Records, 1620–1859. Ed. Arthur Lord. 2 vols. Colonial Society of Massachusetts Publications, vols. 22–23. Boston, 1920–23.

Pope, Robert G. *The Halfway Covenant: Church Membership in Puritan New England*. Princeton, N.J.: Princeton University Press, 1969.

————. "New England Versus the New England Mind: The Myth of Declension." *Journal of Social History* 3 (1969): 95–108.

Porterfield, Amanda. *Female Piety in Puritan New England: The Emergence of Religious Humanism*. New York: Oxford University Press, 1992.

Powell, Sumner Chilton. *Puritan Village: the Formation of a New England Town*. Middletown, Conn.: Wesleyan University Press, 1963.

Powell, Walter Louis, ed. "Edward Taylor's Westfield: An Edition of the Westfield 'Town Records.' " Ph.D. diss., Kent State University, 1982.

Prince, Thomas. *A Chronological History of New-England in the Form of Annals* (1736). Reprint. Boston: Cummings, Hilliard, 1826.

————. "Diary of the Rev. Thomas Prince, 1737." Ed. Albert Matthews. Colonial Society of Massachusetts Publications, vol. 19. Boston, 1918: 331–65.

————. *Earthquakes the Works of God and Tokens of his Just Displeasure*. Boston, 1727.

————. "The Endless Increase of Christ's Government." In *Six Sermons by the Late Thomas Prince*. Edinburgh, 1785.

————. *A Funeral Sermon on the Reverend Mr. Nathaniel Williams*. Boston, 1738.

————. *The People of New-England Put in Mind of the Righteous Acts of the Lord to Them and Their Fathers*. Boston, 1730.

————. *A Sermon Delivered by Thomas Prince . . . at his Ordination*. Boston, 1718.

————. "Some Account of the Late Revival of Religion in Boston." *The Christian History* 2 (Boston, 1745): 374–415.

————. *Vade Mecum for America: or, A Companion for Traders and Travellers*. Boston, 1731.

Pruitt, Betty Hobbs. "Self-Sufficiency and the Agricultural Economy of Eighteenth-Century Massachusetts." *WMQ* 41 (1984): 333–64.

Raimo, John William. "Spiritual Harvest: The Anglo-American Revival in Boston, Massachusetts, and Bristol, England, 1739–42." Ph.D. diss., University of Wisconsin, 1974.

Ramsbottom, Mary MacManus. "Religious Society and the Family in Charlestown, Massachusetts, 1630–1740." Ph.D. diss., Yale University, 1987.

Records of Old South Church and Congregation, 1669–1766. Records of the Old South Church, Boston. Congregational Library. Boston, Massachusetts. Microfilm.

Restad, Penne. *Christmas in America: A History.* New York: Oxford University Press, 1995.

Robbins, Chandler [of Plymouth]. *A Reply to Some Essays Lately Published by John Cotton, Esq.* Boston, 1773.

———. *Some Brief Remarks on a Piece Published by John Cotton.* Boston, 1774.

Robbins, Chandler [of Boston]. *A History of the Second Church, or Old North, in Boston.* Boston, 1852.

Roberts, Oliver Ayer. *History of . . . the Ancient and Honorable Artillery Company of Massachusetts, 1637–1888.* 4 vols. Boston: A. Mudge, 1895–1901.

Roe, Albert S., and Robert F. Trent. "Robert Sanderson and the Founding of the Boston Silversmiths' Trade." In *New England Begins: The Seventeenth Century,* 3:480–500. 3 vols. Boston: Museum of Fine Arts, 1982.

Ronda, James P. "Generations of Faith: The Christian Indians of Martha's Vineyard." *WMQ* 38 (1981): 369–94.

Rowe, Karen E. *Saint and Singer: Edward Taylor's Typology and the Poetics of Meditation.* Cambridge: Cambridge University Press, 1986.

Rowlandson, Mary. "The Sovereignty and Goodness of God" (1682). In Alden T. Vaughan and Edward W. Clark, eds., *Puritans Among the Indians: Accounts of Captivity and Redemption, 1676–1724,* pp. 29–75. Cambridge, Mass.: Harvard University Press, 1981.

Rutman, Darrett B. "Assessing the Little Communities of Early America." *WMQ* 43 (1986): 163–78.

———. *Husbandmen of Plymouth: Farms and Villages in the Old Colony, 1620–1692.* Boston: Plimouth Plantation, Beacon, 1967.

———. *Winthrop's Boston: Portrait of a Puritan Town, 1630–1649.* Chapel Hill: University of North Carolina Press, 1965.

Sargent, Mark L. "William Bradford's 'Dialogue' with History." *NEQ* 65 (1992): 389–421.

Savage, James. *A Genealogical Dictionary of the First Settlers of New England.* 2 vols. Boston: Little, Brown, 1860.

Scheick, William J. *The Will and the Word: The Poetry of Edward Taylor.* Athens: University of Georgia Press, 1974.

Schmidt, Leigh Eric. *Consumer Rites: The Buying and Selling of American Holidays.* Princeton, N. J.: Princeton University Press, 1995.

———. *Holy Fairs: Scottish Communions and American Revivals in the Early Modern Period.* Princeton, N. J.: Princeton University Press, 1989.

———. " 'A Second and Glorious Reformation': The New Light Extremism of Andrew Croswell." *WMQ* 43 (1986): 214–44.

Schuldiner, Michael. "The Rise of Consciousness: The Sacramental Debate Between Edward Taylor and Solomon Stoddard." In *Gifts and Works: The Post-Conversion Paradigm and Spiritual Controversy in Seventeenth-Century Massachusetts.* Macon, Georgia: Mercer University Press, 1991.

Schweninger, Lee. *John Winthrop.* Boston: Twayne, 1990.

Scobey, David M. "Revising the Errand: New England's Ways and the Puritan Sense of the Past." *WMQ* 41 (1984): 3–31.

Scottow, Joshua. *A Narrative of the Planting of the Massachusetts Colony*. Boston, 1694.

———. *Old Men's Tears for Their Own Declensions* (1691). Reprint. Boston, 1733.

Second Congregational Church, Newport, Rhode Island. Record Book, 1725–1772, and Second Congregational Church Records, 1728–[?]. Ms. Vols. 836E and 838B. Newport Historical Society. Newport, Rhode Island.

Selement, George. *Keepers of the Vineyard: The Puritan Ministry and Collective Culture in Colonial New England*. Lanham, Maryland: University Press of America, 1984.

———. "Publication and the Puritan Minister." *WMQ* 37 (1980): 219–41.

Sellar, W. C., and R. J. Yeatman. *1066 and All That*. London: Methuen, 1930.

Sewall, Joseph. *Christ Victorious over the Powers of Darkness, by the Light of His Preached Gospel*. Boston, 1733.

———. *The Duty, Character and Reward of Christ's Faithful Servants, . . . Preached . . . after the Funeral of the Reverend Mr. Thomas Prince*. Boston, 1758.

———. *The Holy Spirit the Gift of God our Heavenly Father, to them that Ask Him*. Boston, 1728.

Sewall, Samuel. *The Diary of Samuel Sewall, 1674–1729*. Ed. M. Halsey Thomas. 2 vols. New York: Farrar, Straus, and Giroux, 1973.

———. "Letter-Book of Samuel Sewall." 2 vols. *MHSC*, 6th ser., 1–2. Boston, 1886–1888.

———. *Phaenomena Quaedam Apocalyptica Ad Aspectum Novi Orbis Configurata*. 2d ed. Boston, 1727.

Shea, Daniel B. *Spiritual Autobiography in Early America*. Rev. ed. Madison: University of Wisconsin Press, 1988.

Shepard, Thomas. *The Church Membership of Children and their Right to Baptism*. Cambridge, Mass., 1662.

———. *God's Plot: The Paradoxes of Puritan Piety, Being the Autobiography and Journal of Thomas Shepard*. Ed. Michael McGiffert. Amherst: University of Massachusetts Press, 1972.

———. *The Parable of the Ten Virgins Opened and Applied*. 1636–1640. Vol. 2 of *The Works of Thomas Shepard*. Ed. John Albro. Boston: Doctrinal Tract and Book Society, 1853. Reprint. New York: AMS Press, 1967.

———. *Thomas Shepard's Confessions*. Ed. George Selement and Bruce Woolley. Colonial Society of Massachusetts Publications, vol. 58. Boston, 1981.

Shepard, Thomas, Jr. *Eye-Salve, or a Watchword from our Lord Jesus Christ to His Churches*. Cambridge, Mass., 1673.

Shipton, Clifford K., *Biographical Sketches of Those Who Attended Harvard College*. Vols. 4–17 of *Sibley's Harvard Graduates*. Cambridge, Mass.: Harvard University Press, 1933; Boston: Massachusetts Historical Society, 1937–1970.

Shipton, Clifford K. and James E. Mooney. *National Index of American Imprints through 1800: The Short-Title Evans*. 2 vols. Worcester, Mass.: American Antiquarian Society, 1969.

Sibley, John Langdon. *Biographical Sketches of Graduates of Harvard University*. 3 vols. Cambridge, Mass.: Charles William Sever, 1873–1885.

Silver, Rollo G. "Publishing in Boston, 1726–1757: The Accounts of Daniel Henchman." *AASP* 66 (1956): 17–36.

Silverman, Kenneth. *The Life and Times of Cotton Mather*. New York: Harper and Row, 1984.

Simmons, Richard C. "The Founding of the Third Church in Boston." *WMQ* 26 (1969): 241–52.

Smith, Daniel Scott. "The Demographic History of Colonial New England." *Journal of Economic History* 32 (1972): 165–83.

Smith, Joseph H., ed. *Colonial Justice in Western Massachusetts (1639–1702): The Pynchon Court Record*. Cambridge, Mass., 1961.

Smolinski, Reiner, ed. *The Threefold Paradise of Cotton Mather: An Edition of "Triparadisus."* Athens: University of Georgia Press, 1995.

"South Church Booke for Sacramental Contributions, 1708." Records of Sacramental Contributions, 1708–1798. Records of the Old South Church, Boston. C SAC I, Shelf 7. Congregational Library. Boston, Massachusetts. Microfilm.

Spaeth, Donald Arragon. "Parsons and Parishioners: Lay-Clerical Conflict and Popular Piety in Wiltshire Villages, 1660–1740." Ph.D. diss., Brown University, 1985.

Spencer, Ivor Debenham. "Christmas, the Upstart." *NEQ* 8 (1935): 498–517.

Spufford, Margaret. *Contrasting Communities: English Villagers in the Sixteenth and Seventeenth Centuries*. Cambridge: Cambridge University Press, 1974.

Stanford, Donald E. "Edward Taylor Versus the 'Young Cockerill' Benjamin Ruggles: A Hitherto Unpublished Episode from the Annals of Early New England Church History." *NEQ* 44 (1971): 459–68.

Starr, Kevin. *Americans and the California Dream, 1850–1915*. New York: Oxford University Press, 1973.

Stavely, Keith W. F. "Roger Williams and the Enclosed Gardens of New England." In Francis J. Bremer, ed., *Puritanism: Transatlantic Perspectives on a Seventeenth-Century Anglo-American Faith*, pp. 257–74. Boston: Massachusetts Historical Society, 1993.

Stearns, Raymond P. *The Strenuous Puritan: Hugh Peters, 1598–1660*. Urbana: University of Illinois Press, 1954.

Stiles, Ezra. *A Discourse on the Christian Union*. Boston, 1761.

Stiles, Henry R. *History and Genealogy of Ancient Windsor*. New York, 1859.

Stoddard, Solomon. *The Doctrine of the Instituted Churches Explained and Improved from the Word of God*. London, 1700.

Stoever, William K. B. *'A Faire and Easie Way to Heaven': Covenant Theology and Antinomianism in Early Massachusetts*. Middletown, Conn.: Wesleyan University Press, 1978.

Stout, Harry S. *The Divine Dramatist: George Whitefield and the Rise of Modern Evangelicalism*. Grand Rapids, Mich.: William B. Eerdmans, 1991.

———. *The New England Soul: Preaching and Religious Culture in Colonial New England*. New York: Oxford University Press, 1986.

Stout, Harry S., and Peter Onuf. "James Davenport and the Great Awakening in New London." *Journal of American History* 71 (1983): 556–78.

Street, Nicholas, in the Name of the Church at New Haven, to the First Church in Boston. 12 October 1668. Two Letters concerning John Davenport. Records of the Old South Church, Boston. Shelf 13. Congregational Library. Boston, Massachusetts.

Sweeney, Kevin. "River Gods and Related Minor Deities: The Williams Family and the Connecticut River Valley, 1637–1790." Ph.D. diss., Yale University, 1986.

Taylor, Edward. *Christographia*. Ed. Norman S. Grabo. New Haven: Yale University Press, 1962.

———. Commonplace Book. Notebook containing entries and copies of papers from 1638 to 1725. Massachusetts Historical Society. Boston, Massachusetts. Microfilm.

———. *The Diary of Edward Taylor*. Ed. Francis Murphy. Springfield, Mass.: Connecticut Valley Historical Museum, 1964.

———. *Edward Taylor vs. Solomon Stoddard: The Nature of the Lord's Supper*. Ed. Thomas M. and Virginia L. Davis. Vol. 2 of *The Unpublished Writings of Edward Taylor*. Boston: Twayne Publishers, 1981.

———. *Edward Taylor's "Church Records" and Related Sermons*. Ed. Thomas M. and Virginia L. Davis. Vol 1. of *The Unpublished Writings of Edward Taylor*. Boston: Twayne Publishers, 1981.

———. "Edward Taylor's Elegy on Deacon David Dewey." Ed. Thomas M. Davis. *AASP* 96 (1986): 75–84.

———. *Edward Taylor's Minor Poetry*. Ed. Thomas M. and Virginia L. Davis. Vol. 3 of *The Unpublished Writings of Edward Taylor*. Boston: Twayne Publishers, 1981.

———. *Edward Taylor's Treatise Concerning the Lord's Supper*. Ed. Norman S. Grabo. East Lansing: Michigan State University Press, 1966.

———. *The Poems of Edward Taylor*. Ed. Donald E. Stanford. New Haven: Yale University Press, 1960.

———. *A Transcript of Edward Taylor's Metrical History of Christianity*. Ed. Donald E. Stanford. Facsimile Reprint. Ann Arbor, Mich.: University Microfilms, 1978.

———. *Upon the Types of the Old Testament*. Ed. Charles W. Mignon. 2 vols. Lincoln: University of Nebraska Press, 1989.

Taylor, Jeremy. *The Worthy Communicant, or, A Discourse of the Nature, Effects, and Blessings Consequent to the Worthy Receiving of the Lords Supper*. London, 1661.

Taylor, Mark William. "Regional Diversity in a New England Microcosm: Seventeenth-Century Hampshire County, Massachusetts." Unpublished paper, Historic Deerfield Summer Institute, 1988.

Thayer, Eli. *The New England Emigrant Aid Company*. Worcester: E.P. Rice, 1887.

Thompson, Roger. *Mobility and Migration: East Anglian Founders of New England, 1629–1640*. Amherst: University of Massachusetts Press, 1994.

Thwing, Annie Haven. *The Crooked & Narrow Streets of the Town of Boston, 1630–1822*. Boston: Marshall Jones, 1920.

Tipson, Baird. "Invisible Saints: The 'Judgment of Charity' in the Early New England Churches." *Church History* 44 (1975): 1–12.

Todd, Margo. "Puritan Self-Fashioning." In Francis J. Bremer, ed., *Puritanism: Transatlantic Perspectives on a Seventeenth-Century Anglo-American Faith*, pp. 57–87. Boston: Massachusetts Historical Society, 1993.

Toulouse, Teresa. *The Art of Prophesying: New England Sermons and the Shaping of Belief*. Athens: University of Georgia Press, 1987.

Tracy, Joseph. *The Great Awakening: A History of the Revival of Religion in the Time of Edwards and Whitefield*. Boston: Tappan and Dennett, 1842.

Tracy, Patricia J. *Jonathan Edwards, Pastor: Religion and Society in Eighteenth-Century Northampton*. New York: Hill and Wang, 1979.

Trumbull, James R. *History of Northampton*. 2 vols. Northampton, Mass.: Gazette Printing, 1898–1902.

Tucker, Bruce. "The Reinvention of New England, 1691–1770." *NEQ* 59 (1986): 315–40.

Twitchell, Joseph. *John Winthrop: First Governor of the Massachusetts Colony*. New York: Dodd, Mead, 1891.

Updegraff, Harlan. *The Origins of the Moving School in Massachusetts*. Reprint. New York: Arno Press, 1969.

Updike, Wilkins. *History of the Episcopal Church in Narragansett, Rhode Island*. New York: Henry M. Onderdonk, 1847.

Van De Wetering, John E. "Thomas Prince: Puritan Polemicist." Ph.D. diss., University of Washington, 1959.

Van Dyken, Seymour. *Samuel Willard, 1640–1707: Preacher of Orthodoxy in an Era of Change*. Grand Rapids, Mich.: Wm. B. Eerdmans, 1972.

Vickers, Daniel. "Competency and Competition: Economic Culture in Early America." *WMQ* 47 (1990): 3–29.

———. *Farmers and Fishermen: Two Centuries of Work in Essex County, Massachusetts, 1630–1830*. Chapel Hill: University of North Carolina Press, 1994.

Walker, Williston. *The Creeds and Platforms of Congregationalism* (1893). Reprint. Introd. Douglas Horton. Boston: Pilgrim Press, 1960.

Walsh, James. "The Great Awakening in the First Congregational Church of Woodbury, Connecticut." *WMQ* 28 (1971): 543–62.

Ward, Barbara McLean. " 'In a Feasting Posture': Communion Vessels and Community Values in Seventeenth- and Eighteenth-Century New England." *Winterthur Portfolio* 23 (1988): 1–24.

Ward, Nathaniel. *The Simple Cobler of Aggawam in America* (1648). Reprint. Boston, 1713.

Weber, Donald. *Rhetoric and History in Revolutionary New England*. New York: Oxford University Press, 1988.

Weis, Frederick Lewis. *The Colonial Clergy and the Colonial Churches of New England*. Publications of the Society of the Descendants of the Colonial Clergy, vol. 2. Lancaster, Mass., 1936.

Wendell, Barrett. *Cotton Mather, The Puritan Priest*. New York: Dodd, Mead, 1891.

Westerkamp, Marilyn J. *Triumph of the Laity: Scots-Irish Piety and the Great Awakening, 1625–1760*. New York: Oxford University Press, 1988.

White, Hayden. *Metahistory: The Historical Imagination in Nineteenth-Century Europe*. Baltimore: Johns Hopkins University Press, 1973.

Whitefield, George. *George Whitefield's Journals*. London: Banner of Truth Trust, 1960.

Whitehill, Walter Muir. *Boston: A Topographical History*. 2d ed. Cambridge, Mass.: Harvard University Press, 1968.

Whitmore, W. H., ed. *The Andros Tracts*. 3 vols. Prince Society Publications, 5–7. Boston, 1868–74.

Wigglesworth, Michael. *The Day of Doom; or, A Poetical Description of the Great End and Last Judgment* (1662). Ed. Kenneth B. Murdock. New York: Spiral Press, 1929.

———. *The Diary of Michael Wigglesworth 1653–1657: The Conscience of a Puritan*. Ed. Edmund S. Morgan. New York: Harper Torchbooks, 1965.

Wigglesworth, Samuel. "An Essay for Reviving Religion" (1733). In *The Great Awakening: Documents Illustrating the Crisis and its Consequences*, pp. 3–7. Ed. Alan Heimert and Perry Miller. Indianapolis: Bobbs-Merrill, 1967.

Willard, Samuel. *All Plots against God and his People Detected and Defeated*. Boston, 1684.

———. *The Barren Fig Trees Doom*. Boston, 1691.

———. *Brief Directions to a Young Scholar Designing the Ministry, for the Study of Divinity*. Boston, 1735.

———. "A Brief Discourse Concerning that Ceremony of Laying the Hands on the Bible in Swearing." In W. H. Whitmore, ed., *The Andros Tracts*, 1:179–92. 3 vols. Prince Society Publications, 5–7. Boston, 1868–74.

———. *A Compleat Body of Divinity in Two Hundred and Fifty Expository Lectures on the Assembly's Shorter Catechism*. Boston, 1726.

———. *Covenant-Keeping the Way to Blessedness*. 1682. Published jointly with *The Child's Portion*. Boston, 1684.

———. *The Duty of a People that have Renewed their Covenant with God*. Boston, 1680.

———. *The High Esteem Which God hath of the Death of his Saints*. Boston, 1683.

———. *Impenitent Sinners Warned of their Misery and Summoned to Judgment*. Boston, 1698.

———. *Morality Not to be Relied on for Life*. Boston, 1700.

———. *Ne Sutor Ultra Crepidam: Or Brief Animadversions Upon the New England Anabaptists Late Fallacious Narrative*. Boston, 1681.

———. *The Necessity of Sincerity in Renewing the Covenant*. Boston, 1680.

———. *The Righteous Man's Death, a Presage of Evil Approaching*. Boston, 1684.

———. *A Sermon Preached upon Ezekiel 22:30, 31*. Boston, 1679.

———. *Several Brief Sacramental Meditations Preparatory for Communion*. Boston, 1711.

———. *The Sinfulness of Worshipping God with Men's Institutions*. Boston, 1691.

Williams, Raymond. *Keywords: A Vocabulary of Culture and Society*. Rev. ed. New York: Oxford University Press, 1983.

Willingham, William F. "Religious Conversion in the Second Society of Windham, Connecticut, 1723–43: A Case Study." *Societas* 6 (1976): 109–20.

Willison, George F. *Saints and Strangers.* New York: Reynal and Hitchcock, 1945.

Wilson, Douglas. "Web of Secrecy: Goffe, Whalley, and the Legend of Hadley." *NEQ* 60 (1987): 515–48.

Winship, George Parker. *A Representative Massachusetts Puritan, Increase Mather.* Cambridge, Mass.: Harvard University Press, 1931.

Winsor, Justin, ed. *A Memorial History of Boston.* 4 vols. Boston, 1880–81.

Winthrop, John. *The History of New England from 1630 to 1649.* Ed. James Savage. 2 vols. Boston, 1825. Reprint. New York: Arno Press, 1972.

———. "A Modell of Christian Charity." 1630. In *Winthrop Papers,* vol. 2, 1623–1630, pp. 282–95. Boston: Massachusetts Historical Society, 1931.

Winthrop, Wait Still. *Some Meditations Concerning Our Honorable Gentlemen and Fellow-Souldiers.* Boston, 1675.

The Winthrop Papers. 6 vols. to date. Boston: Massachusetts Historical Society, 1929– .

Wise, John. *The Churches Quarrel Espoused.* Boston, 1710.

———. *Vindication of the Government of New-England Churches.* Boston, 1717.

Withey, Lynne. *Urban Growth in Colonial Rhode Island.* Albany: State University of New York Press, 1984.

Wood, Joseph S. "Village and Community in Early Colonial New England." In Robert Blair St. George, ed., *Material Life in America, 1600–1800,* pp. 159–70. Boston: Northeastern University Press, 1988.

Worthley, Harold Field. *An Inventory of the Records of the Particular (Congregational) Churches of Massachusetts, Gathered 1620–1805.* Harvard Theological Studies 25. Cambridge, Mass.: Harvard University Press, 1970.

Youngs, J. William T., Jr. *God's Messengers: Religious Leadership in Colonial New England, 1700–1750.* Baltimore: Johns Hopkins University Press, 1976.

Ziff, Larzer. *The Career of John Cotton: Puritanism and the American Experience.* Princeton, N.J.: Princeton University Press, 1962.

———. "The Salem Puritans in the 'Free Aire of the New World.'" *Huntington Library Quarterly* 20 (1957): 373–84.

Zuckerman, Michael. *Peaceable Kingdoms: New England Towns in the Eighteenth Century.* New York: Knopf, 1970.

Index

In this index an "f" after a number indicates a separate reference on the next page, and an "ff" indicates separate references on the next two pages. A continuous discussion over two or more pages is indicated by a span of page numbers, e.g., "57–59." *Passim* is used for a cluster of references in close but not consecutive sequence.

Act of Uniformity, 24, 27, 56
Adams, William, 58
Allen, James, 27, 36, 46, 170
Allin, Edward, 71
Allin, John, 40
Ancient and Honourable Artillery Company, 70
Andros, Edmund, 148, 177–80
Anglicans, *see* Church of England
Antinomian controversy, 26, 74
Arminianism, 222
Ashley, David, 59, 99
Atlantic economy, 24f

Ballantine, John, 222f
Baptism, 29, 35, 105f, 129, 131
Baptists, 131, 164, 175
Belcher, Andrew, 87, 179
Belcher, Jonathan, 225f, 233f, 293–94n
Bellingham, Richard, 26, 41, 44, 46
Bennington, Vermont, 223
Biography, 12–15, 18, 75

Books, devotional, 1f, 81, 90–95, 138–40, 227f, 243n
Boston, Lincolnshire, 2
Boston, Massachusetts, 25, 96, 129, 140, 169; publishing in, 1, 91f, 138–40; economic development, 3, 70–74, 79; population, 38, 86; cultural conflict in, 174–84; as evangelical center, 185, 188, 229; Great Awakening in, 224–29. *See also* Third Church, Boston
Boston Latin School, 89
Boston Thursday Lecture, 32f, 79, 89
Bradford, William, 4–6, 13, 15, 17, 236
Bradstreet, Simon, 26, 30, 179
Brattle, Thomas, 69
Brattle, William, 134
Brattle Street Church, 169–72, 184, 222
Breck, Robert, 222
Brewer, Daniel, 196, 208, 213
Brewster, William, 13
Bromfield, Edward, 76, 78–80, 89f, 116, 174, 182, 187

Bromfield, Edward, Jr., 80
Brookfield, Massachusetts, 53
Bull, Nehemiah, 216f, 220f
Bunyan, John, 92, 111
Bush, Abigail Lee, 97, 194, 204
Bush, Samuel, 97, 202–5
Butcher, Allwin, 92
Butcher, Elizabeth, 92–95, 118, 226
Byfield, Nathaniel, 181

Cambridge, Massachusetts, 10, 56f
Cambridge Platform, 7, 11, 26, 49, 53, 63,
    121, 164, 209
Capitalism, see Commerce
Catechism, 92f, 127
Charity, 168f, 187f, 228f
Charles I, 8
Charles II, 24, 26f, 175f
Charlestown, Massachusetts, 41, 45
Charter, see Massachusetts Bay Charter
Chauncy, Charles, 45, 57
Chauncy, Nathaniel, 54
Chiever, Ezekiel, 87, 89, 167f
Chiever, Thomas, 167
Christian History, 224, 227f
Christmas, 173f, 182f
Church councils, 31, 37–40, 161, 166f, 200
Church covenants, 35, 41–42, 254n
Church discipline, 29, 36, 84–88, 191, 198f,
    202–13, 216, 287n
Church of England, 8, 10, 18, 24ff, 28, 111,
    176–84; in Boston, 74, 85, 89, 164f,
    171–80 passim
Church polity, 9, 21, 25f, 28, 121. See also
    Cambridge Platform; Congregational-
    ism; Presbyterianism
Clap, Nathaniel, 189, 232–33
Clark, William, 129
Cleaveland, John, 225
Clergy, 17, 20, 24, 120, 124–30, 138,
    140–44, 150, 227–29. See also individual
    clergymen by name
Clerical associations, 171–73, 283–84n
Clerical salaries, 2, 123–24, 128–29, 145,
    197, 274n. See also under individual clergy-
    men by name
Cole, Nathan, 226, 234

Colman, Benjamin, 90, 134, 170f, 184,
    187, 221
Commerce, 11, 16–20, 72–74, 234,
    268–69n
Communion, see Lord's Supper
Communion silver, 82–83, 113–14
Community, 16–17, 235, 239, 266n
Competency, 99, 103
Complacency, 110–11, 130, 156
Congregationalism, 8, 31, 37, 157, 172. See
    also Church polity; Presbyterianism
Connecticut, 27–28
Connecticut Valley, 52–53, 63, 66, 102, 156,
    213, 223–24
Consociations of churches, 172–73
Consumer culture, 271n
Conversion, narratives of, 35, 63, 107–12,
    131, 157, 270n, 273n
Cooke, Aaron, 59–63 passim
Cooper, William, 171
Cotton, John, 1–3, 13, 18f, 26, 32, 156, 178
Cotton, John, Jr., 138, 229
Cotton, Josiah, 189
Councils, church, see Church councils
Courts, see Hampshire County Court;
    Judicial system
Covenant renewal, 48, 131, 137, 176
Covenants, church, see Church covenants
Cromwell, Oliver, 148
Croswell, Andrew, 225
Cultural conflict, 181–84
Currency problems, 102–3
Curwin, George, 90

Dartmouth, Massachusetts, 228, 231f
Davenport, James, 225
Davenport, John, 8, 12, 18, 86, 130, 174,
    253n; and First Church schism, 27–49
    passim, 165–66; compared to Edward
    Taylor, 56, 65
Davis, William, 30, 39
Dawes, William, 70
Declension, 4–7, 12–19 passim, 244n
Deerfield, Massachusetts, 53, 97, 201
Delbanco, Andrew, 10
Denominations, 236
Devotional literature, see Books, devotional

Devotional meetings, 81–82, 112, 227
Dewey, Abigail, 213
Dewey, David, 117–18, 155, 201
Dewey, Hepzibah, 114–15
Dewey, Jedediah, 61, 223–24
Dewey, Josiah, 61, 107, 110–16 *passim*, 145, 155
Dewey, Thomas, 58, 61, 99, 193–94
Dewey family, 62–63, 98, 100, 107, 160
Dominion of New England, 177, 180
Dorchester, Massachusetts, 54, 181
Dudley, Thomas, 230
Dummer, Jeremiah, 184

Early Piety; Exemplified in Elizabeth Butcher of Boston, 92–95, 118
Earthquake of 1727, 140–41
Economic contention, 99–100, 103, 193–94, 197, 267–68n
Ecumenicism, *see* Interchurch fellowship
Education, 2, 11. *See also* Boston Latin School; Harvard College; Westfield schools; Yale College
Edwards, Jonathan, 218f, 220–21
Eliot, Jacob, 36, 70, 76f, 167
Eliot, John, 186
Endecott, John, 26
Enfield, Connecticut, 53
Evangelism, 3, 111, 153, 156, 228–30, 234–35. *See also under* Third Church, Boston
Excommunication, 86
Exemplary lives, *see* Biography
Eyre, John, 179

Family piety, 78–80, 108–9
Fast days, 113, 177, 199–200
First Church, Boston, 46f, 58, 80, 167, 169; schism in, 22–40 *passim*
First generation, 7–10, 12, 18, 25
Fitch, Elizabeth, 61
Fitch, James, 63
Flacius, Matthias, 149
Fort St. George's, Maine, 187
Foxe, John, 13, 149, 160
Franklin, Josiah, 81
Frary, Theophilus, 69, 85, 179
Funerals, 179, 181–82
Fur trade, 52, 98

Garden metaphor, 67–68, 110, 131–32, 153–55, 165
Gerrish, Samuel, 91, 94f, 139
Glover, Pelatiah, 63
Graves, Thomas, 56–57
Great Awakening, 1, 21, 141, 219, 231–36 *passim*; in Westfield, 220–24; in Boston, 224–29
Great Migration, 1, 8
Grecian, Dorcas, 178
Green, Bartholomew, 91, 139
Green, John, 184
Groton, Massachusetts, 123, 138
Gunn, Thomas, 60

Hadley, Massachusetts, 53, 63, 222
Halfway Covenant, 6, 11f, 130, 185, 223, 234, 248n; and First Church schism, 23–35 *passim*; in Third Church, 42, 45, 48, 50, 82, 94, 120; in Connecticut Valley, 53, 55, 105, 152; and garden metaphor, 67, 69, 110
Hampshire County Court, 101, 193, 196, 203
Hanchett, John, 197
Hartford, Connecticut, 52ff, 156
Harvard College, 19, 123, 128, 170f; and clerical training, 11, 56, 58, 187, 232, 283n
Hatfield, Massachusetts, 62, 106, 114
Haugh, Atherton, 126
Hayward, Experience, 70
Hayward, John, 71
Henchman, Daniel, 92, 139, 228
Hill, James, 85
Hoar, Leonard, 123
Hooker, Richard, 216ff
Hooker, Thomas, 28, 52, 54, 156
Hubbard, William, 230
Hull, Hannah, 76
Hull, John, 29–30, 39, 58, 69, 75, 83, 175
Hull, Massachusetts, 228
Hunt, Timothy Dwight, 238
Hutchinson, Anne, 26, 74

Independents, *see* Congregationalism
Indian Bible, 186
Indian missions, 165, 186–88
Ingerson, John, 107

Interchurch fellowship, 41–42, 49, 65–66, 165–74, 237

James I, 180–81
James II, 148
Johnson, Edward, 230
Joyliffe, Anna, 178
Joyliffe, John, 179
Judd, Roger, 85–86
Judgment of charity, 35, 133
Judicial system, 11, 101, 210–11. *See also* Hampshire County Court

Keith, George, 285n
Keller, Karl, 155, 161
Kellogg, Steven, 199–200, 204, 212ff
King, Fearnot, 99f
King Philip's War, 59, 61, 148, 168
King's Chapel, 89, 181
Kingston, Rhode Island, 189
Knight, Sarah Kemble, 232
Kuhn, Thomas, 6

Laity, 20, 50; in Boston, 26–27, 88–92, 166–69, 171, 178, 185–90, 227–29; in Westfield, 107–12, 114–18, 208–10. *See also* Third Church, Boston; Westfield church
Lancaster, Massachusetts, 168
Land bank, 103
Laud, William, 8, 25
Lebanon, Connecticut, 116
Lecture Days, 112–13. *See also* Boston Thursday Lecture
Lee, Abigail, 97
Lee, John, 202f
Lee, Sarah, 202f
Lee, Walter, 202ff
Leverett, John (major-general), 26, 39, 41
Leverett, John (Harvard College president), 134, 181
Levin, David, 14
Lilley, Edward, 179
Lockridge, Kenneth, 266n
Loomis, Samuel, 60, 107
Lord's Supper, 29, 253n; in Boston, 34–37, 46, 82–84, 131, 174; in Westfield, 106, 150–52, 157–59, 201, 206, 212
Lyde, Deborah, 181

Malden, Massachusetts, 167
Marlborough, Massachusetts, 226
Massachusetts Charter of 1629, 176–77
Massachusetts Charter of 1691, 171
Massachusetts General Court, 54, 58f, 62, 173, 176–77, 193
Mather, Cotton, 87, 125, 135, 157ff, 184, 234, 236; as historian, 13ff, 75, 139, 160, 230f
Mather, Eleazar, 55, 58
Mather, Increase, 14, 48, 57, 126, 136, 151, 159, 179f; and religious controversy, 87, 157–58, 170, 173, 177, 184
Mather, Richard, 14, 39
Mather, Samuel, 196
Mawdsley, John, 62, 96, 107–10, 112, 156, 193
Mawdsley, Joseph, 101, 199–200, 204, 210ff, 214
Mayhew, Thomas, 90
Means of grace, 10, 78–95 *passim*, 109, 112, 118, 185, 226–29, 247n, 260n
Meetinghouse, *see under* Third Church, Boston; Westfield church
Merchants, *see* Commerce
Middle way, 28–30, 48, 120, 163–64
Middletown, Connecticut, 226
Miller, Perry, 6, 14, 30, 246n
Missionary work, *see* Evangelism
Mitchell, Jonathan, 29, 121
Moody, Samuel, 233
Moxon, George, 55

Nantucket, Massachusetts, 228
Navigation Acts, 24
Netmaker, John, 182
New England, 108, 110–11, 130, 139–40, 229–34, 238
New England Company, 186
New England Emigrant Aid Company, 238
New England Society of San Francisco, 238
New Haven, Connecticut, 8, 27, 30, 32–34
New Lights, 223
New North Church, Boston, 174
Newport, Rhode Island, 189, 231ff
New South Church, Boston, 184
Nicholson, Francis, 174, 182

Noble, Thomas, 201, 207
Northampton, Massachusetts, 53, 60, 63, 101, 158–59, 198; church polity in, 55, 106, 157, 172, 196; revivals in, 218, 220, 222, 229
Northfield, Massachusetts, 53
Norton, John, 13, 26–30 passim, 43, 45, 121, 165
Norton, Mary, 43, 45, 75
Norwich, Connecticut, 61, 63

Oakes, Urian, 47
Occult beliefs, 271n
Old North Church, see Second Church, Boston
Old South Church, see Third Church, Boston
Oliver, Daniel, 186f
Oliver, Mary, 88
Oliver, Nathaniel, 179
Oliver, Peter, 39, 69f
Oppositional mentality, 174–75, 179
Owen, John, 31, 91, 123
Oxenbridge, John, 46f

Parliament, 9
Particular Baptists, see Baptists
Partridge, Samuel, 203–14 passim
Pastoral duties, see Clergy and individual clergymen by name
Pemberton, Ebenezer, 86–88, 121, 123, 127ff, 134, 138, 169, 213
Penn, James, 31–39 passim, 46
Peter, Hugh, 91, 140
Pew ownership, 84, 113
Phelps, George, 60
Phelps, Isaac, 102, 107, 198, 201–16 passim
Pilgrim's Progress, 92, 111
Plenitude of means, see Means of grace
Plymouth church, 4, 21, 138, 229
Plymouth colony, 4, 7, 15, 236
Pomery, Ebenezer, 102, 198f, 203f, 210–11
Pomery, Joseph, 194
Preparation, 142, 219–24 passim, 232–34, 270n
Presbyterianism, 9, 53f, 151, 172, 195–97. See also Church polity; Congregationalism
Primitivism, 7

Prince, Thomas, 94, 123, 183, 189; as pastor, 128–29; and sacramental evangelism, 134–37; and revivals, 141, 224–25, 227–28; as historian, 139ff, 161, 231, 237–38
Proposals of 1705, 172–73, 284n
Providence, Rhode Island, 189
Publishing, see Books, devotional and under individual authors by name
Puritan movement, 8, 103, 129–30, 217–18; in England, 3, 8ff, 18, 25, 151, 172, 180–81, 229; in New England, 3, 28, 53–54, 84, 180–84, 229–30. See also Congregationalism; Presbyterianism
Pynchon, John, 52–53, 62f, 97, 100, 102
Pynchon, William, 52, 54

Quakers, 164, 175

Rainsford, Edward, 36, 70, 75, 122, 130–31
Randolph, Edward, 148, 176f
Ratcliffe, Robert, 177, 179
Rawson, Edward, 70
Rebellion of 1689, 179–80
Reforming Synod of 1679, 47, 138, 167, 209
Restoration, of Charles II, 10–11, 24, 175
Revivals, 140–44, 157, 217, 220, 226–28
Rhode Island, 165, 188–90, 232–33
Rock, Mary, 80
Rogers, John, 90
Rogers, John, Jr., 91
Root, John, 107
Rowlandson, Joseph, 175
Rowlandson, Mary, 168, 282n
Roxbury, Massachusetts, 52
Royal commission of 1664, 27
Ruggles, Benjamin, 195–97
Ruling elders, 121–22
Russell, John, 63
Rutman, Darrett, 14

Sabbath, 174
Sacramental evangelism, 133–37
Sacraments, see Baptism; Lord's Supper
St. Botolph's Church, Boston, Lincolnshire, 18
Salter, Aeneas, 182
Salter, William, 69

Sanderson, Robert, 83
Savage, Thomas, 39, 70, 74–75, 85
Savoy Confession, 47
Scottish Presbyterians, 276n
Scottish Society for Propagating Christian
    Knowledge, 187
Scottow, Joshua, 14, 29–30, 69, 71, 76f, 91
Seccombe, Joseph, 187–88
Second Church, Boston, 32, 43, 184
Selement, George, 138
Separatism, 8f, 25, 34, 37, 223
Sergeant, Peter, 128, 179f, 186
Sewall, Elizabeth ("Betty"), 126–27
Sewall, Joseph, 77, 80, 88, 118, 182–83,
    187, 189; as pastor, 93ff, 128f; and sacra-
    mental evangelism, 134–37; and revivals,
    225, 227
Sewall, Samuel, 82, 83, 117, 128, 160, 175,
    186; and Edward Taylor, 57–58, 96, 195,
    214; as lay leader, 75ff, 81–95 passim, 116;
    and Third Church clergy, 88, 125–27,
    169, 213; promotes interchurch fellow-
    ship, 167–74 passim, 189, 233; opposes
    Church of England, 178–84 passim
Sewall, Samuel, Jr., 126
Shepard, Thomas, 10, 12, 28, 68, 81, 121,
    140, 156, 228
Shepard, Thomas, Jr., 166
Shrimpton, Samuel, 74
Shute, Samuel, 183
Silver (communion vessels), 82–83, 113–14
Simsbury, Connecticut, 103
Smallpox, 140, 194, 215
Smith, Benjamin, 203–13 passim
Smith, Thomas, 197
South Church, see Third Church, Boston
Spiritual economy, 2–3, 239
Springfield, Massachusetts, 17, 52f, 54–55,
    63, 101, 207, 222
Stiles, Ezra, 148, 231, 236–38
Stiles, Isaac, 215–16
Stiles, Keziah Taylor, 216
Stoddard, Anthony, 26, 32, 90, 186
Stoddard, Solomon, 55, 172, 196; and
    Westfield, 60, 63, 65, 200, 207; and
    Edward Taylor, 113, 147, 156–60, 195,
    201; and revivals, 218, 222, 228f
Stone, Samuel, 156

Stoughton, William, 181
Stout, Harry, 133–34
Street, Nicholas, 34, 42
Suffield, Connecticut, 114, 195–97
Synod of 1662, see Halfway Covenant
Synods, 31, 166. See also Cambridge Plat-
    form; Halfway Covenant; Reforming
    Synod of 1679

Taylor, Edward, 56–57, 99, 203, 206,
    210–11; family life, 55, 61, 194, 215–16,
    277n; on church polity, 58–67 passim,
    196; life in Westfield, 59, 96, 144, 159,
    195; salary disputes, 62, 103, 145–46,
    197–98; as pastor, 104, 106f, 112–18
    passim, 147, 150, 153–54; spiritual life of,
    108, 111, 154–55; as author/poet, 115–16,
    148–50, 152, 160–61; and Solomon
    Stoddard, 157–60, 195, 201; and church
    discipline, 192–213 passim; and revivals,
    220f, 223, 233f
Taylor, Eldad, 216
Taylor, Elizabeth Fitch, 194
Taylor, Ruth Wyllys, 194
Taylor, Sarah, 181
Taylor, William, 181
Tennent, Gilbert, 224
Thacher, Thomas, 45–47, 49, 121f, 125–26,
    165–66, 175
Third Church, Boston: and Halfway
    Covenant, 23–24; founding controver-
    sies, 40–49 passim; meetinghouse, 42–45,
    84; compared to Westfield church, 64,
    65–66, 112–14, 213; and garden meta-
    phor, 67–68; and commerce, 69–74,
    234; promotes interchurch fellowship,
    165–73, 237; charity in, 168–69, 187–88,
    228–29; opposes Church of England,
    177–84; promotes evangelism, 185–90;
    Great Awakening in, 224–229;
—laity of: 166–69, 178–90 passim; as
    church leaders, 74–78; and family piety,
    78–79; and devotional meetings, 81–82;
    and Lord's Supper, 82–84; and church
    discipline, 84–88; and public morality,
    87–88; and publication, 91–95
—clergy of: salaries, 122–25; as pastors,
    125–29; and sacramental evangelism,

129–37; and publication, 138–40; and promotion of revivals, 140–43
Torrey, Samuel, 189–90
Tribalism, 111, 113, 117, 264n, 272n
Truesdale, Richard, 36, 69
Tyng, Edward, 41
Typology, 160–61

United Colonies, 186
Usher, Hezekiah, 30, 39, 69
Usher, Hezekiah, Mrs., 168

Vane, Henry, 26

Walter, Isaac, 126
Ward, Nathaniel, 92
Warham, John, 52, 54, 156
Weller, Nathaniel, 145, 201
Westfield, Massachusetts, 1, 194–95; settlement of, 52–55; and Edward Taylor, 58–59, 147, 161; economic development of, 61–62, 96–104 passim, 267n; schools in, 62, 100–102; town government in, 100–102; population dispersal in, 96–98, 100–102, 214–15
Westfield church, 20, 111, 235–36; founding of, 59–66 passim; laity of, 104–5, 107, 111, 114, 158–59; compared with Third Church, Boston, 112–14, 234–36; impoverishment of, 113–14; and Connecticut Valley churches, 156, 159; discipline in, 192–213 passim; abandons conversion narratives, 216; and Great Awakening, 220–24, 234
West Haven, Connecticut, 216
Westminster Confession, 63, 164, 171
Whitefield, George, 141, 221–22, 224–26, 232–34
Whiting, Joseph, 59ff, 99

Wigglesworth, Michael, 155
Wigglesworth, Samuel, 187
Willard, Eunice, 124
Willard, Josiah, 225
Willard, Samuel, 123, 128, 228; on church polity, 48–49, 131–32; as preacher, 75, 79f; as author/publications of, 81, 90ff, 127, 136–38, 152; on church discipline, 85–86; salary, 124, 129, 147; as pastor, 126–27, 137–38; and sacramental evangelism, 130–34; opposes radical sectarians, 131, 175–76; promotes interchurch fellowship, 167, 170–73, 237; opposes Church of England, 176–80
Williams, Nathaniel, 85, 88–89
Williams, Nathaniel, Jr. (Boston Latin School Master), 88–89, 116
Williams, William, 196
Willoughby, Francis, 41
Wilson, John, 9, 26f, 30, 32, 80
Wilton, David, 60
Winchell, David, 194, 197
Windsor, Connecticut, 52ff, 63, 156, 193
Winthrop, John, 9, 13f, 17, 26, 28, 43, 45, 165
Winthrop, John, Jr., 14
Winthrop, Katherine Brattle, 90
Winthrop, Mercy, 126
Winthrop, Waitstill, 91, 179f, 182
Wise, John, 173
Women: and conversion, 19; and family piety, 80; in Westfield church, 105–6; in Third Church, Boston, 178
Woodbridge, John, 54, 207f, 211, 213
Worcester, Massachusetts, 226

Yale College, 184, 216, 232
York, Maine, 233

Library of Congress Cataloging-in-Publication Data

Peterson, Mark A., 1960–
    The price of redemption : the spiritual economy of Puritan
New England / Mark A. Peterson.
        p.   cm.
    Originally presented as the author's thesis (doctoral)—
Harvard University.
    Includes bibliographical references and index.
    ISBN 0–8047–2912–3 (cloth : alk. paper)
    1. Spirituality—Puritans—History.   2. Economics—Reli-
gious aspects—Puritans—History of doctrines.   3. Puri-
tans—Massachusetts—History.   4. Third Church (Boston,
Mass.)—History.   5. Westfield Church (Mass.)—History.
6. Great awakening.   7. Boston (Mass.)—Church history.
8. Westfield (Mass.)—Church history.   9. Massachusetts—
Church history—17th century.   10. Massachusetts—
Church history—18th century.   I. Title.
BX 9355.M4P48   1998
285'.9'0974409032—dc21   97–33712
                                                                    CIP